S0-AHN-528

780.0711 Sch Mil
Miller.
Heinrich Schutz, a
 bibliography of the...

The Lorette Wilmot Library
Nazareth College of Rochester
WITHDRAWN

HEINRICH SCHÜTZ

RECENT TITLES IN THE MUSIC REFERENCE COLLECTION
Series Advisers: *Donald L. Hixon*
                 Adrienne Fried Block

Music for Oboe, Oboe D'Amore, and English Horn: A Bibliography of
Materials at the Library of Congress
Virginia Snodgrass Gifford, compiler

A Bibliography of Nineteenth-Century American Piano Music:
With Location Sources and Composer Biography-Index
John Gillespie and Anna Gillespie

The Resource Book of Jewish Music: A Bibliographical and Topical
Guide to the Book and Journal Literature and Program Materials
Irene Heskes, compiler

American Vocal Chamber Music, 1945-1980: An Annotated Bibliography
Patricia Lust, compiler

Concert and Opera Singers: A Bibliography of Biographical Materials
Robert H. Cowden, compiler

Music History from the Late Roman through the Gothic Periods, 313-1425:
A Documented Chronology
Blanche Gangwere

Guide to the Hymns and Tunes of American Methodism
Samuel J. Rogal, compiler

Musical Settings of American Poetry: A Bibliography
Michael Hovland, compiler

HEINRICH SCHÜTZ

*A Bibliography of the Collected Works
and Performing Editions*

Compiled by
D. Douglas Miller
and Anne L. Highsmith

Music Reference Collection, Number 9

GREENWOOD PRESS
New York • Westport, Connecticut • London

WITHDRAWN
LORETTE WILMOT LIBRARY
NAZARETH COLLEGE

LIBRARY OF CONGRESS CATALOGING-IN-PUBLICATION DATA

Miller, D. Douglas.
  Heinrich Schütz, a bibliography of the collected
works and performing editions.

  (Music reference collection, ISSN 0736-7740 ; no. 9)
  Bibliography: p.
  Includes index.
  1. Schütz, Heinrich, 1585-1672—Bibliography.
I. Highsmith, Anne L.   II. Title.   III. Series.
ML134.S412M5   1986   016.783'092'4   86-7610
ISBN 0-313-24884-2 (lib. bdg. : alk. paper)

Copyright © 1986 by D. Douglas Miller and Anne L. Highsmith

All rights reserved. No portion of this book may be
reproduced, by any process or technique, without the
express written consent of the publisher.

Library of Congress Catalog Card Number: 86-7610
ISBN: 0-313-24884-2
ISSN: 0736-7740

First published in 1986

Greenwood Press, Inc.
88 Post Road West, Westport, Connecticut 06881

Printed in the United States of America

The paper used in this book complies with the
Permanent Paper Standard issued by the National
Information Standards Organization (Z39.48-1984).

10 9 8 7 6 5 4 3 2 1

780.0711
Sch
mil

To the family and friends

who made it possible

CONTENTS

Preface   ix
Acknowledgments   xi
Bibliographic Conventions   xiii
List of Abbreviations   xvii

Bibliography   3

Title Index   247
Source Index   259
Performing Forces Index   265
  Solos or solo ensembles   265
  Choruses   271

PREFACE

The performer or scholar wishing to perform or study the
works of Heinrich Schütz is well served by available editions of
Schütz's five hundred works. No fewer than three collected works
projects have been undertaken; performing editions resulting from those
projects and editions of individual works issued by nearly eighty
publishers provide a wealth of performing materials. At times they
also provide a source of confusion for a conductor attempting to select
a suitable edition for use, since as many as twenty editions exist for
a few popular works.

The authors have compiled this bibliography in order to provide
a reference which will:

1. Identify certain basic information about each work by Schütz.
This information has been determined primarily by consulting the
collected works editions. (See the sample citation in the
Bibliographic Conventions section below for information recorded.)

2. Identify editions which exist for each work.

3. Provide bibliographic information regarding each edition. (See
the sample citation below.)

4. Provide indexes which allow a user to locate works based on the
criteria of title, textual source, or performing forces.

The project has been accomplished using the powerful data
base management system SPIRES (Stanford Public Information Retrieval
System) available at the Computation Center of the Pennsylvania State
University. The data base has been designed so that on-line searches
can be undertaken for any of the information elements recorded by using
Boolean operators and keyword searching. Readers interested in
inquiring about such searches are invited to write to the authors at
218 Music Building, Pennsylvania State University, University Park, PA
16802.

The organization of Schütz's works in this volume follows the SWV (Schütz-Werke-Verzeichnis) numbering of Werner Bittinger's catalogue. Decisions to include or exclude works have been based on the assessments of authenticity in the works list by Joshua Rifkin and Derek McCulloch in the Schütz article in *New Groves.* The authors have then recorded information only for editions which they actually have in hand. These include all published volumes of the three collected works projects (Breitkopf, Bärenreiter, and Hänssler) and approximately 750 performing editions obtained by contacting all publishers with Schütz editions listed in *Choral Music in Print.* The authors acknowledge with gratitude the helpful response of those publishers. In the case of the Bärenreiter and Hänssler editions, which consist largely of offprints of published or projected collected works volumes, all available editions were purchased for inclusion. The authors invite the continued assistance of publishers in identifying additional editions not included in this volume.

In addition to the citations for each work, three indexes have been provided. The first is a title index which directs the reader to the SWV number of a work or works. Included are original titles, secondary titles, collection titles, and translated titles in the case of performing editions. In certain instances more than one work bear the same title. The second index indicates text sources for all works. The sources listed in the citation for the work and in the source index indicate the textual source which Schütz set, rather than the source from which Schütz's text might be ultimately derived. The sources for SWV 301, therefore, are cited as St. Ambrose's "Veni redemptor gentium" and Luther's "Nun komm, der Heiden Heiland" even though the Lutheran text is a translation of the Ambrosian. Biblical chapter and verse numbering follow the Revised Standard Version except in the cases of apocryphal books, where the numbering follows the Vulgate.

The third index lists works according to performing forces employed. Because the assignment of a solo voice or several choral voices to a given line is a decision which may vary from performance to performance, the user is encouraged to consult both the "solo or solo ensembles" and the "choruses" portions of the index. Schütz repeatedly emphasized in the prefaces to the various collections that a number of different performing force possibilities existed; this index can list only a few of those possibilities. Very often a given line might possibly be a solo-voice, choral-voice, instrumental, solo/instrumental, or choral/instrumental line and the instrument(s) employed are often undesignated or interchangeable. Thus the enormous range of variations which can result from these options defies comprehensive treatment within the scope of a short index.

ACKNOWLEDGMENTS

The authors gratefully acknowledge the support provided for this project by the following:

The Institute for the Arts and Humanistic Studies of the Pennsylvania State University.

The Pennsylvania State University College of Arts and Architecture, School of Music, Computation Center, and Pattee Library.

Texas A&M University Sterling C. Evans Library Research Committee.

BIBLIOGRAPHIC CONVENTIONS

In order to describe the information provided in this volume, a sample citation appears below, followed by a description of each element and the conventions employed by the authors.

Sample Citation:

SWV 25 (1)

[Psalmen Davids. Aus der Tiefe, ruf ich Herr, zu dir] (2)

    Sacred German text. (3) Sources: Psalm 130. Gloria Patri. (4)

    For coro favorito I and II (SATB/SATB) and basso continuo. (5)

    Ranges of voice parts: b-e2, a-a1, d-e1, E-c1/ e1-e2, a-a1, c-e1,

    E-a. (6) Duration: short. (7)

1(8)Aus der Tiefe, ruf ich, Herr, zu dir. -- In SGA. -- 1886. -- Bd. 2,

    p. 47-53.(9)

      Edited by Philipp Spitta. Figured bass not realized. (10)

    Original German text. (11) Notes in German. (12)

2   Aus der Tiefe, ruf ich Herr, zu dir. -- In NSA. -- 1971. -- Bd. 23,

    p. 73-84. Pub. no.: BA4475. (13)

    Edited by Wilhelm Ehmann; figured bass realized by Johannes

    H.E. Koch. German text. Notes in German and English.

    Transposed up M2. (14)

This is part of the citation for SWV 25, "Aus der Tiefe, ruf ich Herr, zu dir," from the *Psalmen Davids* collection. For the full citation, see p. 15.

(1) SWV number as assigned by Werner Bittinger in the Schütz-Werke-Verzeichnis.

(2) Uniform title for the work. The uniform title begins with the name of the collection if the work was originally published in a collection. SWV numbers may be added at the end of the uniform title to distinguish works with the same title within the same collection. If the edition being cataloged is a selection rather than the complete work, the SWV number is repeated and the uniform title cites the selection being cataloged.

(3) Indicates whether the text on which the work is based is secular or sacred in nature and the language of the original text.

(4) Textual sources on which the work is based.

(5) Vocal and instrumental forces necessary to perform the work. The slash mark indicates that the eight choral voices function as two SATB choruses. Names of voice parts reflect the clefs employed by Schutz and include Soprano (S), Mezzo soprano (M), Alto (A), Tenor (T), Baritone (R), and Bass (B). "Soprano" includes both parts employing the G clef on the second line and the C clef on the fifth line. "Bass" includes parts employing the F clef on both the fourth line (bass clef) and fifth line (sub-bass clef).

(6) Ranges of voice parts. These are based on the original notated pitch as reflected in the Spitta edition. The notation employed labels the octave ascending from middle c as "c1" to "b1"; the next higher octave is labelled "c2"; the next lower octave as "c." The slash mark separates the two choruses.

(7) The duration of the piece in performance. Four minutes or less is designated "short"; five to eight minutes is "medium"; more than eight minutes is "long".

(8) Number of the edition being cataloged. Edition numbers 1-5 are reserved for specific editions as follows:

    1 SGA Heinrich Schütz : sämtlicher Werke. -- Leipzig : Breitkopf & Härtel, 1885-1927.
    2 NSA Neue Ausgabe sämtlicher Werke. -- Kassel : Bärenreiter, 1955- .
    3   Bärenreiter performing edition, one based on the NSA if available.
    4 SSA Stuttgarter Schütz-Ausgabe. -- Neuhausen-Stuttgart : Hänssler, 1971- .
    5   Hänssler performing edition, one based on the SSA if available.

Editions numbers higher than 5 have no special significance.

Editions which comprise only selections of the work are numbered to appear after editions of the full work.

(9) Publication information.

(10) Notes on editor and continuo realization. If the work was originally written with a continuo part, the reader should assume that the editor provided a continuo realization unless otherwise stated.

(11) Languages of text for that edition.

(12) Notes designed to aid the conductor in performing the work.

(13) Publisher's catalog number.

(14) Indicates whether the performing edition has been transposed from the ranges provided in (6). If no transposition is listed, then the performing edition is at original pitch.

The group of citations for some works may be followed by a note which begins, "Other editions". This note contains citations to Bärenreiter and Hänssler performing editions which the authors did not have in hand but which are listed in the current publisher's catalogs. Bärenreiter and Hänssler editions are reflected in this note because of their high quality and their publishers' efforts to provide a comprehensive listing of Schütz's works.

LIST OF ABBREVIATIONS

A	Alto voice
B	Bass voice
M	Mezzo-soprano voice
NSA	Neue Ausgabe sämtlicher Werke. -- Kassel : Bärenreiter, 1955- . (Neue Schütz Ausgabe)
Pub. no.	Publisher's catalog number
R	Baritone voice
S	Soprano voice
SGA	Heinrich Schütz : sämtlicher Werke. -- Leipzig : Breitkopf & Härtel, 1885-1927. (Schütz Gesamt Ausgabe)*
SSA	Stuttgarter Schütz-Ausgabe. -- Neuhausen-Stuttgart : Hänssler, 1971-.
SWV	Schütz-Werke-Verzeichnis : (SWV). -- Kassel : Bärenreiter, 1960.
T	Tenor voice

* The practice of citing these editions as NSA and SGA follows that established by Werner Bittinger in the Schütz-Werke-Verzeichnis.

HEINRICH SCHÜTZ

BIBLIOGRAPHY

SWV 1

[Madrigals. O primavera, gioventù de l'anno]

    Secular Italian text. Sources: Guarini, Battista. Pastor fido.
      For chorus (SSATB) a cappella. Ranges of voice parts: c#1-f2,
    c1-f2, e-a1, c-f1, F-d1. Duration: medium.

1   O primavera, gioventù de l'anno. -- In SGA. -- 1890. -- Bd. 9, p.
    5-9.
      Edited by Philipp Spitta. Original Italian text. Notes in German.

2   SWV 1. -- In NSA. -- 1962. -- Bd. 22, p. 1-8. Pub. no.: Bärenreiter
    3663.
      Edited by Hans Joachim Moser. Italian text with German
    translation. Notes in German and English.

3   O primavera, gioventù de l'anno. -- Kassel : Bärenreiter, c1963.
    Pub. no.: Bärenreiter-Ausgabe 2851.
      Edited by H.J. Moser. Italian text with German translation.

4   O primavera. -- In SSA. -- c1984. -- Bd. 1, p. 1-7. Pub. no.: HE
    20.915.
      Edited by Siegfried Schmalzriedt. Italian text. Notes in German
    and English.

    Other editions: Hänssler HE20.001.

SWV 2

[Madrigals. O dolcezze amarissime d'amore]

    Secular Italian text. Sources: Guarini, Battista. Pastor fido.
      For chorus (SSATB) a cappella. Ranges of voice parts: c1-g2,
    c#1-f2, d-bflat1, c-f1, F-bflat. Duration: short.

1   O dolcezze amarissime d'amore. -- In SGA. -- 1890. -- Bd. 9, p.
    9-13.
      Edited by Philipp Spitta. Original Italian text. Notes in German.

2   SWV 2. -- In NSA. -- 1962. -- Bd. 22, p. 9-15. Pub. no.: Bärenreiter
     3663.
     Edited by Hans Joachim Moser. Italian text with German
     translation. Notes in German and English.

3   O dolcezze amarissime d'amore. -- Kassel : Bärenreiter, c1963. Pub.
     no.: Bärenreiter-Ausgabe 2851.
     Edited by H.J. Moser. Italian text with German translation.

4   O dolcezze amarissime. -- In SSA. -- c1984. -- Bd. 1, p. 8-12. Pub.
     no.: HE 20.915.
     Edited by Siegfried Schmalzriedt. Italian text. Notes in German
     and English.

     Other editions: Hänssler HE20.002.

SWV 3

[Madrigals. Selve beate, se sospirando in flebili susurri]

     Secular Italian text. Sources: Guarini, Battista. Pastor fido.
     For chorus (SSATB) a cappella. Ranges of voice parts: c#1-g2,
     a-f2, e-bflat1, c#-g1, G-bflat. Duration: short.

1   Selve beate, se sospirando in flebili susurri. -- In SGA. -- 1890.
     -- Bd. 9, p. 13-17.
     Edited by Philipp Spitta. Original Italian text. Notes in German.

2   SWV 3. -- In NSA. -- 1962. -- Bd. 22, p. 16-23. Pub. no.:
     Bärenreiter 3663.
     Edited by Hans Joachim Moser. Italian text with German
     translation. Notes in German and English.

3   Selve beate. -- Kassel : Bärenreiter, c1963. Pub. no.:
     Bärenreiter-Ausgabe 2852.
     Edited by H.J. Moser. Italian text with German translation.

4   Selve beate. -- In SSA. -- c1984. -- Bd. 1, p. 13-19. Pub. no.: HE
     20.915.
     Edited by Siegfried Schmalzriedt. Italian text. Notes in German
     and English.

     Other editions: Hänssler HE20.003.

SWV 4

[Madrigals. Alma afflitta, che fai?]

     Secular Italian text. Sources: Marino, Giambattista. Partita
     dell'amata.
     For chorus (SATTB) a cappella. Ranges of voice parts: b-e2, e-b1,
     c-f1, c-e1, G-a. Duration: short.

1   Alma afflitta che fai?. -- In SGA. -- 1890. -- Bd. 9, p. 18-22.
     Edited by Philipp Spitta. Original Italian text. Notes in German.

2   SWV 4. -- In NSA. -- 1962. -- Bd. 22, p. 24-30. Pub. no.:
Bärenreiter 3663.
   Edited by Hans Joachim Moser. Italian text with German
translation. Notes in German and English.

3   Alma afflitta, che fai. -- Kassel : Bärenreiter, c1962. Pub. no.:
Bärenreiter-Ausgabe 2853.
   Edited by H.J. Moser. Italian text with German translation.

4   Alma afflitta, che fai?. -- In SSA. -- c1984. -- Bd. 1, p. 20-25.
Pub. no.: HE 20.915.
   Edited by Siegfried Schmalzriedt. Italian text. Notes in German
and English.

   Other editions: Hänssler HE20.004.

SWV 5

[Madrigals. Cosi morir debb'io]

   Secular Italian text. Sources: Guarini, Battista. Pastor fido.
   For chorus (SATTB) a cappella. Ranges of voice parts: cl-e2, d-bl,
c-el, c-el, F-dl. Duration: short.

1   Cosi morir debb'io. -- In SGA. -- 1890. -- Bd. 9, p. 23-26.
   Edited by Philipp Spitta. Original Italian text. Notes in German.

2   SWV 5. -- In NSA. -- 1962. -- Bd. 22, p. 31-36. Pub. no.:
Bärenreiter 3663.
   Edited by Hans Joachim Moser. Italian text with German
translation. Notes in German and English.

3   Cosi morir debb'io. -- Kassel : Bärenreiter, c1962. Pub. no.:
Bärenreiter-Ausgabe 2854.
   Edited by H.J. Moser. Italian text with German translation.

4   Cosi morir debb'io. -- In SSA. -- c1984. -- Bd. 1, p. 26-31. Pub.
no.: HE 20.915.
   Edited by Siegfried Schmalzriedt. Italian text. Notes in German
and English.

   Other editions: Hänssler HE20.005.

SWV 6

[Madrigals. D'orrida selce alpina]

   Secular Italian text. Sources: Aligieri, Alessandro. D'orrida selce
alpina.
   For chorus (SMATB) a cappella. Ranges of voice parts: el-e2,
g-c#2, e-al, d-el, E-b. Duration: short.

1   D'orrida selce alpina. -- In SGA. -- 1890. -- Bd. 9, p. 27-30.
   Edited by Philipp Spitta. Original Italian text. Notes in German.

2   SWV 6. -- In NSA. -- 1962. -- Bd. 22, p. 37-42. Pub. no.:
     Bärenreiter 3663.
        Edited by Hans Joachim Moser. Italian text with German
     translation. Notes in German and English.

3   D'orrida selce alpina. -- Kassel : Bärenreiter, c1962. Pub. no.:
     Bärenreiter-Ausgabe 2855.
        Edited by H.J. Moser. Italian text with German translation.

4   D'orrida selce alpina. -- In SSA. -- c1984. -- Bd. 1, p. 32-37. Pub.
     no.: HE 20.915.
        Edited by Siegfried Schmalzriedt. Italian text. Notes in German
     and English.

        Other editions: Hänssler HE20.006.

SWV 7

[Madrigals. Ride la primavera]

     Secular Italian text. Sources: Marino, Giambattista. Stagioni
     contrarie alla sua ninfa.
        For chorus (SSMAR) a cappella. Ranges of voice parts: f1-a2,
     d1-a2, g-d2, d-a1, G-d1. Duration: short.

1   Ride la primavera. -- In SGA. -- 1890. -- Bd. 9, p. 31-35.
        Edited by Philipp Spitta. Original Italian text. Notes in German.

2   SWV 7. -- In NSA. -- 1962. -- Bd. 22, p. 43-50. Pub. no.:
     Bärenreiter 3663.
        Edited by Hans Joachim Moser. Italian text with German
     translation. Notes in German and English. Transposed down M2.

3   Ride la primavera. -- Kassel : Bärenreiter, c1963. Pub. no.:
     Bärenreiter-Ausgabe 2856.
        Edited by H.J. Moser. Italian text with German translation.
     Transposed down M2.

4   Ride la primavera. -- In SSA. -- c1984. -- Bd. 1, p. 38-44. Pub.
     no.: HE 20.915.
        Edited by Siegfried Schmalzriedt. Italian text. Notes in German
     and English.

6   Ride la primavera. -- London : Schott, c1952. Pub. no.: C 38126.
        Italian text.

        Other editions: Hänssler HE20.007.

SWV 8

[Madrigals. Fuggi, o mio core]

Secular Italian text. Sources: Marino, Giambattista. Bella mano veduta.
For chorus (SSMAR) a cappella. Ranges of voice parts: f1-b2, e1-b2, a-d2, g-a1, G-e1. Duration: short.

1   Fuggi o mio core. -- In SGA. -- 1890. -- Bd. 9, p. 35-40.
Edited by Philipp Spitta. Original Italian text. Notes in German.

2   SWV 8. -- In NSA. -- 1962. -- Bd. 22, p. 51-60. Pub. no.:
Bärenreiter 3663.
Edited by Hans Joachim Moser. Italian text with German translation. Notes in German and English. Transposed down M2.

3   Fuggi, o mio core. -- Kassel : Bärenreiter, c1963. Pub. no.:
Bärenreiter-Ausgabe 2857.
Edited by H.J. Moser. Italian text with German translation. Transposed down M2.

4   Fuggi, fuggi, o mio core!. -- In SSA. -- c1984. -- Bd. 1, p. 45-51.
Pub. no.: HE 20.915.
Edited by Siegfried Schmalzriedt. Italian text. Notes in German and English.

Other editions: Hänssler HE20.008.

SWV 9

[Madrigals. Feritevi, ferite, viperette mordacci]

Secular Italian text. Sources: Marino, Giambattista. Guerra di baci.
For chorus (SSATB) a cappella. Ranges of voice parts: c1-f2, bflat-f2, f-a1, A-f1, F-bflat. Duration: short.

1   Feritevi, ferite, viperette mordacci. -- In SGA. -- 1890. -- Bd. 9, p. 41-46.
Edited by Philipp Spitta. Original Italian text. Notes in German.

2   SWV 9. -- In NSA. -- 1962. -- Bd. 22, p. 61-69. Pub. no.:
Bärenreiter 3663.
Edited by Hans Joachim Moser. Italian text with German translation. Notes in German and English.

3   Feritevi, ferite, viperette mordacci. -- Kassel : Bärenreiter, c1962. Pub. no.: Bärenreiter-Ausgabe 2858.
Edited by H.J. Moser. Italian text with German translation.

4   Feritevi, ferite. -- In SSA. -- c1984. -- Bd. 1, p. 52-59. Pub. no.:
HE 20.915.
Edited by Siegfried Schmalzriedt. Italian text. Notes in German and English.

Other editions: Hänssler HE20.009.

SWV 10

[Madrigals. Fiamma ch'allacia e laccio]

Secular Italian text. Sources: Gatti, Alessandro. Fiamma ch'allacia e laccio.
For chorus (SSATB) a cappella. Ranges of voice parts: c1-f2, bflat-f2, f-a1, B-g1, E-c1. Duration: short.

1   Fiamma ch'allacia e laccio. -- In SGA. -- 1890. -- Bd. 9, p. 46-50.
Edited by Philipp Spitta. Original Italian text. Notes in German.

2   SWV 10. -- In NSA. -- 1962. -- Bd. 22, p. 70-76. Pub. no.:
Bärenreiter 3663.
Edited by Hans Joachim Moser. Italian text with German translation. Notes in German and English.

3   Fiamma ch'allaccia e laccio. -- Kassel : Bärenreiter, c1962. Pub.
no.: Bärenreiter-Ausgabe 2859.
Edited by H.J. Moser. Italian text with German translation.

4   Fiamma ch'allaccia. -- In SSA. -- c1984. -- Bd. 1, p. 60-65. Pub.
no.: HE 20.915.
Edited by Siegfried Schmalzriedt. Italian text. Notes in German and English.

Other editions: Hänssler HE20.010.

SWV 11

[Madrigals. Quella damma son io]

Secular Italian text. Sources: Guarini, Battista. Pastor fido.
For chorus (SSATB) a cappella. Ranges of voice parts: c#1-e2, c1-e2, g-a1, d-f1, G-d1. Duration: short.

1   Quella damma son io. -- In SGA. -- 1890. -- Bd. 9, p. 50-53.
Edited by Philipp Spitta. Original Italian text. Notes in German.

2   SWV 11. -- In NSA. -- 1962. -- Bd. 22, p. 77-81. Pub. no.:
Bärenreiter 3663.
Edited by Hans Joachim Moser. Italian text with German translation. Notes in German and English.

3   Quella damma son io. -- Kassel : Bärenreiter, c1962. Pub. no.:
Bärenreiter-Ausgabe 2860.
Edited by H.J. Moser. Italian text with German translation.

4   Quella damma son io. -- In SSA. -- c1984. -- Bd. 1, p. 66-69. Pub.
no.: HE 20.915.
Edited by Siegfried Schmalzriedt. Italian text. Notes in German and English.

Other editions: Hänssler HE20.011.

SWV 12

[Madrigals. Mi saluta costei]

    Secular Italian text. Sources: Marino, Giambattista. Saluto nocevole.
    For chorus (SSMAR) a cappella. Ranges of voice parts: dl-a2, dl-a2, g-d2, e-al, G-dl. Duration: short.

1   Mi saluta costei. -- In SGA. -- 1890. -- Bd. 9, p. 53-57.
    Edited by Philipp Spitta. Original Italian text. Notes in German.

2   SWV 12. -- In NSA. -- 1962. -- Bd. 22, p. 82-88. Pub. no.: Bärenreiter 3663.
    Edited by Hans Joachim Moser. Italian text with German translation. Notes in German and English. Transposed down M2.

3   Mi saluta costei. -- Kassel : Bärenreiter, c1962. Pub. no.: Bärenreiter-Ausgabe 2861.
    Edited by H.J. Moser. Italian text with German translation. Transposed down M2.

4   Mi saluta costei. -- In SSA. -- c1984. -- Bd. 1, p. 70-76. Pub. no.: HE 20.915.
    Edited by Siegfried Schmalzriedt. Italian text. Notes in German and English.

    Other editions: Hänssler HE20.012.

SWV 13

[Madrigals. Io moro, ecco ch'io moro]

    Secular Italian text. Sources: Marino, Giambattista. Bacio chiesto con arguzia.
    For chorus (SSMAR) a cappella. Ranges of voice parts: fl-b2, dl-bflat2, g-eflat2, e-bflatl, G-eflatl. Duration: short.

1   Jo moro, ecco ch'io moro. -- In SGA. -- 1890. -- Bd. 9, p. 57-61.
    Edited by Philipp Spitta. Original Italian text. Notes in German.

2   SWV 13. -- In NSA. -- 1962. -- Bd. 22, p. 89-95. Pub. no.: Bärenreiter 3663.
    Edited by Hans Joachim Moser. Italian text with German translation. Notes in German and English. Transposed down M2.

3   Io moro, ecco ch'io moro. -- Kassel : Bärenreiter, c1962. Pub. no.: Bärenreiter-Ausgabe 2862.
    Edited by H.J. Moser. Italian text with German translation. Transposed down M2.

4   Io moro, ecco ch'io moro. -- In SSA. -- c1984. -- Bd. 1, p. 77-83. Pub. no.: HE 20.915.
    Edited by Siegfried Schmalzriedt. Italian text. Notes in German and English.

Other editions: Hänssler HE20.013.

SWV 14

[Madrigals. Sospir che del bel petto]

Secular Italian text. Sources: Marino, Giambattista. Sospiro della sua donna.
For chorus (SSMAR) a cappella. Ranges of voice parts: e1-bflat2, d1-g2, g-d2, d-a1, F-d1. Duration: short.

1   Sospir che del bel petto. -- In SGA. -- 1890. -- Bd. 9, p. 61-65.
Edited by Philipp Spitta. Original Italian text. Notes in German.

2   SWV 14. -- In NSA. -- 1962. -- Bd. 22, p. 96-102. Pub. no.:
Bärenreiter 3663.
Edited by Hans Joachim Moser. Italian text with German translation. Notes in German and English. Transposed down M2.

3   Sospir che del bel petto. -- Kassel : Bärenreiter, c1962. Pub. no.:
Bärenreiter-Ausgabe 2863.
Edited by H.J. Moser. Italian text with German translation.
Transposed down M2.

4   Sospir, che del bel petto. -- In SSA. -- c1984. -- Bd. 1, p. 84-89.
Pub. no.: HE 20.915.
Edited by Siegfried Schmalzriedt. Italian text. Notes in German and English.

Other editions: Hänssler HE20.014.

SWV 15

[Madrigals. Dunque addio, care selve]

Secular Italian text. Sources: Guarini, Battista. Pastor fido.
For chorus (SSMAR) a cappella. Ranges of voice parts: d1-bflat2, d1-g2, g-c2, d-a1, G-d1. Duration: short.

1   Dunque addio, care selve. -- In SGA. -- 1890. -- Bd. 9, p. 65-69.
Edited by Philipp Spitta. Original Italian text. Notes in German.

2   SWV 15. -- In NSA. -- 1962. -- Bd. 22, p. 103-109. Pub. no.:
Bärenreiter 3663.
Edited by Hans Joachim Moser. Italian text with German translation. Notes in German and English. Transposed down M2.

3   Dunque addio, care selve. -- Kassel : Bärenreiter, c1962. Pub. no.:
Bärenreiter-Ausgabe 2864.
Edited by H.J. Moser. Italian text with German translation.
Transposed down M2.

4   Dunque addio, care selve. -- In SSA. -- c1984. -- Bd. 1, p. 90-96.
    Pub. no.: HE 20.915.
       Edited by Siegfried Schmalzriedt. Italian text. Notes in German
    and English.

    Other editions: Hänssler HE20.015.

SWV 16

[Madrigals. Tornate o cari baci]

    Secular Italian text. Sources: Marino, Giambattista. Baci cari.
       For chorus (SSATB) a cappella. Ranges of voice parts: d1-g2,
    d1-e2, g-b1, c-f1, G-c1. Duration: short.

1   Tornate o cari baci. -- In SGA. -- 1890. -- Bd. 9, p. 69-72.
       Edited by Philipp Spitta. Original Italian text. Notes in German.

2   SWV 16. -- In NSA. -- 1962. -- Bd. 22, p. 110-115. Pub. no.:
    Bärenreiter 3663.
       Edited by Hans Joachim Moser. Italian text with German
    translation. Notes in German and English.

3   Tornate o cari baci. -- Kassel : Bärenreiter, c1963. Pub. no.:
    Bärenreiter-Ausgabe 2865.
       Edited by H.J. Moser. Italian text with German translation.

4   Tornate, o cari baci. -- In SSA. -- c1984. -- Bd. 1, p. 97-101. Pub.
    no.: HE 20.915.
       Edited by Siegfried Schmalzriedt. Italian text. Notes in German
    and English.

    Other editions: Hänssler HE20.016.

SWV 17

[Madrigals. Di marmo siete voi]

    Secular Italian text. Sources: Marino, Giambattista. Somiglianza tra
    l'amante e l'amata.
       For chorus (SSMAR) a cappella. Ranges of voice parts: d1-a2,
    e1-a2, g-d2, e-a1, A-d1. Duration: short.

1   Di marmo siete voi. -- In SGA. -- 1890. -- Bd. 9, p. 73-76.
       Edited by Philipp Spitta. Original Italian text. Notes in German.

2   SWV 17. -- In NSA. -- 1962. -- Bd. 22, p. 116-122. Pub. no.:
    Bärenreiter 3663.
       Edited by Hans Joachim Moser. Italian text with German
    translation. Notes in German and English. Transposed down M2.

3   Di marmo siete voi. -- Kassel : Bärenreiter, c1963. Pub. no.:
    Bärenreiter-Ausgabe 2866.
       Edited by H.J. Moser. Italian text with German translation.
    Transposed down M2.

4   Di marmo siete voi. -- In SSA. -- c1984. -- Bd. 1, p. 102-106. Pub.
    no.: HE 20.915.
    Edited by Siegfried Schmalzriedt. Italian text. Notes in German
    and English.

    Other editions: Hänssler HE20.017.

SWV 18

[Madrigals. Giunto è pur, Lidia]

    Secular Italian text. Sources: Marino, Giambattista. Partita
    dell'amante.
    For chorus (SSMAR) a cappella. Ranges of voice parts: el-a2,
    dl-f2, g-c2, g-al, A-dl. Duration: short.

1   Giunto è pur, Lidia, giunto. -- In SGA. -- 1890. -- Bd. 9, p. 76-79.
    Edited by Philipp Spitta. Original Italian text. Notes in German.

2   SWV 18. -- In NSA. -- 1962. -- Bd. 22, p. 123-128. Pub. no.:
    Bärenreiter 3663.
    Edited by Hans Joachim Moser. Italian text with German
    translation. Notes in German and English. Transposed down M2.

3   Giunto è pur, Lidia. -- Kassel : Bärenreiter, c1962. Pub. no.:
    Bärenreiter-Ausgabe 2867.
    Edited by H.J. Moser. Italian text with German translation.
    Transposed down M2.

4   Giunto è pur, Lidia. -- In SSA. -- c1984. -- Bd. 1, p. 107-111. Pub.
    no.: HE 20.915.
    Edited by Siegfried Schmalzriedt. Italian text. Notes in German
    and English.

    Other editions: Hänssler HE20.018.

SWV 19

[Madrigals. Vasto mar, nel cui seno]

    Secular Italian text.
    For chorus (SATB/SATB) a cappella. Ranges of voice parts: cl-f2,
    g-al, c-el, D-bflat/ cl-f2, e-bl, c-gl, D-cl. Duration: short.

1   Vasto mar, nel cui seno. -- In SGA. -- 1890. -- Bd. 9, p. 80-85.
    Edited by Philipp Spitta. Original Italian text. Notes in German.

2   SWV 19. -- In NSA. -- 1962. -- Bd. 22, p. 129-140. Pub. no.:
    Bärenreiter 3663.
    Edited by Hans Joachim Moser. Italian text with German
    translation. Notes in German and English.

3   Vasto mar. -- Kassel : Bärenreiter, c1962. Pub. no.:
    Bärenreiter-Ausgabe 2868.
    Edited by H.J. Moser. Italian text with German translation.

4   Vasto Mar. -- In SSA. -- c1984. -- Bd. 1, p. 112-123. Pub. no.: HE
     20.915.
        Edited by Siegfried Schmalzriedt. Italian text. Notes in German
     and English.

        Other editions: Hänssler HE20.019.

SWV 20

[Wort Jesus Syrach]

        Sacred German text. Sources: Apocrypha. Ecclesiasticus 26:1-4.
     Apocrypha. Ecclesiasticus 26:21.
        For chorus (SATB) and coro capella of tenor and 3 cornetti with 3
     optional voices (SSM) and basso continuo. Ranges of voice parts:
     c1-g2, g-a1, c-f1, D-c1/ d-d1. Duration: medium.

1   Die Wort Jesus Syrach : wol dem der ein tugendsam Weib hat. -- In
     SGA. -- 1893. -- Bd. 14, p. 111-126.
        Edited by Philipp Spitta. Figured bass not realized. Original
     German text. Notes in German.

SWV 21

[Concertos, SWV 21]

        Sacred German text. Sources: Proverbs 18:22. Proverbs 19:14.
        For chorus I (T voice and 3 trombones or bassoons), chorus II (T
     voice and 3 cornetti or violins), and chorus III (SSB) with basso
     continuo. Ranges of voice parts: c-f1/ c-f1/ d1-f2, d1-f2, G-g.
     Duration: medium.

1   Concert mit 11. Stimmen : Haus und Güter erbet man von Eltern.
     -- In SGA. -- 1893. -- Bd. 14, p. 129-139.
        Edited by Philipp Spitta. Figured bass not realized. Original
     German text. Notes in German.

SWV 22

[Psalmen Davids. Herr sprach zu meinem Herren]

        Sacred German text. Sources: Psalm 110. Gloria Patri.
        For coro favorito I and II (SATB/SATB) and basso continuo with
     optional coro capella (SSATB) and/or instruments. Ranges of voice
     parts: d1-eflat2, a-g1, d-e1, F-bflat/ d1-eflat2, a-a1, d-f1,
     F-bflat/ a1-a2, d1-eflat2, a-a1, d-d1, C-eflat. Duration: medium.

1   Der Herr sprach zu meinem Herren. -- In SGA. -- 1886. -- Bd. 2, p.
     7-20.
        Edited by Philipp Spitta. Figured bass not realized. Original
     German text. Notes in German.

2   Der Herr sprach zu meinem Herren. -- In NSA. -- 1971. -- Bd. 23, p.
     1-22. Pub. no.: BA4475.
     German text. Edited by Wilhelm Ehmann; figured bass realized by
     Wolfgang Dissel. Notes in German and English.

     Other editions: Bärenreiter BA5911.

SWV 23

[Psalmen Davids. Warum toben die Heiden]

     Sacred German text. Sources: Psalm 2. Gloria Patri.
     For coro favorito I and II (SATB/SATB) and basso continuo with
     optional coro capella I and II (SSAB/SSAB) and/or instruments.
     Ranges of voice parts: c1-f2, g-a1, d-f1, F-bflat/ a-f2, d-bflat1,
     c-g1,F-d1/ d1-a2, d1-d2, f-g1, D-eflat/ d1-a2, d1-d2, g-a1, C-g.
     Duration: medium.

1   Warum toben die Heiden. -- In SGA. -- 1886. -- Bd. 2, p. 21-38.
     Edited by Philipp Spitta. Figured bass not realized. Original
     German text. Notes in German.

2   Warum toben die Heiden. -- In NSA. -- 1971. -- Bd. 23, p. 23-52.
     Pub. no.: BA4475.
     German text. Edited by Wilhelm Ehmann; figured bass realized by
     Johannes H.E. Koch. Notes in German and English.

3   Warum toben die Heiden. -- Kassel : Bärenreiter, c1971. Pub. no.:
     Bärenreiter-Ausgabe 1716.
     Edited by Wilhelm Ehmann; continuo realized by Johann H.E. Koch.
     German text. Notes in German and English.

SWV 24

[Psalmen Davids. Ach Herr, straf mich nicht in deinem Zorn]

     Sacred German text. Sources: Psalm 6. Gloria Patri.
     For coro favorito I and II (SATB/SATB) and basso continuo. Ranges
     of voice parts: b-f2, g-a1, d-e1, E-a/ b-e2, e-a1, c-e1, E-a.
     Duration: medium.

1   Ach Herr, straf mich nicht in deinem Zorn. -- In SGA. -- 1886. --
     Bd. 2, p. 39-46.
     Edited by Philipp Spitta. Figured bass not realized. Original
     German text. Notes in German.

2   Ach Herr, straf mich nicht in deinem Zorn. -- In NSA. -- 1971. --
     Bd. 23, p. 53-72. Pub. no.: BA4475.
     Edited by Wilhelm Ehmann. German text. Edited by Wilhelm Ehmann;
     figured bass realized by Heinz Dieter Pharrherr.

3   Ach Herr, straf mich nicht in deinem Zorn. -- Kassel : Bärenreiter,
     c1967. Pub. no.: Bärenreiter-Ausgabe 1718.
     Edited by Wilhelm Ehmann; continuo realized by Heinz Dieter
     Pharrherr. German text. Notes in German and English.

5 Ach Herr, straf mich nicht in deinem Zorn = O Lord, in thy wrath
   rebuke me not. -- Neuhausen-Stuttgart : Hänssler, c1974. Pub. no.:
   HE 20.024.
       Edited by Günter Graulich; continuo realized by Paul Horn. German
   text with English translation. Notes in German and English.

       Other editions: Hänssler 1.070.

SWV 25

[Psalmen Davids. Aus der Tiefe, ruf ich Herr, zu dir]

    Sacred German text. Sources: Psalm 130. Gloria Patri.
       For coro favorito I and II (SATB/SATB) and basso continuo. Ranges
    of voice parts: b-e2, a-a1, d-e1, E-c1/ e1-e2, a-a1, c-e1, E-a.
    Duration: short.

1 Aus der Tiefe, ruf ich, Herr, zu dir. -- In SGA. -- 1886. -- Bd. 2,
   p. 47-53.
       Edited by Philipp Spitta. Figured bass not realized. Original
   German text. Notes in German.

2 Aus der Tiefe, ruf ich Herr, zu dir. -- In NSA. -- 1971. -- Bd. 23,
   p. 73-84. Pub. no.: BA4475.
       Edited by Wilhelm Ehmann; figured bass realized by Johannes H.E.
   Koch. German text. Notes in German and English. Transposed up M2.

3 Aus der Tiefe, ruf ich Herr, zu dir. -- Kassel : Bärenreiter, c1983.
   Pub. no.: Bärenreiter-Ausgabe 1717.
       Edited by Wilhelm Ehmann; continuo realized by Johann H.E. Koch.
   German text. Transposed up M2.

5 Aus der Tiefe, ruf ich Herr, zu dir = From the depths have I cried
   to thee, Lord. -- Neuhausen-Stuttgart : Hänssler, c1969. Pub. no.:
   HE 20.025.
       Edited by Günter Graulich; continuo realized by Paul Horn. German
   text with English translation. Notes in German and English.

SWV 26

[Psalmen Davids. Ich freu mich des, das mir geredt ist]

    Sacred German text. Sources: Psalm 122. Gloria Patri.
       For coro favorito I and II (SATB/SATB) and basso continuo with
    optional coro capella I and II (SSMB/SSMB) and/or instruments.
    Ranges of voice parts: b-e2, g-b1, d-f1, F-b/ b-e2, d-a1, d-f1,
    E-c1/ g1-a2, g1-e2, a-d1, C-a/ a1-a2, c1-e2, a-d2, C-g2. Duration:
    long.

1 Ich freu mich des, das mir geredt ist. -- In SGA. -- 1886. -- Bd. 2,
   p. 54-71.
       Edited by Philipp Spitta. Figured bass not realized. Original
   German text. Notes in German.

2   Ich freu mich des, das mir geredt ist. -- In NSA. -- 1971. -- Bd.
     23, p. 85-112. Pub. no.: BA4475.
     Edited by Wilhelm Ehmann; figured bass realized by Johannes H.E.
     Koch. German text. Notes in German and English.

3   Ich freu mich des, das mir geredt ist. -- Kassel : Bärenreiter,
     c1956. Pub. no.: Bärenreiter-Ausgabe 1715.
     Edited by Wilhelm Ehmann; continuo realized by Johann H.E. Koch.
     German text. Notes in German.

SWV 27

[Psalmen Davids. Herr, unser Herrscher, wie herrlich ist dein Nam]

    Sacred German text. Sources: Psalm 8. Gloria Patri.
    For coro favorito I and II (SSAT/ATRB) and basso continuo with
    optional coro capella (SSATB) and/or instruments. Ranges of voice
    parts: d1-f2, d1-e2, f-a1, a-f1/ b-a1, c-f1, A-d1, E-c1/ g1-a2,
    d1-d2, c1-a1, e-d1, C-d. Duration: medium.

1   Herr, unser Herrscher, wie herrlich ist dein Nam. -- In SGA. --
     1886. -- Bd. 2, p. 72-90.
     Edited by Philipp Spitta. Figured bass not realized. Original
     German text. Notes in German.

2   Herr, unser Herrscher. -- In NSA. -- 1971. -- Bd. 23, p. 113-134.
     Pub. no.: BA 4475.
     Edited by Wilhelm Ehmann; continuo realized by Walter Simon Huber.
     German text. Notes in German and English.

3   Herr, unser Herrscher. -- Kassel : Bärenreiter, c1964. Pub. no.:
     Bärenreiter-Ausgabe 2399.
     Edited by Walter Simon Huber. German text. Notes in German.

SWV 28

[Psalmen Davids. Wohl dem, der nicht wandelt im Rat]

    Sacred German text. Sources: Psalm 1. Gloria Patri.
    For coro favorito I and II (SMAR/ATTB) and basso continuo. Ranges
    of voice parts: d1-g2, g-d2, f-a1, G-eflat1/ d-a1, c-d1, c-e1,
    D-bflat. Duration: medium.

1   Wohl dem, der nicht wandelt im Rath der Gottlosen. -- In SGA. --
     1886. -- Bd. 2, p. 91-103.
     Edited by Philipp Spitta. Figured bass not realized. Original
     German text. Notes in German.

2   Wohl dem, der nicht wandelt im Rat. -- In NSA. -- 1971. -- Bd. 23,
     p. 135-154. Pub. no.: BA 4475.
     Edited by Wilhelm Ehmann; continuo realized by Wolfgang Dissel.
     German text. Notes in German and English.

5   Wohl dem, der nicht wandelt im Rat der Gottlosen = Blessed they who
     keep not the law of the ungodly. -- Neuhausen-Stuttgart : Hänssler,
     c1974. Pub. no.: HE 20.028.
        Edited by Günter Graulich; continuo realized by Paul Horn. German
     text with English translation. Notes in German and English.

     Other editions: Bärenreiter BA5912.

SWV 29

[Psalmen Davids. Wie lieblich sind deine Wohnungen]

     Sacred German text. Sources: Psalm 84.
        For coro favorito I and II (SSAR/TTRB) and basso continuo. Ranges
     of voice parts: f#1-g2, bflat-d2, g-a1, A-f1/ d-f1, c-d1, Bflat-d1,
     D-g. Duration: medium.

1   Wie lieblich sind deine Wohnunge, Herre Zebaoth. -- In SGA. -- 1886.
     -- Bd. 2, p. 104-119.
        Edited by Philipp Spitta. Figured bass not realized. Original
     German text. Notes in German.

2   Wie lieblich sind deine Wohnungen. -- In NSA. -- 1971. -- Bd. 23, p.
     155-177. Pub. no.: BA4475.
        Edited by Wilhelm Ehmann; figured bass realized by Johannes H.E.
     Koch. German text. Notes in German and English. Transposed up M2.

3   Wie lieblich sind deine Wohnungen, Herr Zebaoth. -- Kassel :
     Bärenreiter, c1956. Pub. no.: Bärenreiter-Ausgabe 1714.
        Edited by Wilhelm Ehmann; continuo realized by Johann H.E. Koch.
     German text. Notes in German. Transposed up M2.

5   Wie lieblich sind deine Wohnungen = O how fair are all thy courts.
     -- Neuhausen-Stuttgart : Hänssler, c1968. Pub. no.: HE 20.029.
        Edited by Günter Graulich; continuo realized by Paul Horn. German
     text with English translation. Notes in German and English.

6   How lovely is thine own dwelling place. -- New York : G. Schirmer,
     c1957. Pub. no.: Ed. 2265.
        Edited by William H. Reese. German text with English translation.
     Notes in English.

SWV 30

[Psalmen Davids. Wohl dem, der den Herren fürchtet, SWV 30]

     Sacred German text. Sources: Psalm 128. Gloria Patri.
        For coro favorito I and II (SSAT/ATRB) and basso continuo. Ranges
     of voice parts: c1-f2, a-f2, g-a1, A-e1/ g-a1, c-f1, A-c1, D-a.
     Duration: medium.

1   Wohl dem, der den Herren fürchtet. -- In SGA. -- 1886. -- Bd. 2, p.
     120-129.
        Edited by Philipp Spitta. Figured bass not realized. Original
     German text. Notes in German.

2   Wohl dem, der den Herren fürchtet. -- In NSA. -- 1971. -- Bd. 23, p. 178-194. Pub. no.: BA4475.
      Edited by Wilhelm Ehmann; figured bass realized by Heinz Dieter Pharrherr. German text. Notes in German and English. Transposed up M2.

5   Wohl dem, der den Herren fürchtet = Blessed are all those who fear God. -- Neuhausen-Stuttgart : Hänssler, c1973. Pub. no.: HE 20.030.
      Edited by Günter Graulich; continuo realized by Paul Horn. German text with English translation. Notes in German and English.

      Other editions: Bärenreiter BA5913.

SWV 31

[Psalmen Davids. Ich hebe meine Augen auf zu den Bergen]

      Sacred German text. Sources: Psalm 121.
      For coro favorito (SATB), coro capella (SATB) and basso continuo with optional coro capella (SATB) at times doubling the coro favorito. Ranges of voice parts: c1-f2, f-a1, c-f1, D-c1/ c1-e2, g-a1, A-f#1, D-d1/ c1-f2, f-a1, c-e1, D-c1. Duration: medium.

1   Ich hebe meine Augen auf zu den Bergen. -- In SGA. -- 1886. -- Bd. 2, p. 130-142.
      Edited by Philipp Spitta. Figured bass not realized. Original German text. Notes in German.

2   Ich hebe meine Augen auf. -- In NSA. -- 1979. -- Bd. 24, p. 1-23. Pub. no.: BA4476.
      Edited by Wilhelm Ehmann; figured bass realized by Horst Soenke. German text. Notes in German and English. Transposed up M2.

3   Ich hebe meine Augen auf zu den Bergen. -- Kassel : Bärenreiter, c1956. Pub. no.: Bärenreiter-Ausgabe 1713.
      Edited by Wilhelm Ehmann; continuo realized by Horst Soenke. German text. Notes in German. Transposed up M2.

5   Ich hebe meine Augen auf zu den Bergen = I lift up mine eyes to the hills. -- Neuhausen-Stuttgart : Hänssler, c1969. Pub. no.: HE 20.031.
      Edited by Günter Graulich; continuo realized by Paul Horn. German text with English translation. Notes in German and English.

SWV 32

[Psalmen Davids. Danket dem Herren, denn er ist freundlich, SWV 32]

      Sacred German text. Sources: Psalm 136.
      For coro favorito I and II (SSMT/ATTB) and basso continuo with optional coro capella I and II (SATB/SSMT) and/or instruments. Ranges of voice parts: g1-a2, d1-f2, a-d2, A-g1/ g-a1, c-f1, c-e1, D-a/ d1-e2, g-a1, c-e1, F-a/ g1-a2, f1-e2, bflat-b1, d-e1. Duration: medium.

1   Danket dem Herren, denn er ist freundlich. -- In SGA. -- 1886. --
     Bd. 2, p. 143-170.
     Edited by Philipp Spitta. Figured bass not realized. Original
     German text. Notes in German.

2   Danket dem Herren, denn er ist freundlich. -- In NSA. -- 1979. --
     Bd. 24, p. 24-64. Pub. no.: BA 4476.
     Edited by Wilhelm Ehmann; continuo realized by Heinrich Ehmann.
     German text. Notes in German and English.

SWV 33

[Psalmen Davids. Herr ist mein Hirt]

     Sacred German text. Sources: Psalm 23.
     For coro favorito (SSAT/SATB) and basso continuo with optional
     coro capella (SSAT) at times doubling the coro favorito. Ranges of
     voice parts: d1-g2, a-d2, f-a1, Bflat-f1/ e1-d2, a-a1, d-f1,
     F-bflat/ f1-g2, a-d2, g-g1, c-c1. Duration: medium.

1   Der Herr ist mein Hirt, mir wird nichts mangeln. -- In SGA. -- 1886.
     -- Bd. 2, p. 171-179.
     Edited by Philipp Spitta. Figured bass not realized. Original
     German text. Notes in German.

2   Der Herr ist mein Hirt. -- In NSA. -- 1979. -- Bd. 24, p. 65-86.
     Pub. no.: BA 4476.
     Edited by Wilhelm Ehmann; continuo realized by Heinrich Ehmann.
     German text. Notes in German and English.

5   Der Herr ist mein Hirt. -- Neuhausen-Stuttgart : Hänssler, c1970.
     Pub. no.: HE 20.033/02.
     Edited by Günter Graulich; continuo realized by Paul Horn. German
     text with English translation.

SWV 34

[Psalmen Davids. Ich danke dem Herrn von ganzem Herzen]

     Sacred German text. Sources: Psalm 111. Gloria Patri.
     For coro favorito I and II (SATB/SATB) and basso continuo with
     optional coro capella I and II (SMAB/SMAB) and/or instruments.
     Ranges of voice parts: b-f2, g-a1, a-e1, D-bflat/ a-f2, f-a1, c-f1,
     D-a/ f-bflat2, d1-d2, g-a1, C-g/ f1-a2, a-d2, f-bflat1, C-g.
     Duration: medium.

1   Ich danke dem Herrn von ganzem Herzen. -- In SGA. -- 1886. -- Bd. 2,
     p. 180-205.
     Edited by Philipp Spitta. Figured bass not realized. Original
     German text. Notes in German.

2   Ich danke dem Herrn. -- In NSA. -- 1979. -- Bd. 24, p. 87-122. Pub.
     no.: BA4476.
     Edited by Wilhelm Ehmann; figured bass realized by Heinrich
     Ehmann. German text. Notes in German and English.

3   Ich danke dem Herrn von ganzem Herzen. -- Kassel : Bärenreiter,
c1979. Pub. no.: BA 5920.
    Edited by Wilhelm Ehmann; continuo realized by Heinrich Ehmann.
German text.

SWV 35

[Psalmen Davids. Singet dem Herrn ein neues Lied]

    Sacred German text. Sources: Psalm 98. Gloria Patri.
    For coro favorito I and II (SATB/SATB) and basso continuo. Ranges
of voice parts: c1-f2, e-a1, A-d1, D-c1/ c1-f2, f-a1, A-f1, F-bflat.
Duration: medium.

1   Singet dem Herrn ein neues Lied. -- In SGA. -- 1887. -- Bd. 3, p.
3-15.
    Edited by Philipp Spitta. Figured bass not realized. Original
German text. Notes in German.

2   Singet dem Herrn ein neues Lied. -- In NSA. -- 1979. -- Bd. 24, p.
123-144. Pub. no.: BA4476.
    Edited by Wilhelm Ehmann; figured bass realized by Heinrich
Ehmann. German text. Notes in German and English. Transposed up M2.

3   Singet dem Herrn ein neues Lied. -- Kassel : Bärenreiter, c1962.
Pub. no.: Bärenreiter 2398.
    Edited by Albert Thate. Continuo line not included. German text.
Transposed up M2.

5   Singet dem Herrn ein neues Lied = Sing to the Lord a new song. --
Neuhausen-Stuttgart : Hänssler, c1969. Pub. no.: HE 20.035.
    Edited by Günter Graulich; continuo realized by Paul Horn. German
text with English translation. Notes in German and English.

SWV 36

[Psalmen Davids. Jauchzet dem Herren, alle Welt, SWV 36]

    Sacred German text. Sources: Psalm 100. Gloria Patri.
    For coro favorito I and II (SATB/SATB), each chorus accompanied by
basso continuo. Ranges of voice parts: a-f1, f-a1, c-d1, F-d1/ a-f2,
f-a1, c-d1, F-d1. Duration: medium.

1   Jauchzet dem Herren, alle Welt. -- In SGA. -- 1887. -- Bd. 3, p.
16-24.
    Edited by Philipp Spitta. Figured bass not realized. Original
German text. Notes in German.

2   Jauchzet dem Herren. -- In NSA. -- 1979. -- Bd. 24, p. 145-176. Pub.
no.: BA4476.
    German text. Edited by Wilhelm Ehmann; figured bass realized by
Heinrich Ehmann. Notes in German and English. Transposed up M2.

3   Jauchzet dem Herren alle Welt. -- Kassel : Bärenreiter, c1963. Pub.
     no.: Bärenreiter 480.
     German text. Transposed up M2.

5   Jauchzet dem Herrn. -- Neuhausen-Stuttgart : Hänssler, c1968. Pub.
     no.: HE 1.021.
     German text. Transposed up M2.

6   Sing and be joyful. -- Winona, Minn. : H. Leonard, c1981. Pub. no.:
     08681800.
     Edited by Rod Walker. English text. Transposed up M2.

7   Psalm 100. -- Bryn Mawr, Pa. : T. Presser, c1951. Pub. no.:
     312-40084.
     Edited by George Lynn. German text with English translation.
     Transposed up M2.

8   Jauchzet dem Herren, alle Welt. -- Kassel : Bärenreiter, c1969. Pub.
     no.: Bärenreiter 5914.
     Early version of SWV 36 for triple choir. Edited by Werner Breig.
     German text. Notes in German and English.

9   Jauchzet dem Herren, alle Welt. -- In NSA. -- Kassel : Bärenreiter,
     1971. -- Bd. 28, p. 61-88. Pub. no.: BA4480.
     Edited by Werner Breig. German text. Notes in German and English.
     Early setting of SWV 36 for triple choir.

     Other editions: Hänssler 44.145.

SWV 37

[Psalmen Davids. An den Wassern zu Babel sassen wir]

     Sacred German text. Sources: Psalm 137. Gloria Patri.
     For coro favorito I and II (SATB/SATB) and basso continuo. Ranges
     of voice parts: e1-e2, g#-a1, e-g1, G-c1/ c#1-e2, d-a1, d-f1, G-c1.
     Duration: medium.

1   An den Wassern zu Babel sassen wir und weinten. -- In SGA. -- 1887.
     -- Bd. 3, p. 25-33.
     Edited by Philipp Spitta. Figured bass not realized. Original
     German text. Notes in German.

2   An den Wassern zu Babel. -- In NSA. -- 1979. -- Bd. 24, p. 177-193.
     Pub. no.: BA4476.
     Edited by Wilhelm Ehmann; figured bass realized by Heinrich
     Ehmann. German text. Notes in German and English.

3   An den Wassern zu Babel. -- Kassel : Bärenreiter, c1979. Pub. no.:
     BA 6238.
     Edited by Wilhelm Ehmann; continuo realized by Heinrich Ehmann.
     German text.

SWV 38

[Psalmen Davids. Alleluia! Lobet den Herrn in seinem Heiligtum]

Sacred German text. Sources: Psalm 150.
For coro favorito I and II (SATB/SATB) and basso continuo with
optional coro capella I (3 cornetti and trombone or 3 violins and
bassoon or SSMB chorus) and coro capella II (cornetto or flute and 2
trombones and trombone or bassoon or SATB chorus). Ranges of voice
parts: f1-f2, a-a1, c-f1, G-c1/ c1-f2, e-a1, c-f1, D-a/ e1-a2,
e1-e2, g-e2, C-g/ d1-e2, a-g1, d-f1, C-e. Duration: long.

1   Alleluia! Lobet den Herrn in seinem Heiligthum. -- In SGA. -- 1887.
    -- Bd. 3, p. 34-76.
    Edited by Philipp Spitta. Figured bass not realized. Original
    German text. Notes in German.

2   Alleluja! Lobet den Herren. -- In NSA. -- 1981. -- Bd. 25, p. 3-64.
    Pub. no.: BA4477.
    Edited by Wilhelm Ehmann; figured bass realized by Heinrich
    Ehmann. German text. Notes in German and English.

6   Psalm 150 from Psalmen Davids, Dresden 1619. -- North Easton, Mass.
    : Robert King Music Co., c1958. Pub. no.: MFB no. 601.
    Edited by Theodore Marier. German text with English translation.
    Notes in English.

7   Alleluia, lobet den Herren = Alleluia, worship Jehovah. -- London :
    Oxford University Press, Music Dept., c1978.
    Edited by Paul Steinitz. German text with English translation.
    Notes in English.

SWV 39

[Psalmen Davids. Lobe den Herrn, meine Seele]

Sacred German text. Sources: Psalm 103:1-4.
For coro favorito (SATB), coro capella (SATB) and basso continuo
with optional coro capella at times doubling the coro favorito.
Ranges of voice parts: d1-f2, f-bflat1, c-g1, F-bflat/ d1-d2, a-g1,
d-d1, F-bflat. Duration: medium.

1   Lobe den Herrn, meine Seele. -- In SGA. -- 1887. -- Bd. 3, p. 77-88.
    Edited by Philipp Spitta. Figured bass not realized. Original
    German text. Notes in German.

2   Lobe den Herren, meine Seele. -- In NSA. -- 1980. -- Bd. 25, p.
    65-78. Pub. no.: BA4477.
    Edited by Wilhelm Ehmann; continuo realized by Friedrich
    Rabenschlag. German text. Notes in German and English. Transposed up
    M2.

3   Lobe den Herren, meine Seele. -- Kassel : Bärenreiter, c1962. Pub.
    no.: Bärenreiter-Ausgabe 1588.
       Edited by Friedrich Rabenschlag. German text. Notes in German and
    English. Transposed up M2.

5   Lobe den Herren, meine Seele. -- Neuhausen-Stuttgart : Hänssler,
    c1967. Pub. no.: HE 1.040.
       Edited by Emil Kübler. German text. Notes in German. Transposed up
    M2.

6   Praise ye the Lord, my soul = Lobe den Herren, meine Seele. -- Bryn
    Mawr, Pa. : T. Presser, c1974. Pub. no.: 312-41056.
       Edited by Walter Ehret. German text with English translation.
    Notes in English. Transposed up M2.

7   Sing, o my soul, the Father's praises = Lobe den Herren, meine
    Seele. -- New York : S. Fox, 1967. Pub. no.: CM 28.
       Edited by Roger Granville. German text with English translation.
    Transposed up M2.

8   Lobe den Herren, meine Seele. -- Neuhausen-Stuttgart : Hänssler,
    c1962. Pub. no.: HE 1.018.
       Chorus score. Edited by Albrecht Hermann. German text. Transposed
    up M2.

       Other editions: Hänssler 2.047.

SWV 40

[Psalmen Davids. Ist nicht Ephraim mein teurer Sohn?]

       Sacred German text. Sources: Jeremiah 31:20.
       For coro favorito I (SMAT cornetti or SM or T solo plus trombone
    and 2 cornetti), coro favorito II (A solo plus 3 trombones) and
    basso continuo with optional coro capella I and II (SATB/SATB).
    Ranges of voice parts: d1-f2, c1-c2, c-f1/ g-a1/ d1-f2, c1-a1, d-e1,
    G-a/ d1-d2, bflat-a1, d-f1, F-d1. Duration: medium.

1   Ist nicht Ephraim mein theurer Sohn. -- In SGA. -- 1887. -- Bd. 3,
    p. 89-100.
       Edited by Philipp Spitta. Figured bass not realized. Original
    German text. Notes in German.

2   Ist nicht Ephraim mein teurer Sohn. -- In NSA. -- 1981. -- Bd. 25,
    p. 79-96. Pub. no.: BA4477.
       Edited by Wilhelm Ehmann; figured bass realized by Heinrich
    Ehmann. German text. Notes in German and English.

6   Ist nicht Ephraim mein teurer Sohn? = Is not Ephraim my precious
    son?. -- London : Oxford University Press, Music Dept., c1971.
       Edited by Paul Steinitz. German text with English translation.
    Notes in English.

7   Ist nicht Ephraim mein teurer Sohn? = Is not Ephraim my precious
    son?. -- London : Oxford University Press, Music Dept., c1971.
      Chorus score. Edited by Paul Steinitz. German text with English
    translation.

      Other editions: Hänssler 1.473.

SWV 41

[Psalmen Davids. Nun lob, mein Seel, den Herren]

      Sacred German text. Sources: Graumann, Johann. Nun lob, mein Seel,
    den Herren.
      For coro favorito I and II (SATB/SATB) and basso continuo with
    optional coro capella I (2 violins, 2 violas, double bass) and coro
    capella II (4 cornetti and trombone). Ranges of voice parts: d1-e2,
    f#-b1, c#-f#1, D-a/ d1-e2, g-a1, c#-e1, D-a. Duration: long.

1   Nun lob mein Seele den Herren. -- In SGA. -- 1887. -- Bd. 3, p.
    101-132.
      Edited by Philipp Spitta. Figured bass not realized. Original
    German text. Notes in German.

2   Nun lob, mein Seel, den Herren. -- In NSA. -- 1981. -- Bd. 25, p.
    97-134. Pub. no.: BA4477.
      Edited by Wilhelm Ehmann; figured bass realized by Werner
    Bittinger. German text. Notes in German and English.

3   Nun lob, mein Seel, den Herren. -- Kassel : Bärenreiter, c1963. Pub.
    no.: Bärenreiter-Ausgabe 3465.
      Edited by Wilhelm Ehmann; continuo realized by Werner Bittinger.
    German text. Notes in German.

6   Nun lob, mein Seel, den Herren. -- Neuhausen-Stuttgart : Hänssler,
    c1968. Pub. no.: HE 1.044.
      Edited by Hans Grischkat. German text. Notes in German. Transposed
    up m3.

SWV 42

[Psalmen Davids. Die mit Tränen säen]

      Sacred German text. Sources: Psalm 126:5-6.
      For two choruses, each consisting of soprano and tenor soloists
    and 3 trombones, and basso continuo. Ranges of voice parts: d1-e2,
    c#-f1/ c1-e2, c-e1. Duration: medium.

1   Die mit Thränen säen. -- In SGA. -- 1887. -- Bd. 3, p. 133-141.
      Edited by Philipp Spitta. Figured bass not realized. Original
    German text. Notes in German.

2   Die mit Tränen säen. -- In NSA. -- 1981. -- Bd. 25, p. 135-160. Pub.
    no.: BA4477.
      Edited by Wilhelm Ehmann; figured bass realized by Heinrich
    Ehmann. German text. Notes in German and English. Transposed up M2.

3   Die mit Tränen säen. -- Kassel : Bärenreiter, c1972. Pub. no.:
     Bärenreiter-Ausgabe 5918.
        Edited by Wilhelm Ehmann; continuo realized by Heinrich Ehmann.
     German text. Notes in German and English. Transposed up M2.

5   Die mit Tränen säen = He who weeping soweth. -- Neuhausen-Stuttgart
     : Hänssler, c1983. Pub. no.: HE 20.042/02.
        Edited by Günter Graulich; continuo realized by Paul Horn. German
     text with English translation.

     Other editions: Hänssler 1.022.

SWV 43

[Psalmen Davids. Nicht uns, Herr, sondern deinem Namen gib Ehre]

     Sacred German text. Sources: Psalm 115.
        For chorus I (tenor solo and 3 cornetti), chorus II (SATB), chorus
     III (alto solo and 3 trombones) and basso continuo. Ranges of voice
     parts: c-e1/ c1-e2, f-a1, d-e1, F-a/ a-a1. Duration: medium.

1   Nicht uns, Herr, nicht uns. -- In SGA. -- 1887. -- Bd. 3, p.
     142-166.
        Edited by Philipp Spitta. Figured bass not realized. Original
     German text. Notes in German.

2   Nicht uns, Herr, sondern deinem Name gib Ehre. -- In NSA. -- 1981.
     -- Bd. 25, p. 161-203. Pub. no.: BA4477.
        Edited by Wilhelm Ehmann; figured bass realized by Heinrich
     Ehmann. German text. Notes in German and English.

     Other editions: Hänssler 1.043.

SWV 44

[Psalmen Davids. Wohl dem, der den Herren fürchtet, SWV 44]

     Sacred German text. Sources: Psalm 128.
        For coro favorito I (tenor soloist and 4 cornetti), coro favorito
     II (alto soloist, violin, and 3 trombones), coro capella I (SATB),
     optional coro capella II (SATB) and basso continuo. Ranges of voice
     parts: c-e1/ g-a1/ c1-f2, f-a1, c-e1, F-a/ e1-f2, g-a1, A-e1, E-a.
     Duration: short.

1   Der 128. Psalm. -- In SGA. -- 1887. -- Bd. 3, p. 167-181.
        Edited by Philipp Spitta. Figured bass not realized. Original
     German text. Notes in German.

SWV 45

[Psalmen Davids. Danket dem Herren, denn er ist freundlich, SWV 45]

Sacred German text. Sources: Psalm 136.
For coro favorito I (SSAT), coro favorito II (alto soloist and 3 trombones), coro favorito III (trombetta and timpani), coro capella (SSATB) and basso continuo. Ranges of voice parts: g1-a2, d1-e2, g-a1, e-e1, F-a/ g-a1 / e1-g2, c1-e2, e-a1, c-e1. Duration: medium.

1   Der 136. Psalm. -- In SGA. -- 1887. -- Bd. 3, p. 182-216.
    Edited by Philipp Spitta. Figured bass not realized. Original German text. Notes in German.

3   Danket dem Herren, denn er ist freundlich. -- Kassel : Bärenreiter, c1954. Pub. no.: Bärenreiter-Ausgabe 1710.
    Edited by Wilhelm Ehmann; continuo realized by Johann H.E. Koch. German text. Notes in German. Transposed down m3.

SWV 46

[Psalmen Davids. Zion spricht, der Herr hat mich verlassen]

Sacred German text. Sources: Isaiah 49:14-16.
For coro favorito I (soprano and tenor soloists with 3 cornetti and bassoon), coro favorito II (soprano and tenor soloists with 4 trombones) and basso continuo with optional coro capella I and II (SATB/SATB). Ranges of voice parts: c1-f2, d-f1/ b-d2, B-e1/ f1-f2, a-a1, d-e1, D-a/ c1-e2, g-a1, A-d1, D-a. Duration: medium.

1   Zion spricht, der Herr hat mich verlassen. -- In SGA. -- 1887. -- Bd. 3, p. 217-238.
    Edited by Philipp Spitta. Figured bass not realized. Original German text. Notes in German.

SWV 47

[Psalmen Davids. Jauchzet dem Herren, SWV 47]

Sacred German text. Sources: Psalm 96:11. Psalm 98:4-6. Psalm 117. Psalm 148:1. Psalm 150:4.
For coro favorito I (alto and tenor soli with 2 traversa or 2 cornetti and bassoon), coro favorito II (soprano and tenor soli with lute), coro favorito III (soprano solo with violin and 3 viols), and basso continuo with optional coro capella (SSATB). Ranges of voice parts: g-a1, c-e1/ e1-e2, d-g1/ d1-g2/ d2-a2, g1-e2, a-a1, g-e1, F-a. Duration: long.

1   Jauchzet dem Herren. -- In SGA. -- 1887. -- Bd. 3, p. 239-282.
    Edited by Philipp Spitta. Figured bass not realized. Original German text. Notes in German.

5   Jauchzet dem Herren alle Welt = Show yourselves joyful to the Lord.
    -- Neuhausen-Stuttgart : Hänssler, c1974. Pub. no.: HE 20.047/01.
      Edited by Günter Graulich; continuo realized by Paul Horn. German
    text with English translation. Notes in German and English.

      Other editions: Hänssler 1.041.

SWV 48

[Psalm 133]

      Sacred German text. Sources: Psalm 133:1-3.
      For chorus (SSATB), instruments (cornetto or violin, violin or
    flute, double bass or bassoon), and basso continuo. Ranges of voice
    parts: g-g2, b-f2, g-a1, Bflat-f1, F-d1. Duration: medium.

1   Der 133. Psalm. -- In SGA. -- 1893. -- Bd. 14, p. 143-155.
      Edited by Philipp Spitta. Figured bass not realized. Original
    German text. Notes in German.

SWV 49

[Syncharma musicum]

      Sacred Latin and German text. Sources: Schutz, Heinrich. Syncharma
    musicum.
      For chorus I (tenor soloist and 3 cornettos or 2 cornettos and
    trombone), chorus II (tenor soloist and 3 bassoons), and chorus III
    (SSSB) with basso continuo. Ranges of voice parts: c-eflat1/
    d-g1/f1-g2, c1-f2, c1-f2, F-bflat. Duration: medium.

1   Syncharma musicum. -- In SGA. -- 1893. -- Bd. 15, p. 1-16.
      Edited by Philipp Spitta. Figured bass not realized. Original
    Latin and German text. Notes in German.

2   Syncharma musicum. -- In NSA. -- 1971. -- Bd. 38, p. 22-47. Pub.
    no.: BA4490.
      Edited by Werner Bittinger. Latin and German text. Notes in German
    and English.

SWV 50

[Historia der Auferstehung Jesu Christi]

      Sacred German text. Sources: Corinthians, 1st, 15:57. John 20:2-17.
    John 20:19-23. Luke 23:55-56. Luke 24:1. Luke 24:3-35. Luke 24
    :37-38. Mark 16:1-6. Mark 16:8-11. Mark 16:13-14. Matthew 28:2-4.
    Matthew 28:6-15.

For evangelist (tenor and four viols da gamba), three women (SSS), two angels in the sepulchre (TT), Mary Magdalena (SS), two angels (TT), Jesus (AT), young man (AA), high priests (TRB), Cleophas (T), other disciple (T), chorus (SSATTB), and double chorus (SATB/SATB). Ranges of voice parts: c-f1/ e1-f2, d1,f2, d1-f2/ d-g1, d-d1/ a-f2, c1-e2/ g-d1, f#-a/ d-a1, Bflat-f1/ a-a1, f#-a1/ d-e1, c-a, F-f/ d-g1/ B-e1/ c#1-e2, a-e2, g-a1, d-f1, c-e1, D-a/ d1-D2, A-G1, C-E1, D-A/ C1-E2, A-A1, A-E1, E-A. Duration: long.

1   Historia von der Auferstehung Jesu Christi. -- In SGA. -- 1885. -- Bd. 1, p. 5-46.
     Edited by Philipp Spitta. Figured bass not realized. Original German text. Notes in German.

2   Historia der Auferstehung Jesu Christi. -- 2., durchgesehene Auflage. -- In NSA. -- 1956. -- Bd. 3. Pub. no.: Bärenreiter-Ausgabe 242.
     Edited by Walter Simon Huber. Text in German and Latin. German words in Gothic type. Solo parts in plainsong notation. Notes in German.

5   Historia der Auferstehung Jesu Christi = Account of the Resurrection of Jesus Christ. -- Neuhausen-Stuttgart : Hänssler, c1968. Pub. no.: HE 20.050/01.
     Edited by Günter Graulich. Continuo realized by Paul Horn. Solo parts in plainsong notation. German text with English translation.

6   Auferstehungs-Historie = Histoire de la Resurrection = Resurrection history. -- London ; New York : E. Eulenberg, [19--]. Pub. no.: Edition Eulenburg no. 980.
     Edited by Fritz Stein; figured bass not realized. German text. Notes in German.

SWV 50

[Historia der Auferstehung Jesu Christi. Gott sei Dank]

7   Gott sei Dank, der uns den Sieg gegeben hat. -- Neuhausen-Stuttgart : Hänssler, c1968. Pub. no.: HE 20.050/10.
     For chorus (SATB/SATB), tenor solo, and basso continuo. Concluding chorus of Historia der Auferstehung Jesu Christi. Edited by Günter Graulich; continuo realized by Paul Horn. German text with English translation.

SWV 51

[Psalm 116]

    Sacred German text. Sources: Psalm 116.
    For chorus (SSATB) a cappella. Ranges of voice parts: a-f2, a-f2, d-a1, A-f1, D-c1. Duration: long.

1   Der 166. Psalm. -- In SGA. -- 1892. -- Bd. 12, p. 3-20.
    Edited by Philipp Spitta. Original German text. Notes in German.

2   Das ist mir lieb, dass der Herr mein Stimm und Flehen höret. -- In
    NSA. -- 1971. -- Bd. 28, p. 89-117. Pub. no.: Bärenreiter Ausgabe
    BA4480.
    Edited by Werner Breig. German text. Notes in German.

3   Der 116. Psalm. -- Kassel : Bärenreiter, [1931?]. Pub. no.:
    Bärenreiter-Ausgabe 485.
    Edited by Fritz Holle. German text. Words in Gothic type.

5   Psalm 116 : Das ist mir lieb, dass der Herr mein Stimm und Flehen
    höret : I love the Lord. -- Neuhausen-Stuttgart : Hänssler, c1967.
    Pub. no.: HE 20.051/01.
    Edited by Günter Graulich. German text with English translation.
    Notes in German and English.

SWV 52

[Kläglicher Abschied]

    Secular German text. Sources: Schütz, Heinrich. Kläglicher Abschied.
    Solo for soprano with basso continuo. Range of voice part: d1-e2.
    Duration: short.

1   Grimmige Gruft, so hast du dann. -- In SGA. -- 1927. -- Bd. 18, p.
    116.
    Edited by Heinrich Spitta. Figured bass not realized. Original
    German text. Notes in German.

2   Kläglicher Abschied. -- In NSA. -- 1970. -- Bd. 37, p. 4-5. Pub.
    no.: BA4489.
    Edited by Werner Bittinger. German text. Notes in German and
    English.

SWV 53

[Cantiones sacrae. O bone, o dulcis, o benigne Jesu]

    Sacred Latin text. Sources: Meditationes Augustini.
    For chorus (SMAR) with optional basso continuo. Ranges of voice
    parts: f#1-a2, g-d2, f#-a1, A-d1. Duration: short.

1   O bone, o dulcis. -- In SGA. -- 1887. -- Bd. 4, p. 5-7.
    Edited by Philipp Spitta. Figured bass not realized. Original
    Latin text. Notes in German.

2   O bone, o dulcis = O guter, o lieber, freundlicher Herr Jesu. -- In
    NSA. -- 1960. -- Bd. 8, p. 1-5. Pub. no.: Bärenreiter-Ausgabe 1950.
    Edited by Gottfried Grote. Latin text with German translation.
    Notes in German. Transposed down M2.

3   O bone, o dulcis = O guter, o lieber, freundlicher Herr Jesu. -- In
    Cantiones sacrae. -- Kassel : Bärenreiter, [19--]. -- Motette Nr.
    1-3, p. [1]-5. Pub. no.: Bärenreiter-Ausgabe 1953.
      Edited by Gottfried Grote. Latin text with German translation.
    Transposed down M2.

6   O bone, o dulcis, o benigne Jesu = O guter, o lieber, freundlicher
    Herr Jesu. -- In Selections from Cantiones sacrae. -- New York :
    Belwin Mills, [19--]. -- v. 1, p. [1]-5. Pub. no.: Kalmus vocal
    scores 6441.
      Latin text with German translation. Transposed down M2.

SWV 54

[Cantiones sacrae. Et ne despicias humiliter te petentem]

      Sacred Latin text. Sources: Meditationes Augustini.
      For chorus (SMAR) with optional basso continuo. Ranges of voice
    parts: d1-g2, g-c#2, d-a1, G-d1. Duration: short.

1   Et ne despicias. -- In SGA. -- 1887. -- Bd. 4, p. 8-9.
      Edited by Philipp Spitta. Figured bass not realized. Original
    Latin text. Notes in German.

2   Et ne despicias = Ach Herr, verwirf mich nicht. -- In NSA. -- 1960.
    -- Bd. 8, p. 6-8. Pub. no.: Bärenreiter-Ausgabe 1950.
      Edited by Gottfried Grote. Latin text with German translation.
    Notes in German. Transposed down M2.

3   Et ne despicias = Ach Herr, verwirf mich nicht. -- In Cantiones
    sacrae. -- Kassel : Bärenreiter, [19--]. -- Motette Nr. 1-3, p. 6-8.
    Pub. no.: Bärenreiter-Ausgabe 1953.
      Edited by Gottfried Grote. Latin text with German translation.
    Transposed down M2.

6   Ach Herr, verwirf mich nicht. -- In Selections from Cantiones
    sacrae. -- New York : Belwin Mills, [19--]. -- v. 1, p. 6-8. Pub.
    no.: Kalmus vocal scores 6441.
      Latin text with German translation. Transposed down M2.

SWV 55

[Cantiones sacrae. Deus misereatur nostri]

      Sacred Latin text. Sources: Psalm 67:1.
      For chorus (SMAR) with optional basso continuo. Ranges of voice
    parts: d1-a2, c1-d2, f#-a1, A-f1. Duration: short.

1   Deus misereatur nobis. -- In SGA. -- 1887. -- Bd. 4, p. 10-12.
      Edited by Philipp Spitta. Figured bass not realized. Original
    Latin text. Notes in German.

2   Deus misereatur nostri = Herr Gott, hilf und erbarm dich unser. --
     In NSA. -- 1960. -- Bd. 8, p. 9-12. Pub. no.: Bärenreiter-Ausgabe
     1950.
        Edited by Gottfried Grote. Latin text with German translation.
     Notes in German. Transposed down m3.

3   Deus, misereatur nostri = Herr Gott, hilf und erbarm dich unser. --
     In Cantiones sacrae. -- Kassel : Bärenreiter, [19--]. -- Motette Nr.
     1-3, p. 9-12. Pub. no.: Bärenreiter-Ausgabe 1953.
        Edited by Gottfried Grote. Latin text with German translation.
     Transposed down m3.

6   Deus, misereatur nostri = Herr Gott, hilf und erbarm dich unser. --
     In Selections from Cantiones sacrae. -- New York : Belwin Mills,
     [19--]. -- v. 1, p. 9-12. Pub. no.: Kalmus vocal scores 6441.
        Latin text with German translation. Transposed down m3.

7   Oh Lord, have mercy upon us = Deus misereatur nostri. -- Minneapolis
     : Schmitt, Hall & McCreary, c1959. Pub. no.: no. 1401.
        Edited by Johannes Riedel. Latin text with English translation.
     Transposed down M2.

8   Deus, misereatur nostri = God, be merciful unto us. -- New York : G.
     Schirmer, c1970. Pub. no.: G. Schirmer octavo no. 11969.
        Edited by Maynard Klein. Latin text with English translation.
     Transposed down m3.

9   Deus, misereatur nostri = O God, be merciful unto us. -- [S.1] :
     Tetra Music Corp., c1975. Pub. no.: A.B. 742.
        Edited by Walter Ehret. Latin text with English translation.
     Transposed down m3.

SWV 56

[Cantiones sacrae. Quid commisisti, o dulcissime puer?]

     Sacred Latin text. Sources: Meditationes Augustini.
        For chorus (SATB) with optional basso continuo. Ranges of voice
     parts: d1-e2, e-a1, c-e1, G-b. Duration: short.

1   Quid commisisti. -- In SGA. -- 1887. -- Bd. 4, p. 12-16.
        Edited by Philipp Spitta. Figured bass not realized. Original
     Latin text. Notes in German.

2   Quid commisisti, o dulcissime puer = Was hast du verwirket,
     liebster, freundlicher Herre. -- In NSA. -- 1960. -- Bd. 8, p.
     13-21. Pub. no.: Bärenreiter-Ausgabe 1950.
        Edited by Gottfried Grote. Latin text with German translation.
     Notes in German. Transposed up M2.

3   Quid commisisti, o dulcissime puer = Was hast du verwirket,
     liebster, freundlicher Herre. -- In Cantiones sacrae. -- Kassel :
     Bärenreiter, c1956. -- Motetten Nr. 4-8, p. [1]-9. Pub. no.:
     Bärenreiter-Ausgabe 1954.
        Edited by Gottfried Grote. Latin text with German translation.
     Transposed up M2.

SWV 57

[Cantiones sacrae. Ego sum tui plaga doloris]

Sacred Latin text. Sources: Meditationes Augustini.
For chorus (SATB) with optional basso continuo. Ranges of voice
parts: d1-e2, g-a1, c-e1, G-c. Duration: short.

1   Ego sum tui plaga doloris. -- In SGA. -- 1887. -- Bd. 4, p. 17-19.
    Edited by Philipp Spitta. Figured bass not realized. Original
    Latin text. Notes in German.

2   Ego sum tui plaga doloris = Ich, o ich bin die Qual deiner
    Schmerzen. -- In NSA. -- 1960. -- Bd. 8, p. 21-27. Pub. no.:
    Bärenreiter-Ausgabe 1950.
    Edited by Gottfried Grote. Latin text with German translation.
    Notes in German. Transposed up M2.

3   Ego sum tui plaga doloris = Ich, o ich bin die Qual deiner
    Schmerzen. -- In Cantiones sacrae. -- Kassel : Bärenreiter, c1956.
    -- Motetten Nr. 4-8, p. 9-15. Pub. no.: Bärenreiter-Ausgabe 1954.
    Edited by Gottfried Grote. Latin text with German translation.
    Transposed up M2.

6   Ego sum tui plaga doloris. -- Bryn Mawr, Pa. : T. Presser, c1958.
    Pub. no.: 312-40368.
    Edited by George Lynn. Latin text with English translation.

SWV 58

[Cantiones sacrae. Ego enim inique egi]

Sacred Latin text. Sources: Meditationes Augustini.
For chorus (SATB), with optional basso continuo. Ranges of voice
parts: c#1-f2, g-a1, d-g1, E-c1. Duration: medium.

1   Ego enim inique egi. -- In SGA. -- 1887. -- Bd. 4, p. 20-24.
    Edited by Philipp Spitta. Figured bass not realized. Original
    Latin text. Notes in German.

2   Ego enim inique egi = Ich, nur ich bin der Missetäter. -- In NSA. --
    1960. -- Bd. 8, p. 27-35. Pub. no.: Bärenreiter-Ausgabe 1950.
    Edited by Gottfried Grote. Latin text with German translation.
    Notes in German. Transposed up M2.

3   Ego enim inique egi = Ich, nur ich bin der Missetäter. -- In Kassel
    : Bärenreiter, c1956. -- Motetten Nr. 4-8, p. 15-23. Pub. no.:
    Bärenreiter-Ausgabe 1954.
    Edited by Gottfried Grote. Latin text with German translation.
    Transposed up M2.

SWV 59

[Cantiones sacrae. Quo, nate Dei, quo tua descendit humilitas]

Sacred Latin text. Sources: Meditationes Augustini.
For chorus (SATB) with optional basso continuo. Ranges of voice
parts: a-e2, a-b1, d-e1, E-c1. Duration: short.

1   Quo, nate Dei. -- In SGA. -- 1887. -- Bd. 4, p. 24-27.
    Edited by Philipp Spitta. Figured bass not realized. Original
Latin text. Notes in German.

2   Quo, nate Dei, quo tua descendit humilitas = O Sohn des Höchsten,
    wie tief hast du wollen erniedrigt sein. -- In NSA. -- 1960. -- Bd.
    8, p. 36-41. Pub. no.: Bärenreiter-Ausgabe 1950.
    Edited by Gottfried Grote. Latin text with German translation.
Notes in German. Transposed up M2.

3   Quo, nate dei, quo tua descendit humilitas = O Sohn des Höchsten,
    wie tief hast du wollen erniedrigt sein. -- In Cantiones sacrae. --
    Kassel : Bärenreiter, c1956. -- Motetten Nr. 4-8, p. 24-29. Pub.
    no.: Bärenreiter-Ausgabe 1954.
    Edited by Gottfried Grote. Latin text with German translation.
Transposed up M2.

SWV 60

[Cantiones sacrae. Calicem salutaris accipiam]

Sacred Latin text. Sources: Psalm 116:13-14.
For chorus (SATB) with optional basso continuo. Ranges of voice
parts: c#1-f2, g-a1, d-g1, G-bflat. Duration: short.

1   Calicem salutaris accipiam. -- In SGA. -- 1887. -- Bd. 4, p. 27-30.
    Edited by Philipp Spitta. Figured bass not realized. Original
Latin text. Notes in German.

2   Calicem salutaris accipiam = Ich will den Kelch des Heiles nehmen
    mit Dank. -- In NSA. -- 1960. -- Bd. 8, p. 42-48. Pub. no.:
    Bärenreiter-Ausgabe 1950.
    Edited by Gottfried Grote. Latin text with German translation.
Notes in German. Transposed up M2.

3   Calicem salutaris accipiam = Ich will den Kelch des Heiles nehmen
    mit Dank. -- In Cantiones sacrae. -- Kassel : Bärenreiter, c1956. --
    Motetten Nr. 4-8, p. 30-36. Pub. no.: Bärenreiter-Ausgabe 1954.
    Edited by Gottfried Grote. Latin text with German translation.
Transposed up M2.

SWV 61

[Cantiones sacrae. Verba mea auribus percipe, Domine]

Sacred Latin text. Sources: Psalm 5:1-2.
For chorus (SATB) with optional basso continuo. Ranges of voice
parts: d1-e2, f-a1, c-f1, F-d1. Duration: short.

1   Verba mea auribus percipe. -- In SGA. -- 1887. -- Bd. 4, p. 31-33.
    Edited by Philipp Spitta. Figured bass not realized. Original
    Latin text. Notes in German.

2   Verba mea auribus percipe = Meine Worte höre in Gnaden an. -- In
    NSA. -- 1960. -- Bd. 8, p. 49-54. Pub. no.: Bärenreiter-Ausgabe
    1950.
    Edited by Gottfried Grote. Latin text with German translation.
    Notes in German. Transposed up M2.

3   Verba mea auribus percipe = Meine Worte höre in Gnaden an. --
    Cantiones sacrae. -- Kassel : Bärenreiter, [19--]. -- Motetten Nr.
    9-10, p. [1]-6. Pub. no.: Bärenreiter-Ausgabe 1959.
    Edited by Gottfried Grote. Latin text with German translation.
    Transposed up M2.

6   Verba mea auribus percipe = Meine Worte höre in Gnaden an. -- In
    Selections from Cantiones sacrae. -- New York : Belwin Mills,
    [19--]. -- v. 1, p. [1]-6. Pub. no.: Kalmus vocal scores 6441.
    Latin text with German translation. Transposed up M2.

7   Hearken unto my cry = Verba mea auribus percipe. -- [S.l.] : Tetra
    Music Corp., c1972. Pub. no.: A.B. 715.
    Edited by Walter Ehret. Latin text with English translation.
    Transposed up M2.

SWV 62

[Cantiones sacrae. Quoniam ad te clamabo, Domine]

Sacred Latin text. Sources: Psalm 5:2-3.
For chorus (SATB) with optional basso continuo. Ranges of voice
parts: d1-f2, d-g1, d-f1, D-d1. Duration: short.

1   Quoniam ad te clamabo. -- In SGA. -- 1887. -- Bd. 4, p. 33-35.
    Edited by Philipp Spitta. Figured bass not realized. Original
    Latin text. Notes in German.

2   Quoniam ad te clamabo = O nimm an mein Gebet. -- In NSA. -- 1960. --
    Bd. 8, p. 54-60. Pub. no.: Bärenreiter-Ausgabe 1950.
    Edited by Gottfried Grote. Latin text with German translation.
    Notes in German. Transposed up M2.

3   Quoniam ad te clamabo = O nimm an mein täglich Klagen. -- Cantiones
     sacrae. -- Kassel : Bärenreiter, [19--]. -- Motetten Nr. 9-10, p.
     6-12. Pub. no.: Bärenreiter-Ausgabe 1959.
     Edited by Gottfried Grote. Latin text with German translation.
     Transposed up M2.

6   O nimm mein täglich Klagen. -- In Selections from Cantiones sacrae.
     -- New York : Belwin Mills, [19--]. -- v. 1, p. 6-12. Pub. no.:
     Kalmus vocal scores 6441.
     Latin text with German translation. Transposed up M2.

SWV 63

[Cantiones sacrae. Ego dormio, et cor meum vigilat]

     Sacred Latin text. Sources: Song of Solomon 5:2.
     For chorus (SATB) with optional basso continuo. Ranges of voice
     parts: c1-f2, d-a1, c-g1, F-c1. Duration: medium.

1   Ego dormio, et cor meum vigilat. -- In SGA. -- 1887. -- Bd. 4, p.
     36-40.
     Edited by Philipp Spitta. Figured bass not realized. Original
     Latin text. Notes in German.

2   Ego dormio, et cor meum vigilat = Wenn ich schlafend ruh, wachet
     doch mein liebend Herz. -- In NSA. -- 1960. -- Bd. 8, p. 61-69. Pub.
     no.: Bärenreiter-Ausgabe 1950.
     Edited by Gottfried Grote. Latin text with German translation.
     Notes in German. Transposed up M2.

3   Ego dormio = Wenn ich schlafend ruh. -- In Cantiones sacrae. Kassel
     : Bärenreiter, c1956. -- Motetten Nr. 11-12, p. [1]-9. Pub. no.:
     Bärenreiter-Ausgabe 1960.
     Edited by Gottfried Grote. Latin text with German translation.
     Transposed up M2.

SWV 64

[Cantiones sacrae. Vulnerasti cor meum, filia charissima]

     Sacred Latin text. Sources: Song of Solomon 4:9.
     For chorus (SATB) with optional basso continuo. Ranges of voice
     parts: c1-g2, e-a1, c-f1, F-a. Duration: short.

1   Vulnerasti cor meum. -- In SGA. -- 1887. -- Bd. 4, p. 40-44.
     Edited by Philipp Spitta. Figured bass not realized. Original
     Latin text. Notes in German.

2   Vulnerasti cor meum = Hast verwundet mein Herze. -- In NSA. -- 1960.
     -- Bd. 8, p. 69-76. Pub. no.: Bärenreiter-Ausgabe 1950.
     Edited by Gottfried Grote. Latin text with German translation.
     Notes in German. Transposed up M2.

3   Vulnerasti cor meum = Hast verwundet mein Herze. -- In Cantiones
    sacrae. Kassel : Bärenreiter, c1956. -- Motetten Nr. 11-12, p. 9-16.
    Pub. no.: Bärenreiter-Ausgabe 1960.
       Edited by Gottfried Grote. Latin text with German translation.
    Transposed up M2.

SWV 65

[Cantiones sacrae. Heu mihi, Domine, quia peccavi nimis]

    Sacred Latin text. Sources: Heu mihi Domino, qui peccavi nimis.
       For chorus (SATB) with optional basso continuo. Ranges of voice
    parts: c1-e2, g-a1, A-f1, F-c1. Duration: medium.

1   Heu mihi, Domine. -- In SGA. -- 1887. -- Bd. 4, p. 45-49.
       Edited by Philipp Spitta. Figured bass not realized. Original
    Latin text. Notes in German.

2   Heu mihi, Domine = O weh mir, Herr, mein Gott. -- In NSA. -- 1960.
    -- Bd. 8, p. 77-85. Pub. no.: Bärenreiter-Ausgabe 1950.
       Edited by Gottfried Grote. Latin text with German translation.
    Notes in German. Transposed up M2.

3   Heu mihi, Domine = O weh mir, Herr, mein Gott. -- In Cantiones
    sacrae. -- Kassel : Bärenreiter, c1951. -- Motetten Nr. 13-14, p.
    [1]-9. Pub. no.: Bärenreiter-Ausgabe 1964.
       Edited by Gottfried Grote. Latin text with German translation.
    Transposed up M2.

6   Heu mihi, Domine = O weh mir, Herr, mein Gott. -- In Selections from
    Cantiones sacrae. -- New York : Kalmus, [19--]. -- v. 2, p. [1]-9.
       Latin text with German translation. Transposed up M2.

7   Heu mihi, Domine = O weh mir, Herr, mein Gott. -- New York : Kalmus,
    [19--].
       Latin text with German translation. Transposed up M2.

SWV 66

[Cantiones sacrae. In te, Domine, speravi]

    Sacred Latin text. Sources: Psalm 31:1-2.
       For chorus (SSMT) with optional basso continuo. Ranges of voice
    parts: f1-a2, c1-e2, g-c1, B-e1. Duration: short.

1   In te, Domine, speravi. -- In SGA. -- 1887. -- Bd. 4, p. 49-52.
       Edited by Philipp Spitta. Figured bass not realized. Original
    Latin text. Notes in German.

2   In te, Domine, speravi = In dich, Gott, hab ich gehoffet. -- In NSA.
    -- 1960. -- Bd. 8, p. 86-92. Pub. no.: Bärenreiter-Ausgabe 1950.
       Edited by Gottfried Grote. Latin text with German translation.
    Notes in German. Transposed down M3.

3   In te, Domine, speravi = In dich hab ich gehoffet. -- In Cantiones
     sacrae. -- Kassel : Bärenreiter, c1951. -- Motetten Nr. 13-14, p.
     10-16. Pub. no.: Bärenreiter-Ausgabe 1964.
          Edited by Gottfried Grote. Latin text with German translation.
     Transposed down M3.

6   In te, Domine, speravi = In dich, Gott, hab ich gehoffet. -- In
     Selections from Cantiones sacrae. -- New York : Kalmus, [19--]. --
     v. 2, p. 10-16.
          Latin text with German translation. Transposed down M3.

7   In te, Domine, speravi = In dich, Gott, hab ich gehoffet. -- New
     York : Kalmus, [19--].
          Latin text with German translation. Transposed down M3.

8   In thee, O Lord, do I put my trust = In te domine, speravi. -- New
     York : Chappell, c1967. Pub. no.: 6142.
          Edited by Walter Ehret. Latin text with English translation.
     Transposed down m3.

SWV 67

[Cantiones sacrae. Dulcissime et benignissime Christe]

     Sacred Latin text. Sources: Meditationes Augustini.
          For chorus (SSMT) with optional basso continuo. Ranges of voice
     parts: f#1-a2, b-e2, g-c2, c-e1. Duration: short.

1   Dulcissime et benignissime Christe. -- In SGA. -- 1887. -- Bd. 4, p.
     53-56.
          Edited by Philipp Spitta. Figured bass not realized. Original
     Latin text. Notes in German.

2   Dulcissime et benignissime Christe = Du liebster Herr, du
     Allergütigster, Christe. -- In NSA. -- 1960. -- Bd. 8, p. 93-100.
     Pub. no.: Bärenreiter-Ausgabe 1950.
          Edited by Gottfried Grote. Latin text with German translation.
     Notes in German. Transposed down M2.

3   Dulcissime et benignissime Christe = Du liebster Herr, du
     Allergütigster, Christe. -- In Cantiones sacrae. -- Kassel :
     Bärenreiter, c1960. -- Motette Nr. 15. Pub. no.:
     Bärenreiter-Ausgabe 1965.
          Edited by Gottfried Grote. Latin text with German translation.
     Transposed down M2.

6   Dulcissime et benignissime Christe = Du liebster Herr, du
     Allergütigster, Christe. -- In Selections from Cantiones sacrae. --
     New York : Kalmus, [19--]. -- v. 2, p. 17-24.
          Latin text with German translation. Transposed down M2.

7   Dulcissime et benignissime Christe. -- New York : Kalmus, [19--].
          Latin text with German translation. Transposed down M2.

SWV 68

[Cantiones sacrae. Sicut Moses serpentem in deserto exaltavit]

Sacred Latin text. Sources: John 3:14-15.
For chorus (SATB) with optional basso continuo. Ranges of voice
parts: cl-g2, f-al, c-gl, F-cl. Duration: short.

1   Sicut Moses serpentem. -- In SGA. -- 1887. -- Bd. 4, p. 56-60.
    Edited by Philipp Spitta. Figured bass not realized. Original
    Latin text. Notes in German.

2   Sicut Moses serpentem in deserto exaltavit = So wie Moses die
    Schlange in der Wüste hat erhöhet. -- In NSA. -- 1960. -- Bd. 8, p.
    101-108. Pub. no.: Bärenreiter-Ausgabe 1950.
    Edited by Gottfried Grote. Latin text with German translation.
    Notes in German. Transposed up M2.

3   Sicut Moses serpentem in deserto exaltavit = So wie Moses die
    Schlange in der Wüste hat erhöhet. -- In Cantiones sacrae. -- Kassel
    : Bärenreiter, [19--]. -- Motette Nr. 16. Pub. no.:
    Bärenreiter-Ausgabe 1966.
    Edited by Gottfried Grote. Latin text with German translation.
    Transposed up M2.

6   Sicut Moses serpentem in deserto exaltavit = So wie Moses die
    Schlange in der Wüste hat erhöhet. -- In Selections from Cantiones
    sacrae. -- New York : Kalmus, [19--]. -- v. 2, p. 25-32.
    Latin text with German translation. Transposed up M2.

7   Sicut Moses serpentem in deserto exaltavit. -- New York : Kalmus,
    [19--].
    Latin text with German translation. Transposed up M2.

SWV 69

[Cantiones sacrae. Spes mea, Christe Deus]

Sacred Latin text. Sources: Meditationes Augustini.
For chorus (SATB) with optional basso continuo. Ranges of voice
parts: cl-e2, g-gl, c-el, D-a. Duration: short.

1   Spes mea, Christe Deus. -- In SGA. -- 1887. -- Bd. 4, p. 61-64.
    Edited by Philipp Spitta. Figured bass not realized. Original
    Latin text. Notes in German.

2   Spes mea, Christe Deus = O meine Hoffnung, Jesus. -- In NSA. --
    1960. -- Bd. 8, p. 109-115. Pub. no.: Bärenreiter-Ausgabe 1950.
    Edited by Gottfried Grote. Latin text with German translation.
    Notes in German. Transposed up m3.

3   Spes mea, Christe Deus = O meine Hoffnung, Jesus. -- In Cantiones
     sacrae. -- Kassel : Bärenreiter, [19--]. -- Motetten Nr. 17-18, p.
     [1]-7. Pub. no.: Bärenreiter-Ausgabe 1967.
        Edited by Gottfried Grote. Latin text with German translation.
     Transposed up m3.

6   Spes mea, Christe Deus = O meine Hoffnung, Jesus. -- In Selections
     from Cantiones sacrae. -- New York : Kalmus, [19--]. -- v. 3, p.
     [1]-7.
        Latin text with German translation. Transposed up m3.

7   Spea mea, Christe Deus. -- New York : Kalmus, [19--].
        Latin text with German translation. Transposed up m3.

8   Thou art my hope, Christ Jesus = Spes mea, Christe Deus. -- Bryn
     Mawr, Pa. : T. Presser, c1980. Pub. no.: 312-41259.
        Edited by Walter Ehret. Latin text with English translation.
     Transposed up M2.

SWV 70

[Cantiones sacrae. Turbabor, sed non perturbabor]

     Sacred Latin text. Sources: Meditationes Augustini.
        For chorus (SATB) with optional basso continuo. Ranges of voice
     parts: c1-e2, g-a1, d-g1, F-c1.

1   Turbabor, sed non perturbabor. -- In SGA. -- 1887. -- Bd. 4, p.
     64-66.
        Edited by Philipp Spitta. Figured bass not realized. Original
     Latin text. Notes in German.

2   Turbabor, sed non perturbabor = Furcht störet, doch nicht zerstöret
     den Trost. -- In NSA. -- 1960. -- Bd. 8, p. 116-120. Pub. no.:
     Bärenreiter-Ausgabe 1950.
        Edited by Gottfried Grote. Latin text with German translation.
     Notes in German. Transposed up M2.

3   Turbabor, sed non pertubabor = Furcht störet. -- In Cantiones
     sacrae. -- Kassel : Bärenreiter, [19--]. -- Motetten Nr. 17-18, p.
     8-12. Pub. no.: Bärenreiter-Ausgabe 1967.
        Edited by Gottfried Grote. Latin text with German translation.
     Transposed up M2.

6   Turbabor, sed non perturbabor = Furcht störet, doch nichts zerstöret
     den Trost. -- In Selections from Cantiones sacrae. -- New York :
     Kalmus, [19--] -- v. 3, p. 8-12.
        Latin text with German translation. Transposed up M2.

7   Turbabor, sed non perturbabor. -- New York : Kalmus, [19--].
        Latin text with German translation. Transposed up M2.

SWV 71

[Cantiones sacrae. Ad Dominum cum tribularer]

> Sacred Latin text. Sources: Psalm 120:1-2.
> For chorus (SATB) with optional basso continuo. Ranges of voice
> parts: d1-f2, f-a1, c-g1, G-c1. Duration: short.

1   Ad Dominum cum tribularer. -- In SGA. -- 1887. -- Bd. 4, p. 66-69.
> Edited by Philipp Spitta. Figured bass not realized. Original
> Latin text. Notes in German.

2   Ad Dominum cum tribularer = Ich rief zum Herrn. -- In NSA. -- 1960.
-- Bd. 8, p. 121-127. Pub. no.: Bärenreiter-Ausgabe 1950.
> Edited by Gottfried Grote. Latin text with German translation.
> Notes in German. Transposed up M2.

3   Ad dominum cum tribularer = Ich rief zum Herrn. -- In Cantiones
sacrae. -- Kassel : Bärenreiter, c1958. -- Motetten Nr. 19-20, p.
[1]-7. Pub. no.: Bärenreiter-Ausgabe 1961.
> Edited by Gottfried Grote. Latin text with German translation.
> Transposed up M2.

SWV 72

[Cantiones sacrae. Quid detur tibi aut quid apponatur tibi]

> Sacred Latin text. Sources: Psalm 120:3-4.
> For chorus (SATB) with optional basso continuo. Ranges of voice
> parts: d1-e2, g-a1, d-f1, G-bflat. Duration: short.

1   Quid detur tibi. -- In SGA. -- 1887. -- Bd. 4, p. 69-72.
> Edited by Philipp Spitta. Figured bass not realized. Original
> Latin text. Notes in German.

2   Quid detur tibi = Was er dir geben möge. -- In NSA. -- 1960. -- Bd.
8, p. 127-132. Pub. no.: Bärenreiter-Ausgabe 1950.
> Edited by Gottfried Grote. Latin text with German translation.
> Notes in German. Transposed up M2.

3   Quid detur tibi = Was er dir geben, was er dir beschere möge. -- In
Cantiones sacrae. -- Kassel : Bärenreiter, c1958. -- Motetten Nr.
19-20, p. 7-12. Pub. no.: Bärenreiter-Ausgabe 1961.
> Edited by Gottfried Grote. Latin text with German translation.
> Transposed up M2.

SWV 73

[Cantiones sacrae. Aspice pater piissimum filium]

> Sacred Latin text. Sources: Meditationes Augustini.
> For chorus (SATB) with optional basso continuo. Ranges of voice
> parts: c#1-e2, g-a1, c#-e1, G-c1. Duration: short.

1   Aspice pater piissimum filium. -- In SGA. -- 1887. -- Bd. 4, p.
     72-76.
        Edited by Philipp Spitta. Figured bass not realized. Original
     Latin text. Notes in German.

2   Aspice pater piissimum filium = Schaue doch, Vater, den Sohn. -- In
     NSA. -- 1960. -- Bd. 9, p. 1-8. Pub. no.: Bärenreiter-Ausgabe 1955.
        Edited by Gottfried Grote. Latin text with German translation.
     Notes in German. Transposed up M2.

3   Aspice, pater = Schaue doch, Vater. -- In Cantiones sacrae. --
     Kassel : Bärenreiter, c1958. -- Motetten Nr. 21-23, p. [1]-8. Pub.
     no.: Bärenreiter-Ausgabe 1958.
        Edited by Gottfried Grote. Latin text with German translation.
     Transposed up M2.

SWV 74

[Cantiones sacrae. Nonne hic est, mi Domine, innocens ille]

     Sacred Latin text. Sources: Meditationes Augustini.
        For chorus (SATB) with optional basso continuo. Ranges of voice
     parts: d1-g2, a-c2, d-g1, G-c1. Duration: short.

1   Nonne hic est, mi Domine. -- In SGA. -- 1887. -- Bd. 4, p. 76-78.
        Edited by Philipp Spitta. Figured bass not realized. Original
     Latin text. Notes in German.

2   Nonne hic est, mi Domine, innocens ille = Ohn alle Schuld. -- In
     NSA. -- 1960. -- Bd. 9, p. 9-12. Pub. no.: Bärenreiter-Ausgabe 1955.
        Edited by Gottfried Grote. Latin text with German translation.
     Notes in German. Transposed up M2.

3   Nonne hic est = Ohn alle Schuld. -- In Cantiones sacrae. -- Kassel :
     Bärenreiter, c1958. -- Motetten Nr. 21-23, p. 9-12. Pub. no.:
     Bärenreiter-Ausgabe 1958.
        Edited by Gottfried Grote. Latin text with German translation.
     Transposed up M2.

SWV 75

[Cantiones sacrae. Reduc, Domine Deus meus, oculos majestatis tuae]

     Sacred Latin text. Sources: Meditationes Augustini.
        For chorus (SATB) with optional basso continuo. Ranges of voice
     parts: c1-g2, e-a1, c-e1, E-c1. Duration: short.

1   Reduc, Domine Deus meus. -- In SGA. -- 1887. -- Bd. 4, p. 79-83.
        Edited by Philipp Spitta. Figured bass not realized. Original
     Latin text. Notes in German.

2   Reduc, Domine deus meus, oculos = Wende, du unser Richter, deinen
    Blick. -- In NSA -- 1960. -- Bd. 9, p. 13-20. Pub. no.:
    Bärenreiter-Ausgabe 1955.
        Edited by Gottfried Grote. Latin text with German translation.
    Notes in German. Transposed up M2.

3   Reduc, domine deus meus = Wende, du unser Richter. -- In Cantiones
    sacrae. -- Kassel : Bärenreiter, c1958. -- Motetten Nr. 21-23, p.
    13-20. Pub. no.: Bärenreiter-Ausgabe 1958.
        Edited by Gottfried Grote. Latin text with German translation.
    Transposed up M2.

SWV 76

[Cantiones sacrae. Supereminet omnem scientiam]

    Sacred Latin text. Sources: Meditationes Augustini.
    For chorus (SMAR) with optional basso continuo. Ranges of voice
    parts: el-a2, f-d2, d-bflat1, A-d1. Duration: medium.

1   Supereminet omnem scientiam. -- In SGA. -- 1887. -- Bd. 4, p. 83-89.
        Edited by Philipp Spitta. Figured bass not realized. Original
    Latin text. Notes in German.

2   Supereminet omnem scientiam = Über alle Erkenntnis erhebet sich. --
    In NSA. -- 1960. -- Bd. 9, p. 21-31. Pub. no.: Bärenreiter-Ausgabe
    1955.
        Edited by Gottfried Grote. Latin text with German translation.
    Notes in German. Transposed down M2.

3   Supereminet omnen scientiam = Über alle Erkenntnis erhebet sich. --
    In Cantiones sacrae. -- Kassel : Bärenreiter, c1958. -- Motetten
    Nr. 24-25, p. [1]-11. Pub. no.: Bärenreiter-Ausgabe 1968.
        Edited by Gottfried Grote. Latin text with German translation.
    Transposed down M2.

6   Supereminet omnem scientiam = Über alle Erkenntnis erhebet sich. --
    In Selections from Cantiones sacrae. -- New York : Kalmus, [19--].
    -- v. 4, p. [1]-11.
        Latin text with German translation. Transposed down M2.

7   Supereminet omnem scientiam. -- New York : Kalmus, [19--].
        Latin text with German translation. Transposed down M2.

SWV 77

[Cantiones sacrae. Pro hoc magno mysterio]

    Sacred Latin text. Sources: Meditationes Augustini.
    For chorus (SMAR) with optional basso continuo. Ranges of voice
    parts: fl-f2, bflat-c2, f-al, A-d1. Duration: short.

1   Pro hoc magno mysterio. -- In SGA. -- 1887. -- Bd. 4, p. 89-92.
        Edited by Philipp Spitta. Figured bass not realized. Original
    Latin text. Notes in German.

2　Pro hoc magno mysterio = Für solch grosses Mysterium. -- In NSA. --
1960. -- Bd. 9, p. 31-36. Pub. no.: Bärenreiter-Ausgabe 1955.
　　Edited by Gottfried Grote. Latin text with German translation.
Notes in German. Transposed down M2.

3　Pro hoc magno mysterio = Für solch grosses Mysterium. -- In
Cantiones sacrae. -- Kassel : Bärenreiter, c1958. -- Motetten Nr.
24-25, p. 11-16. Pub. no.: Bärenreiter-Ausgabe 1968.
　　Edited by Gottfried Grote. Latin text with German translation.
Transposed down M2.

6　Für solch grosses Mysterium. -- In Selections from Cantiones sacrae.
-- New York : Kalmus, [19--]. -- v. 4, p. 11-16.
　　Latin text with German translation. Transposed down M2.

7　Pro hoc magno mysterio. -- New York : Kalmus, [19--].
　　Latin text with German translation. Transposed down M2.

SWV 78

[Cantiones sacrae. Domine, non est exaltatum cor meum]

　　Sacred Latin text. Sources: Psalm 131:1.
　　For chorus (SATB) with optional basso continuo. Ranges of voice
parts: c1-f2, g-bflat1, c-f1, F-d1. Duration: short.

1　Domine, non est exaltatum. -- In SGA. -- 1887. -- Bd. 4, p. 92-96.
　　Edited by Philipp Spitta. Figured bass not realized. Original
Latin text. Notes in German.

2　Domine, non est exaltatum cor meum = Herr, mein Gott, nicht
vermessen dränget mein Herze. -- In NSA. -- 1960. -- Bd. 9, p.
37-44. Pub. no.: Bärenreiter-Ausgabe 1955.
　　Edited by Gottfried Grote. Latin text with German translation.
Notes in German. Transposed up M2.

6　Domine, non est exaltatum cor meum = Herr, mein Gott, nicht
vermessen dränget mein Herze. -- In Selections from Cantiones
sacrae. -- New York : Kalmus, [19--]. -- v. 4, p. [1]-8.
　　Latin text with German translation. Transposed up M2.

7　Domine, non ext exaltatum cor meum. -- New York : Kalmus, [19--].
　　Latin text with German translation. Transposed up M2.

8　Lamb of God = Domine, non est exaltatum cor meum. -- Minneapolis :
Schmitt, Hall, & McCreary, c1959. Pub. no.: no. 1402.
　　Edited by Johannes Riedel. Latin text with English translation.

　　Other editions: Bärenreiter BA1971.

SWV 79

[Cantiones sacrae. Si non humiliter sentiebam]

> Sacred Latin text. Sources: Psalm 131:2.
> For chorus (SATB) with optional basso continuo. Ranges of voice parts: a-f2, f-al, d-g1, E-dl. Duration: short.

1   Si non humiliter sentiebam. -- In SGA. -- 1887. -- Bd. 4, p. 96-99.
     Edited by Philipp Spitta. Figured bass not realized. Original Latin text. Notes in German.

2   Si non humiliter sentiebam = Demütig will ich mich dir ergeben. --
In NSA. -- 1960. -- Bd. 9, p. 44-50. Pub. no.: Bärenreiter-Ausgabe 1955.
     Edited by Gottfried Grote. Latin text with German translation. Notes in German. Transposed up M2.

6   Demütig will ich mich dir ergeben. -- In Selections from Cantiones sacrae. -- New York : Kalmus, [19--]. -- v. 4, p. 8-14.
     Latin text with German translation. Transposed up M2.

> Other editions: Bärenreiter BA1971.

SWV 80

[Cantiones sacrae. Speret Israel in Domino]

> Sacred Latin text. Sources: Psalm 131:3.
> For chorus (SATB) with optional basso continuo. Ranges of voice parts: c#1-e2, f#-al, d-el, D-bflat. Duration: short.

1   Speret Israel in Domino. -- In SGA. -- 1887. -- Bd. 4, p. 100-101.
     Edited by Philipp Spitta. Figured bass not realized. Original Latin text. Notes in German.

2   Speret Israel in Domino = Hoffe, Israel. -- In NSA. -- 1960. -- Bd. 9, p. 50-52. Pub. no.: Bärenreiter-Ausgabe 1955.
     Edited by Gottfried Grote. Latin text with German translation. Notes in German. Transposed up M2.

6   Hoffe, Israel. -- In Selections from Cantiones sacrae. -- New York : Kalmus, [19--]. -- v. 4, p. 14-16.
     Latin text with German translation. Transposed up M2.

> Other editions: Bärenreiter BA1971.

SWV 81

[Cantiones sacrae. Cantate Domino canticum novum]

> Sacred Latin text. Sources: Psalm 149:1-3.
> For chorus (SMAR) with optional basso continuo. Ranges of voice parts: fl-bflat2, a-d2, f#-al, c-dl. 4

1   Cantate Domino canticum novum. -- In SGA. -- 1887. -- Bd. 4, p.
    101-108.
        Edited by Philipp Spitta. Figured bass not realized. Original
    Latin text. Notes in German.

2   Cantate Domino canticum novum = Singet ein neues Lied, jauchzet dem
    Herrn. -- In NSA. -- 1960. -- Bd. 9, p. 53-64. Pub. no.:
    Bärenreiter-Ausgabe 1955.
        Edited by Gottfried Grote. Latin text with German translation.
    Notes in German. Transposed down M2.

3   Cantate Domino canticum novum = Singet ein neues Lied, jauchzet dem
    Herren. -- Kassel : Bärenreiter, c1960. Pub. no.:
    Bärenreiter-Ausgabe 1969.
        Edited by Gottfried Grote. Latin text with German translation.
    Transposed down M2.

5   Cantate Domino canticum novum. -- Neuhausen-Stuttgart : Hänssler,
    c1969. Pub. no.: HE 20.081/10.
        For chorus (SATB). Edited by Günter Graulich. Continuo realized by
    Paul Horn. Latin text with German translation. Transposed down P4.

6   Cantate Domino canticum novum = Singet ein neues Lied, jauchzet dem
    Herrn. -- In Selections from Cantiones sacrae. -- New York : Kalmus,
    [19--]. -- v. 3, p. 13-24.
        Latin text with German translation. Transposed down M2.

7   Cantate Domino = O sing ye unto the Lord. -- Toronto : G.V.
    Thompson, c1973. Pub. no.: E.I.2001.
        Edited by Elmer Iseler. Latin text.

8   Cantate Domino canticum novum = Singet ein neues Lied, jauchzet dem
    Herrn. -- New York : Kalmus, [197-?].
        Latin text with German translation. Transposed down M2.

9   Cantate Domino = O sing ye unto the Lord. -- New York : Bourne,
    c1959. Pub. no.: ES33.
        Edited by Norman Greyson. Latin text with English translation.

10 Cantate Domino = O sing ye unto the Lord. -- New York : G. Schirmer,
    c1941. Pub. no.: G. Schirmer octavo no. 8678.
        Edited by Lowell P. Beveridge. Latin text and English text adapted
    by L.P.B. from the Book of Common Prayer.

11 Cantate Domino. -- Bryn Mawr, Pa. : T. Presser, c1983. Pub. no.:
    312-41427.
        Edited by George Lynn. Latin text with English translation.

SWV 82

[Cantiones sacrae. Inter brachia Salvatoris mei]

    Sacred Latin text. Sources: Manuale Augustini.
    For chorus (SATB) with optional basso continuo. Ranges of voice
parts: c1-f2, f-bflat 1, c-g1, F-c1. Duration: medium.

1   Inter brachia Salvatoris mei. -- In SGA. -- 1887. -- Bd. 4, p.
     108-114.
       Edited by Philipp Spitta. Figured bass not realized. Original
     Latin text. Notes in German.

2   Inter brachia Salvatoris mei = In den Armen des Heilandes und
     Herren. -- In NSA. -- 1960. -- Bd. 9, p. 65-76. Pub. no.:
     Bärenreiter-Ausgabe 1955.
       Edited by Gottfried Grote. Latin text with German translation.
     Notes in German. Transposed up M2.

3   Inter brachia salvatoris mei = In den Armen des Heilandes und
     Herren. -- In Cantiones sacrae. -- Kassel : Bärenreiter, [19--].
     Motette Nr. 30. Pub. no.: Bärenreiter-Ausgabe 1970.
       Edited by Gottfried Grote. Latin text with German translation.
     Transposed up M2.

6   Inter brachia salvatoris mei = In den Armen des Heilandes und
     Herren. -- In Selections from Cantiones sacrae. -- New York :
     Kalmus, [19--]. -- v. 4, p. [1]-12.
     Latin text with German translation. Transposed up M2.

SWV 83

[Cantiones sacrae. Veni, rogo, in cor meum]

     Sacred Latin text. Sources: Manuale Augustini.
       For chorus (SSMT) with optional basso continuo. Ranges of voice
     parts: d1-a2, b-e2, f#-d2, B-g1. Duration: medium.

1   Veni, rogo, in cor meum. -- In SGA. -- 1887. -- Bd. 4, p. 115-119.
       Edited by Philipp Spitta. Figured bass not realized. Original
     Latin text. Notes in German.

2   Veni, rogo, in cor meum = Komm, ich bitt dich, in mein Herze. -- In
     NSA. -- 1960. -- Bd. 9, p. 77-84. Pub. no.: Bärenreiter-Ausgabe
     1955.
       Edited by Gottfried Grote. Latin text with German translation.
     Notes in German. Transposed down M2.

3   Veni, rogo, in cor meum = Komm, ich bitt dich, in mein Herze. -- In
     Cantiones sacrae. -- Kassel : Bärenreiter, c1955. -- Motette Nr.
     31. Pub. no.: Bärenreiter-Ausgabe 1951.
       Edited by Gottfried Grote. Latin text with German translation.
     Transposed down M2.

SWV 84

[Cantiones sacrae. Ecce advocatus meus]

     Sacred Latin text. Sources: Meditationes Augustini.
       For chorus (SATB) with basso continuo. Ranges of voice parts:
     e1-e2, f#-a1, c-f1, D-c1. Duration: short.

1   Ecce advocatus meus. -- In SGA. -- 1887. -- Bd. 4, p. 119-123.
     Edited by Philipp Spitta. Figured bass not realized. Original
     Latin text. Notes in German.

2   Ecce advocatus meus = Siehe, mein Fürsprecher ist im Himmel. -- In
     NSA. -- 1960. -- Bd. 9, p. 85-92. Pub. no.: Bärenreiter-Ausgabe
     1955.
     Edited by Gottfried Grote. Latin text with German translation.
     Notes in German. Transposed up m3.

3   Ecce advocatus meus = Siehe, mein Fürsprecher. -- In Cantiones
     sacrae. -- Kassel : Bärenreiter, c1955. -- Motette Nr. 32. Pub.
     no.: Bärenreiter-Ausgabe 1962.
     Edited by Gottfried Grote. Latin text with German translation.
     Transposed up m3.

SWV 85

[Cantiones sacrae. Domine, ne in furore tuo arguas me]

     Sacred Latin text. Sources: Psalm 6:1-4.
     For chorus (SATB) with basso continuo. Ranges of voice parts:
     c1-g2, g-g1, c-f1, G-a. Duration: short.

1   Domine, ne in furore tuo. -- In SGA. -- 1887. -- Bd. 4, p. 124-127.
     Edited by Philipp Spitta. Figured bass not realized. Original
     Latin text. Notes in German.

2   Domine, ne in furore tuo arguas me = Herr, mein Gott, ach nicht in
     deinem Zorne. -- In NSA. -- 1960. -- Bd. 9, p. 93-99. Pub. no.:
     Bärenreiter-Ausgabe 1955.
     Edited by Gottfried Grote. Latin text with German translation.
     Notes in German. Transposed up M2.

3   Domine, ne in furore tuo = Herr mein Gott, ach nicht in deinem
     Zorne. -- In Cantiones sacrae. -- Kassel : Bärenreiter, c1955. --
     Motetten Nr. 33-35, p. [1]-7. Pub. no.: Bärenreiter-Ausgabe 1952.
     Edited by Gottfried Grote. Latin text with German translation.
     Transposed up M2.

SWV 86

[Cantiones sacrae. Quoniam non est in morte qui memor sit tui]

     Sacred Latin text. Sources: Psalm 6:5-7.
     For chorus (ATB) with basso continuo. Ranges of voice parts: g-a1,
     d-f1, G-c1. Duration: short.

1   Quoniam non est in morte. -- In SGA. -- 1887. -- Bd. 4, p. 127-130.
     Edited by Philipp Spitta. Figured bass not realized. Original
     Latin text. Notes in German.

2   Quoniam non est in morte qui memor sit tui = Höre mich, Herr. -- In
    NSA. -- 1960. -- Bd. 9, p. 99-106. Pub. no.: Bärenreiter-Ausgabe
    1955.
       Edited by Gottfried Grote. Latin text with German translation.
    Notes in German. Transposed up M2.

3   Quoniam non est in morte = Höre mich, bei den Toten. -- In Cantiones
    sacrae. -- Kassel : Bärenreiter, c1955. -- Motetten Nr. 33-35, p.
    7-14. Pub. no.: Bärenreiter-Ausgabe 1952.
       Edited by Gottfried Grote. Latin text with German translation.
    Transposed up M2.

SWV 87

[Cantiones sacrae. Discedite a me omnes operamini]

    Sacred Latin text. Sources: Psalm 6:8-10.
    For chorus (SATB) with basso continuo. Ranges of voice parts:
    bflat-d2, d-a1, Bflat-eflat1, F-bflat. Duration: short.

1   Discedite a me omnes. -- In SGA. -- 1887. -- Bd. 4, p. 130-134.
       Edited by Philipp Spitta. Figured bass not realized. Original
    Latin text. Notes in German.

2   Discedite a me = Weichet hinweg von mir. -- In NSA. -- 1960. -- Bd.
    9, p. 107-115. Pub. no.: Bärenreiter-Ausgabe 1955.
       Edited by Gottfried Grote. Latin text with German translation.
    Notes in German. Transposed up M2.

3   Discedite a me = Weichet hinweg von mir. -- In Cantiones sacrae. --
    Kassel : Bärenreiter, c1955. -- Motetten Nr. 33-35, p. 15-23. Pub.
    no.: Bärenreiter-Ausgabe 1952.
       Edited by Gottfried Grote. Latin text with German translation.
    Transposed up M2.

SWV 88

[Cantiones sacrae. Oculi omnium in te sperant, Domine]

    Sacred Latin text. Sources: Psalm 145:15-16.
    For chorus (SSMT) with optional basso continuo. Ranges of voice
    parts: g1g2, c1-d2, g-a1, c-bflat. Duration: short.

1   Oculi omnium in te sperant. -- In SGA. -- 1887. -- Bd. 4, p. 135.
       Edited by Philipp Spitta. Figured bass not realized. Original
    Latin text. Notes in German.

2   Oculi omnium in te sperant, Domine = Aller augen warten auf dich,
    Herr. -- In NSA. -- 1960. -- Bd. 9, p. 116-117. Pub. no.:
    Bärenreiter-Ausgabe 1955.
       Edited by Gottfried Grote. Latin text with German translation.
    Notes in German. Transposed down m3.

3   Oculi omnium in te sperant, Domine. -- In Cantiones sacrae. --
    Kassel : Bärenreiter, c1958. -- Motetten Nr. 36-40, p. [1]-2. Pub.
    no.: Bärenreiter-Ausgabe 1963.
       Edited by Gottfried Grote. Latin text. Transposed down m3.

6   Oculi omnium. -- Augsburg : A. Böhm, [19--]. Pub. no.: 6324.
       Latin text. Transposed down m3.

7   O may the eyes of all = Oculi omnium. -- Bryn Mawr, Pa. : T.
    Presser, c1965. Pub. no.: 312-41382.
       Edited by Arnold Payson. Latin text with English translation.
    Transposed down m3.

8   Oculi omnium in te sperant Domine = The eyes of all wait upon thee.
    -- Ft. Lauderdale : Plymouth Music Co., c1981. Pub. no.: SC-57.
       Edited by Larry D. Wyatt. Latin text with English translation.
    Transposed down m3.

SWV 89

[Cantiones sacrae. Pater noster, SWV 89]

    Sacred Latin text. Sources: Lord's prayer.
       For chorus (SSMT) with optional basso continuo. Ranges of voice
    parts: d1-a2, c1-d2, f-c2, A-f1. Duration: short.

1   Pater noster, qui es in coelis. -- In SGA. -- 1887. -- Bd. 4, p.
    136-139.
       Edited by Philipp Spitta. Figured bass not realized. Original
    Latin text. Notes in German.

2   Pater noster, qui es in coelis = Vater unser. -- In NSA. -- 1960. --
    Bd. 9, p. 117-121. Pub. no.: Bärenreiter-Ausgabe 1955.
       Edited by Gottfried Grote. Latin text with German translation.
    Notes in German. Transposed down m3.

3   Pater noster. -- In Cantiones sacrae. -- Kassel : Bärenreiter,
    c1958. -- Motetten Nr. 36-40, p. 2-6. Pub. no.: Bärenreiter-Ausgabe
    1963.
       Edited by Gottfried Grote. Latin text. Transposed down m3.

6   Pater noster = Our Father. -- Ft. Lauderdale : Plymouth Music Co.,
    c1981. Pub. no.: SC-58.
       Edited by Larry D. Wyatt. Latin text with English translation.
    Transposed down m3.

SWV 90

[Cantiones sacrae. Domine Deus, pater coelestis, benedic nobis]

    Sacred Latin text. Sources: Domine Deus, pater coelestis, benedic
    nobis.
       For chorus (SSMT) with optional basso continuo. Ranges of voice
    parts: f1-g2, c1-eflat2, g-a1, Bflat-c1. Duration: short.

1   Domine Deus, pater coelestis. -- In SGA. -- 1887. -- Bd. 4, p.
     139-140.
     Edited by Philipp Spitta. Figured bass not realized. Original
     Latin text. Notes in German.

2   Domine Deus, pater coelestis = Herr Gott himmlischer Vater. -- In
     NSA. -- 1960. -- Bd. 9, p. 121-123. Pub. no.: Bärenreiter-Ausgabe
     1955.
     Edited by Gottfried Grote. Latin text with German translation.
     Notes in German. Transposed down m3.

3   Domine deus, pater coelestis. -- In Cantiones sacrae. -- Kassel :
     Bärenreiter, c1958. -- Motetten Nr. 36-40, p. 6-8. Pub. no.:
     Bärenreiter-Ausgabe 1963.
     Edited by Gottfried Grote. Latin text. Transposed down m3.

6   Domine Deus, pater coelestis = Lord God our Father. -- Ft.
     Lauderdale : Plymouth Music Co., c1981. Pub. no.: SC-57.
     Edited by Larry D. Wyatt. Latin text with English translation.
     Transposed down m3.

SWV 91

[Cantiones sacrae. Confitemini Domino, quoniam ipse bonus]

     Sacred Latin text. Sources: Psalm 136:1. Psalm 136:25. Psalm 147
     :9-11.
     For chorus (SSMT) with optional basso continuo. Ranges of voice
     parts: gl-a2, dl-d2, bflat-bflat1, d-f1. Duration: short.

1   Confitemini Domino, quoniam ipse bonus. -- In SGA. -- 1887. -- Bd.
     4, p. 141-142.
     Edited by Philipp Spitta. Figured bass not realized. Original
     Latin text. Notes in German.

2   Confitemini Domino = Danket dem Herrn. -- In NSA. -- 1960. -- Bd. 9,
     p. 123-125. Pub. no.: Bärenreiter-Ausgabe 1955.
     Edited by Gottfried Grote. Latin text with German translation.
     Notes in German. Transposed down m3.

3   Confitemini domino. -- In Cantiones sacrae. -- Kassel : Bärenreiter,
     c1958. -- Motetten Nr. 36-40, p. 8-10. Pub. no.:
     Bärenreiter-Ausgabe 1963.
     Edited by Gottfried Grote. Latin text. Transposed down m3.

SWV 92

[Cantiones sacrae. Pater noster, SWV 92]

     Sacred Latin text. Sources: Lord's prayer.
     For chorus (SSMT) with optional basso continuo. Ranges of voice
     parts: dl-a2, cl-d2, f-c2, A-f1. Duration: short.

1   Pater noster, qui es in coelis. -- In SGA. -- 1887. -- Bd. 4, p.
    136-139.
    Edited by Philipp Spitta. Figured bass not realized. Original
    Latin text. Notes in German.

2   Pater noster, qui es in coelis = Vater unser. -- In NSA. -- 1960. --
    Bd. 9, p. 117-121. Pub. no.: Bärenreiter-Ausgabe 1955.
    Edited by Gottfried Grote. Latin text with German translation.
    Notes in German. Transposed down m3.

SWV 93

[Cantiones sacrae. Gratias agimus tibi, Domine Deus Pater]

    Sacred Latin text. Sources: Domine Deus, pater coelestis, benedic
    nobis.
    For chorus (SSMT) with optional basso continuo. Ranges of voice
    parts: f1-g2, bflat-d2, g-c2, Bflat-d1. Duration: short.

1   Gratias agimus tibi. -- In SGA. -- 1887. -- Bd. 4, p. 143-144.
    Edited by Philipp Spitta. Figured bass not realized. Original
    Latin text. Notes in German.

2   Gratias agimus tibi Domine = Wir danken dir, Herr Gott himmlischer
    Vater. -- In NSA. -- 1960. -- Bd. 9, p. 126-127. Pub. no.:
    Bärenreiter-Ausgabe 1955.
    Edited by Gottfried Grote. Latin text with German translation.
    Notes in German. Transposed down m3.

3   Gratias agimus tibi. -- In Cantiones sacrae. -- Kassel :
    Bärenreiter, c1958. -- Motetten Nr. 36-40, p. 11-12. Pub. no.:
    Bärenreiter-Ausgabe 1963.
    Edited by Gottfried Grote. Latin text. Transposed down m3.

SWV 94

[De vitae fugacitate]

    Sacred German text. Sources: Leon, Johann. Ich hab mein Sach Gott
    heimgestellt.
    For chorus (SSATB) and basso continuo. Ranges of voice parts:
    d1-f2, c1-g2, g-bflat1, d-g1, F-bflat. Duration: long.

1   De vitae fugacitate. -- In SGA. -- 1892. -- Bd. 12, p. 37-52.
    Edited by Philip Spitta. Figured bass not realized. Original
    German text. Notes in German by P. Spitta.

2   Ich hab mein Sach Gott heimgestellt. -- In NSA. -- 1970. -- Bd. 31,
    p. 26-56. Pub. no.: BA4483.
    Edited by Werner Breig. German text. Notes in German and English.

    Other editions: Bärenreiter BA3532.

SWV 95

[Ultima verba Psalmi 23]

   Sacred German text. Sources: Psalm 23:6.
   For chorus (SSMATR) and basso continuo, 3 voices of which have
   been reconstructed. Ranges of voice parts: g1-a2, c1-eflat2, g-d2,
   f-al, eflat-g1, G-bflat. Duration: medium.

1   Gutes und Barmherzigkeit : [fragment]. -- In SGA. -- 1927. -- Bd.
    18, p. xvii.
       Edited by Heinrich Spitta. Figured bass not realized. Original
    German text. Notes in German by Philip Spitta.

2   Gutes und Barmherzigkeit. -- In NSA. -- 1970. -- Bd. 31, p. 13-25.
    Pub. no.: BA4483.
       Edited by Werner Breig. German text. Notes in German and English.

3   Gutes und Barmherzigkeit werden mir folgen mein Leben lang. Kassel :
    Bärenreiter, [19--]. Pub. no.: Bärenreiter-Ausgabe 986.
       Edited by Hans Joachim Moser; continuo realized by Max Seiffert.
    German text. Words in Gothic type.

SWV 96

[Glück zu dem Helikon]

   Secular German text. Sources: Opitz, Martin. Glück zu dem Helikon.
      Duet (AT) with basso continuo. Ranges of voice parts: g-g1, f-d1.
   Duration: short.

1   Aria : Glück zu dem Helikon. -- In SGA. -- 1893. -- Bd. 15, p. 83.
       Edited by Philip Spitta. Figured bass not realized. Original
    German text. Notes in German by Philip Spitta.

2   Glück zu dem Helikon. -- In NSA. -- 1970. -- Bd. 37, p. 6. Pub. no.:
    BA4489.
       Edited by Werner Bittinger. German text. Notes in German and
    English. Transposed up M2.

SWV 97

[Beckerscher Psalter. Wer nicht sitzt im Gottlosen Rat]

   Sacred German text. Sources: Psalm 1.
   For chorus (SMAR) and optional continuo. Ranges of voice parts:
   fl-g2, dl-c2, a-g1, Bflat-c1. Duration: short.

1   I. -- In SGA. -- 1894. -- Bd. 16, p. 11.
       Edited by Philipp Spitta. Figured bass not realized. Original
    German text. Notes in German.

2   Wer nicht sitzt im Gottlosen Rat. -- In NSA. -- 1957. -- Bd. 6, p.
     1. Pub. no.: Bärenreiter Ausgabe 984.
       Edited by Walter Blankenburg. German text. Words in Gothic type.
     Notes in German.

6   Psalm 1. -- Bryn Mawr, Pa. : Mercury Music Corp., c1952. Pub. no.:
     352-00143.
       Edited by George Lynn. English text. Transposed down m3.

SWV 98

[Beckerscher Psalter. Was haben doch die Leut im Sinn]

     Sacred German text. Sources: Psalm 2.
     For chorus (SATB) and optional continuo. Ranges of voice parts:
     f1-g2, c1-bflat1, e-f1, G-bflat. Duration: short.

1   II. -- In SGA. -- 1894. -- Bd. 16, p. 12.
       Edited by Philipp Spitta. Figured bass not realized. Original
     German text. Notes in German.

2   Was haben doch die Leut im Sinn. -- In NSA. -- 1957. -- Bd. 6, p. 2.
     Pub. no.: Bärenreiter Ausgabe 984.
       Edited by Walter Blankenburg. German text. Words in Gothic type.
     Notes in German.

SWV 99

[Beckerscher Psalter. Ach wie gross ist der Feinde Rott]

     Sacred German text. Sources: Psalm 3.
     For chorus (SATB) and optional continuo. Ranges of voice parts:
     e1-d2, a-a1, g-d1, G-a. Duration: short.

1   III. -- In SGA. -- 1894. -- Bd. 16, p. 12-13.
       Edited by Philipp Spitta. Figured bass not realized. Original
     German text. Notes in German.

2   Ach wie gross ist der Feinde Rott. -- In NSA. -- 1957. -- Bd. 6, p.
     3. Pub. no.: Bärenreiter Ausgabe 984.
       Edited by Walter Blankenburg. German text. Words in Gothic type.
     Notes in German.

SWV 100

[Beckerscher Psalter. Erhör mich, wenn ich ruf zu dir]

     Sacred German text. Sources: Psalm 4.
     For chorus (SATB) and optional continuo. Ranges of voice parts:
     d1-d2, g-g1, d-d1, F-g. Duration: short.

1   IV. -- In SGA. -- 1894. -- Bd. 16, p. 13.
       Edited by Philipp Spitta. Figured bass not realized. Original
     German text. Notes in German.

LORETTE WILMOT LIBRARY
NAZARETH COLLEGE

2 Erhör mich, wenn ich ruf zu dir. -- In NSA. -- 1957. -- Bd. 6, p. 4.
Pub. no.: Bärenreiter Ausgabe 984.
Edited by Walter Blankenburg. German text. Words in Gothic type.
Notes in German.

SWV 101

[Beckerscher Psalter. Herr hör, was ich will bitten dich]

Sacred German text. Sources: Psalm 5.
For chorus (SMAR) and optional continuo. Ranges of voice parts:
al-g2, dl-d2, f-al, A-dl. Duration: short.

1 V. -- In SGA. -- 1894. -- Bd. 16, p. 14.
Edited by Philipp Spitta. Figured bass not realized. Original
German text. Notes in German.

2 Herr hör, was ich will bitten dich. -- In NSA. -- 1957. -- Bd. 6, p.
5. Pub. no.: Bärenreiter Ausgabe 984.
Edited by Walter Blankenburg. German text. Words in Gothic type.
Notes in German.

SWV 102

[Beckerscher Psalter. Ach Herr, mein Gott, straf mich doch nicht]

Sacred German text. Sources: Psalm 6.
For chorus (SATB) and optional continuo. Ranges of voice parts:
cl-c2, a-gl, d-dl, F-a. Duration: short.

1 VI. -- In SGA. -- 1894. -- Bd. 16, p. 14-15.
Edited by Philipp Spitta. Figured bass not realized. Original
German text. Notes in German.

2 Ach Herr, mein Gott, straf mich doch nicht. -- In NSA. -- 1957. --
Bd. 6, p. 6. Pub. no.: Bärenreiter Ausgabe 984.
Edited by Walter Blankenburg. German text. Words in Gothic type.
Notes in German.

6 Psalm 6. -- In Seven penitential psalms. -- G.I.A. Publications,
c1974. -- p. 4-5. Pub. no.: G-1912.
Edited by Daniel G. Reuning. Figured bass not realized. German
text with English translation. Notes in English.

SWV 103

[Beckerscher Psalter. Auf dich trau ich, mein Herr und Gott]

Sacred German text. Sources: Psalm 7.
For chorus (SATB) and optional continuo. Ranges of voice parts:
dl-d2, g-gl, d-dl, F-g. Duration: short.

1   VII. -- In SGA. -- 1894. -- Bd. 16, p. 15.
      Edited by Philipp Spitta. Figured bass not realized. Original
German text. Notes in German.

2   Auf dich trau ich, mein Herr und Gott. -- In NSA. -- 1957. -- Bd. 6,
p. 7. Pub. no.: Bärenreiter Ausgabe 984.
      Edited by Walter Blankenburg. German text. Words in Gothic type.
Notes in German.

SWV 104

[Beckerscher Psalter. Mit Dank wir sollen loben]

     Sacred German text. Sources: Psalm 8.
      For chorus (SATB) and optional continuo. Ranges of voice parts:
g1-f2, c-g1, f-eflat1, G-bflat. Duration: short.

1   VIII. -- In SGA. -- 1894. -- Bd. 16, p. 16.
      Edited by Philipp Spitta. Figured bass not realized. Original
German text. Notes in German.

2   Mit Dank wir sollen loben. -- In NSA. -- 1957. -- Bd. 6, p. 8. Pub.
no.: Bärenreiter Ausgabe 984.
      Edited by Walter Blankenburg. German text. Words in Gothic type.
Notes in German.

3   Psalm 8. -- In Kleiner Liedpsalter. -- Kassel : Bärenreiter, c1976.
-- p. 2. Pub. no.: BA 6231.
      Edited by Walter Blankenburg. Figured bass not realized. German
text.

5   Mit Dank wir sollen loben. -- Stuttgart : Hänssler, [19--]. Pub.
no.: 6.174.
      Figured bass not realized. German text.

      Other editions: Hänssler 2.028.

SWV 105

[Beckerscher Psalter. Mit fröhlichem Gemüte]

     Sacred German text. Sources: Psalm 9.
      For chorus (SMAR) and optional continuo. Ranges of voice parts:
g1-g2, f1-bflat1, a-g1, Bflat-d1. Duration: short.

1   IX. -- In SGA. -- 1894. -- Bd. 16, p. 16-17.
      Edited by Philipp Spitta. Figured bass not realized. Original
German text. Notes in German.

2   Mit fröhlichem Gemüte. -- In NSA. -- 1957. -- Bd. 6, p. 9. Pub. no.:
Bärenreiter Ausgabe 984.
      Edited by Walter Blankenburg. German text. Words in Gothic type.
Notes in German.

SWV 106

[Beckerscher Psalter. Wie meinst du's doch, ach Herr mein Gott]

    Sacred German text. Sources: Psalm 10.
    For chorus (SATB) and optional continuo. Ranges of voice parts:
d1-f2, a-bflat1, f-g1, G-bflat. Duration: short.

1   X. -- In SGA. -- 1894. -- Bd. 16, p. 17.
    Edited by Philipp Spitta. Figured bass not realized. Original
German text. Notes in German.

2   Wie meinst du's doch, ach Herr mein Gott. -- In NSA. -- 1957. -- Bd.
6, p. 10. Pub. no.: Bärenreiter Ausgabe 984.
    Edited by Walter Blankenburg. German text. Words in Gothic type.
Notes in German.

SWV 107

[Beckerscher Psalter. Ich trau auf Gott, was solls denn sein]

    Sacred German text. Sources: Psalm 11.
    For chorus (SATB) and optional continuo. Ranges of voice parts:
d1-f2, a-a1, d-d1, G-a. Duration: short.

1   XI. -- In SGA. -- 1894. -- Bd. 16, p. 18.
    Edited by Philipp Spitta. Figured bass not realized. Original
German text. Notes in German.

2   Ich trau auf Gott. -- In NSA. -- 1957. -- Bd. 6, p. 11. Pub. no.:
Bärenreiter Ausgabe 984.
    Edited by Walter Blankenburg. German text. Words in Gothic type.
Notes in German.

SWV 108

[Beckerscher Psalter. Ach Gott vom Himmel, sieh darein]

    Sacred German text. Sources: Psalm 12.
    For chorus (SATB) and optional continuo. Ranges of voice parts:
d1-d2, a-g1, f-eflat1, G-g. Duration: short.

1   XII. -- In SGA. -- 1894. -- Bd. 16, p. 18-19.
    Edited by Philipp Spitta. Figured bass not realized. Original
German text. Notes in German.

2   Ach Gott vom Himmel, sieh darein. -- In NSA. -- 1957. -- Bd. 6, p.
12. Pub. no.: Bärenreiter Ausgabe 984.
    Edited by Walter Blankenburg. German text. Words in Gothic type.
Notes in German.

SWV 109

[Beckerscher Psalter. Ach Herr, wie lang willst du denn noch]

   Sacred German text. Sources: Psalm 13.
   For chorus (SATB) and optional continuo. Ranges of voice parts:
   dl-f2, a-al, d-dl, F-bflat. Duration: short.

1   XIII. -- In SGA. -- 1894. -- Bd. 16, p. 19.
    Edited by Philipp Spitta. Figured bass not realized. Original
    German text. Notes in German.

2   Ach Herr, wie lang willst du denn noch. -- In NSA. -- 1957. -- Bd.
    6, p. 13. Pub. no.: Bärenreiter Ausgabe 984.
    Edited by Walter Blankenburg. German text. Words in Gothic type.
    Notes in German.

    Other editions: Bärenreiter BA843.

SWV 110

[Beckerscher Psalter. Es spricht der Unweisen Mund wohl, SWV 110]

   Sacred German text. Sources: Psalm 14.
   For chorus (SATB) and optional continuo. Ranges of voice parts:
   el-f2, bflat-gl, f-dl, Bflat-bflat. Duration: short.

1   XIV. -- In SGA. -- 1894. -- Bd. 16, p. 20.
    Edited by Philipp Spitta. Figured bass not realized. Original
    German text. Notes in German.

2   Es spricht der Unweisen Mund wohl, SWV 110. -- In NSA. -- 1957. --
    Bd. 6, p. 14. Pub. no.: Bärenreiter Ausgabe 984.
    Edited by Walter Blankenburg. German text. Words in Gothic type.
    Notes in German.

SWV 111

[Beckerscher Psalter. Wer wird, Herr, in der Hütten dein]

   Sacred German text. Sources: Psalm 15.
   For chorus (SATB) and optional continuo. Ranges of voice parts:
   el-f2, b-al, g-fl, A-cl. Duration: short.

1   XV. -- In SGA. -- 1894. -- Bd. 16, p. 20-21.
    Edited by Philipp Spitta. Figured bass not realized. Original
    German text. Notes in German.

2   Wer wird, Herr, in der Hütten dein. -- In NSA. -- 1957. -- Bd. 6, p.
    15. Pub. no.: Bärenreiter Ausgabe 984.
    Edited by Walter Blankenburg. German text. Words in Gothic type.
    Notes in German.

5   Lobt Gott, den Herrn der Herrlichkeit. -- Stuttgart : Hänssler,
[19--]. Pub. no.: 6.188.
    Figured bass not realized. German text. Music of SWV 111 with
different text.

SWV 112

[Beckerscher Psalter. Bewahr mich, Gott, ich trau auf dich]

    Sacred German text. Sources: Psalm 16.
    For chorus (SATB) and optional continuo. Ranges of voice parts:
c1-d2, g-g1, d-d1, F-a. Duration: short.

1   XVI. -- In SGA. -- 1894. -- Bd. 16, p. 21.
    Edited by Philipp Spitta. Figured bass not realized. Original
German text. Notes in German.

2   Bewahr mich, Gott, ich trau auf dich. -- In NSA. -- 1957. -- Bd. 6,
p. 16. Pub. no.: Bärenreiter Ausgabe 984.
    Edited by Walter Blankenburg. German text. Words in Gothic type.
Notes in German.

SWV 113

[Beckerscher Psalter. Herr Gott, erhör die Grechtigkeit]

    Sacred German text. Sources: Psalm 17.
    For chorus (SATB) and optional continuo. Ranges of voice parts:
d1-d2, g-g1, d#-e1, E-g. Duration: short.

1   XVII. -- In SGA. -- 1894. -- Bd. 16, p. 22.
    Edited by Philipp Spitta. Figured bass not realized. Original
German text. Notes in German.

2   Herr Gott, erhör die Gerechtigkeit. -- In NSA. -- 1957. -- Bd. 6, p.
17. Pub. no.: Bärenreiter Ausgabe 984.
    Edited by Walter Blankenburg. German text. Words in Gothic type.
Notes in German.

SWV 114

[Beckerscher Psalter. Ich lieb dich, Herr, von Herzen sehr]

    Sacred German text. Sources: Psalm 18.
    For chorus (SATB) and optional continuo. Ranges of voice parts:
d1-e2, a-g1, e-e1, G-a. Duration: short.

1   XVIII. -- In SGA. -- 1894. -- Bd. 16, p. 23.
    Edited by Philipp Spitta. Figured bass not realized. Original
German text. Notes in German.

2   Ich lieb dich, Herr, von Herzen sehr. -- In NSA. -- 1957. -- Bd. 6, p. 18. Pub. no.: Bärenreiter Ausgabe 984.
Edited by Walter Blankenburg. German text. Words in Gothic type. Notes in German.

3   Psalm 18. -- In Kleiner Liedpsalter. -- Kassel : Bärenreiter, c1976. -- p. 3. Pub. no.: BA 6231.
Edited by Walter Blankenburg. Figured bass not realized. German text.

5   Ich lieb dich, Herr, von Herzen sehr. -- In Die Psalmen Davids. -- Neuhausen-Stuttgart : Hänssler, c1967. -- p. 3. Pub. no.: HE 2.004.
Edited by Emil Kubler. Figured bass not realized. German text.

6   Ich lieb dich, Herr, von Herzen sehr. -- Stuttgart : Hänssler, c1968. Pub. no.: HE 6.022.
Figured bass not realized. German text.

SWV 115

[Beckerscher Psalter. Himmel, Herr, preisen sehr]

Sacred German text. Sources: Psalm 19.
For chorus (SATB) and optional continuo. Ranges of voice parts: c1-e2, a-g1, e-c1, F-a. Duration: short.

1   XIX. -- In SGA. -- 1894. -- Bd. 16, p. 23.
Edited by Philipp Spitta. Figured bass not realized. Original German text. Notes in German.

2   Die Himmel, Herr, preisen sehr. -- In NSA. -- 1957. -- Bd. 6, p. 19. Pub. no.: Bärenreiter Ausgabe 984.
Edited by Walter Blankenburg. German text. Words in Gothic type. Notes in German.

5   Die Himmel, Herr, preisen sehr. -- In Die Psalmen Davids. -- Neuhausen-Stuttgart : Hänssler, c1967. -- p. 4. Pub. no.: HE 2.004.
Edited by Emil Kubler. Figured bass not realized. German text.

6   Die Himmel, Herr, preisen sehr. -- Stuttgart : Hänssler, c1968. Pub. no.: HE 6.022.
Figured bass not realized. German text.

SWV 116

[Beckerscher Psalter. Herr erhor dich in der Not]

Sacred German text. Sources: Psalm 20.
For chorus (SATB) and optional continuo. Ranges of voice parts: d1-d2, b-a1, d-e1, G-b. Duration: short.

1   XX. -- In SGA. -- 1894. -- Bd. 16, p. 24.
Edited by Philipp Spitta. Figured bass not realized. Original German text. Notes in German.

2   Der Herr erhör dich in der Not. -- In NSA. -- 1957. -- Bd. 6, p. 20.
    Pub. no.: Bärenreiter Ausgabe 984.
    Edited by Walter Blankenburg. German text. Words in Gothic type.
    Notes in German.

5   Der Herr erhör dich in der Not. -- In Die Psalmen Davids. --
    Neuhausen-Stuttgart : Hänssler, c1967. -- p. 5. Pub. no.: HE 2.004.
    Edited by Emil Kübler. Figured bass not realized. German text.

6   Der Herr erhör dich in der Not. -- Stuttgart : Hänssler, [19--].
    Pub. no.: J 042 K.
    Figured bass not realized. German text.

7   Psalm XX. -- In Four psalms. -- New York : Music Press, [19--]. --
    p. 1-2. Pub. no.: D.C.S. no. 6.
    Edited by Paul Boepple. Figured bass not realized. German text
    with English translation. Notes in English.

8   May God attend thee in thy distress = Der Herr erhör dich in der
    Not. -- In Three chorales. -- Fort Lauderdale, Fla. : Music 70,
    c1975. -- p. 5-7. Pub. no.: M70-153.
    Edited by John Kingsbury. German text with English translation.

    Other editions: Hänssler 6.023.

SWV 117

[Beckerscher Psalter. Hoch freuet sich der König]

    Sacred German text. Sources: Psalm 21.
    For chorus (SATB) and optional continuo. Ranges of voice parts:
    d1-e2, a-g1, d-d1, E-g. Duration: short.

1   XXI. -- In SGA. -- 1894. -- Bd. 16, p. 24-25.
    Edited by Philipp Spitta. Figured bass not realized. Original
    German text. Notes in German.

2   Hoch freuet sich der König. -- In NSA. -- 1957. -- Bd. 6, p. 21.
    Pub. no.: Bärenreiter Ausgabe 984.
    Edited by Walter Blankenburg. German text. Words in Gothic type.
    Notes in German.

SWV 118

[Beckerscher Psalter. Mein Gott, mein Gott, ach Herr mein Gott]

    Sacred German text. Sources: Psalm 22.
    For chorus (SATB) and optional continuo. Ranges of voice parts:
    e1-f2, a-a1, e-f1, G-bflat. Duration: short.

1   XXII. -- In SGA. -- 1894. -- Bd. 16, p. 25.
    Edited by Philipp Spitta. Figured bass not realized. Original
    German text. Notes in German.

2   Mein Gott, mein Gott. -- In NSA. -- 1957. -- Bd. 6, p. 22. Pub. no.:
     Bärenreiter Ausgabe 984.
     Edited by Walter Blankenburg. German text. Words in Gothic type.
     Notes in German.

SWV 119

[Beckerscher Psalter. Ich will verkündgen in der Gmein]

     Sacred German text. Sources: Psalm 22.
     For chorus (SATB) and optional continuo. Ranges of voice parts:
     d1-f2, a-g1, c-c1, F-g. Duration: short.

1   XXII. -- In SGA. -- 1894. -- Bd. 16, p. 26.
     Edited by Philipp Spitta. Figured bass not realized. Original
     German text. Notes in German.

2   Ich will verkündgen in der Gmein. -- In NSA. -- 1957. -- Bd. 6, p.
     23. Pub. no.: Bärenreiter Ausgabe 984.
     Edited by Walter Blankenburg. German text. Words in Gothic type.
     Notes in German.

SWV 120

[Beckerscher Psalter. Herr ist mein getreuer Hirt]

     Sacred German text. Sources: Psalm 23.
     For chorus (SATB) and optional continuo. Ranges of voice parts:
     d1-f2, g-a1, e-f1, F-d1. Duration: short.

1   XXIII. -- In SGA. -- 1894. -- Bd. 16, p. 27.
     Edited by Philipp Spitta. Figured bass not realized. Original
     German text. Notes in German.

2   Der Herr ist mein getreuer Hirt. -- In NSA. -- 1957. -- Bd. 6, p.
     24. Pub. no.: Bärenreiter Ausgabe 984.
     Edited by Walter Blankenburg. German text. Words in Gothic type.
     Notes in German.

5   Der Herr ist mein getreuer Hirt. -- Stuttgart : Hänssler, [19--].
     Figured bass not realized. German text.

6   Psalm 23. -- In Four psalms. -- Springfield, Ohio : Chantry Music
     Press, c1959. -- p. 4-5. Pub. no.: CLA 598.
     Edited by Ulrich S. Leupold. English text. Notes in English.

     Other editions: Bärenreiter BA834.

SWV 121

[Beckerscher Psalter. Erd und was sich auf ihr regt]

> Sacred German text. Sources: Psalm 24.
> For chorus (SATB) and optional continuo. Ranges of voice parts:
> c1-f2, a-g1, e-d1, G-f. Duration: short.

1　XXIV. -- In SGA. -- 1894. -- Bd. 16, p. 28.
　　Edited by Philipp Spitta. Figured bass not realized. Original
　　German text. Notes in German.

2　Erd und was sich auf ihr regt. -- In NSA. -- 1957. -- Bd. 6, p. 25.
　　Pub. no.: Bärenreiter Ausgabe 984.
　　Edited by Walter Blankenburg. German text. Words in Gothic type.
　　Notes in German.

3　Psalm 24. -- In Kleiner Liedpsalter. -- Kassel : Bärenreiter, c1976.
　　-- p. 4. Pub. no.: BA 6231.
　　Edited by Walter Blankenburg. Figured bass not realized. German
　　text.

5　Die Erd und was sich auf ihr regt. -- In Die Psalmen Davids. --
　　Neuhausen-Stuttgart : Hänssler, c1967. -- p. 6. Pub. no.: HE 2.004.
　　Edited by Emil Kübler. Figured bass not realized. German text.

6　Die Erd und was sich auf ihr regt. -- Stuttgart : Hänssler, [19--].
　　Pub. no.: J 043 K.
　　Figured bass not realized. German text.

> Other editions: Hänssler 2.022; 6.023.

SWV 122

[Beckerscher Psalter. Nach dir verlangt mich, Herr mein Gott]

> Sacred German text. Sources: Psalm 25.
> For chorus (SATB) and optional continuo. Ranges of voice parts:
> d1-f2, b-a1, d-e1, F-a. Duration: short.

1　XXV. -- In SGA. -- 1894. -- Bd. 16, p. 28-29.
　　Edited by Philipp Spitta. Figured bass not realized. Original
　　German text. Notes in German.

2　Nach dir verlangt mich, Herr mein Gott. -- In NSA. -- 1957. -- Bd.
　　6, p. 26. Pub. no.: Bärenreiter Ausgabe 984.
　　Edited by Walter Blankenburg. German text. Words in Gothic type.
　　Notes in German.

3　Psalm 25. -- In Kleiner Liedpsalter. -- Kassel : Bärenreiter, c1976.
　　-- p. 5. Pub. no.: BA 6231.
　　Edited by Walter Blankenburg. Figured bass not realized. German
　　text.

SWV 123

[Beckerscher Psalter. Herr, schaff mir Recht, nimm dich mein an]

    Sacred German text. Sources: Psalm 26.
    For chorus (SATB) and optional continuo. Ranges of voice parts:
    c1-d2, a-a1, e-e1, F-a. Duration: short.

1   XXVI. -- In SGA. -- 1894. -- Bd. 16, p. 29.
      Edited by Philipp Spitta. Figured bass not realized. Original
    German text. Notes in German.

2   Herr, schaff mir Recht. -- In NSA. -- 1957. -- Bd. 6, p. 27. Pub.
    no.: Bärenreiter Ausgabe 984.
      Edited by Walter Blankenburg. German text. Words in Gothic type.
    Notes in German.

SWV 124

[Beckerscher Psalter. Mein Licht und Heil ist Gott der Herr]

    Sacred German text. Sources: Psalm 27.
    For chorus (SATB) and optional continuo. Ranges of voice parts:
    c1-e2, a-g1, d-d1, F-a. Duration: short.

1   XXVII. -- In SGA. -- 1894. -- Bd. 16, p. 30.
      Edited by Philipp Spitta. Figured bass not realized. Original
    German text. Notes in German.

2   Mein Licht und Heil ist Gott der Herr. -- In NSA. -- 1957. -- Bd. 6,
    p. 28. Pub. no.: Bärenreiter Ausgabe 984.
      Edited by Walter Blankenburg. German text. Words in Gothic type.
    Notes in German.

3   Psalm 27. -- In Kleiner Liedpsalter. -- Kassel : Bärenreiter, c1976.
    -- p. 6. Pub. no.: BA 6231.
      Edited by Walter Blankenburg. Figured bass not realized. German
    text.

SWV 125

[Beckerscher Psalter. Ich ruf zu dir, Herr Gott, mein Hort]

    Sacred German text. Sources: Psalm 28.
    For chorus (SATB) and optional continuo. Ranges of voice parts:
    e1-e2, b-a1, g-e1, G-a. Duration: short.

1   XXVIII. -- In SGA. -- 1894. -- Bd. 16, p. 31.
      Edited by Philipp Spitta. Figured bass not realized. Original
    German text. Notes in German.

2   Ich ruf zu dir, Herr Gott, mein Hort. -- In NSA. -- 1957. -- Bd. 6,
     p. 29. Pub. no.: Bärenreiter Ausgabe 984.
     Edited by Walter Blankenburg. German text. Words in Gothic type.
     Notes in German.

SWV 126

[Beckerscher Psalter. Bringt Ehr und Preis dem Herren]

     Sacred German text. Sources: Psalm 29.
     For chorus (SATB) and optional continuo. Ranges of voice parts:
     c1-f2, a-g1, e-eflat1, F-bflat. Duration: short.

1   XXIX. -- In SGA. -- 1894. -- Bd. 16, p. 32-33.
     Edited by Philipp Spitta. Figured bass not realized. Original
     German text. Notes in German.

2   Bringt Ehr und Preis dem Herren. -- In NSA. -- 1957. -- Bd. 6, p.
     30. Pub. no.: Bärenreiter Ausgabe 984.
     Edited by Walter Blankenburg. German text. Words in Gothic type.
     Notes in German.

3   Psalm 29. -- In Kleiner Liedpsalter. -- Kassel : Bärenreiter, c1976.
     -- p. 7. Pub. no.: BA 6231.
     Edited by Walter Blankenburg. Figured bass not realized. German
     text.

5   Bringt Ehr und Preis dem Herren. -- In Die Psalmen Davids. --
     Neuhausen-Stuttgart : Hänssler, c1967. -- p. 7. Pub. no.: HE 2.004.
     Edited by Emil Kübler. Figured bass not realized. German text.

6   Bringt Ehr und Preis dem Herren. -- Stuttgart : Hänssler, c1962.
     Pub. no.: HE 6.024.
     Figured bass not realized. German text.

7   Psalm 29. -- Bryn Mawr, Pa. : T. Presser, c1950. Pub. no.:
     312-40072.
     Edited by George Lynn. English text.

SWV 127

[Beckerscher Psalter. Ich preis dich, Herr, zu aller Stund]

     Sacred German text. Sources: Psalm 30.
     For chorus (SATB) and optional continuo. Ranges of voice parts:
     c1-d2, g-g1, d-d1 F-g. Duration: short.

1   XXX. -- In SGA. -- 1894. -- Bd. 16, p. 33.
     Edited by Philipp Spitta. Figured bass not realized. Original
     German text. Notes in German.

2   Ich preis dich, Herr, zu aller Stund. -- In NSA. -- 1957. -- Bd. 6,
     p. 31. Pub. no.: Bärenreiter Ausgabe 984.
     Edited by Walter Blankenburg. German text. Words in Gothic type.
     Notes in German.

SWV 128

[Beckerscher Psalter. In dich hab ich gehoffet, Herr]

    Sacred German text. Sources: Psalm 31.
    For chorus (SATB) and optional continuo. Ranges of voice parts:
    f1-c2, c1-g1, e-eflat1, F-g. Duration: short.

1   XXXI. -- In SGA. -- 1894. -- Bd. 16, p. 34.
    Edited by Philipp Spitta. Figured bass not realized. Original
German text. Notes in German.

2   In dich hab ich gehoffet, Herr. -- In NSA. -- 1957. -- Bd. 6, p. 32.
Pub. no.: Bärenreiter Ausgabe 984.
    Edited by Walter Blankenburg. German text. Words in Gothic type.
Notes in German.

5   In dich hab ich gehoffet, Herr. -- Neuhausen-Stuttgart : Hänssler,
c1966. Pub. no.: HE 6.175.
    Figured bass not realized. German text.

SWV 129

[Beckerscher Psalter. Mensch vor Gott wohl selig ist]

    Sacred German text. Sources: Psalm 32.
    For chorus (SATB) and optional continuo. Ranges of voice parts:
    c#1-f2, a-a1, e-d1, F-c1. Duration: short.

1   XXXII. -- In SGA. -- 1894. -- Bd. 16, p. 34-35.
    Edited by Philipp Spitta. Figured bass not realized. Original
German text. Notes in German.

2   Der Mensch vor Gott wohl selig ist. -- In NSA. -- 1957. -- Bd. 6, p.
33. Pub. no.: Bärenreiter Ausgabe 984.
    Edited by Walter Blankenburg. German text. Words in Gothic type.
Notes in German.

6   Psalm 32. -- In Seven penitential psalms. -- G.I.A. Publications,
c1974. -- p. 6-7. Pub. no.: G-1912.
    Edited by Daniel G. Reuning. Figured bass not realized. German
text with English translation. Notes in English.

SWV 130

[Beckerscher Psalter. Freut euch des Herrn, ihr Christen all]

    Sacred German text. Sources: Psalm 33.
    For chorus (SATB) and optional continuo. Ranges of voice parts:
    f1-f2, c1-g1, f-c1, Bflat-bflat. Duration: short.

1   XXXIII. -- In SGA. -- 1894. -- Bd. 16, p. 35.
    Edited by Philipp Spitta. Figured bass not realized. Original
German text. Notes in German.

2   Freut euch des Herrn, ihr Christen all. -- In NSA. -- 1957. -- Bd.
     6, p. 34. Pub. no.: Bärenreiter Ausgabe 984.
     Edited by Walter Blankenburg. German text. Words in Gothic type.
     Notes in German.

3   Psalm 33. -- In Kleiner Liedpsalter. -- Kassel : Bärenreiter, c1976.
     -- p. 8. Pub. no.: BA 6231.
     Edited by Walter Blankenburg. Figured bass not realized. German
     text.

5   Freut euch des Herrn, ihr Christen all. -- In Die Psalmen Davids. --
     Neuhausen-Stuttgart : Hänssler, c1967. -- p. 8. Pub. no.: HE 2.004.
     Edited by Emil Kübler. Figured bass not realized. German text.

6   Freut euch des Herrn, ihr Christen all. -- Neuhausen-Stuttgart :
     Hänssler, [19--]. Pub. no.: 6.020.
     Figured bass not realized. German text.

7   Freut euch des Herrn, ihr Christen all. -- Stuttgart : Hänssler,
     c1962. Pub. no.: HE 6.024.
     Figured bass not realized. German text.

8   Freuet euch des Herrn, ihr Christen all. -- Neuhausen-Stuttgart :
     Hänssler, c1962.
     Figured bass not realized. German text.

     Other editions: Hänssler 8.039; 44.169.

SWV 131

[Beckerscher Psalter. Ich will bei meinem Leben]

     Sacred German text. Sources: Psalm 34.
     For chorus (SATB) and optional continuo. Ranges of voice parts:
     el-f2, bflat-gl, f-dl, G-a. Duration: short.

1   XXXIV. -- In SGA. -- 1894. -- Bd. 16, p. 36.
     Edited by Philipp Spitta. Figured bass not realized. Original
     German text. Notes in German.

2   Ich will bei meinem Leben. -- In NSA. -- 1957. -- Bd. 6, p. 35. Pub.
     no.: Bärenreiter Ausgabe 984.
     Edited by Walter Blankenburg. German text. Words in Gothic type.
     Notes in German.

5   Ich will bei meinem Leben rühmen den Herren mein. -- In Die Psalmen
     Davids. -- Neuhausen-Stuttgart : Hänssler, c1967. -- p. 9. Pub. no.:
     HE 2.004.
     Edited by Emil Kübler. Figured bass not realized. German text.

6   Ich will, so lang ich lebe. -- Neuhausen-Stuttgart : Hänssler,
     c1966. Pub. no.: HE 6.175.
     Figured bass not realized. German text.

7 Ich will, so lang ich lebe. -- Stuttgart : Hänssler, c1966. Pub. no.: HE 6.278.
Figured bass not realized. German text.

8 Von Gott ich will nicht lassen. -- Stuttgart : Hänssler, [19--].
Pub. no.: 6.017.
Figured bass not realized. German text. Uses text of SWV 366, Ludwig Helmbold's Von Gott ich will nicht lassen.

9 Ich will bei meinem Leben rühmen den Herren mein. -- Stuttgart : Hänssler, [19--]. Pub. no.: 6.025.
Figured bass not realized. German text.

Other editions: Hänssler FH1928; 2.014.

SWV 132

[Beckerscher Psalter. Herr, hader mit den Hadrern mein]

Sacred German text. Sources: Psalm 35.
For chorus (SATB) and optional continuo. Ranges of voice parts: c1-e2, g-g1, e-d1, G-a. Duration: short.

1 XXXV. -- In SGA. -- 1894. -- Bd. 16, p. 36-37.
Edited by Philipp Spitta. Figured bass not realized. Original German text. Notes in German.

2 Herr, hader mit den Hadrern mein. -- In NSA. -- 1957. -- Bd. 6, p. 36. Pub. no.: Bärenreiter Ausgabe 984.
Edited by Walter Blankenburg. German text. Words in Gothic type. Notes in German.

SWV 133

[Beckerscher Psalter. Ich sags von Grund meins Herzen frei]

Sacred German text. Sources: Psalm 36.
For chorus (SATB) and optional continuo. Ranges of voice parts: f1-f2, bflat-g1, e-d1, F-g. Duration: short.

1 XXXVI. -- In SGA. -- 1894. -- Bd. 16, p. 37.
Edited by Philipp Spitta. Figured bass not realized. Original German text. Notes in German.

2 So weit, Herr Gott, der Himmel reicht. -- In NSA. -- 1957. -- Bd. 6, p. 37. Pub. no.: Bärenreiter Ausgabe 984.
Edited by Walter Blankenburg. German text. Words in Gothic type. Notes in German.

3 Psalm 36. -- In Kleiner Liedpsalter. -- Kassel : Bärenreiter, c1976. -- p. 9. Pub. no.: BA 6231.
Edited by Walter Blankenburg. Figured bass not realized. German text.

SWV 134

[Beckerscher Psalter. Erzürn dich nicht so sehre]

Sacred German text. Sources: Psalm 37.
For chorus (SATB) and optional continuo. Ranges of voice parts:
c1-c2, a-f1, d-c1, F-f. Duration: short.

1   XXXVII. -- In SGA. -- 1894. -- Bd. 16, p. 38.
    Edited by Philipp Spitta. Figured bass not realized. Original
    German text. Notes in German.

2   Erzürn dich nicht so sehre. -- In NSA. -- 1957. -- Bd. 6, p. 38.
    Pub. no.: Bärenreiter Ausgabe 984.
    Edited by Walter Blankenburg. German text. Words in Gothic type.
    Notes in German.

SWV 135

[Beckerscher Psalter. Herr, straf mich nicht in deinem Zorn]

Sacred German text. Sources: Psalm 38.
For chorus (SATB) and optional continuo. Ranges of voice parts:
c1-e2, a-a1, d-d1, G-g. Duration: short.

1   XXXVIII. -- In SGA. -- 1894. -- Bd. 16, p. 38-39.
    Edited by Philipp Spitta. Figured bass not realized. Original
    German text. Notes in German.

2   Herr, straf mich nicht in deinem Zorn. -- In NSA. -- 1957. -- Bd. 6,
    p. 39. Pub. no.: Bärenreiter Ausgabe 984.
    Edited by Walter Blankenburg. German text. Words in Gothic type.
    Notes in German.

6   Psalm 38. -- In Seven penitential psalms. -- G.I.A. Publications,
    c1974. -- p. 8-9. Pub. no.: G-1912.
    Edited by Daniel G. Reuning. Figured bass not realized. German
    text with English translation. Notes in English.

SWV 136

[Beckerscher Psalter. In meinem Herzen hab ich mir]

Sacred German text. Sources: Psalm 39.
For chorus (SATB) and optional continuo. Ranges of voice parts:
d1-f2, f-a1, f-f1, G-bflat. Duration: short.

1   XXXIX. -- In SGA. -- 1894. -- Bd. 16, p. 39-40.
    Edited by Philipp Spitta. Figured bass not realized. Original
    German text. Notes in German.

2   Ich bin verstummet ganz und still. -- In NSA. -- 1957. -- Bd. 6, p.
     40. Pub. no.: Bärenreiter Ausgabe 984.
     Edited by Walter Blankenburg. German text. Words in Gothic type.
     Notes in German.

3   Psalm 39. -- In Kleiner Liedpsalter. -- Kassel : Bärenreiter, c1976.
     -- p. 10. Pub. no.: BA 6231.
     Edited by Walter Blankenburg. Figured bass not realized. German
     text.

5   Ich bin verstummet ganz und still. -- In Die Psalmen Davids. --
     Neuhausen-Stuttgart : Hänssler, c1967. -- p. 11. Pub. no.: HE 2.004.
     Edited by Emil Kübler. Figured bass not realized. German text.

6   Ich bin verstummet ganz und still. -- Stuttgart : Hänssler, [19--].
     Pub. no.: J 048 K.
     Figured bass not realized. German text.

     Other editions: Hänssler FH1928; 6.026.

SWV 137

[Beckerscher Psalter. Ich harrete des Herren]

     Sacred German text. Sources: Psalm 40.
     For chorus (SATB) and optional continuo. Ranges of voice parts:
     c1-d2, g-f1, d-d1, G-f. Duration: short.

1   XL. -- In SGA. -- 1894. -- Bd. 16, p. 40.
     Edited by Philipp Spitta. Figured bass not realized. Original
     German text. Notes in German.

2   Ich harrete des Herren. -- In NSA. -- 1957. -- Bd. 6, p. 41. Pub.
     no.: Bärenreiter Ausgabe 984.
     Edited by Walter Blankenburg. German text. Words in Gothic type.
     Notes in German.

5   Ich harrete des Herren. -- In Die Psalmen Davids. --
     Neuhausen-Stuttgart : Hänssler, c1967. -- p. 10. Pub. no.: HE 2.004.
     Edited by Emil Kübler. Figured bass not realized. German text.

6   Ich harrete des Herren. -- Stuttgart : Hänssler, [19--]. Pub. no.:
     6.025.
     Figured bass not realized. German text.

7   Ich harrete des Herren. -- Stuttgart : Hänssler, [19--]. Pub. no.:
     1926.
     Figured bass not realized. German text. Words in Gothic type.
     Transposed up M2.

SWV 138

[Beckerscher Psalter. Wohl mag der sein ein selig Mann]

Sacred German text. Sources: Psalm 41.
For chorus (SATB) and optional continuo. Ranges of voice parts:
f1-f2, d1-a1, f-f1, Bflat-c1. Duration: short.

1   XLI. -- In SGA. -- 1894. -- Bd. 16, p. 41.
     Edited by Philipp Spitta. Figured bass not realized. Original
     German text. Notes in German.

2   Wohl mag der sein ein selig Mann. -- In NSA. -- 1957. -- Bd. 6, p.
     42. Pub. no.: Bärenreiter Ausgabe 984.
     Edited by Walter Blankenburg. German text. Words in Gothic type.
     Notes in German.

SWV 139

[Beckerscher Psalter. Gleichwie ein Hirsch eilt mit Begier]

Sacred German text. Sources: Psalm 42.
For chorus (SATB) and optional continuo. Ranges of voice parts:
c1-f2, g-g1, e-d1, F-bflat. Duration: short.

1   XLII. -- In SGA. -- 1894. -- Bd. 16, p. 41-42.
     Edited by Philipp Spitta. Figured bass not realized. Original
     German text. Notes in German.

2   Gleichwie ein Hirsch eilt mit Begier. -- In NSA. -- 1957. -- Bd. 6,
     p. 43. Pub. no.: Bärenreiter Ausgabe 984.
     Edited by Walter Blankenburg. German text. Words in Gothic type.
     Notes in German.

SWV 140

[Beckerscher Psalter. Gott, führ mein Sach und richte mich]

Sacred German text. Sources: Psalm 43.
For chorus (SATB) and optional continuo. Ranges of voice parts:
c1-e2, b-g1, e-d1, F-a. Duration: short.

1   XLIII. -- In SGA. -- 1894. -- Bd. 16, p. 42-43.
     Edited by Philipp Spitta. Figured bass not realized. Original
     German text. Notes in German.

2   Gott, führ mein Sach und richte mich. -- In NSA. -- 1957. -- Bd. 6,
     p. 44. Pub. no.: Bärenreiter Ausgabe 984.
     Edited by Walter Blankenburg. German text. Words in Gothic type.
     Notes in German.

3   Psalm 43. -- In Kleiner Liedpsalter. -- Kassel : Bärenreiter, c1976.
     -- p. 11. Pub. no.: BA 6231.
     Edited by Walter Blankenburg. Figured bass not realized. German
     text.

SWV 141

[Beckerscher Psalter. Wir haben, Herr, mit Fleiss gehört]

     Sacred German text. Sources: Psalm 44.
     For chorus (SATB) and optional continuo. Ranges of voice parts:
     d1-f2, c1-a1, f-g1, A-bflat. Duration: short.

1   XLIV. -- In SGA. -- 1894. -- Bd. 16, p. 43.
     Edited by Philipp Spitta. Figured bass not realized. Original
     German text. Notes in German.

2   Wir haben, Herr, mit Fleiss gehort. -- In NSA. -- 1957. -- Bd. 6, p.
     45. Pub. no.: Bärenreiter Ausgabe 984.
     Edited by Walter Blankenburg. German text. Words in Gothic type.
     Notes in German.

SWV 142

[Beckerscher Psalter. Mein Herz dichtet ein Lied mit Fleiss]

     Sacred German text. Sources: Psalm 45.
     For chorus (SATB) and optional continuo. Ranges of voice parts:
     d1-f2, g-a1, f-f1, G-bflat. Duration: short.

1   XLV. -- In SGA. -- 1894. -- Bd. 16, p. 44.
     Edited by Philipp Spitta. Figured bass not realized. Original
     German text. Notes in German.

2   Mein Herz dichtet ein Lied. -- In NSA. -- 1957. -- Bd. 6, p. 46.
     Pub. no.: Bärenreiter Ausgabe 984.
     Edited by Walter Blankenburg. German text. Words in Gothic type.
     Notes in German.

5   Mein Herz dichtet ein Lied. -- In Die Psalmen Davids. --
     Neuhausen-Stuttgart : Hänssler, c1967. -- p. 12. Pub. no.: HE 2.004.
     Edited by Emil Kübler. Figured bass not realized. German text.

6   Mein Herz dichtet ein Lied. -- Stuttgart : Hänssler, [19--]. Pub.
     no.: J 049 K.
     Figured bass not realized. German text.

     Other editions: Hänssler 6.026.

SWV 143

[Beckerscher Psalter. Feste Burg ist unser Gott]

> Sacred German text. Sources: Psalm 46.
> For chorus (SATB) and optional continuo. Ranges of voice parts:
> c1-c2, g-g1, e-e1, F-a. Duration: short.

1   XLVI. -- In SGA. -- 1894. -- Bd. 16, p. 45.
    Edited by Philipp Spitta. Figured bass not realized. Original
    German text. Notes in German.

2   Ein feste Burg ist unser Gott. -- In NSA. -- 1957. -- Bd. 6, p. 47.
    Pub. no.: Bärenreiter Ausgabe 984.
    Edited by Walter Blankenburg. German text. Words in Gothic type.
    Notes in German.

> Other editions: Hänssler 44.591.

SWV 144

[Beckerscher Psalter. Frohlockt mit Freud, ihr Völker all]

> Sacred German text. Sources: Psalm 47.
> For chorus (SATB) and optional continuo. Ranges of voice parts:
> g1-e2, c1-a1, e-e1, F-c1. Duration: short.

1   XLVII. -- In SGA. -- 1894. -- Bd. 16, p. 46.
    Edited by Philipp Spitta. Figured bass not realized. Original
    German text. Notes in German.

2   Frohlockt mit Freud, ihr Völker all. -- In NSA. -- 1957. -- Bd. 6,
    p. 48-49. Pub. no.: Bärenreiter Ausgabe 984.
    Edited by Walter Blankenburg. German text. Words in Gothic type.
    Notes in German.

5   Frohlockt mit Freud. -- In Die Psalmen Davids. --
    Neuhausen-Stuttgart : Hänssler, c1967. -- p. 13. Pub. no.: HE 2.004.
    Edited by Emil Kübler. Figured bass not realized. German text.

6   Frohlockt mit Freud!. -- Stuttgart : Hänssler, [19--]. Pub. no.: H
    1927 H.
    Figured bass not realized. German text. Words in Gothic type.

7   Frohlockt mit Freud, ihr Völker all. -- Stuttgart : Hänssler,
    [19--]. Pub. no.: HE 6.128.
    Figured bass not realized. German text.

8   Frohlockt mit Freud, ihr Völker all. -- Stuttgart : Hänssler,
    [19--]. Pub. no.: HE 6.027.
    Figured bass not realized. German text.

> Other editions: Hänssler 2.029; 6.029.

SWV 145

[Beckerscher Psalter. Gross ist der Herr und hoch gepreist]

Sacred German text. Sources: Psalm 48.
For chorus (SATB) and optional continuo. Ranges of voice parts:
dl-e2, cl-al, f-fl, F-b. Duration: short.

1 XLVIII. -- In SGA. -- 1894. -- Bd. 16, p. 46-47.
   Edited by Philipp Spitta. Figured bass not realized. Original
   German text. Notes in German.

2 Gross ist der Herr und hoch. -- In NSA. -- 1957. -- Bd. 6, p. 49.
   Pub. no.: Bärenreiter Ausgabe 984.
   Edited by Walter Blankenburg. German text. Words in Gothic type.
   Notes in German.

5 Gross ist der Herr und hoch gepreist. -- In Die Psalmen Davids. --
   Neuhausen-Stuttgart : Hänssler, c1967. -- p. 14. Pub. no.: HE 2.004.
   Edited by Emil Kübler. Figured bass not realized. German text.

6 Gross ist der Herr und hoch gepreist. -- Stuttgart : Hänssler,
   [19--]. Pub. no.: HE 6.027.
   Figured bass not realized. German text.

   Other editions: Hänssler 2.049.

SWV 146

[Beckerscher Psalter. Hört zu, ihr Völker insgemein]

Sacred German text. Sources: Psalm 49.
For chorus (SATB) and optional continuo. Ranges of voice parts:
dl-e2, g-al, g-gl, G-a. Duration: short.

1 XLIX. -- In SGA. -- 1894. -- Bd. 16, p. 47.
   Edited by Philipp Spitta. Figured bass not realized. Original
   German text. Notes in German.

2 Hört zu, ihr Völker insgemein. -- In NSA. -- 1957. -- Bd. 6, p. 50.
   Pub. no.: Bärenreiter Ausgabe 984.
   Edited by Walter Blankenburg. German text. Words in Gothic type.
   Notes in German.

SWV 147

[Beckerscher Psalter. Gott unser Herr, mächtig durchs Wort]

Sacred German text. Sources: Psalm 50.
For chorus (SATB) and optional continuo. Ranges of voice parts:
cl-e2, g-al, d-dl, G-bflat. Duration: short.

1   L. -- In SGA. -- 1894. -- Bd. 16, p. 48.
     Edited by Philipp Spitta. Figured bass not realized. Original
German text. Notes in German.

2   Gott unser Herr, mächtig durchs Wort. -- In NSA. -- 1957. -- Bd. 6,
p. 51. Pub. no.: Bärenreiter Ausgabe 984.
     Edited by Walter Blankenburg. German text. Words in Gothic type.
Notes in German.

3   Psalm 50. -- In Kleiner Liedpsalter. -- Kassel : Bärenreiter, c1976.
-- p. 12. Pub. no.: BA 6231.
     Edited by Walter Blankenburg. Figured bass not realized. German
text.

5   Gott unser Herr, mächtig durchs Wort. -- In Die Psalmen Davids. --
Neuhausen-Stuttgart : Hänssler, c1967. -- p. 15. Pub. no.: HE 2.004.
     Edited by Emil Kübler. Figured bass not realized. German text.

6   Gott unser Herr, mächtig durchs Wort. -- Stuttgart : Hänssler,
[19--]. Pub. no.: J 052 K.
     Figured bass not realized. German text.

     Other editions: Hänssler 6.028.

SWV 148

[Beckerscher Psalter. Erbarm dich mein, o Herre Gott]

     Sacred German text. Sources: Psalm 51.
     For chorus (SATB) and optional continuo. Ranges of voice parts:
c1-c2, g-f1, d-e1, F-a. Duration: short.

1   LI. -- In SGA. -- 1894. -- Bd. 16, p. 48-49.
     Edited by Philipp Spitta. Figured bass not realized. Original
German text. Notes in German.

2   Erbarm dich mein, o Herre Gott. -- In NSA. -- 1957. -- Bd. 6, p. 52.
Pub. no.: Bärenreiter Ausgabe 984.
     Edited by Walter Blankenburg. German text. Words in Gothic type.
Notes in German.

5   Erbarm dich mein, o Herre Gott. -- In Die Psalmen Davids. --
Neuhausen-Stuttgart : Hänssler, c1967. -- p. 16. Pub. no.: HE 2.004.
     Edited by Emil Kübler. Figured bass not realized. German text.

6   Psalm 51. -- In Seven penitential psalms. -- G.I.A. Publications,
c1974. -- p. 10-11. Pub. no.: G-1912.
     Edited by Daniel G. Reuning. Figured bass not realized. German
text with English translation. Notes in English.

7   Erbarm dich mein, o Herre Gott. -- Stuttgart : Hänssler, [19--].
Pub. no.: J 053 K.
     Figured bass not realized. German text.

     Other editions: Hänssler 6.028.

SWV 149

[Beckerscher Psalter. Was trotzst denn du, Tyrann, so hoch]

    Sacred German text. Sources: Psalm 52.
      For chorus (SATB) and optional continuo. Ranges of voice parts:
    d1-eflat2, f-g1, f-eflat1, G-bflat. Duration: short.

1   LII. -- In SGA. -- 1894. -- Bd. 16, p. 49.
      Edited by Philipp Spitta. Figured bass not realized. Original
German text. Notes in German.

2   Was trotzst denn du, Tyrann, so hoch. -- In NSA. -- 1957. -- Bd. 6,
p. 53. Pub. no.: Bärenreiter Ausgabe 984.
      Edited by Walter Blankenburg. German text. Words in Gothic type.
Notes in German.

SWV 150

[Beckerscher Psalter. Es spricht der Unweisen Mund wohl, SWV 150]

    Sacred German text. Sources: Psalm 53.
      For chorus (SATB) and optional continuo. Ranges of voice parts:
    e1-f2, bflat-g1, f-d1, Bflat-bflat. Duration: short.

1   LIII. -- In SGA. -- 1894. -- Bd. 16, p. 20.
      Edited by Philipp Spitta. Figured bass not realized. Original
German text. Notes in German.

2   Es spricht der Unweisen Mund wohl, SWV 150. -- In NSA. -- 1957. --
Bd. 6, p. 14. Pub. no.: Bärenreiter Ausgabe 984.
      Edited by Walter Blankenburg. German text. Words in Gothic type.
Notes in German.

SWV 151

[Beckerscher Psalter. Hilf mir, Gott, durch den Namen dein]

    Sacred German text. Sources: Psalm 54.
      For chorus (SATB) and optional continuo. Ranges of voice parts:
    f1-eflat2, bflat-g1, f#-eflat1, Bflat-bflat. Duration: short.

1   LIV. -- In SGA. -- 1894. -- Bd. 16, p. 50.
      Edited by Philipp Spitta. Figured bass not realized. Original
German text. Notes in German.

2   Hilf mir, Gott, durch den Namen dein. -- In NSA. -- 1957. -- Bd. 6,
p. 54. Pub. no.: Bärenreiter Ausgabe 984.
      Edited by Walter Blankenburg. German text. Words in Gothic type.
Notes in German.

3   Psalm 54. -- In Kleiner Liedpsalter. -- Kassel : Bärenreiter, c1976.
     -- p. 13. Pub. no.: BA 6231.
       Edited by Walter Blankenburg. Figured bass not realized. German
     text.

SWV 152

[Beckerscher Psalter. Erhör mein Gbet, du treuer Gott]

     Sacred German text. Sources: Psalm 55.
       For chorus (SATB) and optional continuo. Ranges of voice parts:
     f#1-f2, bflat-g1, f-eflat1, G-c1. Duration: short.

1   LV. -- In SGA. -- 1894. -- Bd. 16, p. 50-51.
       Edited by Philipp Spitta. Figured bass not realized. Original
     German text. Notes in German.

2   Erhör mein Gbet, du treuer Gott. -- In NSA. -- 1957. -- Bd. 6, p.
     55. Pub. no.: Bärenreiter Ausgabe 984.
       Edited by Walter Blankenburg. German text. Words in Gothic type.
     Notes in German.

SWV 153

[Beckerscher Psalter. Herr Gott, erzeig mir Hilf und Gnad]

     Sacred German text. Sources: Psalm 56.
       For chorus (SATB) and optional continuo. Ranges of voice parts:
     c1-e2, a-g1, g-e1, F-c1. Duration: short.

1   LVI. -- In SGA. -- 1894. -- Bd. 16, p. 51.
       Edited by Philipp Spitta. Figured bass not realized. Original
     German text. Notes in German.

2   Herr Gott, erzeig mir Hülf und Gnad. -- In NSA. -- 1957. -- Bd. 6,
     p. 56. Pub. no.: Bärenreiter Ausgabe 984.
       Edited by Walter Blankenburg. German text. Words in Gothic type.
     Notes in German.

3   Psalm 56. -- In Kleiner Liedpsalter. -- Kassel : Bärenreiter, c1976.
     -- p. 14. Pub. no.: BA 6231.
       Edited by Walter Blankenburg. Figured bass not realized. German
     text.

5   Herr Gott, erzeig mir Hilf und Gnad. -- In Die Psalmen Davids. --
     Neuhausen-Stuttgart : Hänssler, c1967. -- p. 17. Pub. no.: HE 2.004.
       Edited by Emil Kübler. Figured bass not realized. German text.

6   Herr Gott, erzeig mir Hilf und Gnad. -- Stuttgart : Hänssler,
     [19--].
       Figured bass not realized. German text.

     Other editions: Hänssler 6.029.

SWV 154

[Beckerscher Psalter. Sei mir gnädig, o Gott, mein Herr]

>Sacred German text. Sources: Psalm 57.
>For chorus (SATB) and optional continuo. Ranges of voice parts:
>d1-f2, g-g1, f-eflat1, G-bflat. Duration: short.

1   LVII. -- In SGA. -- 1894. -- Bd. 16, p. 52.
    Edited by Philipp Spitta. Figured bass not realized. Original
    German text. Notes in German.

2   Sei mir gnädig, o Gott, mein Herr. -- In NSA. -- 1957. -- Bd. 6, p.
    57. Pub. no.: Bärenreiter Ausgabe 984.
    Edited by Walter Blankenburg. German text. Words in Gothic type.
    Notes in German.

SWV 155

[Beckerscher Psalter. Wie nun, ihr Herren, seid ihr stumm]

>Sacred German text. Sources: Psalm 58.
>For chorus (SATB) and optional continuo. Ranges of voice parts:
>d1-e2, a-g1, f-e1, F-a. Duration: short.

1   LVIII. -- In SGA. -- 1894. -- Bd. 16, p. 53.
    Edited by Philipp Spitta. Figured bass not realized. Original
    German text. Notes in German.

2   Wie nun, ihr Herren. -- In NSA. -- 1957. -- Bd. 6, p. 58. Pub. no.:
    Bärenreiter Ausgabe 984.
    Edited by Walter Blankenburg. German text. Words in Gothic type.
    Notes in German.

SWV 156

[Beckerscher Psalter. Ach treuer Gott, sieh doch darein]

>Sacred German text. Sources: Psalm 59.
>For chorus (SATB) and optional continuo. Ranges of voice parts:
>c1-e2, g-g1, e-e1, G-c1. Duration: short.

1   LIX. -- In SGA. -- 1894. -- Bd. 16, p. 53.
    Edited by Philipp Spitta. Figured bass not realized. Original
    German text. Notes in German.

2   Ach treuer Gott, sieh doch darein. -- In NSA. -- 1957. -- Bd. 6,
    p. 59. Pub. no.: Bärenreiter Ausgabe 984.
    Edited by Walter Blankenburg. German text. Words in Gothic type.
    Notes in German.

SWV 157

[Beckerscher Psalter. Ach Gott, der du vor dieser Zeit]

> Sacred German text. Sources: Psalm 60.
> For chorus (SATB) and optional continuo. Ranges of voice parts:
> el-f2, c#1-a1, g-el, A-c1. Duration: short.

1   LX. -- In SGA. -- 1894. -- Bd. 16, p. 54.
    Edited by Philipp Spitta. Figured bass not realized. Original
    German text. Notes in German.

2   Ach Gott, der du vor dieser Zeit. -- In NSA. -- 1957. -- Bd. 6,
    p. 60. Pub. no.: Bärenreiter Ausgabe 984.
    Edited by Walter Blankenburg. German text. Words in Gothic type.
    Notes in German.

5   Ach Gott, der du vor dieser Zeit. -- Stuttgart : Hänssler, [19--].
    Pub. no.: 6.177.
    Figured bass not realized. German text.

SWV 158

[Beckerscher Psalter. Gott, mein Geschrei erhöre]

> Sacred German text. Sources: Psalm 61.
> For chorus (SATB) and optional continuo. Ranges of voice parts:
> fl-f2, cl-al, f-fl G-bflat. Duration: short.

1   LXI. -- In SGA. -- 1894. -- Bd. 16, p. 55.
    Edited by Philipp Spitta. Figured bass not realized. Original
    German text. Notes in German.

2   Gott, mein Geschrei erhöre. -- In NSA. -- 1957. -- Bd. 6, p. 60-61.
    Pub. no.: Bärenreiter Ausgabe 984.
    Edited by Walter Blankenburg. German text. Words in Gothic type.
    Notes in German.

SWV 159

[Beckerscher Psalter. Mein Seel ist still in meinem Gott]

> Sacred German text. Sources: Psalm 62.
> For chorus (SATB) and optional continuo. Ranges of voice parts:
> cl-d2, g-el, e-cl, F-f. Duration: short.

1   LXII. -- In SGA. -- 1894. -- Bd. 16, p. 55-56.
    Edited by Philipp Spitta. Figured bass not realized. Original
    German text. Notes in German.

2   Mein Seel ist still in meinem Gott. -- In NSA. -- 1957. -- Bd. 6, p.
    61. Pub. no.: Bärenreiter Ausgabe 984.
    Edited by Walter Blankenburg. German text. Words in Gothic type.
    Notes in German.

5   Mein Seel ist still in meinem Gott. -- In Die Psalmen Davids. --
    Neuhausen-Stuttgart : Hänssler, c1967. -- p. 18. Pub. no.: HE 2.004.
    Edited by Emil Kübler. Figured bass not realized. German text.

6   Mein Seel ist still in meinem Gott. -- Stuttgart : Hänssler, [19--].
    Figured bass not realized. German text.

    Other editions: Hänssler 6.029.

SWV 160

[Beckerscher Psalter. O Gott, du mein getreuer Gott]

    Sacred German text. Sources: Psalm 63.
    For chorus (SATB) and optional continuo. Ranges of voice parts:
    d1-e2, g-a1, e-d1, E-a. Duration: short.

1   LXIII. -- In SGA. -- 1894. -- Bd. 16, p. 56-57.
    Edited by Philipp Spitta. Figured bass not realized. Original
    German text. Notes in German.

2   O Gott, du mein getreuer Gott. -- In NSA. -- 1957. -- Bd. 6, p. 62.
    Pub. no.: Bärenreiter Ausgabe 984.
    Edited by Walter Blankenburg. German text. Words in Gothic type.
    Notes in German. Transposed up m3.

3   Psalm 63. -- In Kleiner Liedpsalter. -- Kassel : Bärenreiter, c1976.
    -- p. 15. Pub. no.: BA 6231.
    Edited by Walter Blankenburg. Figured bass not realized. German
    text. Transposed up m3.

SWV 161

[Beckerscher Psalter. Erhör mein Stimm, Herr, wenn ich klag]

    Sacred German text. Sources: Psalm 64.
    For chorus (SATB) and optional continuo. Ranges of voice parts:
    g1-e2, d1-a1, g-e1, G-c1. Duration: short.

1   LXIV. -- In SGA. -- 1894. -- Bd. 16, p. 57.
    Edited by Philipp Spitta. Figured bass not realized. Original
    German text. Notes in German.

2   Erhör mein Stimm, Herr, wenn ich klag. -- In NSA. -- 1957. -- Bd. 6,
    p. 63. Pub. no.: Bärenreiter Ausgabe 984.
    Edited by Walter Blankenburg. German text. Words in Gothic type.
    Notes in German.

SWV 162

[Beckerscher Psalter. Gott, man lob dich in der Still]

> Sacred German text. Sources: Psalm 65.
> For chorus (SATB) and optional continuo. Ranges of voice parts:
> c1-d2, a-g1, d-e1, G-a. Duration: short.

1   LXV. -- In SGA. -- 1894. -- Bd. 16, p. 58.
> Edited by Philipp Spitta. Figured bass not realized. Original
> German text. Notes in German.

2   Wohl dem, den Gott hat erwählt. -- In NSA. -- 1957. -- Bd. 6, p. 64.
> Pub. no.: Bärenreiter Ausgabe 984.
> Edited by Walter Blankenburg. German text. Words in Gothic type.
> Notes in German.

SWV 163

[Beckerscher Psalter. Jauchzet Gott alle Lande sehr]

> Sacred German text. Sources: Psalm 66.
> For chorus (SATB) and optional continuo. Ranges of voice parts:
> f#1-f2, bflat-a1, g-f1, G-bflat. Duration: short.

1   LXVI. -- In SGA. -- 1894. -- Bd. 16, p. 59.
> Edited by Philipp Spitta. Figured bass not realized. Original
> German text. Notes in German.

2   Jauchzet Gott alle Lande sehr. -- In NSA. -- 1957. -- Bd. 6, p. 65.
> Pub. no.: Bärenreiter Ausgabe 984.
> Edited by Walter Blankenburg. German text. Words in Gothic type.
> Notes in German.

5   Jauchzet Gott alle Lande sehr. -- In Die Psalmen Davids. --
> Neuhausen-Stuttgart : Hänssler, c1967. -- p. 19. Pub. no.: HE 2.004.
> Edited by Emil Kübler. Figured bass not realized. German text.

6   Jauchzet Gott alle Lande sehr. -- Stuttgart : Hänssler, [19--].
> Figured bass not realized. German text.

7   Den enda gladje, som jag vet = Jauchzet Gott alle Lande sehr. --
> Stockholm : Eriks Musikhandel, c1973. Pub. no.: K. 343.
> Edited by Valdemar Soderholm. Figured bass not realized. Swedish
> text.

> Other editions: Hänssler 2.037; 6.030.

SWV 164

[Beckerscher Psalter. Es woll uns Gott genädig sein]

    Sacred German text. Sources: Psalm 67.
    For chorus (SATB) and optional continuo. Ranges of voice parts:
    cl-e2, g-al, e-el, G-a. Duration: short.

1   LXVII. -- In SGA. -- 1894. -- Bd. 16, p. 59-60.
    Edited by Philipp Spitta. Figured bass not realized. Original
German text. Notes in German.

2   Es woll uns Gott genädig sein. -- In NSA. -- 1957. -- Bd. 6, p. 66.
Pub. no.: Bärenreiter Ausgabe 984.
    Edited by Walter Blankenburg. German text. Words in Gothic type.
Notes in German.

SWV 165

[Beckerscher Psalter. Es steh Gott auf, dass seine Feind plötzlich
    zerstreuet werden]

    Sacred German text. Sources: Psalm 68.
    For chorus (SATB) and optional continuo. Ranges of voice parts:
    dl-f2, g-al, f-dl, F-bflat. Duration: short.

1   LXVIII. -- In SGA. -- 1894. -- Bd. 16, p. 60-61.
    Edited by Philipp Spitta. Figured bass not realized. Original
German text. Notes in German.

2   Es steh Gott auf, dass seine Feind. -- In NSA. -- 1957. -- Bd. 6, p.
67. Pub. no.: Bärenreiter Ausgabe 984.
    Edited by Walter Blankenburg. German text. Words in Gothic type.
Notes in German.

5   Es steh Gott auf, dass seine Feind. -- In Die Psalmen Davids. --
Neuhausen-Stuttgart : Hänssler, c1967. -- p. 20. Pub. no.: HE 2.004.
    Edited by Emil Kübler. Figured bass not realized. German text.

6   Es steh Gott auf, dass seine Feind. -- Stuttgart : Hänssler, [19--].
Figured bass not realized. German text.

    Other editions: Hänssler 2.039; 6.030.

SWV 166

[Beckerscher Psalter. Gott hilf mir, denn das Wasser dringt]

    Sacred German text. Sources: Psalm 69.
    For chorus (SATB) and optional continuo. Ranges of voice parts:
    cl-d2, a-al, f-fl, G-a. Duration: short.

1   LXIX. -- In SGA. -- 1894. -- Bd. 16, p. 61-62.
    Edited by Philipp Spitta. Figured bass not realized. Original
    German text. Notes in German.

2   Gott hilf mir, denn das Wasser dringt. -- In NSA. -- 1957. -- Bd. 6,
    p. 68. Pub. no.: Bärenreiter Ausgabe 984.
    Edited by Walter Blankenburg. German text. Words in Gothic type.
    Notes in German.

SWV 167

[Beckerscher Psalter. Eil Herr, mein Gott, zu retten mich]

    Sacred German text. Sources: Psalm 70.
    For chorus (SATB) and optional continuo. Ranges of voice parts:
    d1-e2, a-a1, d-e1, G-a. Duration: short.

1   LXX. -- In SGA. -- 1894. -- Bd. 16, p. 62.
    Edited by Philipp Spitta. Figured bass not realized. Original
    German text. Notes in German.

2   Eil Herr, mein Gott, zu retten mich. -- In NSA. -- 1957. -- Bd. 6,
    p. 69. Pub. no.: Bärenreiter Ausgabe 984.
    Edited by Walter Blankenburg. German text. Words in Gothic type.
    Notes in German.

SWV 168

[Beckerscher Psalter. Auf dich, Herr, trau ich allezeit]

    Sacred German text. Sources: Psalm 71.
    For chorus (SATB) and optional continuo. Ranges of voice parts:
    e1-f2, c1-g1, d-f1, F-c1. Duration: short.

1   LXXI. -- In SGA. -- 1894. -- Bd. 16, p. 63.
    Edited by Philipp Spitta. Figured bass not realized. Original
    German text. Notes in German.

2   Auf dich, Herr, trau ich allezeit. -- In NSA. -- 1957. -- Bd. 6, p.
    70. Pub. no.: Bärenreiter Ausgabe 984.
    Edited by Walter Blankenburg. German text. Words in Gothic type.
    Notes in German.

    Other editions: Bärenreiter BA844.

SWV 169

[Beckerscher Psalter. Gott, gieb dem König auserkorn Recht]

    Sacred German text. Sources: Psalm 72.
    For chorus (SATB) and optional continuo. Ranges of voice parts:
    f1-eflat2, bflat-g1, f#-eflat1, G-c1. Duration: short.

1   LXXII. -- In SGA. -- 1894. -- Bd. 16, p. 64.
    Edited by Philipp Spitta. Figured bass not realized. Original
    German text. Notes in German.

2   Auf Hügeln, Bergen weit und breit. -- In NSA. -- 1957. -- Bd. 6, p.
    71. Pub. no.: Bärenreiter Ausgabe 984.
    Edited by Walter Blankenburg. German text. Words in Gothic type.
    Notes in German.

SWV 170

[Beckerscher Psalter. Dennoch hat Israel zum Trost]

    Sacred German text. Sources: Psalm 73.
    For chorus (SATB) and optional continuo. Ranges of voice parts:
    d1-d2, a-a1, e-d1, F-a. Duration: short.

1   LXXIII. -- In SGA. -- 1894. -- Bd. 16, p. 64-65.
    Edited by Philipp Spitta. Figured bass not realized. Original
    German text. Notes in German.

2   Dennoch hat Israel zum Trost. -- In NSA. -- 1957. -- Bd. 6, p. 72.
    Pub. no.: Bärenreiter Ausgabe 984.
    Edited by Walter Blankenburg. German text. Words in Gothic type.
    Notes in German. Transposed up M2.

5   Dennoch hat Israel zum Trost. -- In Die Psalmen Davids. --
    Neuhausen-Stuttgart : Hänssler, c1967. -- p. 21. Pub. no.: HE 2.004.
    Edited by Emil Kübler. Figured bass not realized. German text.
    Transposed up M2.

6   Dennoch hat Israel zum Trost. -- Stuttgart : Hänssler, [19--]. Pub.
    no.: J 058 K.
    Figured bass not realized. German text. Transposed up M2.

    Other editions: Hänssler 6.031.

SWV 171

[Beckerscher Psalter. Warum verstösst du uns so gar]

    Sacred German text. Sources: Psalm 74.
    For chorus (SATB) and optional continuo. Ranges of voice parts:
    e1-e2, c1-a1, g#-e1, G-c1. Duration: short.

1   LXXIV. -- In SGA. -- 1894. -- Bd. 16, p. 65.
    Edited by Philipp Spitta. Figured bass not realized. Original
    German text. Notes in German.

2   Warum verstösst du uns so gar. -- In NSA. -- 1957. -- Bd. 6, p. 73.
    Pub. no.: Bärenreiter Ausgabe 984.
    Edited by Walter Blankenburg. German text. Words in Gothic type.
    Notes in German.

SWV 172

[Beckerscher Psalter. Aus unsers Herzens Grunde]

    Sacred German text. Sources: Psalm 75.
      For chorus (SATB) and optional continuo. Ranges of voice parts:
el-eflat2, cl-al, g-el, A-bflat. Duration: short.

1   LXXV. -- In SGA. -- 1894. -- Bd. 16, p. 66.
      Edited by Philipp Spitta. Figured bass not realized. Original
German text. Notes in German.

2   Aus unsers Herzens Grunde. -- In NSA. -- 1957. -- Bd. 6, p. 74. Pub.
no.: Bärenreiter Ausgabe 984.
      Edited by Walter Blankenburg. German text. Words in Gothic type.
Notes in German.

SWV 173

[Beckerscher Psalter. In Juda ist der Herr bekannt]

    Sacred German text. Sources: Psalm 76.
      For chorus (SATB) and optional continuo. Ranges of voice parts:
cl-e2, g-al, e-el, F-a. Duration: short.

1   LXXVI. -- In SGA. -- 1894. -- Bd. 16, p. 67.
      Edited by Philipp Spitta. Figured bass not realized. Original
German text. Notes in German.

2   Wenn sich der Herr Gott Zebaoth. -- In NSA. -- 1957. -- Bd. 6, p.
75. Pub. no.: Bärenreiter Ausgabe 984.
      Edited by Walter Blankenburg. German text. Words in Gothic type.
Notes in German.

SWV 174

[Beckerscher Psalter. Ich ruf zu Gott mit meiner Stimm]

    Sacred German text. Sources: Psalm 77.
      For chorus (SATB) and optional continuo. Ranges of voice parts:
dl-eflat2, a-gl, d-eflatl, G-g. Duration: short.

1   LXXVII. -- In SGA. -- 1894. -- Bd. 16, p. 67-68.
      Edited by Philipp Spitta. Figured bass not realized. Original
German text. Notes in German.

2   Ich ruf zu Gott mit meiner Stimm. -- In NSA. -- 1957. -- Bd. 6, p.
76. Pub. no.: Bärenreiter Ausgabe 984.
      Edited by Walter Blankenburg. German text. Words in Gothic type.
Notes in German.

SWV 175

[Beckerscher Psalter. Hör, mein Volk, mein Gesetz und Weis]

    Sacred German text. Sources: Psalm 78.
    For chorus (SATB) and optional continuo. Ranges of voice parts:
    c1-d2, g-g1, d-e1, F-a. Duration: short.

1   LXXVIII. -- In SGA. -- 1894. -- Bd. 16, p. 68.
    Edited by Philipp Spitta. Figured bass not realized. Original
   German text. Notes in German.

2   Hör, mein Volk, mein Gesetz und Weis. -- In NSA. -- 1957. -- Bd. 6,
   p. 77. Pub. no.: Bärenreiter Ausgabe 984.
    Edited by Walter Blankenburg. German text. Words in Gothic type.
   Notes in German. Transposed up m3.

SWV 176

[Beckerscher Psalter. Ach Herr, es ist der Heiden Heer]

    Sacred German text. Sources: Psalm 79.
    For chorus (SATB) and optional continuo. Ranges of voice parts:
    f1-f2, g-a1, f-f1, G-bflat. Duration: short.

1   LXXIX. -- In SGA. -- 1894. -- Bd. 16, p. 69.
    Edited by Philipp Spitta. Figured bass not realized. Original
   German text. Notes in German.

2   Ach Herr, es ist der Heiden Heer. -- In NSA. -- 1957. -- Bd. 6, p.
   78. Pub. no.: Bärenreiter Ausgabe 984.
    Edited by Walter Blankenburg. German text. Words in Gothic type.
   Notes in German.

SWV 177

[Beckerscher Psalter. Du Hirt Israel, höre uns]

    Sacred German text. Sources: Psalm 80.
    For chorus (SATB) and optional continuo. Ranges of voice parts:
    e1-d2, c1-g1, g#-e1, G-a. Duration: short.

1   LXXX. -- In SGA. -- 1894. -- Bd. 16, p. 69-70.
    Edited by Philipp Spitta. Figured bass not realized. Original
   German text. Notes in German.

2   Tröst uns, Gott, unser Zuversicht. -- In NSA. -- 1957. -- Bd. 6, p.
   79. Pub. no.: Bärenreiter Ausgabe 984.
    Edited by Walter Blankenburg. German text. Words in Gothic type.
   Notes in German.

3   Psalm 80. -- In Kleiner Liedpsalter. -- Kassel : Bärenreiter, c1976.
     -- p. 16. Pub. no.: BA 6231.
        Edited by Walter Blankenburg. Figured bass not realized. German
     text.

SWV 178

[Beckerscher Psalter. Singet mit Freuden unserm Gott]

    Sacred German text. Sources: Psalm 81.
    For chorus (SATB) and optional continuo. Ranges of voice parts:
    d1-f2, b-a1, e-e1, G-c1. Duration: short.

1   LXXXI. -- In SGA. -- 1894. -- Bd. 16, p. 70-71.
        Edited by Philipp Spitta. Figured bass not realized. Original
     German text. Notes in German.

2   Singet mit Freuden unserm Gott. -- In NSA. -- 1957. -- Bd. 6, p. 80.
     Pub. no.: Bärenreiter Ausgabe 984.
        Edited by Walter Blankenburg. German text. Words in Gothic type.
     Notes in German.

        Other editions: Hänssler 6.319.

SWV 179

[Beckerscher Psalter. Merkt auf, die ihr an Gottes Statt]

    Sacred German text. Sources: Psalm 82.
    For chorus (SATB) and optional continuo. Ranges of voice parts:
    d1-d2, b-g1, e-e1, G-g. Duration: short.

1   LXXXII. -- In SGA. -- 1894. -- Bd. 16, p. 71.
        Edited by Philipp Spitta. Figured bass not realized. Original
     German text. Notes in German.

2   Merkt auf, die ihr an Gottes Statt. -- In NSA. -- 1957. -- Bd. 6, p.
     81. Pub. no.: Bärenreiter Ausgabe 984.
        Edited by Walter Blankenburg. German text. Words in Gothic type.
     Notes in German. Transposed up m3.

SWV 180

[Beckerscher Psalter. Gott, schweig du nicht so ganz und gar]

    Sacred German text. Sources: Psalm 83.
    For chorus (SATB) and optional continuo. Ranges of voice parts:
    c1-e2, a-a1, d-d1, F-a. Duration: short.

1   LXXXIII. -- In SGA. -- 1894. -- Bd. 16, p. 72.
        Edited by Philipp Spitta. Figured bass not realized. Original
     German text. Notes in German.

2   Gott, schweig du nicht so ganz und gar. -- In NSA. -- 1957. -- Bd.
     6, p. 82. Pub. no.: Bärenreiter Ausgabe 984.
     Edited by Walter Blankenburg. German text. Words in Gothic type.
     Notes in German.

SWV 181

[Beckerscher Psalter. Wie sehr lieblich und schone]

    Sacred German text. Sources: Psalm 84.
    For chorus (SATB) and optional continuo. Ranges of voice parts:
    d1-d2, g-a1, g-e1, G-g. Duration: short.

1   LXXXIV. -- In SGA. -- 1894. -- Bd. 16, p. 72-73.
     Edited by Philipp Spitta. Figured bass not realized. Original
     German text. Notes in German.

2   Wie sehr lieblich und schöne. -- In NSA. -- 1957. -- Bd. 6, p. 83.
     Pub. no.: Bärenreiter Ausgabe 984.
     Edited by Walter Blankenburg. German text. Words in Gothic type.
     Notes in German. Transposed up M2.

6   How pleasant are thy dwellings = Wie sehr lieblich und schöne. --
     Bryn Mawr, Pa. : T. Presser, c1961. Pub. no.: 312-41428.
     Edited by George Lynn. German text with English translation.

7   Psalm LXX[X]IV. -- In Four psalms. -- New York : Music Press,
     [19--]. -- p. 3-4. Pub. no.: D.C.S. no. 6.
     Edited by Paul Boepple. Figured bass not realized. German text
     with English translation. Notes in English. Transposed up M2.

    Other editions: Hänssler 44.665.

SWV 182

[Beckerscher Psalter. Herr, der du vormals gnädig warst]

    Sacred German text. Sources: Psalm 85.
    For chorus (SATB) and optional continuo. Ranges of voice parts:
    d1-d2, a-a1, d-f1, G-a. Duration: short.

1   LXXXV. -- In SGA. -- 1894. -- Bd. 16, p. 73.
     Edited by Philipp Spitta. Figured bass not realized. Original
     German text. Notes in German.

2   Herr, der du vormals gnädig warst. -- In NSA. -- 1957. -- Bd. 6,
     p. 84. Pub. no.: Bärenreiter Ausgabe 984.
     Edited by Walter Blankenburg. German text. Words in Gothic type.
     Notes in German.

3   Psalm 85. -- Kassel : Bärenreiter, c1951. Pub. no.:
     Bärenreiter-Ausgabe 879.
     Figured bass not realized. German text. Words in Gothic type.

5   Herr, der du vormals hast dein Land. -- In Die Psalmen Davids. --
     Neuhausen-Stuttgart : Hänssler, c1967. -- p. 22. Pub. no.: HE 2.004.
     Edited by Emil Kübler. Figured bass not realized. German text.

6   Herr, der du vormals hast dein Land. -- Stuttgart : Hänssler,
     [19--]. Pub. no.: J 059 K.
     Figured bass not realized. German text.

     Other editions: Hänssler 6.031.

SWV 183

[Beckerscher Psalter. Herr, neig zu mir dein gnädigs Ohr]

     Sacred German text. Sources: Psalm 86.
     For chorus (SATB) and optional continuo. Ranges of voice parts:
     f1-d2, a-g1, f-eflat1, G-g. Duration: short.

1   LXXXVI. -- In SGA. -- 1894. -- Bd. 16, p. 74.
     Edited by Philipp Spitta. Figured bass not realized. Original
     German text. Notes in German.

2   Herr, neig zu mir dein gnädigs Ohr. -- In NSA. -- 1957. -- Bd. 6, p.
     85. Pub. no.: Bärenreiter Ausgabe 984.
     Edited by Walter Blankenburg. German text. Words in Gothic type.
     Notes in German.

SWV 184

[Beckerscher Psalter. Fest ist gegründet Gottes Stadt]

     Sacred German text. Sources: Psalm 87.
     For chorus (SATB) and optional continuo. Ranges of voice parts:
     g1-f2, d1-a1, g-g1, A-d1. Duration: short.

1   LXXXVII. -- In SGA. -- 1894. -- Bd. 16, p. 74-75.
     Edited by Philipp Spitta. Figured bass not realized. Original
     German text. Notes in German.

2   Fest ist gegründet Gottes Stadt. -- In NSA. -- 1957. -- Bd. 6, p.
     86. Pub. no.: Bärenreiter Ausgabe 984.
     Edited by Walter Blankenburg. German text. Words in Gothic type.
     Notes in German.

SWV 185

[Beckerscher Psalter. Herr Gott, mein Heiland, Nacht und Tag]

     Sacred German text. Sources: Psalm 88.
     For chorus (SATB) and optional continuo. Ranges of voice parts:
     d1-c2, a-a1, f-f1, G-c1. Duration: short.

1   LXXXVIII. -- In SGA. -- 1894. -- Bd. 16, p. 75.
     Edited by Philipp Spitta. Figured bass not realized. Original
     German text. Notes in German.

2   Herr Gott, mein Heiland, Nacht und Tag. -- In NSA. -- 1957. -- Bd.
     6, p. 87. Pub. no.: Bärenreiter Ausgabe 984.
     Edited by Walter Blankenburg. German text. Words in Gothic type.
     Notes in German.

SWV 186

[Beckerscher Psalter. Ich will von Gnade singen]

     Sacred German text. Sources: Psalm 89.
     For chorus (SATB) and optional continuo. Ranges of voice parts:
     d1-d2, b-g1, g-e1, G-bflat. Duration: short.

1   LXXXIX : erster Theil. -- In SGA. -- 1894. -- Bd. 16, p. 76.
     Edited by Philipp Spitta. Figured bass not realized. Original
     German text. Notes in German.

2   Ich will von Gnade singen. -- In NSA. -- 1957. -- Bd. 6, p. 88. Pub.
     no.: Bärenreiter Ausgabe 984.
     Edited by Walter Blankenburg. German text. Words in Gothic type.
     Notes in German. Transposed up M2.

3   Psalm 89. -- In Kleiner Liedpsalter. -- Kassel : Bärenreiter, c1976.
     -- p. 17. Pub. no.: BA 6231.
     Edited by Walter Blankenburg. Figured bass not realized. German
     text. Transposed up M2.

SWV 187

[Beckerscher Psalter. Ach Gott, warum verstösst du nun]

     Sacred German text. Sources: Psalm 89.
     For chorus (SATB) and optional continuo. Ranges of voice parts:
     c#1-d2, a-g1, d-f1, F-c1. Duration: short.

1   LXXXIX : andrer Theil. -- In SGA. -- 1894. -- Bd. 16, p. 77.
     Edited by Philipp Spitta. Figured bass not realized. Original
     German text. Notes in German.

2   Ach Gott, warum verstösst du nun. -- In NSA. -- 1957. -- Bd. 6, p.
     89. Pub. no.: Bärenreiter Ausgabe 984.
     Edited by Walter Blankenburg. German text. Words in Gothic type.
     Notes in German.

SWV 188

[Beckerscher Psalter. Herr Gott Vater im höchsten Thron]

    Sacred German text. Sources: Psalm 90.
     For chorus (SATB) and optional continuo. Ranges of voice parts:
c1-eflat2, g-g1, d-d1, F-bflat. Duration: short.

1   XC. -- In SGA. -- 1894. -- Bd. 16, p. 78-79.
     Edited by Philipp Spitta. Figured bass not realized. Original
German text. Notes in German.

2   Herr Gott Vater im höchsten Thron. -- In NSA. -- 1957. -- Bd. 6, p.
90-91. Pub. no.: Bärenreiter Ausgabe 984.
     Edited by Walter Blankenburg. German text. Words in Gothic type.
Notes in German.

SWV 189

[Beckerscher Psalter. Wer sich des Höchsten Schirm vertraut]

    Sacred German text. Sources: Psalm 91.
     For chorus (SATB) and optional continuo. Ranges of voice parts:
d1-e2, b-a1, e-e1, G-a. Duration: short.

1   XCI. -- In SGA. -- 1894. -- Bd. 16, p. 79-80.
     Edited by Philipp Spitta. Figured bass not realized. Original
German text. Notes in German.

2   Wer sich des Höchsten Schirm vertraut. -- In NSA. -- 1957. -- Bd. 6,
p. 92. Pub. no.: Bärenreiter Ausgabe 984.
     Edited by Walter Blankenburg. German text. Words in Gothic type.
Notes in German.

SWV 190

[Beckerscher Psalter. Es ist fürwahr ein köstlich Ding]

    Sacred German text. Sources: Psalm 92.
     For chorus (SATB) and optional continuo. Ranges of voice parts:
g1-f2, b-a1, f#-d1, c-a. Duration: short.

1   XCII. -- In SGA. -- 1894. -- Bd. 16, p. 80.
     Edited by Philipp Spitta. Figured bass not realized. Original
German text. Notes in German.

2   Es ist fürwahr ein köstlich Ding. -- In NSA. -- 1957. -- Bd. 6, p.
93. Pub. no.: Bärenreiter Ausgabe 984.
     Edited by Walter Blankenburg. German text. Words in Gothic type.
Notes in German.

3   Psalm 92. -- In Kleiner Liedpsalter. -- Kassel : Bärenreiter, c1976.
    -- p. 18. Pub. no.: BA 6231.
    Edited by Walter Blankenburg. Figured bass not realized. German
    text.

SWV 191

[Beckerscher Psalter. Herr ist König herrlich schön]

   Sacred German text. Sources: Psalm 93.
   For chorus (SATB) and optional continuo. Ranges of voice parts:
   el-e2, a-a1, g#-f1, A-a. Duration: short.

1   XCIII. -- In SGA. -- 1894. -- Bd. 16, p. 81.
    Edited by Philipp Spitta. Figured bass not realized. Original
    German text. Notes in German.

2   Der Herr ist König herrlich schön. -- In NSA. -- 1957. -- Bd. 6, p.
    94. Pub. no.: Bärenreiter Ausgabe 984.
    Edited by Walter Blankenburg. German text. Words in Gothic type.
    Notes in German.

3   Psalm 93. -- In Kleiner Liedpsalter. -- Kassel : Bärenreiter, c1976.
    -- p. 19. Pub. no.: BA 6231.
    Edited by Walter Blankenburg. Figured bass not realized. German
    text.

5   Der Herr ist König herrlich schön. -- In Die Psalmen Davids. --
    Neuhausen-Stuttgart : Hänssler, c1967. -- p. 4. Pub. no.: HE 2.004.
    Edited by Emil Kübler. Figured bass not realized. German text.

6   Der Herr ist König herrlich schön. -- Stuttgart : Hänssler, c1968.
    Pub. no.: HE 6.022.
    Figured bass not realized. German text.

SWV 192

[Beckerscher Psalter. Herr Gott, dem alle Rach heimfällt]

   Sacred German text. Sources: Psalm 94.
   For chorus (SATB) and optional continuo. Ranges of voice parts:
   cl-e2, b-a1, e-f1, A-b. Duration: short.

1   XCIV. -- In SGA. -- 1894. -- Bd. 16, p. 81-82.
    Edited by Philipp Spitta. Figured bass not realized. Original
    German text. Notes in German.

2   Herr Gott, dem alle Rach heimfällt. -- In NSA. -- 1957. -- Bd. 6, p.
    95. Pub. no.: Bärenreiter Ausgabe 984.
    Edited by Walter Blankenburg. German text. Words in Gothic type.
    Notes in German.

SWV 193

[Beckerscher Psalter. Kommt herzu, lasst uns fröhlich sein]

> Sacred German text. Sources: Psalm 95.
> For chorus (SATB) and optional continuo. Ranges of voice parts:
> f#1-f2, a-a1, e-f1, a-c1. Duration: short.

1 XCV. -- In SGA. -- 1894. -- Bd. 16, p. 82.
   Edited by Philipp Spitta. Figured bass not realized. Original
   German text. Notes in German.

2 Kommt herzu, lasst uns fröhlich sein. -- In NSA. -- 1957. -- Bd. 6,
   p. 96. Pub. no.: Bärenreiter Ausgabe 984.
   Edited by Walter Blankenburg. German text. Words in Gothic type.
   Notes in German. Transposed up M2.

5 Kommt herzu, lasst uns fröhlich sein. -- Neuhausen-Stuttgart :
   Hänssler, c1967. Pub. no.: HE 6.182.
   Figured bass not realized. German text. Transposed up M2.

6 Psalm 95. -- In Four psalms. -- Springfield, Ohio : Chantry Music
   Press, c1959. -- p. 6-7. Pub. no.: CLA 598.
   Edited by Ulrich S. Leupold. English text. Notes in English.

7 Psalm 95. -- In Five psalms of praise and the responsorium. --
   Chicago : G.I.A. Publications, c1973. -- p. 4-5. Pub. no.: G-1790.
   Edited by Daniel G. Reuning. Figured bass not realized. German
   text with English translation. Notes in English. Transposed up M2.

SWV 194

[Beckerscher Psalter. Singet dem Herrn ein neues Lied, SWV 194]

> Sacred German text. Sources: Psalm 96.
> For chorus (SATB) and optional continuo. Ranges of voice parts:
> g1-e2, c1-g1, g-d1, a-c1. Duration: short.

1 XCVI. -- In SGA. -- 1894. -- Bd. 16, p. 83.
   Edited by Philipp Spitta. Figured bass not realized. Original
   German text. Notes in German.

2 Singet dem Herrn ein neues Lied, all Welt. -- In NSA. -- 1957. --
   Bd. 6, p. 97. Pub. no.: Bärenreiter Ausgabe 984.
   Edited by Walter Blankenburg. German text. Words in Gothic type.
   Notes in German.

5 Singet dem Herrn ein neues Lied. -- In Die Psalmen Davids. --
   Neuhausen-Stuttgart : Hänssler, c1967. -- p. 23. Pub. no.: HE 2.004.
   Edited by Emil Kübler. Figured bass not realized. German text.

6 Psalm 96. -- In Four psalms. -- Springfield, Ohio : Chantry Music
   Press, c1959. -- p. 8-9. Pub. no.: CLA 598.
   Edited by Ulrich S. Leupold. English text. Notes in English.

7   Singet dem Herrn ein neues Lied. -- Augsburg : A. Böhm, [19--]. Pub.
no.: 11547.
    Figured bass not realized. German text.

8   Singet dem Herrn ein neues Lied. -- Neuhausen-Stuttgart : Hänssler,
c1966. Pub. no.: HE 6.032.
    Figured bass not realized. German text.

9   Sing a new song. -- Minneapolis : Schmitt Publications, c1975. Pub.
no.: No. 7601.
    Edited by Carol Jennings. Figured bass not realized. Flute
accompaniment added. English text.

10   Sing a new song. -- Melville, N.Y. : Belwin Mills, c1975. Pub. no.:
SCHCH 7601.
    Edited by Carol Jennings. Figured bass not realized. Flute
accompaniment added. English text.

SWV 195

[Beckerscher Psalter. Herr ist König überall]

    Sacred German text. Sources: Psalm 97.
    For chorus (SATB) and optional continuo. Ranges of voice parts:
d1-f2, a-a1, d-f1, G-a. Duration: short.

1   XCVII. -- In SGA. -- 1894. -- Bd. 16, p. 84.
    Edited by Philipp Spitta. Figured bass not realized. Original
German text. Notes in German.

2   Der Herr ist König überall. -- In NSA. -- 1957. -- Bd. 6, p. 98.
Pub. no.: Bärenreiter Ausgabe 984.
    Edited by Walter Blankenburg. German text. Words in Gothic type.
Notes in German.

5   Kommt her, des Königs Aufgebot. -- Stuttgart : Hänssler, [19--].
Pub. no.: F. 2564 H.
    Music of SWV 195 with different text. Figured bass not realized.
German text.

6   Psalm XCVII. -- In Four psalms. -- New York : Music Press, [19--].
-- p. 5-6. Pub. no.: D.C.S. no. 6.
    Edited by Paul Boepple. Figured bass not realized. German text
with English translation. Notes in English.

7   Psalm 97. -- In Four psalms. -- Springfield, Ohio : Chantry Music
Press, c1959. -- p. 10-11. Pub. no.: CLA 598.
    Edited by Ulrich S. Leupold. English text. Notes in English.

8   Der Herr ist König überall. -- Augsburg : A. Böhm, [19--]. Pub. no.:
11545.
    Figured bass not realized. German text.

    Other editions: Bärenreiter BA844; Hänssler 2.014; 2.052; 6.246.

SWV 196

[Beckerscher Psalter. Singet dem Herrn ein neues Lied, SWV 196]

> Sacred German text. Sources: Psalm 98.
> For chorus (SATB) and optional continuo. Ranges of voice parts:
> d1-eflat2, bflat-a1, g-f1, G-bflat. Duration: short.

1   XCVIII. -- In SGA. -- 1894. -- Bd. 16, p. 85.
> Edited by Philipp Spitta. Figured bass not realized. Original
> German text. Notes in German.

2   Singet dem Herrn ein neues Lied, denn durch. -- In NSA. -- 1957. --
> Bd. 6, 99. Pub. no.: Bärenreiter Ausgabe 984.
> Edited by Walter Blankenburg. German text. Words in Gothic type.
> Notes in German.

3   Psalm 98. -- In Kleiner Liedpsalter. -- Kassel : Bärenreiter, c1976.
> -- p. 20. Pub. no.: BA 6231.
> Edited by Walter Blankenburg. Figured bass not realized. German
> text.

5   Singet dem Herrn ein neues Lied. -- In Die Psalmen Davids. --
> Neuhausen-Stuttgart : Hänssler, c1967. -- p. 23. Pub. no.: HE 2.004.
> Edited by Emil Kübler. Figured bass not realized. German text.

6   Psalm 98. -- In Five psalms of praise and the responsorium. --
> Chicago : G.I.A. Publications, c1973. -- p. 6-7. Pub. no.: G-1790.
> Edited by Daniel G. Reuning. Figured bass not realized. German
> text with English translation. Notes in English.

7   Singet dem Herrn ein neues Lied. -- Neuhausen-Stuttgart : Hänssler,
> c1966. Pub. no.: HE 6.032.
> Figured bass not realized. German text.

8   Psalm 98. -- Kassel : Bärenreiter, c1975. Pub. no.:
> Bärenreiter-Ausgabe 785.
> Figured bass not realized. German text. Words in Gothic type.

> Other editions: Hänssler 9.004.

SWV 197

[Beckerscher Psalter. Herr ist König und regiert]

> Sacred German text. Sources: Psalm 99.
> For chorus (SATB) and optional continuo. Ranges of voice parts:
> e1-e2, a-a1, f-f1, G-a. Duration: short.

1   XCIX. -- In SGA. -- 1894. -- Bd. 16, p. 85-86.
> Edited by Philipp Spitta. Figured bass not realized. Original
> German text. Notes in German.

2   Der Herr ist König und regiert. -- In NSA. -- 1957. -- Bd. 6,
     p. 100. Pub. no.: Bärenreiter Ausgabe 984.
     Edited by Walter Blankenburg. German text. Words in Gothic type.
     Notes in German.

3   Psalm 99. -- Kassel : Bärenreiter, c1975. Pub. no.:
     Bärenreiter-Ausgabe 785.
     Figured bass not realized. German text. Words in Gothic type.

SWV 198

[Beckerscher Psalter. Jauchzet dem Herren alle Welt]

     Sacred German text. Sources: Psalm 100.
     For chorus (SATB) and optional continuo. Ranges of voice parts:
     c1-d2, b-g1, d-d1, G-a. Duration: short.

1   C. -- In SGA. -- 1894. -- Bd. 16, p. 86-87.
     Edited by Philipp Spitta. Figured bass not realized. Original
     German text. Notes in German.

2   Jauchzet dem Herren alle Welt. -- In NSA. -- 1957. -- Bd. 6, p.
     100-101. Pub. no.: Bärenreiter Ausgabe 984.
     Edited by Walter Blankenburg. German text. Words in Gothic type.
     Notes in German. Transposed up m3.

3   Psalm 100. -- Kassel : Bärenreiter, c1975. Pub. no.:
     Bärenreiter-Ausgabe 785.
     Figured bass not realized. German text. Words in Gothic type.
     Transposed up m3.

5   Jauchzet dem Herren alle Welt. -- Neuhausen-Stuttgart : Hänssler,
     c1963. Pub. no.: HE 6.180.
     Figured bass not realized. German text. Transposed up M2.

6   Psalm 100. -- In Five psalms of praise and the responsorium. --
     Chicago : G.I.A. Publications, c1973. -- p. 8-9. Pub. no.: G-1790.
     Edited by Daniel G. Reuning. Figured bass not realized. German
     text with English translation. Notes in English. Transposed up m3.

7   Jauchzet dem Herren alle Welt. -- Augsburg : A. Böhm, [19--]. Pub.
     no.: 11546.
     Figured bass not realized. German text. Transposed up M2.

SWV 199

[Beckerscher Psalter. Von Gnad und Recht soll singen]

     Sacred German text. Sources: Psalm 101.
     For chorus (SATB) and optional continuo. Ranges of voice parts:
     f1-eflat2, c1-a1, e-eflat1, F-g. Duration: short.

1   CI. -- In SGA. -- 1894. -- Bd. 16, p. 87.
     Edited by Philipp Spitta. Figured bass not realized. Original
     German text. Notes in German.

2   Von Gnad und Recht soll singen. -- In NSA. -- 1957. -- Bd. 6, p.
101. Pub. no.: Bärenreiter Ausgabe 984.
    Edited by Walter Blankenburg. German text. Words in Gothic type.
Notes in German.

SWV 200

[Beckerscher Psalter. Hör mein Gebet und lass zu dir]

    Sacred German text. Sources: Psalm 102.
    For chorus (SATB) and optional continuo. Ranges of voice parts:
e1-f2, b-a1, e-f1, G-a. Duration: short.

1   CII. -- In SGA. -- 1894. -- Bd. 16, p. 87-88.
    Edited by Philipp Spitta. Figured bass not realized. Original
German text. Notes in German.

2   Hör mein Gebet und lass zu dir. -- In NSA. -- 1957. -- Bd. 6, p.
102. Pub. no.: Bärenreiter Ausgabe 984.
    Edited by Walter Blankenburg. German text. Words in Gothic type.
Notes in German.

3   Psalm 102. -- In Kleiner Liedpsalter. -- Kassel : Bärenreiter,
c1976. -- p. 21. Pub. no.: BA 6231.
    Edited by Walter Blankenburg. Figured bass not realized. German
text.

6   Psalm 102. -- In Seven penitential psalms. -- G.I.A. Publications,
c1974. -- p. 14-15. Pub. no.: G-1912.
    Edited by Daniel G. Reuning. Figured bass not realized. German
text with English translation. Notes in English.

SWV 201

[Beckerscher Psalter. Nun lob, mein Seel, den Herren]

    Sacred German text. Sources: Psalm 103.
    For chorus (SATB) and optional continuo. Ranges of voice parts:
d1-d2, g-g1, A-e1, G-a. Duration: short.

1   CIII. -- In SGA. -- 1894. -- Bd. 16, p. 88-89.
    Edited by Philipp Spitta. Figured bass not realized. Original
German text. Notes in German.

2   Nun lob, mein Seel, den Herren. -- In NSA. -- 1957. -- Bd. 6, p.
103. Pub. no.: Bärenreiter Ausgabe 984.
    Edited by Walter Blankenburg. German text. Words in Gothic type.
Notes in German. Transposed up m3.

3   Nun lob, mein Seel, den Herren. -- Kassel : Bärenreiter, c1970. Pub.
no.: Bärenreiter-Ausgabe 6333.
    Figured bass not realized. German text. Transposed up M2.

6   Be swift to do his will. -- Bryn Mawr, Pa. : T. Presser, c1965. Pub.
    no.: 312-41434.
    Edited by George Lynn. English text. Transposed up M2.

SWV 202

[Beckerscher Psalter. Herr, dich lob die Seele mein]

    Sacred German text. Sources: Psalm 104.
    For chorus (SATB) and optional continuo. Ranges of voice parts:
    el-g2, a-al, e-el, G-bflat. Duration: short.

1   CIV. -- In SGA. -- 1894. -- Bd. 16, p. 90.
    Edited by Philipp Spitta. Figured bass not realized. Original
German text. Notes in German.

2   Herr, dich lob die Seele mein. -- In NSA. -- 1957. -- Bd. 6, p.
    104-105. Pub. no.: Bärenreiter Ausgabe 984.
    Edited by Walter Blankenburg. German text. Words in Gothic type.
Notes in German.

SWV 203

[Beckerscher Psalter. Danket dem Herren, lobt ihn frei]

    Sacred German text. Sources: Psalm 105.
    For chorus (SATB) and optional continuo. Ranges of voice parts:
    dl-c2, cl-fl, g-dl, G-bflat. Duration: short.

1   CV. -- In SGA. -- 1894. -- Bd. 16, p. 90-91.
    Edited by Philipp Spitta. Figured bass not realized. Original
German text. Notes in German.

2   Danket dem Herren, lobt ihn frei. -- In NSA. -- 1957. -- Bd. 6, p.
    105. Pub. no.: Bärenreiter Ausgabe 984.
    Edited by Walter Blankenburg. German text. Words in Gothic type.
Notes in German.

5   Danket dem Herren, lobt ihn frei. -- Stuttgart : Hänssler, [19--].
    Pub. no.: 6.181.
    Figured bass not realized. German text.

6   Psalm 105. -- In Five psalms of praise and the responsorium. --
    Chicago : G.I.A. Publications, c1973. -- p. 10-11. Pub. no.: G-1790.
    Edited by Daniel G. Reuning. Figured bass not realized. German
    text with English translation. Notes in English.

7   Danket dem Herren, lobt ihn frei. -- Stuttgart : Hänssler, [19--].
    Pub. no.: 6.286.
    Figured bass not realized. German text.

    Other editions: Hänssler 6.181.

SWV 204

[Beckerscher Psalter. Danket dem Herrn, erzeigt ihm Ehr]

    Sacred German text. Sources: Psalm 106.
    For chorus (SATB) and optional continuo. Ranges of voice parts:
d1-eflat2, g-a1, g-f1, F-bflat. Duration: short.

1   CVI. -- In SGA. -- 1894. -- Bd. 16, p. 91.
    Edited by Philipp Spitta. Figured bass not realized. Original
German text. Notes in German.

2   Danket dem Herrn, erzeigt ihm Ehr. -- In NSA. -- 1957. -- Bd. 6, p.
106. Pub. no.: Bärenreiter Ausgabe 984.
    Edited by Walter Blankenburg. German text. Words in Gothic type.
Notes in German.

5   Danket dem Herrn, erzeigt ihm Ehr. -- Neuhausen-Stuttgart :
Hänssler, c1967. Pub. no.: HE 6.182.
    Figured bass not realized. German text.

6   Des heilgen Geistes Gnade gross ; Danket dem Herrn. --
Neuhausen-Stuttgart : Hänssler, c1964. Pub. no.: HE 6.203.
    Figured bass not realized. German text.

SWV 205

[Beckerscher Psalter. Danket dem Herren, unserm Gott]

    Sacred German text. Sources: Psalm 107.
    For chorus (SATB) and optional continuo. Ranges of voice parts:
d1-d2, a-g1, f-eflat1, F-bflat. Duration: short.

1   CVII. -- In SGA. -- 1894. -- Bd. 16, p. 92.
    Edited by Philipp Spitta. Figured bass not realized. Original
German text. Notes in German.

2   Danket dem Herren, unserm Gott. -- In NSA. -- 1957. -- Bd. 6, p.
107. Pub. no.: Bärenreiter Ausgabe 984.
    Edited by Walter Blankenburg. German text. Words in Gothic type.
Notes in German.

6   Let the people give thanks. -- New York : Mercury Music Corp.,
c1956. Pub. no.: MC 271.
    Edited by George Lynn. English text. Transposed up M2.

SWV 206

[Beckerscher Psalter. Mit rechtem Ernst und frohem Mut]

    Sacred German text. Sources: Psalm 108.
    For chorus (SATB) and optional continuo. Ranges of voice parts:
c1-e2, b-g1, g-e1, G-a. Duration: short.

1   CVIII. -- In SGA. -- 1894. -- Bd. 16, p. 92-93.
    Edited by Philipp Spitta. Figured bass not realized. Original
German text. Notes in German.

2   Mit rechtem Ernst und frohem Mut. -- In NSA. -- 1957. -- Bd. 6, p.
    108. Pub. no.: Bärenreiter Ausgabe 984.
    Edited by Walter Blankenburg. German text. Words in Gothic type.
Notes in German.

3   Psalm 108. -- In Kleiner Liedpsalter. -- Kassel : Bärenreiter,
    c1976. -- p. 22. Pub. no.: BA 6231.
    Edited by Walter Blankenburg. Figured bass not realized. German
text.

    Other editions: Hänssler 2.037.

SWV 207

[Beckerscher Psalter. Herr Gott, des ich mich rühmte viel]

    Sacred German text. Sources: Psalm 109.
    For chorus (SATB) and optional continuo. Ranges of voice parts:
g1-e2, b-a1, g-e1, G-a. Duration: short.

1   CIX. -- In SGA. -- 1894. -- Bd. 16, p. 93.
    Edited by Philipp Spitta. Figured bass not realized. Original
German text. Notes in German.

2   Herr Gott, des ich mich rühmte viel. -- In NSA. -- 1957. -- Bd. 6,
    p. 109. Pub. no.: Bärenreiter Ausgabe 984.
    Edited by Walter Blankenburg. German text. Words in Gothic type.
Notes in German.

SWV 208

[Beckerscher Psalter. Herr sprach zu meim Herzen]

    Sacred German text. Sources: Psalm 110.
    For chorus (SATB) and optional continuo. Ranges of voice parts:
c1-d2, f-g1, c#-e1, F-g. Duration: short.

1   CX. -- In SGA. -- 1894. -- Bd. 16, p. 94.
    Edited by Philipp Spitta. Figured bass not realized. Original
German text. Notes in German.

2   Der Herr sprach zu meim Herzen. -- In NSA. -- 1957. -- Bd. 6, p.
    110. Pub. no.: Bärenreiter Ausgabe 984.
    Edited by Walter Blankenburg. German text. Words in Gothic type.
Notes in German.

5   Der Herr sprach zu meim Herren. -- In Die Psalmen Davids. --
    Neuhausen-Stuttgart : Hänssler, c1967. -- p. 24. Pub. no.: HE 2.004.
    Edited by Emil Kubler. Figured bass not realized. German text.

6   Der Herr sprach zu meim Herren. -- Neuhausen-Stuttgart : Hänssler,
    c1966. Pub. no.: HE 6.032.
    Figured bass not realized. German text.

SWV 209

[Beckerscher Psalter. Ich will von Herzen danken Gott dem Herren]

    Sacred German text. Sources: Psalm 111.
    For chorus (SATB) and optional continuo. Ranges of voice parts:
    d1-f2, bflat-a1, e-f1, G-bflat. Duration: short.

1   CXI. -- In SGA. -- 1894. -- Bd. 16, p. 94-95.
    Edited by Philipp Spitta. Figured bass not realized. Original
German text. Notes in German.

2   Ich will von Herzen danken. -- In NSA. -- 1957. -- Bd. 6, p. 111.
    Pub. no.: Bärenreiter Ausgabe 984.
    Edited by Walter Blankenburg. German text. Words in Gothic type.
Notes in German.

3   Psalm 111. -- In Kleiner Liedpsalter. -- Kassel : Bärenreiter,
    c1976. -- p. 23. Pub. no.: BA 6231.
    Edited by Walter Blankenburg. Figured bass not realized. German
text.

5   Ich will von Herzen danken Gott dem Herrn. -- In Die Psalmen Davids.
    -- Neuhausen-Stuttgart : Hänssler, c1967. -- p. 25. Pub. no.: HE
    2.004.
    Edited by Emil Kübler. Figured bass not realized. German text.

6   Ich will von Herzen danken Gott dem Herrn. -- Neuhausen-Stuttgart :
    Hänssler, [19--]. Pub. no.: FH 2616.
    Figured bass not realized. German text.

7   Ich will von Herzen danken Gott dem Herrn. -- Stuttgart : Hänssler,
    c1968. Pub. no.: HE 6.033.
    Figured bass not realized. German text.

    Other editions: Hänssler 9.103; 44.723.

SWV 210

[Beckerscher Psalter. Der ist fürwahr ein selig Mann]

    Sacred German text. Sources: Psalm 112.
    For chorus (SATB) and optional continuo. Ranges of voice parts:
    c1-d2, a-g1, d-d1, G-g. Duration: short.

1   CXII. -- In SGA. -- 1894. -- Bd. 16, p. 95-96.
    Edited by Philipp Spitta. Figured bass not realized. Original
German text. Notes in German.

2   Der ist fürwahr ein selig Mann. -- In NSA. -- 1957. -- Bd. 6, p.
    112. Pub. no.: Bärenreiter Ausgabe 984.
       Edited by Walter Blankenburg. German text. Words in Gothic type.
    Notes in German.

SWV 211

[Beckerscher Psalter. Lobet, ihr Knecht, den Herren]

      Sacred German text. Sources: Psalm 113.
         For chorus (SATB) and optional continuo. Ranges of voice parts:
      f1-f2, bflat-bflat1, f#-f1, G-bflat. Duration: short.

1   CXIII. -- In SGA. -- 1894. -- Bd. 16, p. 96-97.
       Edited by Philipp Spitta. Figured bass not realized. Original
    German text. Notes in German.

2   Lobet, ihr Knecht, den Herren. -- In NSA. -- 1957. -- Bd. 6, p.
    112-113. Pub. no.: Bärenreiter Ausgabe 984.
       Edited by Walter Blankenburg. German text. Words in Gothic type.
    Notes in German.

SWV 212

[Beckerscher Psalter. Als das Volk Israel auszog]

      Sacred German text. Sources: Psalm 114.
         For chorus (SATB) and optional continuo. Ranges of voice parts:
      d1-e2, b-a1, g-f#1, G-b. Duration: short.

1   CXIV. -- In SGA. -- 1894. -- Bd. 16, p. 98.
       Edited by Philipp Spitta. Figured bass not realized. Original
    German text. Notes in German.

2   Als das Volk Israel auszog. -- In NSA. -- 1957. -- Bd. 6, p. 114.
    Pub. no.: Bärenreiter Ausgabe 984.
       Edited by Walter Blankenburg. German text. Words in Gothic type.
    Notes in German.

SWV 213

[Beckerscher Psalter. Nicht uns, nicht uns, Herr lieber Gott]

      Sacred German text. Sources: Psalm 115.
         For chorus (SATB) and optional continuo. Ranges of voice parts:
      c1-f2, a-a1, e-e1, F-bflat. Duration: short.

1   CXV. -- In SGA. -- 1894. -- Bd. 16, p. 99.
       Edited by Philipp Spitta. Figured bass not realized. Original
    German text. Notes in German.

2   Nicht uns, nicht uns. -- In NSA. -- 1957. -- Bd. 6, p. 115. Pub.
no.: Bärenreiter Ausgabe 984.
    Edited by Walter Blankenburg. German text. Words in Gothic type.
Notes in German.

SWV 214

[Beckerscher Psalter. Meim Herzen ists ein grosse Freud]

    Sacred German text. Sources: Psalm 116.
    For chorus (SATB) and optional continuo. Ranges of voice parts:
c1-e2, f-g1, d-d1, F-f. Duration: short.

1   CXVI. -- In SGA. -- 1894. -- Bd. 16, p. 100.
    Edited by Philipp Spitta. Figured bass not realized. Original
German text. Notes in German.

2   Meim Herzen ist's ein grosse Freud. -- In NSA. -- 1957. -- Bd. 6, p.
116. Pub. no.: Bärenreiter Ausgabe 984.
    Edited by Walter Blankenburg. German text. Words in Gothic type.
Notes in German.

5   Meim Herzen ist's ein grosse Freud. -- Neuhausen-Stuttgart :
Hänssler, c1967. Pub. no.: HE 6.183.
    Figured bass not realized. German text.

SWV 215

[Beckerscher Psalter. Lobt Gott mit Schall, ihr Heiden all]

    Sacred German text. Sources: Psalm 117.
    For chorus (SATB) and optional continuo. Ranges of voice parts:
f1-f2, g-a1, d-f1, G-c1. Duration: short.

1   CXVII. -- In SGA. -- 1894. -- Bd. 16, p. 100-101.
    Edited by Philipp Spitta. Figured bass not realized. Original
German text. Notes in German.

2   Lobt Gott mit Schall. -- In NSA. -- 1957. -- Bd. 6, p. 116-117. Pub.
no.: Bärenreiter Ausgabe 984.
    Edited by Walter Blankenburg. German text. Words in Gothic type.
Notes in German.

5   Lobt Gott mit Schall, ihr Heiden all. -- Neuhausen-Stuttgart :
Hänssler, c1969. Pub. no.: HE 20.215.
    Edited by Hermann Stern and Günter Graulich. Continuo realized by
Paul Horn. German text with English translation.

6   O praise the Lord, ye people all = Lobt Gott mit Schall. -- New York
: Tetra Music Corp., c1981. Pub. no.: AB 960.
    Edited by Robert Gray. German text with English translation.

7   God's might recall, ye people all = Lobt Gott mit Schall, ihr Heiden
all. -- New York : Bourne, c1975. Pub. no.: ES 122.
    Edited by Norman Greyson. German text with English translation.

Other editions: Hänssler 2.049; 9.005; 44.571.

SWV 216

[Beckerscher Psalter. Lasst uns Gott, unserm Herren]

    Sacred German text. Sources: Psalm 118.
      For chorus (SATB) and optional continuo. Ranges of voice parts:
    cl-e2, g-al, e-f1, G-cl. Duration: short.

1   CXVIII. -- In SGA. -- 1894. -- Bd. 16, p. 102.
      Edited by Philipp Spitta. Figured bass not realized. Original
German text. Notes in German.

2   Lasst uns Gott, unserm Herren. -- In NSA. -- 1957. -- Bd. 6, p.
118-119. Pub. no.: Bärenreiter Ausgabe 984.
      Edited by Walter Blankenburg. German text. Words in Gothic type.
Notes in German.

3   Psalm 118. -- In Kleiner Liedpsalter. -- Kassel : Bärenreiter,
c1976. -- p. 24. Pub. no.: BA 6231.
      Edited by Walter Blankenburg. Figured bass not realized. German
text.

5   Lasst uns Gott unserm Herren. -- In Die Psalmen Davids. --
Neuhausen-Stuttgart : Hänssler, c1967. -- p. 26. Pub. no.: HE 2.004.
      Edited by Emil Kübler. Figured bass not realized. German text.

6   Lasst uns Gott unserm Herren. -- Stuttgart : Hänssler, c1968. Pub.
no.: HE 6.033.
      Figured bass not realized. German text.

SWV 217

[Beckerscher Psalter. Wohl denen, die da leben]

    Sacred German text. Sources: Psalm 119.
      For chorus (SATB) and optional continuo. Ranges of voice parts:
    dl-e2, a-gl, d-dl, G-a. Duration: short.

1   CXIX : erster Theil. -- In SGA. -- 1894. -- Bd. 16, p. 102-103.
      Edited by Philipp Spitta. Figured bass not realized. Original
German text. Notes in German.

2   Wohl denen, die da leben. -- In NSA. -- 1957. -- Bd. 6, p. 119. Pub.
no.: Bärenreiter Ausgabe 984.
      Edited by Walter Blankenburg. German text. Words in Gothic type.
Notes in German.

    Other editions: Bärenreiter BA931.

SWV 218

[Beckerscher Psalter. Tu wohl, Herr, deinem Knechte]

    Sacred German text. Sources: Psalm 119.
    For chorus (SATB) and optional continuo. Ranges of voice parts:
    d1-d2, bflat-g1, f-d1, G-g. Duration: short.

1   CXIX : andrer Theil. -- In SGA. -- 1894. -- Bd. 16, p. 103.
    Edited by Philipp Spitta. Figured bass not realized. Original
    German text. Notes in German.

2   Tu wohl, Herr, deinem Knechte. -- In NSA. -- 1957. -- Bd. 6, p. 120.
    Pub. no.: Bärenreiter Ausgabe 984.
    Edited by Walter Blankenburg. German text. Words in Gothic type.
    Notes in German.

SWV 219

[Beckerscher Psalter. Lass mir Gnad widerfahren]

    Sacred German text. Sources: Psalm 119.
    For chorus (SATB) and optional continuo. Ranges of voice parts:
    d1-d2, b-g1, g-e1, A-a. Duration: short.

1   CXIX : dritter Theil. -- In SGA. -- 1894. -- Bd. 16, p. 104.
    Edited by Philipp Spitta. Figured bass not realized. Original
    German text. Notes in German.

2   Lass mir Gnad widerfahren. -- In NSA. -- 1957. -- Bd. 6, p. 121.
    Pub. no.: Bärenreiter Ausgabe 984.
    Edited by Walter Blankenburg. German text. Words in Gothic type.
    Notes in German.

3   Psalm 119. -- Kassel : Bärenreiter, c1973. Pub. no.:
    Bärenreiter-Ausgabe 931.
    Figured bass not realized. Music of SWV 219 with text from SWV
    217, 218, 219, and 221. German text. Words in Gothic type.

5   Wohl denen, die da wandeln. -- Neuhausen-Stuttgart : Hänssler,
    c1967. Pub. no.: HE 6.183.
    Figured bass not realized. German text.

6   Wohl denen, die da wandeln. -- Stuttgart : Hänssler, [19--]. Pub.
    no.: F.H. 2381.
    Arranged for four-part men's chorus. Music of SWV 219 with text of
    SWV 217. Figured bass not realized. German text. Transposed up m3.

7   Wohl denen, die da wandeln. -- Neuhausen-Stuttgart : Hänssler,
    c1968. Pub. no.: HE 6.289.
    Music of SWV 219 with text of SWV 217. Figured bass not realized.
    German text.

    Other editions: Hänssler 2.014; 2.052; 8.030.

SWV 220

[Beckerscher Psalter. Du tust viel guts beweisen]

    Sacred German text. Sources: Psalm 119.
    For chorus (SATB) and optional continuo. Ranges of voice parts:
    e1-d2, d#1-b1, b-g1, A-b. Duration: short.

1   CXIX : vierter Theil. -- In SGA. -- 1894. -- 16, p. 104-105.
    Edited by Philipp Spitta. Figured bass not realized. Original
German text. Notes in German.

2   Du tust viel guts beweisen. -- In NSA. -- 1957. -- Bd. 6, p. 122.
Pub. no.: Bärenreiter Ausgabe 984.
    Edited by Walter Blankenburg. German text. Words in Gothic type.
Notes in German.

5   Du tust viel Guts beweisen. -- Stuttgart : Hänssler, [19--]. Pub.
no.: 6.184.
    Figured bass not realized. German text.

SWV 221

[Beckerscher Psalter. Dein Wort, Herr, nicht vergehet]

    Sacred German text. Sources: Psalm 119.
    For chorus (SATB) and optional continuo. Ranges of voice parts:
    c1-d2, b-a1, g#-f1, F-c1. Duration: short.

1   CXIX : fünfter Theil. -- In SGA. -- 1894. -- Bd. 16, p. 105.
    Edited by Philipp Spitta. Figured bass not realized. Original
German text. Notes in German.

2   Dein Wort, Herr, nicht vergehet. -- In NSA. -- 1957. -- Bd. 6, p.
123. Pub. no.: Bärenreiter Ausgabe 984.
    Edited by Walter Blankenburg. German text. Words in Gothic type.
Notes in German.

SWV 222

[Beckerscher Psalter. Ich hass die Flattergeister]

    Sacred German text. Sources: Psalm 119.
    For chorus (SATB) and optional continuo. Ranges of voice parts:
    c1-d2, g-g1, e-e1, F-a. Duration: short.

1   CXIX : sechster Theil. -- In SGA. -- 1894. -- Bd. 16, p. 106.
    Edited by Philipp Spitta. Figured bass not realized. Original
German text. Notes in German.

2   Ich hass die Flattergeister. -- In NSA. -- 1957. -- Bd. 6, p. 124.
Pub. no.: Bärenreiter Ausgabe 984.
    Edited by Walter Blankenburg. German text. Words in Gothic type.
Notes in German.

SWV 223

[Beckerscher Psalter. Dir gbührt allein die Ehre]

> Sacred German text. Sources: Psalm 119.
> For chorus (SATB) and optional continuo. Ranges of voice parts:
> c1-d2, a-f1, f-c1, G-g. Duration: short.

1   CXIX : siebenter Theil. -- In SGA. -- 1894. -- Bd. 16, p. 106-107.
    Edited by Philipp Spitta. Figured bass not realized. Original
    German text. Notes in German.

2   Dir gbührt allein die Ehre. -- In NSA. -- 1957. -- Bd. 6, p. 125.
    Pub. no.: Bärenreiter Ausgabe 984.
    Edited by Walter Blankenburg. German text. Words in Gothic type.
    Notes in German.

SWV 224

[Beckerscher Psalter. Fürsten sind meine Feinde]

> Sacred German text. Sources: Psalm 119.
> For chorus (SATB) and optional continuo. Ranges of voice parts:
> c1-e2, a-a1, g-f1, G-c1. Duration: short.

1   CXIX : achter und letzter Theil. -- In SGA. -- 1894. -- Bd. 16, p.
    107.
    Edited by Philipp Spitta. Figured bass not realized. Original
    German text. Notes in German.

2   Die lieben dein Gesetze. -- In NSA. -- 1957. -- Bd. 6, p. 126. Pub.
    no.: Bärenreiter Ausgabe 984.
    Edited by Walter Blankenburg. German text. Words in Gothic type.
    Notes in German.

SWV 225

[Beckerscher Psalter. Ich ruf zu dir, mein Herr und Gott]

> Sacred German text. Sources: Psalm 120.
> For chorus (SATB) and optional continuo. Ranges of voice parts:
> eflat1-eflat2, c1-aflat1, f#-f1, G-bflat. Duration: short.

1   CXX. -- In SGA. -- 1894. -- Bd. 16, p. 108.
    Edited by Philipp Spitta. Figured bass not realized. Original
    German text. Notes in German.

2   Ich ruf zu dir, mein Herr und Gott. -- In NSA. -- 1957. -- Bd. 6, p.
    127. Pub. no.: Bärenreiter Ausgabe 984.
    Edited by Walter Blankenburg. German text. Words in Gothic type.
    Notes in German.

SWV 226

[Beckerscher Psalter. Ich heb mein Augen sehnlich auf]

Sacred German text. Sources: Psalm 121.
For chorus (SATB) and optional continuo. Ranges of voice parts:
d1-d2, g-a1, d-d1, F-d1. Duration: short.

1　CXXI. -- In SGA. -- 1894. -- Bd. 16, p. 108-109.
Edited by Philipp Spitta. Figured bass not realized. Original
German text. Notes in German.

2　Ich heb mein Augen sehnlich auf. -- In NSA. -- 1957. -- Bd. 6, p.
128. Pub. no.: Bärenreiter Ausgabe 984.
Edited by Walter Blankenburg. German text. Words in Gothic type.
Notes in German.

3　Psalm 121. -- Kassel : Bärenreiter, [19--]. Pub. no.:
Bärenreiter-Ausgabe 845.
Figured bass not realized. German text. Words in Gothic type.

5　Ich heb mein Augen sehnlich auf. -- In Die Psalmen Davids. --
Neuhausen-Stuttgart : Hänssler, c1967. -- p. 27. Pub. no.: HE 2.004.
Edited by Emil Kübler. Figured bass not realized. German text.

6　Psalm CXXI. -- In Four psalms. -- New York : Music Press, [19--]. --
p. 7-8. Pub. no.: D.C.S. no. 6.
Edited by Paul Boepple. Figured bass not realized. German text
with English translation. Notes in English. Transposed up M2.

7　Ich heb mein Augen sehnlich auf. -- Stuttgart : Hänssler, c1968.
Pub. no.: HE 6.034.
Figured bass not realized. German text.

8　Mine eyes I lift = Ich hab [sic] mein Augen sehnlich auf. -- In
Three chorales. -- Fort Lauderdale, Fla. : Music 70, c1975. -- p.
8-10. Pub. no.: M70-153.
Edited by John Kingsbury. German text with English translation.
Transposed up M2.

SWV 227

[Beckerscher Psalter. Es ist ein Freud dem Herzen mein]

Sacred German text. Sources: Psalm 122.
For chorus (SATB) and optional continuo. Ranges of voice parts:
d1-f2, a-a1 d-d1, F-a. Duration: short.

1　CXXII. -- In SGA. -- 1894. -- Bd. 16, p. 109.
Edited by Philipp Spitta. Figured bass not realized. Original
German text. Notes in German.

2   Es ist ein Freud dem Herzen mein. -- In NSA. -- 1957. -- Bd. 6, p. 129. Pub. no.: Bärenreiter Ausgabe 984.
     Edited by Walter Blankenburg. German text. Words in Gothic type. Notes in German.

3   Psalm 122. -- In Kleiner Liedpsalter. -- Kassel : Bärenreiter, c1976. -- p. 25. Pub. no.: BA 6231.
     Edited by Walter Blankenburg. Figured bass not realized. German text.

5   Es ist ein Freud dem Herzen mein. -- In Die Psalmen Davids. -- Neuhausen-Stuttgart : Hänssler, c1967. -- p. 28. Pub. no.: HE 2.004.
     Edited by Emil Kübler. Figured bass not realized. German text.

6   Es ist ein Freud dem Herzen mein. -- Stuttgart : Hänssler, c1968. Pub. no.: HE 6.034.
     Figured bass not realized. German text.

7   Psalm 122. -- Kassel : Bärenreiter, c1974. Pub. no.: Bärenreiter-Ausgabe 6321.
     Figured bass not realized. German text.

     Other editions: Hänssler 44.641.

SWV 228

[Beckerscher Psalter. Ich heb mein Augen auf zu dir]

    Sacred German text. Sources: Psalm 123.
     For chorus (SATB) and optional continuo. Ranges of voice parts: f1-d2, d1-a1, g#-f1, A-a. Duration: short.

1   CXXIII. -- In SGA. -- 1894. -- Bd. 16, p. 110.
     Edited by Philipp Spitta. Figured bass not realized. Original German text. Notes in German.

2   Ich heb mein Augen auf zu dir. -- In NSA. -- 1957. -- Bd. 6, p. 130. Pub. no.: Bärenreiter Ausgabe 984.
     Edited by Walter Blankenburg. German text. Words in Gothic type. Notes in German.

SWV 229

[Beckerscher Psalter. Wär Gott nicht mit uns diese Zeit]

    Sacred German text. Sources: Psalm 124.
     For chorus (SATB) and optional continuo. Ranges of voice parts: f1-d2, bflat1-g1, e-eflat1, F-g. Duration: short.

1   CXXIV. -- In SGA. -- 1894. -- Bd. 16, p. 110-111.
     Edited by Philipp Spitta. Figured bass not realized. Original German text. Notes in German.

2 Wär Gott nicht mit uns diese Zeit. -- In NSA. -- 1957. -- Bd. 6, p. 131. Pub. no.: Bärenreiter Ausgabe 984.
   Edited by Walter Blankenburg. German text. Words in Gothic type. Notes in German.

SWV 230

[Beckerscher Psalter. Die nur vertrauend stellen]

   Sacred German text. Sources: Psalm 125.
   For chorus (SATB) and optional continuo. Ranges of voice parts: d1-eflat2, bflat-g1, g-f1, G-aflat. Duration: short.

1 CXXV. -- In SGA. -- 1894. -- Bd. 16, p. 111.
   Edited by Philipp Spitta. Figured bass not realized. Original German text. Notes in German.

2 Die nur vertrauend stellen auf Gott ihr Zuversicht. -- In NSA. -- 1957. -- Bd. 6, p. 132. Pub. no.: Bärenreiter Ausgabe 984.
   Edited by Walter Blankenburg. German text. Words in Gothic type. Notes in German.

SWV 231

[Beckerscher Psalter. Wenn Gott einmal erlösen wird]

   Sacred German text. Sources: Psalm 126.
   For chorus (SATB) and optional continuo. Ranges of voice parts: e1-d2, c1-g1, g#-e1, A-a. Duration: short.

1 CXXVI. -- In SGA. -- 1894. -- Bd. 16, p. 112.
   Edited by Philipp Spitta. Figured bass not realized. Original German text. Notes in German.

2 Wenn Gott einmal erlösen wird. -- In NSA. -- 1957. -- Bd. 6, p. 132-133. Pub. no.: Bärenreiter Ausgabe 984.
   Edited by Walter Blankenburg. German text. Words in Gothic type. Notes in German.

3 Psalm 126. -- In Kleiner Liedpsalter. -- Kassel : Bärenreiter, c1976. -- p. 26. Pub. no.: BA 6231.
   Edited by Walter Blankenburg. Figured bass not realized. German text.

5 Wenn Gott einmal erlösen wird. -- In Die Psalmen Davids. -- Neuhausen-Stuttgart : Hänssler, c1967. -- p. 29. Pub. no.: HE 2.004.
   Edited by Emil Kübler. Figured bass not realized. German text.

6 Wenn Gott einmal erlösen wird. -- Neuhausen-Stuttgart : Hänssler, c1960. Pub. no.: HE 6.035.
   Figured bass not realized. German text.

SWV 232

[Beckerscher Psalter. Wo Gott zum Haus nicht gibt sein Gunst]

    Sacred German text. Sources: Psalm 127.
    For chorus (SATB) and optional continuo. Ranges of voice parts:
f1-f2, c1-a1, e-eflat1, G-bflat. Duration: short.

1   CXXVII. -- In SGA. -- 1894. -- Bd. 16, p. 112-113.
    Edited by Philipp Spitta. Figured bass not realized. Original
German text. Notes in German.

2   Wo Gott zum Haus nicht gibt sein Gunst. -- In NSA. -- 1957. -- Bd.
6, p. 133. Pub. no.: Bärenreiter Ausgabe 984.
    Edited by Walter Blankenburg. German text. Words in Gothic type.
Notes in German.

SWV 233

[Beckerscher Psalter. Wohl dem, der in Gottesfurcht steht]

    Sacred German text. Sources: Psalm 128.
    For chorus (SATB) and optional continuo. Ranges of voice parts:
e1-e2, d1-b1, a-g1, G-g. Duration: short.

1   CXXVIII. -- In SGA. -- 1894. -- Bd. 16, p. 113.
    Edited by Philipp Spitta. Figured bass not realized. Original
German text. Notes in German.

2   Wohl dem, der in Gottesfurcht steht. -- In NSA. -- 1957. -- Bd. 6,
p. 134. Pub. no.: Bärenreiter Ausgabe 984.
    Edited by Walter Blankenburg. German text. Words in Gothic type.
Notes in German.

3   Psalm 128. -- In Kleiner Liedpsalter. -- Kassel : Bärenreiter,
c1976. -- p. 27. Pub. no.: BA 6231.
    Edited by Walter Blankenburg. Figured bass not realized. German
text.

SWV 234

[Beckerscher Psalter. Feind haben mich oft gedrängt]

    Sacred German text. Sources: Psalm 129.
    For chorus (SATB) and optional continuo. Ranges of voice parts:
d1-d2, a-g1, c-eflat1, F#-a. Duration: short.

1   CXXIX. -- In SGA. -- 1894. -- Bd. 16, p. 114.
    Edited by Philipp Spitta. Figured bass not realized. Original
German text. Notes in German.

2   Feind haben mich oft gedrängt. -- In NSA. -- 1957. -- Bd. 6, p.
    134-135. Pub. no.: Bärenreiter Ausgabe 984.
        Edited by Walter Blankenburg. German text. Words in Gothic type.
    Notes in German.

SWV 235

[Beckerscher Psalter. Aus tiefer Not schrei ich zu dir]

    Sacred German text. Sources: Psalm 130.
    For chorus (SATB) and optional continuo. Ranges of voice parts:
    el-d2, b-gl, d-el, E-a. Duration: short.

1   CXXX. -- In SGA. -- 1894. -- Bd. 16, p. 114-115.
        Edited by Philipp Spitta. Figured bass not realized. Original
    German text. Notes in German.

2   Aus tiefer Not schrei ich zu dir. -- In NSA. -- 1957. -- Bd. 6, p.
    135. Pub. no.: Bärenreiter Ausgabe 984.
        Edited by Walter Blankenburg. German text. Words in Gothic type.
    Notes in German.

3   Aus tiefer Not schrei ich zu dir. -- Kassel : Bärenreiter, [19--].
    Pub. no.: Kl. BA 848.
        Figured bass not realized. German text.

6   Psalm 130. -- In Seven penitential psalms. -- G.I.A. Publications,
    c1974. -- p. 16-17. Pub. no.: G-1912.
        Edited by Daniel G. Reuning. Figured bass not realized. German
    text with English translation. Notes in English.

7   Aus tiefer Not. -- Stuttgart : Hänssler, [19--]. Pub. no.: 1926.
        Figured bass not realized. German text. Words in Gothic type.

SWV 236

[Beckerscher Psalter. Herr, mein Gemüt und Sinn du weisst]

    Sacred German text. Sources: Psalm 131.
    For chorus (SATB) and optional continuo. Ranges of voice parts:
    dl-d2, b-gl, f#-fl, F-bflat. Duration: short.

1   CXXXI. -- In SGA. -- 1894. -- Bd. 16, p. 115.
        Edited by Philipp Spitta. Figured bass not realized. Original
    German text. Notes in German.

2   Herr, mein Gemüt und Sinn du weisst. -- In NSA. -- 1957. -- Bd. 6,
    p. 136. Pub. no.: Bärenreiter Ausgabe 984.
        Edited by Walter Blankenburg. German text. Words in Gothic type.
    Notes in German.

SWV 237

[Beckerscher Psalter. In Gnaden, Herr, wollst eindenk sein]

Sacred German text. Sources: Psalm 132.
For chorus (SATB) and optional continuo. Ranges of voice parts:
e1-f2, b-a1, f#-f1, A-a. Duration: short.

1 CXXXII. -- In SGA. -- 1894. -- Bd. 16, p. 116.
Edited by Philipp Spitta. Figured bass not realized. Original
German text. Notes in German.

2 In Gnaden, Herr, wollst eingdenk sein. -- In NSA. -- 1957. -- Bd. 6,
p. 137. Pub. no.: Bärenreiter Ausgabe 984.
Edited by Walter Blankenburg. German text. Words in Gothic type.
Notes in German.

SWV 238

[Beckerscher Psalter. Wie ists so fein, lieblich und schön]

Sacred German text. Sources: Psalm 133.
For chorus (SATB) and optional continuo. Ranges of voice parts:
f#1-f2, d1-a1, g-f1, G-c1. Duration: short.

1 CXXXIII. -- In SGA. -- 1894. -- Bd. 16, p. 116-117.
Edited by Philipp Spitta. Figured bass not realized. Original
German text. Notes in German.

2 Wie ist's so fein, lieblich und schön. -- In NSA. -- 1957. -- Bd. 6,
p. 138. Pub. no.: Bärenreiter Ausgabe 984.
Edited by Walter Blankenburg. German text. Words in Gothic type.
Notes in German.

3 Psalm 133. -- In Kleiner Liedpsalter. -- Kassel : Bärenreiter,
c1976. -- p. 28. Pub. no.: BA 6231.
Edited by Walter Blankenburg. Figured bass not realized. German
text.

SWV 239

[Beckerscher Psalter. Den Herren lobt mit Freuden]

Sacred German text. Sources: Psalm 134.
For chorus (SATB) and optional continuo. Ranges of voice parts:
d1-f2, b-a1, g-e1, G-c1. Duration: short.

1 CXXXIV. -- In SGA. -- 1894. -- Bd. 16, p. 117.
Edited by Philipp Spitta. Figured bass not realized. Original
German text. Notes in German.

2   Den Herren lobt mit Freuden. -- In NSA. -- 1957. -- Bd. 6, p. 138.
     Pub. no.: Bärenreiter Ausgabe 984.
        Edited by Walter Blankenburg. German text. Words in Gothic type.
     Notes in German.

5   Den Herren lobt mit Freuden. -- In Die Psalmen Davids. --
     Neuhausen-Stuttgart : Hänssler, c1967. -- p. 29. Pub. no.: HE 2.004.
        Edited by Emil Kübler. Figured bass not realized. German text.

6   Den Herren lobt mit Freuden. -- Neuhausen-Stuttgart : Hänssler,
     c1960. Pub. no.: HE 6.035.
        Figured bass not realized. German text.

7   Lasst uns den Herren loben. -- Stuttgart : Hänssler, [19--]. Pub.
     no.: F.H. 1425.
        Music of SWV 239 with different text. Figured bass not realized.
     German text.

8   Lasst uns den Herren loben. -- Stuttgart : Hänssler, [19--]. Pub.
     no.: 6.195.
        Music of SWV 239 with different text. Figured bass not realized.
     German text.

SWV 240

[Beckerscher Psalter. Lobt Gott von Herzensgrunde]

     Sacred German text. Sources: Psalm 135.
        For chorus (SATB) and optional continuo. Ranges of voice parts:
     d1-d2, g-a1, d-f1, G-bflat. Duration: short.

1   CXXXV. -- In SGA. -- 1894. -- Bd. 16 , p. 118.
        Edited by Philipp Spitta. Figured bass not realized. Original
     German text. Notes in German.

2   Lobt Gott von Herzensgrunde all. -- In NSA. -- 1957. -- Bd. 6, p.
     139. Pub. no.: Bärenreiter Ausgabe 984.
        Edited by Walter Blankenburg. German text. Words in Gothic type.
     Notes in German. Transposed up M2.

5   Lobt Gott von Herzensgrunde. -- Stuttgart : Hänssler, [19--]. Pub.
     no.: 6.189.
        Figured bass not realized. German text. Transposed up M2.

SWV 241

[Beckerscher Psalter. Danket dem Herren, gebt ihm Ehr]

     Sacred German text. Sources: Psalm 136.
        For chorus (SATB) and optional continuo. Ranges of voice parts:
     f1-f2, c1-a1, g-f#1, Bflat-c1. Duration: short.

1   CXXXVI. -- In SGA. -- 1894. -- Bd. 16, p. 119.
        Edited by Philipp Spitta. Figured bass not realized. Original
     German text. Notes in German.

2   Danket dem Herren, gebt ihm Ehr. -- In NSA. -- 1957. -- Bd. 6, p.
     140. Pub. no.: Bärenreiter Ausgabe 984.
        Edited by Walter Blankenburg. German text. Words in Gothic type.
     Notes in German.

5   Danket dem Herren, gebt ihm Ehr. -- Stuttgart : Hänssler, [19--].
     Pub. no.: 6.190.
        Figured bass not realized. German text.

SWV 242

[Beckerscher Psalter. An Wasserflüssen Babylon]

     Sacred German text. Sources: Psalm 137.
        For chorus (SATB) and optional continuo. Ranges of voice parts:
     c1-d2, bflat-g1, d-f1, G-bflat. Duration: short.

1   CXXXVII. -- In SGA. -- 1894. -- Bd. 16, p. 119-120.
        Edited by Philipp Spitta. Figured bass not realized. Original
     German text. Notes in German.

2   An Wasserflüssen Babylon. -- In NSA. -- 1957. -- Bd. 6, p. 141. Pub.
     no.: Bärenreiter Ausgabe 984.
        Edited by Walter Blankenburg. German text. Words in Gothic type.
     Notes in German.

SWV 243

[Beckerscher Psalter. Aus meines Herzen Grunde]

     Sacred German text. Sources: Psalm 138.
        For chorus (SATB) and optional continuo. Ranges of voice parts:
     c1-e2, g-a1, e-f1, F-a. Duration: short.

1   CXXXVIII. -- In SGA. -- 1894. -- Bd. 16, p. 121.
        Edited by Philipp Spitta. Figured bass not realized. Original
     German text. Notes in German.

2   Aus meines Herzens Grunde. -- In NSA. -- 1957. -- Bd. 6, p. 142.
     Pub. no.: Bärenreiter Ausgabe 984.
        Edited by Walter Blankenburg. German text. Words in Gothic type.
     Notes in German.

3   Ich weiss, woran ich glaube. -- Kassel : Bärenreiter, c1973. Pub.
     no.: Bärenreiter-Ausgabe 931.
        Figured bass not realized. Music of SWV 243 with different text.
     German text. Words in Gothic type.

5   Aus meines Herzens Grunde. -- In Die Psalmen Davids. --
     Neuhausen-Stuttgart : Hänssler, c1967. -- p. 30. Pub. no.: HE 2.004.
        Edited by Emil Kubler. Figured bass not realized. German text.

6   Auf dein Wort will ich trauen. -- Stuttgart : Hänssler, [19--]. Pub.
     no.: 6.020.
        Figured bass not realized. German text.

7   Aus meines Herzens Grunde. -- Neuhausen-Stuttgart : Hänssler, c1960.
     Pub. no.: HE 6.035.
     Figured bass not realized. German text.

     Other editions: Hänssler 2.014.

SWV 244

[Beckerscher Psalter. Herr, du erforschst meine Sinne]

     Sacred German text. Sources: Psalm 139.
     For chorus (SATB) and optional continuo. Ranges of voice parts:
     d1-e2, a-a1, g-f1, A-a. Duration: short.

1   CXXXIX. -- In SGA. -- 1894. -- Bd. 16, p. 121-122.
     Edited by Philipp Spitta. Figured bass not realized. Original
     German text. Notes in German.

2   Herr, du erforschst meine Sinne. -- In NSA. -- 1957. -- Bd. 6, p.
     143. Pub. no.: Bärenreiter Ausgabe 984.
     Edited by Walter Blankenburg. German text. Words in Gothic type.
     Notes in German.

SWV 245

[Beckerscher Psalter. Vor bösen Menschen rette mich]

     Sacred German text. Sources: Psalm 140.
     For chorus (SATB) and optional continuo. Ranges of voice parts:
     c1-e2, g-a1, d-f1, G-a. Duration: short.

1   CXL. -- In SGA. -- 1894. -- Bd. 16, p. 122.
     Edited by Philipp Spitta. Figured bass not realized. Original
     German text. Notes in German.

2   Vor bösen Menschen rette mich. -- In NSA. -- 1957. -- Bd. 6, p. 144.
     Pub. no.: Bärenreiter Ausgabe 984.
     Edited by Walter Blankenburg. German text. Words in Gothic type.
     Notes in German.

SWV 246

[Beckerscher Psalter. Herr, mein Gott, wenn ich ruf zu dir]

     Sacred German text. Sources: Psalm 141.
     For chorus (SATB) and optional continuo. Ranges of voice parts:
     c1-d2, g-a1, d-e1, F-b. Duration: short.

1   CXLI. -- In SGA. -- 1894. -- Bd. 16, p. 123.
     Edited by Philipp Spitta. Figured bass not realized. Original
     German text. Notes in German.

2   Herr, mein Gott, wenn ich ruf zu dir. -- In NSA. -- 1957. -- Bd. 6,
p. 145. Pub. no.: Bärenreiter Ausgabe 984.
Edited by Walter Blankenburg. German text. Words in Gothic type.
Notes in German.

SWV 247

[Beckerscher Psalter. Ich schrei zu meinem lieben Gott]

Sacred German text. Sources: Psalm 142.
For chorus (SATB) and optional continuo. Ranges of voice parts:
d1-eflat2, b-a1, g-f1, G-bflat. Duration: short.

1   CXLII. -- In SGA. -- 1894. -- Bd. 16, p. 124.
Edited by Philipp Spitta. Figured bass not realized. Original
German text. Notes in German.

2   Ich schrei zu meinem lieben Gott. -- In NSA. -- 1957. -- Bd. 6, p.
146. Pub. no.: Bärenreiter Ausgabe 984.
Edited by Walter Blankenburg. German text. Words in Gothic type.
Notes in German.

SWV 248

[Beckerscher Psalter. Herr, mein Gebet erhör in Gnad]

Sacred German text. Sources: Psalm 143.
For chorus (SATB) and optional continuo. Ranges of voice parts:
f1-eflat2, bflat-a1, g-f1, G-bflat. Duration: short.

1   CXLIII. -- In SGA. -- 1894. -- Bd. 16, p. 125.
Edited by Philipp Spitta. Figured bass not realized. Original
German text. Notes in German.

2   Herr, mein Gebet erhör in Gnad. -- In NSA. -- 1957. -- Bd. 6, p.
147. Pub. no.: Bärenreiter Ausgabe 984.
Edited by Walter Blankenburg. German text. Words in Gothic type.
Notes in German.

3   Psalm 143. -- Kassel : Bärenreiter, c1951. Pub. no.:
Bärenreiter-Ausgabe 879.
Figured bass not realized. German text. Words in Gothic type.

5   Herr, mein Gebet erhör in Gnad. -- In Die Psalmen Davids. --
Neuhausen-Stuttgart : Hänssler, c1967. -- p. 31. Pub. no.: HE 2.004.
Edited by Emil Kübler. Figured bass not realized. German text.

6   Psalm 143. -- In Seven penitential psalms. -- G.I.A. Publications,
c1974. -- p. 18-19. Pub. no.: G-1912.
Edited by Daniel G. Reuning. Figured bass not realized. German
text with English translation. Notes in English.

7   Herr, mein Gebet erhör in Gnad. -- Neuhausen-Stuttgart : Hänssler,
c1967. Pub. no.: HE 6.036.
Figured bass not realized. German text.

SWV 249

[Beckerscher Psalter. Gelobet sei der Herr, mein Hort]

    Sacred German text. Sources: Psalm 144.
    For chorus (SATB) and optional continuo. Ranges of voice parts:
    d1-d2, a-a1, e-f1, F-g. Duration: short.

1   CXLIV. -- In SGA. -- 1894. -- Bd. 16, p. 125-126.
    Edited by Philipp Spitta. Figured bass not realized. Original
    German text. Notes in German.

2   Gelobet sei der Herr, mein Hort. -- In NSA. -- 1957. -- Bd. 6, p.
    148. Pub. no.: Bärenreiter Ausgabe 984.
    Edited by Walter Blankenburg. German text. Words in Gothic type.
    Notes in German.

SWV 250

[Beckerscher Psalter. Ich will sehr hoch erhöhen dich]

    Sacred German text. Sources: Psalm 145.
    For chorus (SATB) and optional continuo. Ranges of voice parts:
    f1-eflat2, c1-g1, f-eflat1, G-bflat. Duration: short.

1   CXLV. -- In SGA. -- 1894. -- Bd. 16, p. 126.
    Edited by Philipp Spitta. Figured bass not realized. Original
    German text. Notes in German.

2   Ich will sehr hoch erhöhen dich. -- In NSA. -- 1957. -- Bd. 6, p.
    149. Pub. no.: Bärenreiter Ausgabe 984.
    Edited by Walter Blankenburg. German text. Words in Gothic type.
    Notes in German.

3   Psalm 145. -- In Kleiner Liedpsalter. -- Kassel : Bärenreiter,
    c1976. -- p. 29. Pub. no.: BA 6231.
    Edited by Walter Blankenburg. Figured bass not realized. German
    text.

5   Ich will sehr hoch erhöhen. -- In Die Psalmen Davids. --
    Neuhausen-Stuttgart : Hänssler, c1967. -- p. 32. Pub. no.: HE 2.004.
    Edited by Emil Kübler. Figured bass not realized. German text.

6   Psalm 145. -- Kassel : Bärenreiter, c1974. Pub. no.:
    Bärenreiter-Ausgabe 6321.
    Figured bass not realized. German text.

7   Psalm 145. -- Kassel : Bärenreiter, [19--]. Pub. no.:
    Bärenreiter-Ausgabe 845.
    Figured bass not realized. German text. Words in Gothic type.
    Transposed up M2.

8   Ich will sehr hoch erhöhen. -- Neuhausen-Stuttgart : Hänssler,
    c1967. Pub. no.: HE 6.036.
    Figured bass not realized. German text.

Other editions: Hänssler 44.638.

SWV 251

[Beckerscher Psalter. Mein Seel soll loben Gott den Herrn]

Sacred German text. Sources: Psalm 146.
For chorus (SATB) and optional continuo. Ranges of voice parts:
el-d2, g-gl, f-el, G-a. Duration: short.

1   CXLVI. -- In SGA. -- 1894. -- Bd. 16, p. 127.
     Edited by Philipp Spitta. Figured bass not realized. Original
German text. Notes in German.

2   Mein Seel soll loben Gott den Herrn. -- In NSA. -- 1957. -- Bd. 6,
     p. 150. Pub. no.: Bärenreiter Ausgabe 984.
     Edited by Walter Blankenburg. German text. Words in Gothic type.
Notes in German. Transposed up M2.

5   Mein Seel soll loben Gott den Herrn. -- In Die Psalmen Davids. --
     Neuhausen-Stuttgart : Hänssler, c1967. -- p. 33. Pub. no.: HE 2.004.
     Edited by Emil Kübler. Figured bass not realized. German text.
Transposed up M2.

6   Mein Seel soll loben Gott den Herrn. -- Neuhausen-Stuttgart :
     Hänssler, c1966. Pub. no.: HE 6.037.
     Figured bass not realized. German text. Transposed up M2.

SWV 252

[Beckerscher Psalter. Zu Lob und Ehr mit Freuden singt]

Sacred German text. Sources: Psalm 147.
For chorus (SATB) and optional continuo. Ranges of voice parts:
dl-f2, g-al, d-el, G-cl. Duration: short.

1   CXLVII. -- In SGA. -- 1894. -- Bd. 16, p. 128.
     Edited by Philipp Spitta. Figured bass not realized. Original
German text. Notes in German.

2   Zu Lob und Ehr mit Freuden singt. -- In NSA. -- 1957. -- Bd. 6, p.
     151. Pub. no.: Bärenreiter Ausgabe 984.
     Edited by Walter Blankenburg. German text. Words in Gothic type.
Notes in German.

SWV 253

[Beckerscher Psalter. Lobet, ihr Himmel, Gott den Herrn]

Sacred German text. Sources: Psalm 148.
For chorus (SATB) and optional continuo. Ranges of voice parts:
dl-e2, cl-gl, f#-dl, G-a. Duration: short.

1   CXLVIII. -- In SGA. -- 1894. -- Bd. 16, p. 129.
     Edited by Philipp Spitta. Figured bass not realized. Original
German text. Notes in German.

2   Lobet, ihr Himmel, Gott den Herren. -- In NSA. -- 1957. -- Bd. 6, p.
152. Pub. no.: Bärenreiter Ausgabe 984.
     Edited by Walter Blankenburg. German text. Words in Gothic type.
Notes in German.

5   Lobt, ihr Himmel, Gott den Herrn. -- In Die Psalmen Davids. --
Neuhausen-Stuttgart : Hänssler, c1967. -- p. 33. Pub. no.: HE 2.004.
     Edited by Emil Kübler. Figured bass not realized. German text.

6   Lobt, ihr Himmel, Gott den Herrn. -- Neuhausen-Stuttgart : Hänssler,
c1966. Pub. no.: HE 6.037.
     Figured bass not realized. German text.

SWV 254

[Beckerscher Psalter. Heilige Gemeine]

     Sacred German text. Sources: Psalm 149.
     For chorus (SATB) and optional continuo. Ranges of voice parts:
f1-eflat2, c1-a1, f#-f1, G-bflat. Duration: short.

1   CXLIX. -- In SGA. -- 1894. -- Bd. 16, p. 129-130.
     Edited by Philipp Spitta. Figured bass not realized. Original
German text. Notes in German.

2   Die heilige Gemeine. -- In NSA. -- 1957. -- Bd. 6, p. 153. Pub. no.:
Bärenreiter Ausgabe 984.
     Edited by Walter Blankenburg. German text. Words in Gothic type.
Notes in German.

3   Psalm 149. -- In Kleiner Liedpsalter. -- Kassel : Bärenreiter,
c1976. -- p. 30. Pub. no.: BA 6231.
     Edited by Walter Blankenburg. Figured bass not realized. German
text.

SWV 255

[Beckerscher Psalter. Lobt Gott in seinem Heiligtum]

     Sacred German text. Sources: Psalm 150.
     For chorus (SATB) and optional continuo. Ranges of voice parts:
e1-d2, b-g1, e-d1, E-g. Duration: short.

1   CL. -- In SGA. -- 1894. -- Bd. 16, p. 130.
     Edited by Philipp Spitta. Figured bass not realized. Original
German text. Notes in German.

2   Lobt Gott in seinem Heiligtum. -- In NSA. -- 1957. -- Bd. 6, p. 154.
Pub. no.: Bärenreiter Ausgabe 984.
     Edited by Walter Blankenburg. German text. Words in Gothic type.
Notes in German. Transposed up m3.

3   Psalm 150. -- In Kleiner Liedpsalter. -- Kassel : Bärenreiter,
     c1976. -- p. 31. Pub. no.: BA 6231.
       Edited by Walter Blankenburg. Figured bass not realized. German
     text. Transposed up m3.

5   Lobt Gott in seinem Heiligtum. -- Stuttgart : Hänssler, [19--]. Pub.
     no.: H 1927 H.
       Figured bass not realized. German text. Words in Gothic type.
     Transposed up m3.

6   Psalm 150. -- In Five psalms of praise and the responsorium. --
     Chicago : G.I.A. Publications, c1973. -- p. 12-13. Pub. no.: G-1790.
       Edited by Daniel G. Reuning. Figured bass not realized. German
     text with English translation. Notes in English. Transposed up m3.

7   Psalm 150. -- Stockholm : Eriks Nothandel, [19--]. Pub. no.: AK 850.
       Figured bass not realized. Swedish text. Transposed up m3.

       Other editions: Hänssler 2.039; 2.047.

SWV 256

[Beckerscher Psalter. Responsorium]

       Sacred German text.
       For chorus (SATB) and optional continuo. Ranges of voice parts:
     d1-e2, g-g1, g-d1, G-a. Duration: short.

1   Responsorium. -- In SGA. -- 1894. -- Bd. 16, p. 131.
       Edited by Philipp Spitta. Figured bass not realized. Original
     German text. Notes in German.

2   Alles was Odem hat, lobe den Herren. -- In NSA. -- 1957. -- Bd. 6,
     p. 155. Pub. no.: Bärenreiter Ausgabe 984.
       Edited by Walter Blankenburg. German text. Words in Gothic type.
     Notes in German. Transposed up m3.

5   Responsorium. -- Neuhausen-Stuttgart : Hänssler, c1969. Pub. no.: HE
     20.215.
       Edited by Hermann Stern and Günter Graulich. Continuo realized by
     Paul Horn. German text with English translation.

6   Responsorium. -- In Five psalms of praise and the responsorium. --
     Chicago : G.I.A. Publications, c1973. -- p. 14-15. Pub. no.: G-1790.
       Edited by Daniel G. Reuning. Figured bass not realized. German
     text with English translation. Transposed up m3.

7   Responsorium. -- In Die Psalmen Davids. -- Neuhausen-Stuttgart :
     Hänssler, c1967. -- p. 34. Pub. no.: HE 2.004.
       Edited by Emil Kübler. Figured bass not realized. German text.
     Transposed up m3.

8   Responsorium. -- Neuhausen-Stuttgart : Hänssler, c1966. Pub. no.: HE
     6.037.
       Figured bass not realized. German text. Transposed up m3.

9   Response to the psalms. -- Fremont, Ohio : Chantry Music Press,
    c1962.
      Figured bass not realized. English text. Transposed up m3.

10 Responsorium. -- Stockholm : Eriks Nothandel, [19--]. Pub. no.: AK
    851.
      Figured bass not realized. German text with Swedish translation.
    Transposed up m3.

    Other editions: Hänssler HE20.256.

SWV 257

[Symphoniae sacrae, 1 pars. Paratum cor meum, Deus]

      Sacred Latin text. Sources: Psalm 108:1-3.
      Solo for soprano with 2 violins and continuo. Range of voice part:
    d1-f2. Duration: medium.

1   Paratum cor meum, Deus. -- In SGA. -- 1887. -- Bd. 5, p. 5-10.
      Edited by Philipp Spitta. Figured bass not realized. Notes in
    German. Original Latin text.

2   Paratum cor meum = Mein Herz ist gerüstet. -- In NSA. -- 1957. --
    Bd. 13, p. 9-17. Pub. no.: Bärenreiter Ausgabe 3661.
      Edited by Rudolf Gerber. Latin text with German translation.
    German text in Gothic type. Notes in German.

3   Paratum cor meum, Deus = Mein Herz ist gerüstet, o Gott. -- In
    Symphoniae sacrae I. -- Kassel : Bärenreiter, [19--]. -- Nr. 1. Pub.
    no.: Bärenreiter-Ausgabe 28.
      Edited by Rudolf Gerber. Latin text with German translation.
    German words in Gothic type.

SWV 258

[Symphoniae sacrae, 1 pars. Exultavit cor meum in Domino]

      Sacred Latin text. Sources: Samuel, 1st, 2:1-2.
      Solo for soprano with 2 violins and continuo. Range of voice part:
    c1-f2. Duration: medium.

1   Exultavit cor meum in Domino. -- In SGA. -- 1887. -- Bd. 5, p.
    11-14.
      Edited by Philipp Spitta. Figured bass not realized. Notes in
    German. Original Latin text.

2   Exultavit cor meum = Freude und Glück bewegt mich. -- In NSA. --
    1957. -- Bd. 13, p. 18-26. Pub. no.: Bärenreiter Ausgabe 3661.
      Edited by Rudolf Gerber. Latin text with German translation.
    German text in Gothic type. Notes in German.

3   Exultavit cor meum = Freude und Glück bewegt mich. -- In Symphoniae
     sacrae I. -- Kassel : Bärenreiter, c1956. -- Nr. 2. Pub. no.:
     Bärenreiter-Ausgabe 29.
       Edited by Rudolf Gerber. Latin text with German translation.
     German words in Gothic type.

SWV 259

[Symphoniae sacrae, 1 pars. In te, Domine, speravi]

     Sacred Latin text. Sources: Psalm 31:2-3.
       Solo for alto with violin, bassoon or trombone, and continuo.
     Range of voice part: e-al. Duration: medium.

1   In te Domine speravi. -- In SGA. -- 1887. -- Bd. 5, p. 15-19.
       Edited by Philipp Spitta. Figured bass not realized. Notes in
     German. Original Latin text.

2   In te, Domine, speravi = Dir, o Herr, gilt all mein Hoffen. -- In
     NSA. -- 1957. -- Bd. 13, p. 27-37. Pub. no.: Bärenreiter Ausgabe
     3661.
       Edited by Rudolf Gerber. Latin text with German translation.
     German text in Gothic type. Notes in German. Transposed up P4.

3   In te, Domine, speravi = Dir, o Herr, gilt all mein Hoffen. -- In
     Symphoniae sacrae I. -- Kassel : Bärenreiter, c1956. -- Nr. 3. Pub.
     no.: Bärenreiter-Ausgabe 30.
       Edited by Rudolf Gerber. Latin text with German translation.
     German words in Gothic type. Transposed up P4.

SWV 260

[Symphoniae sacrae, 1 pars. Cantabo Domino in vita mea]

     Sacred Latin text. Sources: Psalm 104:33.
       Solo for tenor with 2 violins and continuo. Range of voice part:
     d-gl. Duration: medium.

1   Cantabo Domino in vita mea. -- In SGA. -- 1887. -- Bd. 5, p. 20-24.
       Edited by Philipp Spitta. Figured bass not realized. Notes in
     German. Original Latin text.

2   Cantabo Domino in vita mea = Ich singe dem Herren. -- In NSA. --
     1957. -- Bd. 13, p. 38-46. Pub. no.: Bärenreiter Ausgabe 3661.
       Edited by Rudolf Gerber. Latin text with German translation.
     German text in Gothic type. Notes in German.

3   Cantabo Domino = Ich singe dem Herrn. -- In Symphoniae sacrae I. --
     Kassel : Bärenreiter, [19--]. -- Nr. 4. Pub. no.:
     Bärenreiter-Ausgabe 31.
       Edited by Rudolf Gerber. Latin text with German translation.
     German words in Gothic type.

SWV 261

[Symphoniae sacrae, 1 pars. Venite ad me omnes qui laboratis]

    Sacred Latin text. Sources: Matthew 11:28-30.
    Solo for tenor with 2 violins and continuo. Range of voice part:
c-gl. Duration: medium.

1   Venite ad me omnes qui laboratis. -- In SGA. -- 0887. -- Bd. 5, p.
    25-31.
       Edited by Philipp Spitta. Figured bass not realized. Notes in
    German. Original Latin text.

2   Venite ad me = Kommt alle zu mir. -- In NSA. -- 1957. -- Bd. 13, p.
    47-58. Pub. no.: Bärenreiter Ausgabe 3661.
       Edited by Rudolf Gerber. Latin text with German translation.
    German text in Gothic type. Notes in German.

3   Venite ad me = Kommt alle zu mir. -- In Symphoniae sacrae I. --
    Kassel : Bärenreiter, [19--]. -- Nr. 5. Pub. no.:
    Bärenreiter-Ausgabe 32.
       Edited by Rudolf Gerber. Latin text with German translation.
    German words in Gothic type.

SWV 262

[Symphoniae sacrae, 1 pars. Jubilate Deo omnis terra]

    Sacred Latin text. Sources: Psalm 100.
    Solo for bass with 2 violins or 2 flutes and continuo. Range of
voice part: D-cl. Duration: medium.

1   Jubilate Deo omnis terra. -- In SGA. -- 1887. -- Bd. 5, p. 31-34.
       Edited by Philipp Spitta. Figured bass not realized. Notes in
    German. Original Latin text.

2   Jubilate Deo omnis terra = Lob und Ehre zollt dem Herren. -- In NSA.
    -- 1957. -- Bd. 13, p. 59-67. Pub. no.: Bärenreiter Ausgabe 3661.
       Edited by Rudolf Gerber. Latin text with German translation.
    German text in Gothic type. Notes in German. Transposed up M3.

3   Jubilate Deo, omnis terra = Lob und Ehre zollt dem Herren, alle
    Völker. -- In Symphoniae sacrae I. -- Kassel : Bärenreiter, c1957.
    -- Nr. 6. Pub. no.: Bärenreiter-Ausgabe 33.
       Edited by Rudolf Gerber. Latin text with German translation.
    German words in Gothic type. Notes in German and English. Transposed
    up M3.

SWV 263

[Symphoniae sacrae, 1 pars. Anima mea liquefacta est]

> Sacred Latin text. Sources: Song of Solomon 2:14. Song of Solomon 5
> :13. Song of Solomon 5:6.
> Duet (TT) with 2 cornettino or 2 fiffaro and continuo. Ranges of
> voice parts: d-f1, c-d1. Duration: short.

1   Anima mea liquefacta est. -- In SGA. -- 1887. -- Bd. 5, p. 35-38.
    Edited by Philipp Spitta. Figured bass not realized. Notes in
    German. Original Latin text.

2   Anima mea liquefacta est = Ach, meine Seele schmilzt in Wonne hin.
    -- In NSA. -- 1957. -- Bd. 13, p. 68-74. Pub. no.: Bärenreiter
    Ausgabe 3661.
    Edited by Rudolf Gerber. Latin text with German translation.
    German text in Gothic type. Notes in German.

3   Anima mea liquefacta est = Ach, meine Seele schmilzt in Wonne hin.
    -- In Symphoniae sacrae I. -- Kassel : Bärenreiter, [19--]. -- Nr.
    7-8, p. 4-10. Pub. no.: Bärenreiter-Ausgabe 34.
    Edited by Rudolf Gerber. Latin text with German translation.
    German words in Gothic type.

SWV 264

[Symphoniae sacrae, 1 pars. Adjuro vos, filiae Hierusalem]

> Sacred Latin text. Sources: Song of Solomon 5:8.
> Duet (TT) with 2 cornettino or 2 fiffaro and continuo. Ranges of
> voice parts: c-f1, B-f1. Duration: short.

1   Adjuro vos, filiae Hierusalem. -- In SGA. -- 1887. -- Bd. 5, p.
    39-41.
    Edited by Philipp Spitta. Figured bass not realized. Notes in
    German. Original Latin text.

2   Adjuro vos, filiae Jerusalem = Ich flehe euch an, Töchter von
    Jerusalem. -- In NSA. -- 1957. -- Bd. 13, p. 75-79. Pub. no.:
    Bärenreiter Ausgabe 3661.
    Edited by Rudolf Gerber. Latin text with German translation.
    German text in Gothic type. Notes in German.

3   Adjuro vos, filiae Jerusalem = Ich flehe euch an, Töchter von
    Jerusalem. -- In Symphoniae sacrae I. -- Kassel : Bärenreiter,
    [19--]. -- Nr. 7-8, p. 11-15. Pub. no.: Bärenreiter-Ausgabe 34.
    Edited by Rudolf Gerber. Latin text with German translation.
    German words in Gothic type.

SWV 265

[Symphoniae sacrae, 1 pars. O quam tu pulchra es, amica mea]

Sacred Latin text. Sources: Song of Solomon 4:1-5. Song of Solomon 5 :2.
Duet (TR) with 2 violins and continuo. Ranges of voice parts: c-g1, c-e1. Duration: medium.

1   O quam tu pulchra es, amica mea. -- In SGA. -- 1887. -- Bd. 5, p. 42-46.
    Edited by Philipp Spitta. Figured bass not realized. Notes in German. Original Latin text.

2   O quam tu pulchra es = O wie berückend, wie schön du bist. -- In NSA. -- 1957. -- Bd. 13, p. 80-87. Pub. no.: Bärenreiter Ausgabe 3661.
    Edited by Rudolf Gerber. Latin text with German translation. German text in Gothic type. Notes in German.

3   O quam tu pulchra es = O, wie berückend, wie schon bist du. -- In Symphoniae sacrae I. -- Kassel : Bärenreiter, [19--]. -- Nr. 9-10, p. 4-11. Pub. no.: Bärenreiter-Ausgabe 35.
    Edited by Rudolf Gerber. Latin text with German translation. German words in Gothic type.

SWV 266

[Symphoniae sacrae, 1 pars. Veni de Libano, amica mea]

Sacred Latin text. Sources: Song of Solomon 2:10. Song of Solomon 4 :8. Song of Solomon 5:2.
Duet (TR) with 2 violins and continuo. Ranges of voice parts: d-f1, d-e1. Duration: short.

1   Veni de Libano, amica mea. -- In SGA. -- 1887. -- Bd. 5, p. 47-52.
    Edited by Philipp Spitta. Figured bass not realized. Notes in German. Original Latin text.

2   Veni de Libano = Steige herab von den Bergen. -- In NSA. -- 1957. -- Bd. 13, p. 88-95. Pub. no.: Bärenreiter Ausgabe 3661.
    Edited by Rudolf Gerber. Latin text with German translation. German text in Gothic type. Notes in German.

3   Veni de Libano = Steige herab von den Bergen. -- In Symphoniae sacrae I. -- Kassel : Bärenreiter, [19--]. -- Nr. 9-10, p. 12-19. Pub. no.: Bärenreiter-Ausgabe 35.
    Edited by Rudolf Gerber. Latin text with German translation. German words in Gothic type.

SWV 267

[Symphoniae sacrae, 1 pars. Benedicam Dominum in omni tempore]

> Sacred Latin text. Sources: Psalm 34:1-3.
> Trio (STB) with cornetto or violin and continuo. Ranges of voice parts: cl-f2, d-fl, F-dl. Duration: short.

1   Benedicam Dominum in omni tempore. -- In SGA. -- 1887. -- Bd. 5, p. 53-58.
    Edited by Philipp Spitta. Figured bass not realized. Notes in German. Original Latin text.

2   Benedicam Dominum in omni tempore = Preisen will ich allezeit den Herren in der Höh. -- In NSA. -- 1965. -- Bd. 14, p. [1]-15. Pub. no.: Bärenreiter Ausgabe BA3667.
    Edited by Gerhard Kirchner. Latin text with German translation. German text in Gothic type. Notes in German and English.

3   Benedicam Domine in omni tempore = Preisen will ich allezeit den Herren in der Höh. -- In Symphoniae sacrae I. -- Kassel : Bärenreiter, c1965. -- Nr. 11-12, p. [7]-21. Pub. no.: Bärenreiter-Ausgabe 36.
    Edited by Gerhard Kirchner. Latin text with German translation. Notes in German and English.

SWV 268

[Symphoniae sacrae, 1 pars. Exquisivi Dominum et exaudivit me]

> Sacred Latin text. Sources: Psalm 34:4-5.
> Trio (STB) with cornetto or violin and continuo. Ranges of voice parts: cl-e2, c-fl, D-cl. Duration: short.

1   Exquisivi Dominum et exaudivit me. -- In SGA. -- 1887. -- Bd. 5, p. 59-64.
    Edited by Philipp Spitta. Figured bass not realized. Notes in German. Original Latin text.

2   Exquisivi Dominum = Als ich Gott den Herrn gesucht. -- In NSA. -- 1965. -- Bd. 14, p. 16-29. Pub. no.: Bärenreiter Ausgabe BA3667.
    Edited by Gerhard Kirchner. Latin text with German translation. German text in Gothic type. Notes in German and English.

3   Exquisivi Dominum = Als ich Gott den Herrn gesucht. -- In Symphoniae sacrae I. -- Kassel : Bärenreiter, c1965. -- Nr. 11-12, p. 22-35. Pub. no.: Bärenreiter-Ausgabe 36.
    Edited by Gerhard Kirchner. Latin text with German translation. Notes in German and English.

SWV 269

[Symphoniae sacrae, 1 pars. Fili mi, Absalon]

Sacred Latin text. Sources: Samuel, 2nd, 18:33.
Solo for bass with 4 trombones or 2 violins and 2 trombones and
continuo. Range of voice part: G-cl. Duration: medium.

1   Fili mi, Absalon. -- In SGA. -- 1887. -- Bd. 5, p. 65-69.
Edited by Philipp Spitta. Figured bass not realized. Notes in
German. Original Latin text.

2   Fili mi, Absalon = Ach, mein Sohn Absalon. -- In NSA. -- 1965. --
Bd. 14, p. 30-39. Pub. no.: Bärenreiter Ausgabe BA3667.
Edited by Rudolf Gerber. Latin text with German translation.
German text in Gothic type. Notes in German and English by Gerhard
Kirchner. Transposed up M2.

Other editions: Bärenreiter BA40.

SWV 270

[Symphoniae sacrae, 1 pars. Attendite, popule meus, legem meam]

Sacred Latin text. Sources: Psalm 78:1-3.
Solo for bass with 4 trombones or 2 violins and 2 trombones and
continuo. Range of voice part: E-cl. Duration: medium.

1   Attendite, popule meus, legem meam. -- In SGA. -- 1887. -- Bd. 5, p.
70-76.
Edited by Philipp Spitta. Figured bass not realized. Notes in
German. Original Latin text.

2   Attendite, popule meus = So höre doch, meine Gemeinde. -- In NSA. --
1965. -- Bd. 14, p. 40-55. Pub. no.: Bärenreiter Ausgabe BA3667.
Edited by Gerhard Kirchner. Latin text with German translation.
German text in Gothic type. Notes in German and English.

3   Attendite, popule meus = So höre doch, meine Gemeinde. -- In
Symphoniae sacrae I. -- Kassel : Bärenreiter, c1965. -- Nr. 14. Pub.
no.: Bärenreiter-Ausgabe 37.
Edited by Gerhard Kirchner. Latin text with German translation.
Notes in German and English.

SWV 271

[Symphoniae sacrae, 1 pars. Domine, labia mea aperies]

Sacred Latin text. Sources: Psalm 51:15.
Duet (ST) with cornetto or violin, trombone, bassoon and continuo.
Ranges of voice parts: cl-g2, B-fl. Duration: medium.

1   Domine, labia mea aperies. -- In SGA. -- 1887. -- Bd. 5, p. 77-82.
     Edited by Philipp Spitta. Figured bass not realized. Notes in
     German. Original Latin text.

2   Domine, labia mea aperies = Öffne du mir meine Lippen, Allmächtiger.
     -- In NSA. -- 1965. -- Bd. 14, p. 56-69. Pub. no.: Bärenreiter
     Ausgabe BA3667.
     Edited by Gerhard Kirchner. Latin text with German translation.
     German text in Gothic type. Notes in German and English.

3   Domine, labia mea aperies = Öffne du mir meine Lippen, Allmächtiger.
     -- In Symphoniae sacrae I. -- Kassel : Bärenreiter, c1965. -- Nr.
     15. Pub. no.: Bärenreiter-Ausgabe 38.
     Edited by Gerhard Kirchner. Latin text with German translation.
     Notes in German and English.

SWV 272

[Symphoniae sacrae, 1 pars. In lectulo per noctes]

     Sacred Latin text. Sources: Song of Solomon 3:1-2.
     Duet (SA) with 3 bassoons or 3 viola da gamba and continuo. Ranges
     of voice parts: c#1-f2, f-a1. Duration: medium.

1   In lectulo per noctes. -- In SGA. -- 1887. -- Bd. 5, p. 83-88.
     Edited by Philipp Spitta. Figured bass not realized. Notes in
     German. Original Latin text.

2   In lectulo per noctes = Des Nachts auf meinem Lager. -- In NSA. --
     1965. -- Bd. 14, p. 70-80. Pub. no.: Bärenreiter Ausgabe BA3667.
     Edited by Gerhard Kirchner. Latin text with German translation.
     German text in Gothic type. Notes in German and English. Transposed
     up M2.

3   In lectulo per noctes = Des Nachts auf meinem Lager. -- In
     Symphoniae sacrae I. -- Kassel : Bärenreiter, c1965. -- Nr. 16-17,
     p. [9]-19. Pub. no.: Bärenreiter-Ausgabe 39.
     Edited by Gerhard Kirchner. Latin text with German translation.
     Notes in German and English. Transposed up M2.

SWV 273

[Symphoniae sacrae, 1 pars. Invenerunt me custodes civitatis]

     Sacred Latin text. Sources: Song of Solomon 3:3-4.
     Duet (SA) with 3 bassoons or 3 viola da gamba and continuo. Ranges
     of voice parts: d1-f2, f#-bflat1. Duration: medium.

1   Invenerunt me custodes civitatis. -- In SGA. -- 1887. -- Bd. 5, p.
     89-95.
     Edited by Philipp Spitta. Figured bass not realized. Notes in
     German. Original Latin text.

2   Invenerunt me custodes civitatis = Und es trafen mich dort in der
    Stadt die Wächter. -- In NSA. -- 1965. -- Bd. 14, p. 81-97. Pub.
    no.: Bärenreiter Ausgabe BA3667.
    Edited by Gerhard Kirchner. Latin text with German translation.
    German text in Gothic type. Notes in German and English. Transposed
    up M2.

3   Invenerunt me custodes civitatis = Und es trafen mich dort in der
    Stadt die Wächter. -- In Symphoniae sacrae I. -- Kassel :
    Bärenreiter, c1965. -- Nr. 16-17, p. 20-36. Pub. no.:
    Bärenreiter-Ausgabe 39.
    Edited by Gerhard Kirchner. Latin text with German translation.
    Notes in German and English. Transposed up M2.

SWV 274

[Symphoniae sacrae, 1 pars. Veni, dilecte mi, in hortum meum]

    Sacred Latin text. Sources: Song of Solomon 4:16. Song of Solomon 5
    :1.
    Trio (SST) with 3 trombones and continuo or quartet (ST/ST) with 2
    trombones and continuo. Ranges of voice parts: c1-g2, (c-e1), c1-g2,
    c-g1. Duration: medium.

1   Veni, dilecte mi, in hortum meum. -- In SGA. -- 1887. -- Bd. 5, p.
    96-102.
    Edited by Philipp Spitta. Figured bass not realized. Notes in
    German. Original Latin text.

2   Veni, dilecte mi = Komm doch, Geliebter mein. -- In NSA. -- 1965. --
    Bd. 14, p. 98-115. Pub. no.: Bärenreiter Ausgabe BA3667.
    Edited by Gerhard Kirchner. Latin text with German translation.
    German text in Gothic type. Notes in German and English.

3   Veni, dilecte mi = Komm doch, Geliebter mein. -- In Symphoniae
    sacrae I. -- Kassel : Bärenreiter, c1965. -- Nr. 18. Pub. no.:
    Bärenreiter-Ausgabe 41.
    Edited by Gerhard Kirchner. Latin text with German translation.
    Notes in German and English.

SWV 275

[Symphoniae sacrae, 1 pars. Buccinate in neomenia tuba]

    Sacred Latin text. Sources: Psalm 81:1. Psalm 81:3. Psalm 98:6.
    Trio (TTB) with cornetto, trombetta or cornetto, bassoon, and
    continuo. Ranges of voice parts: c-g1, c-e1, F-bflat. Duration:
    medium.

1   Buccinate in neomenia tuba. -- In SGA. -- 1887. -- Bd. 5, p.
    103-108.
    Edited by Philipp Spitta. Figured bass not realized. Notes in
    German. Original Latin text.

2   Buccinate in neomenia tuba = Auf und blaset am Fest des Neumonds die
    Tuba. -- In NSA. -- 1965. --, Bd. 14, p. 116-130. Pub. no.:
    Bärenreiter Ausgabe BA3667.
      Edited by Rudolf Gerber. Latin text with German translation.
    German text in Gothic type. Notes in German and English by Gerhard
    Kirchner.

3   Buccinate in neomenia tuba = Auf und blaset am Fest des Neumonds die
    Tuba. -- In Symphoniae sacrae I. -- Kassel : Bärenreiter, c1954. --
    Nr. 19-20, p. 5-18. Pub. no.: Bärenreiter-Ausgabe 42.
      Edited by Rudolf Gerber. Latin text with German translation.
    German words in Gothic type. Notes in German and English.

SWV 276

[Symphoniae sacrae, 1 pars. Jubilate Deo in chordis et organo]

      Sacred Latin text. Sources: Psalm 98:4. Psalm 150:4.
      Trio (TTB) with cornetto, trombetta or cornetto, bassoon, and
    continuo. Ranges of voice parts: d-f1, c-d1, F-c1. Duration: short.

1   Jubilate Deo in chordis et organo. -- In SGA. -- 1887. -- Bd. 5, p.
    109-113.
      Edited by Philipp Spitta. Figured bass not realized. Notes in
    German. Original Latin text.

2   Jubilate Deo in chordis et organo = Lobt den Herren. -- In NSA. --
    1965. -- Bd. 14, p. 131-143. Pub. no.: Bärenreiter Ausgabe BA3667.
      Edited by Rudolf Gerber. Latin text with German translation.
    German text in Gothic type. Notes in German and English by Gerhard
    Kirchner.

3   Jubilate Deo = Lobt den Herrn. -- In Symphoniae sacrae I. -- Kassel
    : Bärenreiter, c1954. -- Nr. 19-20, p. 19-30. Pub. no.:
    Bärenreiter-Ausgabe 42.
      Edited by Rudolf Gerber. Latin text with German translation.
    German words in Gothic type. Notes in German and English.

SWV 277

[Das ist je gewisslich wahr]

      Sacred German text. Sources: Timothy, 1st, 1:15-17.
      For chorus (SSATTB) and basso continuo. Ranges of voice parts:
    d1-g2, c1-e2, f-g1, c-f1, c-e1, F-c1. Duration: medium.

1   Verba D. Pauli, ex. epist. ad Timotheum cap. 1, v. 15 : das ist je
    gewisslich wahr, und ein theuer werthes Wort etc. -- In SGA. --
    1892. -- Bd. 12, p. 25-31.
      Edited by Philipp Spitta. Figured bass not realized. Original
    German text. Notes in German.

2   Das ist je gewisslich wahr. -- In NSA. -- 1970. -- Bd. 31, p. 57-81.
    Pub. no.: BA4483.
      Edited by Werner Breig. German text. Notes in German and English.

SWV 278

[Canconetta, voices (6)]

Secular German text.
Quartet (SSSS) with 2 violins and basso continuo. Ranges of voice
parts: g1-g2, d1-g2, c1-e2, b-e2. Duration: medium.

1   Canconetta : O der grossen Wundertaten. -- In SGA. -- 1927. -- Bd.
    18, p. 135-138.
    Edited by Heinrich Spitta. Figured bass not realized. Original
    German text. Notes in German.

2   O der grossen Wundertaten. -- In NSA. -- 1970. -- Bd. 37, p. 20-34.
    Pub. no.: BA4489.
    Edited by Werner Bittinger. German text. Notes in German and
    English.

SWV 279

[Musicalische Exequien. Nacket bin ich von Mutterleibe kommen]

Sacred German text. Sources: John 1:29. John 3:16. John, 1st, 1:7.
Philippians 1:21. Philippians 3:20-21. Romans 14:8. Apocrypha.
Wisdom of Solomon 3:1-3. Genesis 32:26. Isaiah 1:18. Isaiah 26:20.
Job 1:21. Job 19:25-26. Psalm 73:25-26. Psalm 90:10. Gigas,
Johannes. Ach wie elend ist unsre Zeit. Helmbold, Ludwig. Nun lasst
uns Gott dem Herren. Herman, Nicolaus. Wenn mein Stündlein vorhanden
ist. Leon, Johann. Ich hab mein Sach Gott heimgestellt. Luther,
Martin. Deutsche Litanei. Luther, Martin. Mit Fried und Freud ich
fahr dahin. Luther, Martin. Nun freut euch, lieben Christen gmein.
For solo voices (SSATTB) and basso continuo with optional chorus
(SSATTB). Ranges of voice parts: b-e2, c#1-e2, e-a1, c-f1, c-e1,
D-b/ b-e2, c#1-e2, e-a, c-e1, c-e1, D-g. Duration: long.

1   Concert in Form einer teutschen Begräbnis-Missa. -- In SGA. -- 1892.
    -- Bd. 12, p. 61-97.
    Edited by Philipp Spitta. Figured bass not realized. Original
    German text. Notes in German.

2   Concert in Form einer teutschen Begräbnis-Missa. -- In NSA. -- 1956.
    -- Bd. 4, p. 11-51. Pub. no.: Bärenreiter Ausgabe 250.
    Edited by Friedrich Schöneich. German text. Notes in German.

4   Nacket bin ich von Mutterleibe kommen. -- In SSA. -- c1973. -- Bd.
    8, p. 3-46. Pub. no.: HE 20.908.
    Edited by Günter Graulich. Continuo realized by Paul Horn. German
    text with English translation. Notes in German and English.

5   Nacket bin ich von Mutterleibe kommen. -- Neuhausen-Stuttgart :
    Hänssler, c1972. Pub. no.: HE 20.279/01.
    Edited by Günter Graulich. Continuo realized by Paul Horn. German
    text with English translation. Notes in German and English.

6   Concerto in the form of a German Requiem = Concert in Form einer
      teutschen Begräbnis-Missa. -- In A German Requiem. -- New York : G.
      Schirmer, c1957. -- p. 1-65. Pub. no.: Ed. 2270.
      Edited by Arthur Mendel. German text with English translation.
      Notes in English. Transposed up M2.

7   Concert in Form einer teutschen Begräbnis-Missa. -- In Musikalische
      Exequien. -- Leipzig : VEB Breitkopf & Härtel, 1973. -- p. 1-51.
      Pub. no.: Edition Breitkopf Nr. 4181.
      Edited by Georg Schumann. German text.

SWV 280

[Musicalische Exequien. Herr, wenn ich nur dich habe]

      Sacred German text. Sources: Psalm 73:25-26.
      For double chorus (SATB/SATB) with optional basso continuo. Ranges
      of voice parts: d1-f2, g-a1, B-e1, E-c1/ c#1-e2, e-a1, c-e1, F-a.
      Duration: short.

1   Motette : Herr, wenn ich nur dich habe. -- In SGA. -- 1892. -- Bd.
      12, p. 98-103.
      Edited by Philipp Spitta. Figured bass not realized. Original
      German text. Notes in German.

2   Herr, wenn ich nur dich habe. -- In NSA. -- 1956. -- Bd. 4, p.
      52-59. Pub. no.: Bärenreiter Ausgabe 250.
      Edited by Friedrich Schoneich. German text. Notes in German.

4   Herr, wenn ich nur dich habe. -- In SSA. -- c1973. -- Bd. 8, p.
      49-56. Pub. no.: HE 20.908.
      Edited by Günter Graulich. Continuo realized by Paul Horn. German
      text with English. Notes in German and English.

5   Herr, wenn ich nur dich habe. -- Neuhausen-Stuttgart : Hänssler,
      c1968. Pub. no.: HE 20.280/02.
      Edited by Günter Graulich. Continuo realized by Paul Horn. German
      text with English translation.

6   Lord, and whom but thee have I? = Herr, wenn ich nur dich habe. --
      In A German Requiem. -- New York : G. Schirmer, c1957. -- p. 66-82.
      Pub. no.: Ed. 2270.
      Edited by Arthur Mendel. German text with English translation.
      Notes in English. Transposed up M2.

7   Herr, wenn ich nur dich habe. -- In Musikalische Exequien. --
      Leipzig : VEB Breitkopf & Härtel, 1973. -- p. 52-59. Pub. no.:
      Edition Breitkopf Nr. 4181.
      Edited by Georg Schumann. German text.

SWV 281

[Musicalische Exequien. Herr, nun lässest du deinen Diener]

Sacred German text. Sources: Revelation 14:13. Apocrypha. Wisdom of
Solomon 3:1. Nunc dimittis.
For two choruses (MATTB/SSR) and basso continuo with two optional
doubling choruses (SSR/SSR). Ranges of voice parts: el-c2, g-al,
c-f1, c-d1, F-f/ c#1-f2, c1-f2, G-eflat1. Duration: medium.

1   Canticum B. Simeonis : Herr nun lässest du deinen Diener. -- In SGA.
     -- 1892. -- Bd. 12, p. 104-111.
     Edited by Philipp Spitta. Figured bass not realized. Original
     German text. Notes in German.

2   Canticum B. Simeonis : Herr nun lassest du deinen Diener. -- In NSA.
     -- 1956. -- Bd. 4, p. 60-70. Pub. no.: Bärenreiter Ausgabe 250.
     Edited by Friedrich Schöneich. German text. Notes in German.

4   Herr, nun lässest du deinen Diener in Friede fahren. -- In SSA. --
     c1973. -- Bd. 8, p. 59-69. Pub. no.: HE 20.908.
     Edited by Günter Graulich. Continuo realized by Paul Horn. German
     text with English translation. Notes in German and English.

5   Herr, nun lässest du deinen Diener im Frieden fahren = Nunc
     dimittis. -- Neuhausen-Stuttgart : Hänssler, c1972. Pub. no.: HE
     20.281/02.
     Edited by Günter Graulich. Continuo realized by Paul Horn. German
     text with English translation.

6   Lord, now lettest thou thy servant = Herr, nun lässest du deinen
     Diener. -- In A German Requiem. -- New York : G. Schirmer, c1957. --
     p. 83-106. Pub. no.: Ed. 2270.
     Edited by Arthur Mendel. German text with English translation.
     Notes in English. Transposed up M2.

7   Herr, nun lässest du deinen Diener. -- In Musikalische Exequien. --
     Leipzig : VEB Breitkopf & Härtel, 1973. -- p. 60-70. Pub. no.:
     Edition Breitkopf Nr. 4181.
     Edited by Georg Schumann. German text.

SWV 282

[Kleine geistliche Concerte, 1. Theil. Eile mich, Gott zu erretten]

Sacred German text. Sources: Psalm 70.
Solo for soprano with basso continuo. Range of voice part: cl-g2.
Duration: short.

1   Eile mich, Gott zu erretten. -- In SGA. -- 1887. -- Bd. 6, p. 5-6.
     Edited by Philipp Spitta. Figured bass not realized. Original
     German text. Notes in German.

2   Eile mich, Gott zu erretten. -- In NSA. -- 1963. -- Bd. 10, p.
    [1]-3. Pub. no.: BA3664.
       Edited by Wilhelm Ehmann and Hans Hoffman. German text. Words in
    Gothic type. Notes in German and English.

3   Eile mich, Gott, zu erretten. -- In Kleine geistliche Konzerte. --
    Kassel : Bärenreiter, c1963. -- Heft 1, p. [5]-7. Pub. no.:
    Bärenreiter 1701.
       Edited by Hans Hoffmann. Continuo realized by Fritz Dietrich.
    German text. Words in Gothic type. Notes in German and English by
    Wilhelm Ehmann.

5   Eile mich, Gott zu erretten = Hasten, O Lord, to redeem me. --
    Neuhausen-Stuttgart : Hänssler, c1975. Pub. no.: HE 20.282.
       Edited by Günter Graulich. Continuo realized by Paul Horn. German
    text with English translation.

SWV 283

[Kleine geistliche Concerte, 1. Theil. Bringt her dem Herren, ihr
     Gewaltigen]

    Sacred German text. Sources: Psalm 29:1-2. Psalm 66:4.
       Solo for mezzo-soprano with basso continuo. Range of voice part:
    b-d2. Duration: short.

1   Bringt her dem Herren, ihr Gewaltigen. -- In SGA. -- 1887. -- Bd. 6,
    p. 6-7.
       Edited by Philipp Spitta. Figured bass not realized. Original
    German text. Notes in German.

2   Bringt her dem Herren. -- In NSA. -- 1963. -- Bd. 10, p. 8-10. Pub.
    no.: BA3664.
       Edited by Wilhelm Ehmann and Hans Hoffman. German text. Words in
    Gothic type. Notes in German and English.

3   Bringt her dem Herren. -- In Kleine geistliche Konzerte. -- Kassel :
    Bärenreiter, c1963. -- Heft 1, p. 8-10. Pub. no.: Bärenreiter 1701.
       Edited by Hans Hoffmann. Continuo realized by Fritz Dietrich.
    German text. Words in Gothic type. Notes in German and English by
    Wilhelm Ehmann. Transposed up M2.

6   Give to Jehovah = Bringt her dem Herren. -- Boston, Mass. : E.C.
    Schirmer, c1969. Pub. no.: E.C.S. Choral Music no. 2538.
       Edited by William Herrmann. German text with English translation.
    Transposed up M2.

7   Give God the glory. -- New York : C. Fischer, c1982. Pub. no.:
    CM8161.
       Arranged for chorus (SATB). Edited by Hal H. Hopson. English text.
    Transposed up m3.

8   Bringt her dem Herren. -- In Kleine geistliche Konzerte. -- Kassel :
     Bärenreiter, c1963. -- Heft 2, p. [5]-7. Pub. no.: Bärenreiter 1702.
       Edited by Hans Hoffmann. Continuo realized by Fritz Dietrich.
     German text. Words in Gothic type. Notes in German and English by
     Wilhelm Ehmann.

     Other editions: Hänssler HE20.283.

SWV 284

[Kleine geistliche Concerte, 1. Theil. Ich danke dem Herrn von ganzem
     Herzen]

     Sacred German text. Sources: Psalm 111.
       Solo for alto with basso continuo. Range of voice part: f-bflat1.
     Duration: short.

1   Ich danke dem Herrn von ganzem Herzen. -- In SGA. -- 1887. -- Bd.
     6, p. 7-9.
       Edited by Philipp Spitta. Figured bass not realized. Original
     German text. Notes in German.

2   Ich danke dem Herrn von ganzem Herzen. -- In NSA. -- 1963. -- Bd.
     10, p. 11-15. Pub. no.: BA3664.
       Edited by Wilhelm Ehmann and Hans Hoffman. German text. Words in
     Gothic type. Notes in German and English.

3   Ich danke dem Herrn von ganzem Herzen. -- In Kleine geistliche
     Concerte. -- Kassel : Bärenreiter, c1963. -- Heft 2, p. 8-12. Pub.
     no.: Bärenreiter 1702.
       Edited by Hans Hoffmann. Continuo realized by Fritz Dietrich.
     German text. Words in Gothic type. Notes in German and English by
     Wilhelm Ehmann.

     Other editions: Hänssler HE20.284.

SWV 285

[Kleine geistliche Concerte, 1. Theil. O süsser, o freundlicher, o
     gütiger Herr Jesu Christe]

     Sacred German text. Sources: Manuale Augustini.
       Solo for tenor or soprano with basso continuo. Range of voice
     part: c-g1. Duration: short.

1   O süsser, o freundlicher, o gütiger Herr Jesu Christe. -- In SGA. --
     1887. -- Bd. 6, p. 9-11.
       Edited by Philipp Spitta. Figured bass not realized. Original
     German text. Notes in German.

2   O süsser, o freundlicher. -- In NSA. -- 1963. -- Bd. 10, p. 83-87.
     Pub. no.: BA3664.
       Edited by Wilhelm Ehmann and Hans Hoffman. German text. Words in
     Gothic type. Notes in German and English.

3   O süsser, o freundlicher. -- In Kleine geistliche Konzerte. --
    Kassel : Bärenreiter, c1963. -- Heft 1, p. 11-15. Pub. no.:
    Bärenreiter 1701.
       Edited by Hans Hoffmann. Continuo realized by Fritz Dietrich.
    German text. Words in Gothic type. Notes in German and English by
    Wilhelm Ehmann.

5   O süsser, o freundlicher, o gütiger Herr Jesu Christe. --
    Neuhausen-Stuttgart : Hänssler, c1981. Pub. no.: HE 20.285.
       Edited by Günter Graulich. Continuo realized by Paul Horn. German
    text with English translation.

6   O süsser, o freundlicher. -- Stuttgart : Hänssler, [19--]. Pub. no.:
    H. 3150 H.
       Edited by Hermann Stern. German text. Words in Gothic type.

    Other editions: Hänssler 5.026.

SWV 286

[Kleine geistliche Concerte, 1. Theil. Herr ist gross und sehr löblich]

    Sacred German text. Sources: Psalm 145:3-4.
    Duet (SS) with basso continuo. Ranges of voice parts: c1-e2,
    c1-f2. Duration: short.

1   Der Herr ist gross und sehr löblich. -- In SGA. -- 1887. -- Bd. 6,
    p. 11-13.
       Edited by Philipp Spitta. Figured bass not realized. Original
    German text. Notes in German.

2   Der Herr ist gross. -- In NSA. -- 1963. -- Bd. 10, p. 19-23. Pub.
    no.: BA3664.
       Edited by Wilhelm Ehmann and Hans Hoffman. German text. Words in
    Gothic type. Notes in German and English. Transposed up M2.

3   Der Herr ist gross. -- In Kleine geistliche Konzerte. -- Kassel :
    Bärenreiter, c1963. -- Heft 4, p. [5]-9. Pub. no.: Bärenreiter 1138.
       Edited by Hans Hoffmann. German text. Words in Gothic type. Notes
    in German and English by Wilhelm Ehmann. Transposed up M2.

5   Der Herr ist gross und sehr löblich. -- Neuhausen-Stuttgart :
    Hänssler, c1981. Pub. no.: HE 20.286.
       Edited by Günter Graulich. Continuo realized by Paul Horn. German
    text with English translation.

6   Great is our Lord = Der Herr ist Gross. -- [S.l.] : Mercury Music,
    c1942. Pub. no.: 352-00017.
       Edited by Paul Boepple. German text with English translation.

7   Great is the Lord = Der Herr ist gross. -- New York : McAfee Music
    Corp., c1977. Pub. no.: M8049.
       Edited by Don McAfee. German text with English translation.
    Transposed down M2.

8   Great is the Lord = Der Herr ist gross. -- New York : E.C. Schirmer,
     c1971. Pub. no.: E.C.S. choral music no. 2788.
         Edited by Thomas Dunn. German text with English translation. Notes
     in English.

9   Great is the Lord = Der Herr ist gross. -- In Small sacred
     concertos. -- New York : McAfee Music Corp., c1977. -- p. 4-9. Pub.
     no.: DM119.
         Edited by Don McAfee. German text with English translation. Notes
     in English. Transposed down M2.

SWV 287

[Kleine geistliche Concerte, 1. Theil. O lieber Herre Gott, wecke uns
     auf]

     Sacred German text. Sources: O lieber Herre Gott, wecke uns auf.
     Duet (SS) with basso continuo. Ranges of voice parts: c1-f2,
     c1-f2. Duration: short.

1   O lieber Herre Gott, wecke uns auf. -- In SGA. -- 1887. -- Bd. 6, p.
     13-15.
         Edited by Philipp Spitta. Figured bass not realized. Original
     German text. Notes in German.

2   O lieber Herre Gott. -- In NSA. -- 1963. -- Bd. 10, p. 24-28. Pub.
     no.: BA3664.
         Edited by Wilhelm Ehmann and Hans Hoffman. German text. Words in
     Gothic type. Notes in German and English. Transposed up M2.

3   O lieber Herre Gott. -- In Kleine geistliche Konzerte. -- Kassel :
     Bärenreiter, c1963. -- Heft 4, p. 10-14. Pub. no.: Bärenreiter 1138.
         Edited by Hans Hoffmann. German text. Words in Gothic type. Notes
     in German and English by Wilhelm Ehmann. Transposed up M2.

5   O lieber Herre Gott, wecke uns auf. -- Neuhausen-Stuttgart :
     Hänssler, c1972. Pub. no.: HE 20.287.
         Edited by Günter Graulich. Continuo realized by Paul Horn. German
     text with English translation.

6   O blessed Lord our God = O lieber Herre Gott. -- Boston, Mass. :
     E.C. Schirmer, c1971. Pub. no.: E.C.S. no. 2787.
         Edited by Thomas Dunn. German text with English translation. Notes
     in English. Transposed up M2.

7   O gracious Lord God, may we be vigilant and ready = O lieber Herre
     Gott, wecke uns auf. -- St. Louis, Miss. : Concordia Publishing
     House, c1961. Pub. no.: 98-1558.
         Edited by C. Buell Agey. German text with English translation.

8   O mighty God, Our Lord = O lieber Herre Gott. -- New York : Mercury
     Music, c1944. Pub. no.: D.C.S. no. 18.
         Edited by Paul Boepple. German text with English translation.
     Notes in English.

     Other editions: Hänssler 2.029.

SWV 288

[Kleine geistliche Concerte, 1. Theil. Ihr Heiligen lobsinget dem
    Herren]

Sacred German text. Sources: Psalm 30:4-5.
Duet (SS) with basso continuo. Ranges of voice parts: c#1-e2,
a-e2. Duration: short.

1   Ihr Heiligen lobsinget dem Herren. -- In SGA. -- 1887. -- Bd. 6, p.
    16-17.
    Edited by Philipp Spitta. Figured bass not realized. Original
    German text. Notes in German.

2   Ihr Heiligen, lobsinget dem Herren. -- In NSA. -- 1963. -- Bd. 10,
    p. 29-33. Pub. no.: BA3664.
    Edited by Wilhelm Ehmann and Hans Hoffman. German text. Words in
    Gothic type. Notes in German and English.

3   Ihr Heiligen, lobsinget dem Herren. -- In Kleine geistliche
    Concerte. -- Kassel : Bärenreiter, c1963. -- Heft 6, p. [5]-9. Pub.
    no.: Bärenreiter 1704.
    Edited by Wilhelm Ehmann. Continuo realized by Johannes H.E. Koch.
    German text. Words in Gothic type. Notes in German and English.

5   Ihr Heiligen, lobsinget dem Herren. -- Neuhausen-Stuttgart :
    Hänssler, c1981. Pub. no.: HE 20.288.
    Edited by Günter Graulich. Continuo realized by Paul Horn. German
    text with English translation.

6   Ihr Heiligen, lobsinget dem Herren. -- Stuttgart : Hänssler, [19--].
    Pub. no.: H. 2515 H.
    Edited by Ernst Arfken. German text.

7   Praise ye the Lord = Ihr Heiligen, lobsinget dem Herren. --
    Melville, NY : McAfee Music Corp., c1980. Pub. no.: DMC 8090.
    Edited by Don McAfee. German text with English translation.

8   Praise ye the Lord = Ihr Heiligen, lobsinget dem Herren. -- In Small
    sacred concertos. -- Melville, NY : McAfee Music Corp., c1977. -- p.
    10-15. Pub. no.: DM119.
    Edited by Don McAfee. German text with English translation. Notes
    in English.

    Other editions: Hänssler 5.004.

SWV 289

[Kleine geistliche Concerte, 1. Theil. Erhöre mich, wenn ich dich rufe,
    Gott meiner Gerechtigkeit]

Sacred German text. Sources: Psalm 4:1. Psalm 5:2.
Duet (SS) with basso continuo. Ranges of voice parts: d1-e2,
c#1-e2. Duration: short.

1   Erhöre mich, wenn ich dich rufe, Gott meiner Gerechtigkeit. -- In
     SGA. -- 1887. -- Bd. 6, p. 18-19.
       Edited by Philipp Spitta. Figured bass not realized. Original
     German text. Notes in German.

2   Erhöre mich, wenn ich rufe. -- In NSA. -- 1963. -- Bd. 10, p. 34-37.
     Pub. no.: BA3664.
       Edited by Wilhelm Ehmann and Hans Hoffman. German text. Words in
     Gothic type. Notes in German and English.

3   Erhöre mich, wenn ich rufe. -- In Kleine geistliche Konzerte. --
     Kassel : Bärenreiter, c1963. -- Heft 4, p. 15-18. Pub. no.:
     Bärenreiter 1138.
       Edited by Hans Hoffmann. German text. Words in Gothic type. Notes
     in German and English by Wilhelm Ehmann.

5   Erhöre mich, wenn ich rufe = Give ear to me when I call thee. --
     Neuhausen-Stuttgart : Hänssler, c1981. Pub. no.: HE 20.289/02.
       Edited by Günter Graulich. Continuo realized by Paul Horn. German
     text with English translation.

6   Give ear, O Lord = Erhöre mich, wenn ich rufe. -- Boston, Mass. :
     E.C. Schirmer, c1971. Pub. no.: E.C.S. choral music no. 2789.
       German text with English translation. Notes in English.

7   Give ear, O Lord = Erhöre mich. -- [S.l.] : Mercury Music, c1941.
     Pub. no.: 352-00013.
       Edited by Paul Boepple. German text with English translation.
     Notes in English.

8   Hear me, O Lord = Erhöre mich, wenn ich rufe. -- In Small sacred
     concertos. -- Belwin Mills, NY : McAfee Music, c1977. -- p. 16-20.
     Pub. no.: DM119.
       Edited by Don McAfee. German text with English translation. Notes
     in English. Transposed down M2.

SWV 290

[Kleine geistliche Concerte, 1. Theil. Wohl dem, der nicht wandelt im
     Rat der Gottlosen]

     Sacred German text. Sources: Psalm 1:1-3.
       Duet (SA) with basso continuo. Ranges of voice parts: c1-f2,
     g-bflat1. Duration: medium.

1   Wohl dem, der nicht wandelt im Rat der Gottlosen. -- In SGA. --
     1887. -- Bd. 6, p. 19-22.
       Edited by Philipp Spitta. Figured bass not realized. Original
     German text. Notes in German.

2   Wohl dem, der nicht wandelt im Rat der Gottlosen. -- In NSA. --
     1963. -- Bd. 10, p. 69-74. Pub. no.: BA3664.
       Edited by Wilhelm Ehmann and Hans Hoffman. German text. Words in
     Gothic type. Notes in German and English. Transposed up M2.

3   Wohl dem, der nicht wandelt im Rat der Gottlosen. -- In Kleine
     geistliche Concerte. -- Kassel : Bärenreiter, c1963. -- Heft 20.
     Pub. no.: Bärenreiter 1270.
        Edited by Hans Hoffmann. German text. Words in Gothic type. Notes
     in German and English by Wilhelm Ehmann. Transposed up M2.

5   Wohl dem, der nicht wandelt im Rat der Gottlosen = Blest he who goes
     not after words of the godless. -- Neuhausen-Stuttgart : Hänssler,
     c1982. Pub. no.: HE 20.290/02.
        Edited by Günter Graulich. Continuo realized by Paul Horn. German
     text with English translation.

6   Blessed is he who walks not in the paths of godlessness = Wohl dem,
     der nicht wandelt im Rath der Gottlosen. -- Charlotte, N.C. : Brodt
     Music Co., c1960. Pub. no.: No. WC 1.
        Edited by C. Buell Agey. German text with English translation.
     Transposed up M2.

SWV 291

[Kleine geistliche Concerte, 1. Theil. Schaffe in mir, Gott, ein reines
     Herz]

     Sacred German text. Sources: Psalm 51:10-12.
        Duet (ST) with basso continuo. Ranges of voice parts: c#1-e2,
     c-f1. Duration: short.

1   Schaffe in mir, Gott, ein reines Herz. -- In SGA. -- 1887. -- Bd. 6,
     p. 23-24.
        Edited by Philipp Spitta. Figured bass not realized. Original
     German text. Notes in German.

2   Schaffe in mir, Gott, ein reines Herz. -- In NSA. -- 1963. -- Bd.
     11, p. [1]-4. Pub. no.: BA3665.
        Edited by Wilhelm Ehmann. German text. German words in Gothic
     type. Notes in German and English. Transposed up M2.

5   Schaffe in mir, Gott, ein reines Herz. -- Neuhausen-Stuttgart :
     Hänssler, c1981. Pub. no.: HE 20.291.
        Edited by Günter Graulich. Continuo realized by Paul Horn. German
     text with English translation.

6   Lord, create in me a cleaner heart = Schaffe in mir, Gott, ein
     reines Herz. -- Melville, N.Y. : McAfee Music Corp., c1980. Pub.
     no.: DMC 8091.
        Edited by Don McAfee. German text with English translation.
     Transposed down M2.

7   Schaffe in mir, Gott, ein reines Herz. -- Stuttgart : Hänssler,
     c1967. Pub. no.: HE 5.013.
        Edited by Gerhard Trubel. German text.

8   Lord, create in me a cleaner heart = Schaffe in mir, Gott, ein
     reines Herz. -- In Little sacred concertos. -- Melville, N.Y. :
     McAfee Music Corp., c1977. -- p. 43-48. Pub. no.: DM119.
        Edited by Don McAfee. German text with English translation. Notes
     in English. Transposed down M2.

SWV 292

[Kleine geistliche Concerte, 1. Theil. Herr schauet vom Himmel auf der
        Menschen Kinder]

     Sacred German text. Sources: Psalm 14:2-3.
        Duet (SB) with basso continuo. Ranges of voice parts: c#1-e2,
     G-c1. Duration: short.

1   Der Herr schauet vom Himmel auf der menschen Kinder. -- In SGA. --
     1887. -- Bd. 6, p. 25-26.
        Edited by Philipp Spitta. Figured bass not realized. Original
     German text. Notes in German.

2   Der Herr schauet vom Himmel. -- In NSA. -- 1963. -- Bd. 11, p.
     11-14. Pub. no.: BA3665.
        German text. German words in Gothic type. Edited by Wilhelm
     Ehmann. Transposed up M2.

3   Der Herr schauet vom Himmel. -- In Kleine geistliche Konzerte. --
     Kassel : Bärenreiter, c1963. -- Heft 12, p. 5-8. Pub. no.:
     Bärenreiter 3432.
        Edited by Wilhelm Ehmann. Continuo realized by Horst Soenke.
     German text. Words in Gothic type. Notes in German and English.
     Transposed up M2.

5   Der Herr schauet vom Himmel auf der Menschen Kinder. --
     Neuhausen-Stuttgart : Hänssler, c1981. Pub. no.: HE 20.292.
        Edited by Günter Graulich. Continuo realized by Paul Horn. German
     text with English translation.

6   Der Herr schauet vom Himmel. -- [S.l. : s.n., 19--]. Pub. no.: F.H.
     2514.
        Edited by Ernst Arfken. German text.

        Other editions: Hänssler 5.003.

SWV 293

[Kleine geistliche Concerte, 1. Theil. Lobet den Herren, der zu Zion
        wohnet]

     Sacred German text. Sources: Psalm 9:11-12.
        Duet (AA) with basso continuo. Ranges of voice parts: g-a1, g-a1.
     Duration: short.

1   Lobet den Herren, der zu Zion wohnet. -- In SGA. -- 1887. -- Bd. 6,
    p. 27-28.
    Edited by Philipp Spitta. Figured bass not realized. Original
    German text. Notes in German.

2   Lobet den Herren, der zu Zion wohnet. -- In NSA. -- 1963. -- Bd. 10,
    p. 75-79. Pub. no.: BA3664.
    Edited by Wilhelm Ehmann and Hans Hoffman. German text. Words in
    Gothic type. Notes in German and English. Transposed up m3.

3   Lobet den Herren, der zu Zion wohnet. -- In Kleine geistliche
    Concerte. -- Kassel : Bärenreiter, c1963. -- Heft 6, p. 10-14. Pub.
    no.: Bärenreiter 1704.
    Edited by Wilhelm Ehmann. Continuo realized by Johannes H.E. Koch.
    German text. Words in Gothic type. Notes in German and English.
    Transposed up m3.

5   Lobet den Herren, der zu Zion wohnet. -- Neuhausen-Stuttgart :
    Hänssler, c1981. Pub. no.: HE 20.293.
    Edited by Günter Graulich. Continuo realized by Paul Horn. German
    text with English translation.

6   Praise ye Jehovah = Lobet den Herren, der zu Zion wohnet. -- New
    York : Abingdon Press, c1962. Pub. no.: APM-170.
    Edited by C. Buell Agey. German text with English translation.
    Transposed up P4.

7   Praise to the Lord God = Lobet den Herren, der zu Zion wohnet. -- In
    Small sacred concertos. -- Melville, NY : McAfee Music Corp., c1977.
    -- p. 29-33. Pub. no.: DM119.
    Edited by Don McAfee. German text with English translation. Notes
    in English. Transposed up P4.

SWV 294

[Kleine geistliche Concerte, 1. Theil. Eins bitte ich vom Herren]

    Sacred German text. Sources: Psalm 27:4.
    Duet (TT) with basso continuo. Ranges of voice parts: d-f1, c-f1.
    Duration: short.

1   Eins bitte ich vom Herren. -- In SGA. -- 1887. -- Bd. 6, p. 29-30.
    Edited by Philipp Spitta. Figured bass not realized. Original
    German text. Notes in German.

2   Eins bitte ich vom Herren. -- In NSA. -- 1963. -- Bd. 10, p.
    100-102. Pub. no.: BA3664.
    Edited by Wilhelm Ehmann and Hans Hoffman. German text. Words in
    Gothic type. Notes in German and English.

5   Eins bitte ich vom Herren. -- Neuhausen-Stuttgart : Hänssler, c1981.
    Pub. no.: HE 20.294.
    Edited by Günter Graulich. Continuo realized by Paul Horn. German
    text with English translation.

6   One thing I ask of the Lord = Eins bitte ich vom Herren. --
     Melville, N.Y. : McAfee Music Corp., c1977. Pub. no.: DMC 8059.
        Edited by Don McAfee. German text with English translation.
     Transposed down M2.

7   One thing I ask of the Lord = Eins bitte ich vom Herren. -- In Small
     sacred concertos. -- Melville, N.Y. : McAfee Music Corp., c1977. --
     p. 34-38. Pub. no.: DM119.
        Edited by Don McAfee. German text with English translation. Notes
     in English. Transposed down M2.

SWV 295

[Kleine geistliche Concerte, 1. Theil. O hilf, Christe, Gottes Sohn]

     Sacred German and Latin text. Sources: Weisse, Michael. Christus der
     uns selig macht.
        Duet (TT) with basso continuo. Ranges of voice parts: e-f1, d-f1.
     Duration: short.

1   O hilf, Christe, Gottes Sohn. -- In SGA. -- 1887. -- Bd. 6, p.
     30-31.
        Edited by Philipp Spitta. Figured bass not realized. Original
     German and Latin text. Notes in German.

2   O hilf, Christe, Gottes Sohn = Christe Deus adjuva. -- In NSA. --
     1963. -- Bd. 10, p. 103-105. Pub. no.: BA3664.
        Edited by Wilhelm Ehmann and Hans Hoffman. Text in German and
     Latin. German words in Gothic type. Notes in German and English.

5   O hilf, Christe, Gottes Sohn = Christe Deus adjuva = O help, Christ,
     thou Son of God. -- Neuhausen-Stuttgart : Hänssler, c1977. Pub. no.:
     HE 20.295.
        Edited by Günter Graulich. Continuo realized by Paul Horn. German
     and Latin text.

6   O Jesus, thou Son of God = O hilf, Christe, Gottes Sohn = Christe
     Deus adjuva. -- Melville, N.Y. : McAfee Music Corp., c1971. Pub.
     no.: DMC 8094.
        Edited by Don McAfee. German and Latin text with English
     translation. Transposed down M2.

7   O Jesus, thou Son of God = O hilf, Christe, Gottes Sohn = Christe
     Deus adjuva. -- In Small sacred concertos. -- Melville, N.Y. :
     McAfee Music Corp., c1977. -- p. 39-42. Pub. no.: DM119.
        Edited by Don McAfee. German and Latin text with English
     translation. Notes in English. Transposed down M2.

     Other editions: Hänssler 2.029.

SWV 296

[Kleine geistliche Concerte, 1. Theil. Fürchte dich nicht, ich bin mit
    dir]

    Sacred German text. Sources: Isaiah 41:10.
    Duet (BB) with basso continuo. Ranges of voice parts: E-d1,
    F#-bflat. Duration: short.

1   Fürchte dich nicht, ich bin mit dir. -- In SGA. -- 1887. -- Bd. 6,
    p. 32-33.
    Edited by Philipp Spitta. Figured bass not realized. Original
    German text. Notes in German.

2   Fürchte dich nicht. -- In NSA. -- 1963. -- Bd. 10, p. 112-115. Pub.
    no.: BA3664.
    Edited by Wilhelm Ehmann and Hans Hoffman. German text. Words in
    Gothic type. Notes in German and English.

3   Fürchte dich nicht. -- In Kleine geistliche Konzerte. -- Kassel :
    Bärenreiter, c1963. -- Heft 7, p. 18-21. Pub. no.: Bärenreiter 1705.
    Edited by Wilhelm Ehmann. Continuo realized by Johannes H.E. Koch.
    German text. Words in Gothic type. Notes in German and English.

5   Fürchte dich nicht, ich bin mit dir. -- Neuhausen-Stuttgart :
    Hänssler, c1981. Pub. no.: HE 20.296.
    Edited by Günter Graulich. Continuo realized by Paul Horn. German
    text with English translation.

SWV 297

[Kleine geistliche Concerte, 1. Theil. O Herr hilf, o Herr lass wohl
    gelingen]

    Sacred German text. Sources: Psalm 118:25-26.
    Trio (SST) with basso continuo. Ranges of voice parts: c1-f2,
    c#1-f2, c-f1. Duration: short.

1   O Herr hilf, o Herr lass wohl gelingen. -- In SGA. -- 1887. -- Bd.
    6, p. 33-35.
    Edited by Philipp Spitta. Figured bass not realized. Original
    German text. Notes in German.

2   O Herr hilf. -- In NSA. -- 1963. -- Bd. 11, p. 19-22. Pub. no.:
    BA3665.
    Edited by Wilhelm Ehmann. German text. German words in Gothic
    type. Notes in German and English. Transposed up M2.

5   O Herr hilf, o Herr lass wohl gelingen = O save us Lord. --
    Neuhausen-Stuttgart : Hänssler, c1967. Pub. no.: XX 297.
    Edited by Günter Graulich. Continuo realized by Paul Horn. German
    text with English translation. Notes in German and English.

    Other editions: Bärenreiter BA3431; Hänssler 5.031.

SWV 298

[Kleine geistliche Concerte, 1. Theil. Blut Jesu Christi, des Sohnes
Gottes]

Sacred German text. Sources: John, 1st, 1:7.
Trio (SSB) with basso continuo. Ranges of voice parts: cl-f2,
cl-eflat2, F-cl. Duration: short.

1   Das Blut Jesu Christi, des Sohnes Gottes. -- In SGA. -- 1887. -- Bd.
     6, p. 36-37.
     Edited by Philipp Spitta. Figured bass not realized. Original
     German text. Notes in German.

2   Das Blut Jesu Christi. -- In NSA. -- 1963. -- Bd. 11, p. 30-33. Pub.
     no.: BA3665.
     Edited by Wilhelm Ehmann. German text. German words in Gothic
     type. Notes in German and English. Transposed up M2.

3   Das Blut Jesu Christi. -- In Kleine geistliche Konzerte. -- Kassel :
     Bärenreiter, c1963. -- Heft 12, p. 16-19. Pub. no.: Bärenreiter
     3432.
     Edited by Wilhelm Ehmann. Continuo realized by Horst Soenke.
     German text. Words in Gothic type. Notes in German and English.
     Transposed up M2.

5   Das Blut Jesu Christi. -- Neuhausen-Stuttgart : Hänssler, c1972.
     Pub. no.: HE 20.298.
     Edited by Günter Graulich. Continuo realized by Paul Horn. German
     text with English translation.

     Other editions: Hänssler 5.001.

SWV 299

[Kleine geistliche Concerte, 1. Theil. Gottseligkeit ist zu allen Dingen
nütz]

Sacred German text. Sources: Timothy, 1st, 4:8.
Trio (SSB) with basso continuo. Ranges of voice parts: gl-g2,
fl-g2, c-cl. Duration: short.

1   Die Gottseligkeit ist zu allen Dingen nütz. -- In SGA. -- 1887. --
     Bd. 6, p. 38-39.
     Edited by Philipp Spitta. Figured bass not realized. Original
     German text. Notes in German.

2   Die Gottseligkeit. -- In NSA. -- 1963. -- Bd. 11, p. 34-36. Pub.
     no.: BA3665.
     Edited by Wilhelm Ehmann. German text. German words in Gothic
     type. Notes in German and English. Transposed up m3.

3   Die Gottseligkeit. -- In Kleine geistliche Konzerte. -- Kassel :
    Bärenreiter, c1963. -- Heft 12, p. 9-11. Pub. no.: Bärenreiter 3432.
      Edited by Wilhelm Ehmann. Continuo realized by Horst Soenke.
    German text. Words in Gothic type. Notes in German and English.
    Transposed up m3.

5   Die Gottseligkeit ist zu allen Dingen nütz = The love of God is most
    useful in all things. -- Neuhausen-Stuttgart : Hänssler, c1972. Pub.
    no.: HE 20.299.
      Edited by Günter Graulich. Continuo realized by Paul Horn. German
    text with English translation. Transposed up P4.

SWV 300

[Kleine geistliche Concerte, 1. Theil. Himmel und Erde vergehen]

    Sacred German text. Sources: Luke 21:33.
      Trio (BBB) with basso continuo. Ranges of voice parts: F-d1, C-c1,
    C-c1. Duration: short.

1   Himmel und Erde vergehen. -- In SGA. -- 1887. -- Bd. 6, p. 39-40.
      Edited by Philipp Spitta. Figured bass not realized. Original
    German text. Notes in German.

2   Himmel und Erde vergehen. -- In NSA. -- 1963. -- Bd. 10, p. 134-136.
    Pub. no.: BA3664.
      Edited by Wilhelm Ehmann and Hans Hoffman. German text. Words in
    Gothic type. Notes in German and English. Transposed up M2.

3   Himmel und Erde vergehen. -- In Kleine geistliche Konzerte. --
    Kassel : Bärenreiter, c1963. -- Heft 7, p. 22-24. Pub. no.:
    Bärenreiter 1705.
      Edited by Wilhelm Ehmann. Continuo realized by Johannes H.E. Koch.
    German text. Words in Gothic type. Notes in German and English.
    Transposed up M2.

5   Himmel und Erden vergehen. -- Neuhausen-Stuttgart : Hänssler, c1981.
    Pub. no.: HE 20.300.
      Edited by Günter Graulich. Continuo realized by Paul Horn. German
    text with English translation.

SWV 301

[Kleine geistliche Concerte, 1. Theil. Nun komm, der Heiden Heiland]

    Sacred German and Latin text. Sources: Ambrose, Saint. Veni
    redemptor gentium. Luther, Martin. Nun komm, der Heiden Heiland.
      Quartet (SSBB) with basso continuo. Ranges of voice parts: c#1-g2,
    c1-g2, G-d1, F-g. Duration: short.

1   Nun komm, der Heiden Heiland. -- In SGA. -- 1887. -- Bd. 6, p.
    41-44.
      Edited by Philipp Spitta. Figured bass not realized. Original
    German and Latin text. Notes in German.

2   Nun komm, der Heiden Heiland = Veni redemtor gentium. -- In NSA. --
1963. -- Bd. 11, p. 91-96. Pub. no.: BA3665.
    Edited by Wilhelm Ehmann. Text in German and Latin. German words
in Gothic type. Transposed up M2.

5   Nun komm, der Heiden Heiland = Veni redemtor gentium. --
Neuhausen-Stuttgart : Hänssler, c1981. Pub. no.: HE 20.301.
    Edited by Günter Graulich. Continuo realized by Paul Horn. German
and Latin text.

SWV 302

[Kleine geistliche Concerte, 1. Theil. Kind ist uns geboren]

    Sacred German text. Sources: Isaiah 9:6-7.
    Quartet (SATB) with basso continuo. Ranges of voice parts:
c1-eflat2, f-a1, c-eflat1, F-d1. Duration: medium.

1   Ein Kind ist uns geboren. -- In SGA. -- 1887. -- Bd. 6, p. 44-50.
    Edited by Philipp Spitta. Figured bass not realized. Original
German text. Notes in German.

2   Ein Kind ist uns geboren. -- In NSA. -- 1963. -- Bd. 11, p. 97-103.
Pub. no.: BA3665.
    Edited by Hans Hoffman. German text. German words in Gothic type.
Notes in German and English. Transposed up M3.

3   Ein Kind ist uns geboren. -- In Kleine geistliche Konzerte. --
Kassel : Bärenreiter, c1963. -- Heft 3, p. [5]-11. Pub. no.:
Bärenreiter 1703.
    Edited by Hans Hoffmann. Continuo realized by Karl Grebe. German
text. Words in Gothic type. Notes in German and English by Wilhelm
Ehmann. Transposed up M3.

5   Ein Kind ist uns geboren = A child is born unto us. --
Neuhausen-Stuttgart : Hänssler, c1969. Pub. no.: HE 20.302.
    Edited by Günter Graulich. Continuo realized by Paul Horn. German
text with English translation. Notes in German and English.

6   A child to us is born = Ein Kind ist uns geboren. -- New York : G.
Schirmer, c1961. Pub. no.: 44866.
    Edited by C. Buell Agey. German text with English translation.
Notes in English. Transposed up M2.

SWV 303

[Kleine geistliche Concerte, 1. Theil. Wir gläuben all an einen Gott]

    Sacred German text. Sources: Nicene Creed. German.
    Quartet (SSTB) with basso continuo. Ranges of voice parts: c#1-e2,
a-e2, c-e1, D-c1. Duration: medium.

1   Wir gläuben all an einen Gott. -- In SGA. -- 1887. -- Bd. 6, p.
    50-54.
    Edited by Philipp Spitta. Figured bass not realized. Original
    German text. Notes in German.

2   Wir gläuben all an einen Gott. -- In NSA. -- 1963. -- Bd. 11, p.
    84-90. Pub. no.: BA3665.
    Edited by Hans Hoffman. German text. German words in Gothic type.
    Notes in German and English. Transposed up m3.

3   Wir gläuben all an einen Gott. -- In Kleine geistliche Konzerte. --
    Kassel : Bärenreiter, c1963. -- Heft 3, p. 12-18. Pub. no.:
    Bärenreiter 1703.
    Edited by Hans Hoffmann. Continuo realized by Karl Grebe. German
    text. Words in Gothic type. Notes in German and English by Wilhelm
    Ehmann. Transposed up m3.

    Other editions: Hänssler HE20.303.

SWV 304

[Kleine geistliche Concerte, 1. Theil. Siehe, mein Fürsprecher ist im
    Himmel]

    Sacred German text. Sources: Meditationes Augustini.
    Quartet (SATB) with basso continuo and optional chorus (SATB).
    Ranges of voice parts: d1-e2, f#-a1, c-f1, D-c1/ g1-e2, c1-g1, e-e1,
    D-c1. Duration: short.

1   Siehe, mein Fürsprecher ist im Himmel. -- In SGA. -- 1887. -- Bd. 6,
    p. 54-58.
    Edited by Philipp Spitta. Figured bass not realized. Original
    German text. Notes in German.

2   Siehe, mein Fürsprecher ist im Himmel. -- In NSA. -- 1963. -- Bd.
    11, p. 104-109. Pub. no.: BA3665.
    Edited by Hans Hoffman. German text. German words in Gothic type.
    Notes in German and English. Transposed up m3.

3   Siehe, mein Fürsprecher. -- In Kleine geistliche Konzerte. -- Kassel
    : Bärenreiter, c1963. -- Heft 3, p. 19-24. Pub. no.: Bärenreiter
    1703.
    Edited by Hans Hoffmann. Continuo realized by Karl Grebe. German
    text. Words in Gothic type. Notes in German and English by Wilhelm
    Ehmann. Transposed up m3.

5   Siehe, mein Fürsprecher ist im Himmel = See, I have an advocate in
    Heaven. -- Neuhausen-Stuttgart : Hänssler, c1972. Pub. no.: HE
    20.304.
    Edited by Günter Graulich. Continuo realized by Paul Horn. German
    text with English translation.

SWV 305

[Kleine geistliche Concerte, 1. Theil. Ich hab mein Sach Gott
heimgestellt]

Sacred German and Latin text. Sources: Leon, Johann. Ich hab mein
Sach Gott heimgestellt.
Quintet (SSATB) with basso continuo and optional chorus (SSATB).
Ranges of voice parts: d1-g2, c1-f2, f-bflat1, c-g1, F-bflat.
Duration: long.

1   Ich hab mein Sach Gott heimgestellt. -- In SGA. -- 1887. -- Bd. 6,
    p. 59-88.
    Edited by Philipp Spitta. Figured bass not realized. Original
    German and Latin text. Notes in German.

2   Ich hab mein Sach Gott heimgestellt = Meas dicavi res Deo. -- In
    NSA. -- 1963. -- Bd. 12, p. [1]-35. Pub. no.: BA3666.
    Edited by Wilhelm Ehmann. Text in German and Latin. German words
    in Gothic type. Notes in German and English.

3   Ich hab mein Sach Gott heimgestellt. -- In Kleine geistliche
    Concerte. -- Kassel : Bärenreiter, c1956. -- Heft 10. Pub. no.:
    Bärenreiter 1708.
    Edited by Wilhelm Ehmann. Continuo realized by Johannes H.E. Koch.
    German text. Words in Gothic type. Notes in German.

    Other editions: Hänssler HE20.305.

SWV 306

[Kleine geistliche Concerte, 2. Theil. Ich will den Herren loben
allezeit]

Sacred German text. Sources: Psalm 34:1-4. Psalm 34:6.
Solo for soprano with basso continuo. Range of voice part: c1-g2.
Duration: short.

1   Ich will den Herren loben allezeit. -- In SGA. -- 1887. -- Bd. 6, p.
    93-94.
    Edited by Philipp Spitta. Figured bass not realized. Original
    German text. Notes in German.

2   Ich will den Herren loben allezeit. -- In NSA. -- 1963. -- Bd. 10,
    p. 4-7. Pub. no.: BA3664.
    Edited by Wilhelm Ehmann and Hans Hoffman. German text. Words in
    Gothic type. Notes in German and English.

3   Ich will den Herren loben allezeit. -- In Kleine geistliche
    Concerte. -- Kassel : Bärenreiter, c1963. -- Heft 1, p. 16-19. Pub.
    no.: Bärenreiter 1701.
    Edited by Hans Hoffmann. Continuo realized by Fritz Dietrich.
    German text. Words in Gothic type. Notes in German and English by
    Wilhelm Ehmann.

5   Ich will den Herren loben allezeit. -- Neuhausen-Stuttgart :
Hänssler, c1975. Pub. no.: HE 20.306.
    Edited by Günter Graulich. Continuo realized by Paul Horn. German
text with English translation.

SWV 307

[Kleine geistliche Concerte, 2. Theil. Was hast du verwirket, o du
    allerholdseligster Knab]

    Sacred German text. Sources: Meditationes Augustini.
      Solo for alto with basso continuo. Range of voice part: f-al.
Duration: short.

1   Was hast du verwirket, o du allerholdseligster Knab. -- In SGA. --
1887. -- Bd. 6, p. 94-95.
    Edited by Philipp Spitta. Figured bass not realized. Original
German text. Notes in German.

2   Was hast du verwirket. -- In NSA. -- 1963. -- Bd. 10, p. 16-18. Pub.
no.: BA3664.
    Edited by Wilhelm Ehmann and Hans Hoffman. German text. Words in
Gothic type. Notes in German and English. Transposed up M2.

3   Was hast du verwirket. -- In Kleine geistliche Konzerte. -- Kassel :
Bärenreiter, c1963. -- Heft 2, p. 13-15. Pub. no.: Bärenreiter 1702.
    Edited by Hans Hoffmann. Continuo realized by Fritz Dietrich.
German text. Words in Gothic type. Notes in German and English by
Wilhelm Ehmann. Transposed up M2.

    Other editions: Hänssler HE20.307.

SWV 308

[Kleine geistliche Concerte, 2. Theil. O Jesu, nomen dulce]

    Sacred Latin text. Sources: Jesu, dulcis memoria.
      Solo for tenor with basso continuo. Range of voice part: d-gl.
Duration: short.

1   O Jesu, nomen dulce. -- In SGA. -- 1887. -- Bd. 6, p. 96-97.
    Edited by Philipp Spitta. Figured bass not realized. Original
German text. Notes in German.

2   O Jesu, nomen dulce. -- In NSA. -- 1963. -- Bd. 10, p. 88-90. Pub.
no.: BA3664.
    Edited by Wilhelm Ehmann and Hans Hoffman. Latin text. Notes in
German and English.

3   O Jesu, nomen dulce. -- In Kleine geistliche Konzerte. -- Kassel :
Bärenreiter, c1959. -- Heft 14, p. [5]-7. Pub. no.: Bärenreiter
3434.
    Edited by Wilhelm Ehmann. Continuo realized by Horst Soenke. Latin
text. Notes in German and English.

Other editions: Hänssler HE20.308.

SWV 309

[Kleine geistliche Concerte, 2. Theil. O misericordissime Jesu]

Sacred Latin text. Sources: Meditationes Augustini.
Solo for tenor with basso continuo. Range of voice part: c-g1.
Duration: short.

1   O misericordissime Jesu. -- In SGA. -- 1887. -- Bd. 6, p. 97-98.
Edited by Philipp Spitta. Figured bass not realized. Original
Latin text. Notes in German.

2   O misericordissime Jesu. -- In NSA. -- 1963. -- Bd. 10, p. 91-95.
Pub. no.: BA3664.
Edited by Wilhelm Ehmann and Hans Hoffman. Latin text. Notes in
German and English.

3   O misericordissime Jesu. -- In Kleine geistliche Konzerte. -- Kassel
: Bärenreiter, c1959. -- Heft 14, p. 8-12. Pub. no.: Bärenreiter
3434.
Edited by Wilhelm Ehmann. Continuo realized by Horst Soenke. Latin
text. Notes in German and English.

Other editions: Hänssler HE20.309.

SWV 310

[Kleine geistliche Concerte, 2. Theil. Ich liege und schlafe]

Sacred German text. Sources: Psalm 3:5-8.
Solo for bass with basso continuo. Range of voice part: E-c1.
Duration: short.

1   Ich liege und schlafe, und erwache. -- In SGA. -- 1887. -- Bd. 6, p.
98-99.
Edited by Philipp Spitta. Figured bass not realized. Original
German text. Notes in German.

2   Ich liege und schlafe. -- In NSA. -- 1963. -- Bd. 10, p. 96-99. Pub.
no.: BA3664.
Edited by Wilhelm Ehmann and Hans Hoffman. German text. Words in
Gothic type. Notes in German and English. Transposed up m3.

3   Ich liege und schlafe. -- In Kleine geistliche Konzerte. -- Kassel :
Bärenreiter, c1963. -- Heft 7, p. [5]-8. Pub. no.: Bärenreiter 1705.
Edited by Wilhelm Ehmann. Continuo realized by Johannes H.E. Koch.
German text. Words in Gothic type. Notes in German and English.
Transposed up m3.

5   Ich liege und schlafe. -- Stuttgart : Hänssler, [19--]. Pub. no.: F.
2579 H.
Edited by Gerhard Trubel. German text. Transposed up P4.

Other editions: Hänssler HE20.310; 5.015.

SWV 311

[Kleine geistliche Concerte, 2. Theil. Habe deine Lust an dem Herren]

Sacred German text. Sources: Psalm 37:1-5.
Duet (SS) with basso continuo. Ranges of voice parts: c1-g2,
c1-g2. Duration: medium.

1   Habe deine Lust an dem Herren. -- In SGA. -- 1887. -- Bd. 6, p.
     100-104.
     Edited by Philipp Spitta. Figured bass not realized. Original
     German text. Notes in German.

2   Habe deine Lust an dem Herren. -- In NSA. -- 1963. -- Bd. 10, p.
     38-47. Pub. no.: BA3664.
     Edited by Wilhelm Ehmann and Hans Hoffman. German text. Words in
     Gothic type. Notes in German and English.

3   Habe deine Lust an dem Herren. -- In Kleine geistliche Konzerte. --
     Kassel : Bärenreiter, c1963. -- Heft 4, p. 19-28. Pub. no.:
     Bärenreiter 1138.
     Edited by Hans Hoffmann. German text. Words in Gothic type. Notes
     in German and English by Wilhelm Ehmann.

     Other editions: Hänssler HE20.311.

SWV 312

[Kleine geistliche Concerte, 2. Theil. Herr, ich hoffe darauf, dass du
     so gnädig bist]

Sacred German text. Sources: Psalm 13:5-6.
Duet (SS) with basso continuo. Ranges of voice parts: c1-f2,
bflat-e2. Duration: short.

1   Herr, ich hoffe darauf, dass du so gnädig bist. -- In SGA. -- 1887.
     -- Bd. 6, p. 105-107.
     Edited by Philipp Spitta. Figured bass not realized. Original
     German text. Notes in German.

2   Herr, ich hoffe darauf. -- In NSA. -- 1963. -- Bd. 10, p. 48-52.
     Pub. no.: BA3664.
     Edited by Wilhelm Ehmann and Hans Hoffman. German text. Words in
     Gothic type. Notes in German and English. Transposed up M2.

3   Herr, ich hoffe darauf. -- In Kleine geistliche Konzerte. -- Kassel
     : Bärenreiter, c1963. -- Heft 6, p. 15-19. Pub. no.: Bärenreiter
     1704.
     Edited by Wilhelm Ehmann. Continuo realized by Johannes H.E. Koch.
     German text. Words in Gothic type. Notes in German and English.
     Transposed up M2.

5   Herr, ich hoffe darauf, dass du so gnädig bist. --
     Neuhausen-Stuttgart : Hänssler, c1977. Pub. no.: HE 20.312.
        Edited by Günter Graulich. Continuo realized by Paul Horn. German
     text with English translation.

6   Lord, my hope is in thee = Herr, ich hoffe darauf. -- Melville, N.Y.
     : McAfee Music Corp., c1971. Pub. no.: DMC 8093.
        Edited by Don McAfee. German text with English translation.

7   Lord, my hope is in thee = Herr, ich hoffe darauf. -- In Small
     sacred concertos. -- Melville, N.Y. : McAfee Music Corp., c1977. --
     p. 21-28. Pub. no.: DM119.
        Edited by Don McAfee. German text with English translation. Notes
     in English.

SWV 313

[Kleine geistliche Concerte, 2. Theil. Bone Jesu, verbum Patris]

     Sacred Latin text. Sources: Meditationes Augustini.
        Duet (SS) with basso continuo. Ranges of voice parts: d1-g2,
     c1-g2. Duration: medium.

1   Bone Jesu, verbum Patris. -- In SGA. -- 1887. -- Bd. 6, p. 107-111.
        Edited by Philipp Spitta. Figured bass not realized. Original
     Latin text. Notes in German.

2   Bone Jesu, verbum Patris. -- In NSA. -- 1963. -- Bd. 10, p. 53-62.
     Pub. no.: BA3664.
        Edited by Wilhelm Ehmann and Hans Hoffman. Latin text. Notes in
     German and English.

3   Bone Jesu, verbum Patris. -- In Kleine geistliche Konzerte. --
     Kassel : Bärenreiter, c1963. -- Heft 15, p. [5]-14. Pub. no.:
     Bärenreiter 3435.
        Edited by Wilhelm Ehmann. Continuo realized by Horst Soenke. Latin
     text. Notes in German and English.

     Other editions: Hänssler HE20.313.

SWV 314

[Kleine geistliche Concerte, 2. Theil. Verbum caro factum est]

     Sacred Latin text. Sources: John 1:14.
        Duet (SS) with basso continuo. Ranges of voice parts: c1-g2,
     c1-g2. Duration: medium.

1   Verbum caro factum est. -- In SGA. -- 1887. -- Bd. 6, p. 111-114.
        Edited by Philipp Spitta. Figured bass not realized. Original
     Latin text. Notes in German.

2 Verbum caro factum est. -- In NSA. -- 1963. -- Bd. 10, p. 63-68.
   Pub. no.: BA3664.
   Edited by Wilhelm Ehmann and Hans Hoffman. Latin text. Notes in
   German and English.

3 Verbum caro factum est. -- In Kleine geistliche Konzerte. -- Kassel
   : Bärenreiter, c1963. -- Heft 15, p. 15-20. Pub. no.: Bärenreiter
   3435.
   Edited by Wilhelm Ehmann. Continuo realized by Horst Soenke. Latin
   text. Notes in German and English.

   Other editions: Hänssler HE20.314.

SWV 315

[Kleine geistliche Concerte, 2. Theil. Hodie Christus natus est]

   Sacred Latin text. Sources: Hodie Christus natus est.
   Duet (ST) with basso continuo. Ranges of voice parts: c1-g2, c-g1.
   Duration: short.

1 Hodie Christus natus est. -- In SGA. -- 1887. -- Bd. 6, p. 114-117.
   Edited by Philipp Spitta. Figured bass not realized. Original
   Latin text. Notes in German.

2 Hodie Christus natus est. -- In NSA. -- 1963. -- Bd. 11, p. 5-10.
   Pub. no.: BA3665.
   Edited by Wilhelm Ehmann. Latin text. Notes in German and English.

3 Hodie Christus natus est. -- In Kleine geistliche Konzerte. --
   Kassel : Bärenreiter, c1960. -- Heft 17, p. 9-14. Pub. no.:
   Bärenreiter 3437.
   Edited by Wilhelm Ehmann. Continuo realized by Horst Soenke. Latin
   text. Notes in German and English.

   Other editions: Hänssler HE20.315.

SWV 316

[Kleine geistliche Concerte, 2. Theil. Wann unsre Augen schlafen ein]

   Sacred German and Latin text. Sources: Alber, Erasmus. Christe, der
   du bist der helle Tag.
   Duet (SB) with basso continuo. Ranges of voice parts: c1-g2, D-c1.
   Duration: short.

1 Wann unsre Augen schlafen ein. -- In SGA. -- 1887. -- Bd. 6, p.
   117-119.
   Edited by Philipp Spitta. Figured bass not realized. Original
   German and Latin text. Notes in German.

2 Wann unsre Augen schlafen ein = Quando se claudunt lumina. -- In
   NSA. -- 1963. -- Bd. 11, p. 15-18. Pub. no.: BA3665.
   Edited by Wilhelm Ehmann. Text in German and Latin. German words
   in Gothic type. Transposed up M2.

3   Wann unsre Augen schlafen ein = Quando se claudunt lumina. -- In
    Kleine geistliche Concerte. -- Kassel : Bärenreiter, c1963. -- Heft
    12, p. 12-15. Pub. no.: Bärenreiter 3432.
      Edited by Wilhelm Ehmann. Continuo realized by Horst Soenke.
    German and Latin text. German words in Gothic type. Notes in German
    and English. Transposed up M2.

5   Wann unsre Augen schlafen ein = Quando se claudunt lumina. --
    Neuhausen-Stuttgart : Hänssler, c1983. Pub. no.: HE 20.316/02.
      Edited by Günter Graulich. Continuo realized by Paul Horn. German
    and Latin text.

    Other editions: Hänssler 5.030.

SWV 317

[Kleine geistliche Concerte, 2. Theil. Meister, wir haben die ganze
      Nacht gearbeitet]

    Sacred German text. Sources: Luke 5:5.
      Duet (TT) with basso continuo. Ranges of voice parts: c-el, c-fl.
    Duration: short.

1   Meister, wir haben die ganze Nacht gearbeitet. -- In SGA. -- 1887.
    -- Bd. 6, p. 119-120.
      Edited by Philipp Spitta. Figured bass not realized. Original
    German text. Notes in German.

2   Meister, wir haben die ganze Nacht gearbeitet. -- In NSA. -- 1963.
    -- Bd. 10, p. 106-108. Pub. no.: BA3664.
      Edited by Wilhelm Ehmann and Hans Hoffman. German text. Words in
    Gothic type. Notes in German and English.

5   Meister, wir haben die ganze Nacht gearbeitet = Master, thou
    laboring all the night. -- Neuhausen-Stuttgart : Hänssler, c1983.
    Pub. no.: HE 20.317/02.
      Edited by Günter Graulich. Continuo realized by Paul Horn. German
    text with English translation.

6   Meister, wir haben die ganze Nacht gearbeitet. -- Stuttgart :
    Hänssler, [19--]. Pub. no.: H. 3156 H.
      Edited by Hermann Stern. German text. Words in Gothic type.

    Other editions: Hänssler 5.032.

SWV 318

[Kleine geistliche Concerte, 2. Theil. Furcht des Herren ist der
      Weisheit Anfang]

    Sacred German text. Sources: Psalm 111:10.
      Duet (TT) with basso continuo. Ranges of voice parts: d-fl, d-dl.
    Duration: short.

1   Die Furcht des Herren ist der Weisheit Anfang. -- In SGA. -- 1887.
    -- Bd. 6, p. 120-122.
      Edited by Philipp Spitta. Figured bass not realized. Original
    German text. Notes in German.

2   Die Furcht des Herren. -- In NSA. -- 1963. -- Bd. 10, p. 109-111.
    Pub. no.: BA3664.
      Edited by Wilhelm Ehmann and Hans Hoffman. German text. Words in
    Gothic type. Notes in German and English.

5   Die Furcht des Herren ist der Weisheit Anfang = Fear of the Lord God
    is the source of wisdom. -- Neuhausen-Stuttgart : Hänssler, c1972.
    Pub. no.: HE 20.318.
      Edited by Günter Graulich. Continuo realized by Paul Horn. German
    text with English translation.

    Other editions: Hänssler 5.016.

SWV 319

[Kleine geistliche Concerte, 2. Theil. Ich beuge meine Knie gegen dem
      Vater]

    Sacred German text. Sources: Ephesians 3:14-17.
      Duet (BB) with basso continuo. Ranges of voice parts: F-c1, F-c1.
    Duration: short.

1   Ich beuge meine Knie gegen dem Vater unsers Herren Jesu Christi. --
    In SGA. -- 1887. -- Bd. 6, p. 122-124.
      Edited by Philipp Spitta. Figured bass not realized. Original
    German text. Notes in German.

2   Ich beuge meine Knie. -- In NSA. -- 1963. -- Bd. 10, p. 116-120.
    Pub. no.: BA3664.
      Edited by Wilhelm Ehmann and Hans Hoffman. German text. Words in
    Gothic type. Notes in German and English.

3   Ich beuge meine Knie. -- In Kleine geistliche Konzerte. -- Kassel :
    Bärenreiter, c1963. -- Heft 7, p. 9-13. Pub. no.: Bärenreiter 1705.
      Edited by Wilhelm Ehmann. Continuo realized by Johannes H.E. Koch.
    German text. Words in Gothic type. Notes in German and English.

5   Ich beuge meine Knie gegen den Vater = I bow and bend the knee unto
    the Father of Lord Jesus Christ. -- Neuhausen-Stuttgart : Hänssler,
    c1983. Pub. no.: HE 20.319/02.
      Edited by Günter Graulich. Continuo realized by Paul Horn. German
    text with English translation.

SWV 320

[Kleine geistliche Concerte, 2. Theil. Ich bin jung gewesen und bin alt
      worden]

Sacred German text. Sources: Psalm 37:25.
Duet (BB) with basso continuo. Ranges of voice parts: F-c1,
D-bflat. Duration: short.

1   Ich bin jung gewesen und bin alt worden. -- In SGA. -- 1887. -- Bd.
6, p. 124-126.
Edited by Philipp Spitta. Figured bass not realized. Original
German text. Notes in German.

2   Ich bin jung gewesen. -- In NSA. -- 1963. -- Bd. 10, 121-124. Pub.
no.: BA3664.
Edited by Wilhelm Ehmann and Hans Hoffman. German text. Words in
Gothic type. Notes in German and English. Transposed up M3.

3   Ich bin jung gewesen. -- In Kleine geistliche Konzerte. -- Kassel :
Bärenreiter, c1963. -- Heft 7, p. 14-17. Pub. no.: Bärenreiter 1705.
Edited by Wilhelm Ehmann. Continuo realized by Johannes H.E. Koch.
German text. Words in Gothic type. Notes in German and English.
Transposed up M3.

5   Ich bin jung gewesen und bin alt worden. -- Neuhausen-Stuttgart :
Hänssler, c1983. Pub. no.: HE 20.320/02.
Edited by Günter Graulich. Continuo realized by Paul Horn. German
text with English translation.

SWV 321

[Kleine geistliche Concerte, 2. Theil. Herr, wann ich nur dich habe]

Sacred German text. Sources: Psalm 73:25-26.
Trio (SST) with basso continuo. Ranges of voice parts: c1-f2,
b-f2, c-g1. Duration: short.

1   Herr, wann ich nur dich habe. -- In SGA. -- 1887. -- Bd. 6, p.
126-129.
Edited by Philipp Spitta. Figured bass not realized. Original
German text. Notes in German.

2   Herr, wenn ich nur dich habe. -- In NSA. -- 1963. -- Bd. 11, p.
23-29. Pub. no.: BA3665.
Edited by Wilhelm Ehmann. German text. German words in Gothic
type. Notes in German and English. Transposed up M2.

5   Herr, wann ich nur dich habe = Lord, if I have thee only. --
Neuhausen-Stuttgart : Hänssler, c1977. Pub. no.: HE 20.321/02.
Edited by Günter Graulich. Continuo·realized by Paul Horn. German
text with English translation.

SWV 322

[Kleine geistliche Concerte, 2. Theil. Rorate coeli desuper]

Sacred Latin text. Sources: Isaiah 45:8.
Trio (SSB) with basso continuo. Ranges of voice parts: c#1-g2,
c#1-g2, G-bflat. Duration: short.

1   Rorate coeli desuper. -- In SGA. -- 1887. -- Bd. 6, p. 130-132.
    Edited by Philipp Spitta. Figured bass not realized. Original
    Latin text. Notes in German.

2   Rorate coeli desuper. -- In NSA. -- 1963. -- Bd. 11, p. 37-42. Pub.
    no.: BA3665.
    Edited by Wilhelm Ehmann. Latin text. Notes in German and English.

3   Rorate coeli desuper. -- In Kleine geistliche Konzerte. -- Kassel :
    Bärenreiter, c1960. -- Heft 17, p. 15-20. Pub. no.: Bärenreiter
    3437.
    Edited by Wilhelm Ehmann. Continuo realized by Horst Soenke. Latin
    text. Notes in German and English.

    Other editions: Hänssler HE20.322.

SWV 323

[Kleine geistliche Concerte, 2. Theil. Joseph, du Sohn David]

    Sacred German text. Sources: Matthew 1:20-21.
    Trio (SSR) with basso continuo. Ranges of voice parts: g#1-a2,
    f#1-a2, A-d1. Duration: short.

1   Joseph, du Sohn David. -- In SGA. -- 1887. -- Bd. 6, p. 133-135.
    Edited by Philipp Spitta. Figured bass not realized. Original
    German text. Notes in German.

2   Joseph, du Sohn David. -- In NSA. -- 1963. -- Bd. 11, p. 43-47. Pub.
    no.: BA3665.
    Edited by Wilhelm Ehmann. German text. German words in Gothic
    type. Notes in German and English. Transposed down M2.

3   Joseph, du Sohn David. -- In Kleine geistliche Konzerte. -- Kassel :
    Bärenreiter, c1963. -- Heft 12, p. 20-24. Pub. no.: Bärenreiter
    3432.
    Edited by Wilhelm Ehmann. Continuo realized by Horst Soenke.
    German text. Words in Gothic type. Notes in German and English.
    Transposed down M2.

5   Joseph, du Sohn David, fürchte dich nicht = Joseph, you David's son,
    be not afraid. -- Neuhausen-Stuttgart : Hänssler, c1972. Pub. no.:
    HE 20.323.
    Edited by Günter Graulich. Continuo realized by Paul Horn. German
    text with English translation.

SWV 324

[Kleine geistliche Concerte, 2. Theil. Ich bin die Auferstehung und das
    Leben]

    Sacred German text. Sources: John 11:25-26.
    Trio (TTB) with basso continuo. Ranges of voice parts: c#-g1,
    d-f1, D-b. Duration: short.

1   Ich bin die Auferstehung und das Leben. -- In SGA. -- 1887. -- Bd.
     6, p. 135-139.
     Edited by Philipp Spitta. Figured bass not realized. Original
     German text. Notes in German.

2   Ich bin die Auferstehung. -- In NSA. -- 1963. -- Bd. 10, p. 125-133.
     Pub. no.: BA3664.
     Edited by Wilhelm Ehmann and Hans Hoffman. German text. Words in
     Gothic type. Notes in German and English.

5   Ich bin die Auferstehung und das Leben. -- Neuhausen-Stuttgart :
     Hänssler, c1972. Pub. no.: HE 20.324.
     Edited by Günter Graulich. Continuo realized by Paul Horn. German
     text with English translation.

SWV 325

[Kleine geistliche Concerte, 2. Theil. Seele Christi heilige mich]

     Sacred German text. Sources: Seele Christi heilige mich.
     Trio (ATB) with basso continuo. Ranges of voice parts: f-a1, d-e1,
     F-c1. Duration: short.

1   Die Seele Christi heilige mich. -- In SGA. -- 1887. -- Bd. 6, p.
     139-143.
     Edited by Philipp Spitta. Figured bass not realized. Original
     German text. Notes in German.

2   Die Seele Christi heilige mich. -- In NSA. -- 1963. -- Bd. 11, p.
     48-54. Pub. no.: BA3665.
     Edited by Wilhelm Ehmann. German text. German words in Gothic
     type. Notes in German and English.

5   Die Seele Christi heilige mich = The soul of Christ now sanctify me.
     -- Neuhausen-Stuttgart : Hänssler, c1983. Pub. no.: HE 20.325/02.
     Edited by Günter Graulich. Continuo realized by Paul Horn. German
     text with English translation.

SWV 326

[Kleine geistliche Concerte, 2. Theil. Ich ruf zu dir, Herr Jesu Christ]

     Sacred German and Latin text. Sources: Agricola, Johann. Ich ruf zu
     dir, Herr Jesu Christ. Stiehler, Caspar. Te Christe supplex invoco.
     Quartet (SSSR) with basso continuo. Ranges of voice parts: d1-g2,
     bflat-g2, d1-eflat2, G-eflat1. Duration: short.

1   Ich ruf zu dir, Herr Jesu Christ. -- In SGA. -- 1887. -- Bd. 6, p.
     144-146.
     Edited by Philipp Spitta. Figured bass not realized. Original
     German and Latin text. Notes in German.

2   Ich ruf zu dir, Herr Jesu Christ = Te Christe supplex invoco. -- In
     NSA. -- 1963. -- Bd. 11, p. 55-59.
        Text in German and Latin. German words in Gothic type. Edited by
     Wilhelm Ehmann.

5   Ich ruf zu dir, Herr Jesu Christ = Te Christe supplex invoco = I
     call to thee, Lord Jesu Christ. -- Neuhausen-Stuttgart : Hänssler,
     c1972. Pub. no.: HE 20.326.
        Edited by Günter Graulich. Continuo realized by Paul Horn. German
     and Latin text.

SWV 327

[Kleine geistliche Concerte, 2. Theil. Allein Gott in der Höh sei Ehr]

     Sacred German text. Sources: Decius, Nicolaus. Allein Gott in der
     Höh sei Ehr.
        Quartet (SSTT) with basso continuo. Ranges of voice parts: d1-e2,
     e1-e2, e-e1, c-e1. Duration: medium.

1   Allein Gott in der Höh sei Ehr. -- In SGA. -- 1887. -- Bd. 6, p.
     147-153.
        Edited by Philipp Spitta. Figured bass not realized. Original
     German text. Notes in German.

2   Allein Gott in der Höh sei Ehr. -- In NSA. -- 1963. -- Bd. 11, p.
     60-68. Pub. no.: BA3665.
        Edited by Wilhelm Ehmann. German text. German words in Gothic
     type. Notes in German and English. Transposed up M2.

5   Allein Gott in der Höh sei Ehr = To God alone on high be praise. --
     Neuhausen-Stuttgart : Hänssler, c1983. Pub. no.: HE 20.327/02.
        Edited by Günter Graulich. Continuo realized by Paul Horn. German
     text with English translation.

SWV 328

[Kleine geistliche Concerte, 2. Theil. Veni, sancte Spiritus]

     Sacred Latin text. Sources: Veni sancte Spiritus.
        Quartet (SSTT) with basso continuo. Ranges of voice parts: d1-f2,
     c1-f2, c-g1, A-f1. Duration: medium.

1   Veni, sancte spiritus. -- In SGA. -- 1887. -- Bd. 6, p. 153-159.
        Edited by Philipp Spitta. Figured bass not realized. Original
     Latin text. Notes in German.

2   Veni, sancte spiritus. -- In NSA. -- 1963. -- Bd. 11, p. 69-83.
     Pub no.: BA3665.
        Edited by Wilhelm Ehmann. Latin text. Notes in German and English.

3 Veni, sancte Spiritus. -- In Kleine geistliche Konzerte. -- Kassel :
Bärenreiter, c1960. -- Heft 17, p. 21-35. Pub. no.: Bärenreiter
3437.
Edited by Wilhelm Ehmann. Continuo realized by Horst Soenke. Latin
text. Notes in German and English.

Other editions: Hänssler HE20.328.

SWV 329

[Kleine geistliche Concerte, 2. Theil. Ist Gott für uns, wer mag wider
uns sein?]

Sacred German text. Sources: Romans 8:31-34.
Quartet (SATB) with basso continuo. Ranges of voice parts: d1-f2,
f-a1, d-f1, F-c1. Duration: short.

1 Ist Gott für uns, wer mag wider uns sein?. -- In SGA. -- 1887. --
Bd. 6, p. 160-164.
Edited by Philipp Spitta. Figured bass not realized. Original
German text. Notes in German.

2 Ist Gott für uns. -- In NSA. -- 1963. -- Bd. 11, p. 110-116. Pub.
no.: BA3665.
Edited by Wilhelm Ehmann. German text. German words in Gothic
type. Notes in German and English. Transposed up M2.

5 Ist Gott für uns, wer mag wider uns sein = With God for us, who can
be against us?. -- Neuhausen-Stuttgart : Hänssler, c1972. Pub. no.:
HE 20.329.
Edited by Günter Graulich. Continuo realized by Paul Horn. German
text with English translation.

6 Is God for us. -- Springfield, Ohio : Chantry Music Press, c1949.
Edited by Ludwig Leneh. German text with English translation.

Other editions: Bärenreiter BA1706; Hänssler 1.009.

SWV 330

[Kleine geistliche Concerte, 2. Theil. Wer will uns scheiden von der
Liebe Gottes?]

Sacred German text. Sources: Romans 8:35. Romans 8:38-39.
Quartet (SATB) with basso continuo. Ranges of voice parts: c1-d2,
a-bflat1, d-f#1, Eflat-bflat. Duration: short.

1 Wer will uns scheiden von der Liebe Gottes?. -- In SGA. -- 1887. --
Bd. 6, p. 164-168.
Edited by Philipp Spitta. Figured bass not realized. Original
German text. Notes in German.

2   Wer will uns scheiden von der Liebe Gottes?. -- In NSA. -- 1963. --
    Bd. 11, p. 117-122. Pub. no.: BA3665.
    Edited by Wilhelm Ehmann. German text. German words in Gothic
    type. Notes in German and English. Transposed up M2.

5   Wer will uns scheiden von der Liebe Gottes = Who then can part us
    from the love God gives us?. -- Neuhausen-Stuttgart : Hänssler,
    c1972. Pub. no.: HE 20.330/02.
    Edited by Günter Graulich. Continuo realized by Paul Horn. German
    text with English translation.

6   Who shall separate us from the love of God? = Wer will uns scheiden
    von der Liebe Gottes?. -- New York : G. Schirmer, c1961. Pub. no.:
    G. Schirmer octavo no. 10874.
    Edited by C. Buell Agey. German text with English translation.
    Transposed up M2.

7   Who shall separate us? = Wer will uns scheiden. -- New York : S.
    Fox, c1965. Pub. no.: CM11.
    Edited by Roger Granville. German text with English translation.

8   Who shall separate us. -- Springfield, Ohio : Chantry Music Presss,
    c1949.
    Edited by Ulrich S. Leupold. German text with English translation.

    Other editions: Bärenreiter BA1706.

SWV 331

[Kleine geistliche Concerte, 2. Theil. Stimm des Herren gehet auf den
    Wassern]

    Sacred German text. Sources: Psalm 29:3-9.
    Quartet (SATB) with basso continuo. Ranges of voice parts: d1-e2,
    f-a1, d-f1, F-bflat. Duration: medium.

1   Die Stimm des Herren gehet auf den Wassern. -- In SGA. -- 1887. --
    Bd. 6, p. 169-174.
    Edited by Philipp Spitta. Figured bass not realized. Original
    German text. Notes in German.

2   Die Stimm des Herren gehet auf den Wassern. -- In NSA. -- 1963. --
    Bd. 11, p. 123-130. Pub. no.: BA3665.
    Edited by Wilhelm Ehmann. German text. German words in Gothic
    type. Notes in German and English. Transposed up M2.

5   Die Stimm des Herren gehet auf den Wassern. -- Neuhausen-Stuttgart :
    Hänssler, c1977. Pub. no.: HE 20.331/02.
    Edited by Günter Graulich. Continuo realized by Paul Horn. German
    text with English translation.

6   The voice of the Lord sounds upon the waters = Die Stimme des Herren
    gehet auf den Wassern. -- New York : Mercury Music Corp., c1963.
    Pub. no.: MC407.
    Edited by C. Buell Agey. German text with English translation.

Other editions: Bärenreiter BA1706.

SWV 332

[Kleine geistliche Concerte, 2. Theil. Jubilate Deo omnis terra]

Sacred German text. Sources: Psalm 100.
Quartet (SATB) with basso continuo. Ranges of voice parts: c1-g2,
g-a1, f-f1, E-bflat. Duration: medium.

1   Jubilate Deo omnis terra. -- In SGA. -- 1887. -- Bd. 6, p. 174-184.
    Edited by Philipp Spitta. Figured bass not realized. Original
    German text. Notes in German.

2   Jubilate Deo. -- In NSA. -- 1963. -- Bd. 11, p. 131-151. Pub. no.:
    BA3665.
    Edited by Wilhelm Ehmann. Latin text. Notes in German and English.
    Transposed up M2.

3   Jubilate Deo. -- In Kleine geistliche Konzerte. -- Kassel :
    Bärenreiter, c1963. -- Heft 18. Pub. no.: Bärenreiter 3438.
    Edited by Wilhelm Ehmann. Continuo realized by Horst Soenke. Latin
    text. Notes in German and English. Transposed up M2.

    Other editions: Hänssler HE20.332.

SWV 333

[Kleine geistliche Concerte, 2. Theil. Sei gegrüsset Maria, du
    holdselige]

Sacred German text. Sources: Luke 1:28-38.
Duet (SA) with basso continuo, 5 unspecified instruments, and 3
other soli (ATB) or chorus (SSATB). Ranges of voice parts: d1-f2,
e1-f2, g-bflat1, e-e1, F-e. Duration: medium.

1   Sei gegrüsset Maria, du holdselige. -- In SGA. -- 1887. -- Bd. 6, p.
    184-190.
    Edited by Philipp Spitta. Figured bass not realized. Original
    German text. Notes in German.

2   Sei gegrüsset Maria. -- In NSA. -- 1963. -- Bd. 12, p. 36-46. Pub.
    no.: BA3666.
    Edited by Wilhelm Ehmann. German text. Words in Gothic type. Notes
    in German and English. Transposed up M2.

3   Sei gegrüsset, Maria. -- In Kleine geistliche Konzerte. -- Kassel :
    Bärenreiter, c1963. -- Heft 13. Pub. no.: Bärenreiter 3433.
    Edited by Wilhelm Ehmann. Continuo realized by Horst Soenke.
    German text. Words in Gothic type. Notes in German and English.
    Transposed up M2.

5   Sei gegrüsset Maria, du holdselige = The Annunciation. --
    Neuhausen-Stuttgart : Hänssler, c1967. Pub. no.: XX 333.
    Edited by Günter Graulich. Continuo realized by Paul Horn. German
    text with English translation. Notes in German and English.

6   The Annunciation according to St. Luke. -- New York : G. Schirmer, c1968. Pub. no.: Ed. 2753.
    Edited by C. Buell Agey. German text with English translation. Notes in English. Transposed up M2.

SWV 334

[Kleine geistliche Concerte, 2. Theil. Ave Maria, gratia plena]

    Sacred Latin text. Sources: Luke 1:28-38.
    Duet (SA) with basso continuo, 5 unspecified instruments, and 3 other soli (ATB) or chorus (SSATB). Ranges of voice parts: d1-f2, e1-f2, g-bflat1, g-a1, F-e. Duration: medium.

1   Das XXVIII. Concert des zweiten Theils in der vom Componisten selbst vorgenommen lateinischen Text. -- In SGA. -- 1887. -- Bd. 6, p. 219-225.
    Edited by Philipp Spitta. Figured bass not realized. Original Latin text. Notes in German.

2   Ave Maria. -- In NSA. -- 1963. -- Bd. 12, p. 47-57. Pub. no.: BA3666.
    Edited by Wilhelm Ehmann. Latin text. Notes in German and English. Transposed up M2.

3   Ave, Maria. -- In Kleine geistliche Konzerte. -- Kassel : Bärenreiter, c1959. -- Heft 16. Pub. no.: Bärenreiter 3436.
    Edited by Wilhelm Ehmann. Continuo realized by Horst Soenke. Latin text. Notes in German and English. Transposed up M2.

5   Ave Maria, gratia plena. -- Neuhausen-Stuttgart : Hänssler, c1967. Pub. no.: XX 334.
    Edited by Günter Graulich. Continuo realized by Paul Horn. Latin text. Notes in German and English.

SWV 335

[Kleine geistliche Concerte, 2. Theil. Was betrübst du dich, meine Seele]

    Sacred German text. Sources: Psalm 42:11.
    Quintet (SSATB) with basso continuo. Ranges of voice parts: d1-g2, c1-f2, g-a1, c-f1, G-c1. Duration: short.

1   Was betrübst du dich, meine Seele. -- In SGA. -- 1887. -- Bd. 6, p. 191-196.
    Edited by Philipp Spitta. Figured bass not realized. Original German text. Notes in German.

2   Was betrübst du dich, meine Seele. -- In NSA. -- 1963. -- Bd. 12, p. 58-68. Pub. no.: BA3666.
    Edited by Wilhelm Ehmann. German text. Words in Gothic type. Notes in German and English.

5   Was betrübst du dich, meine Seele = What has bowed you down, o my
spirit. -- Neuhausen-Stuttgart : Hänssler, c1974. Pub. no.: HE
20.335.
Edited by Günter Graulich. Continuo realized by Paul Horn. German
text with English translation.

Other editions: Bärenreiter BA1706.

SWV 336

[Kleine geistliche Concerte, 2. Theil. Quemadmodum desiderat cervus ad
fontes aquarum]

Sacred Latin text. Sources: Soliloquia Augustini.
Quintet (SATTB) with basso continuo. Ranges of voice parts: c1-f2,
f-a1, c-g1, c-e1, D-bflat. Duration: medium.

1   Quemadmodum desiderat cervus ad fontes aquarum. -- In SGA. -- 1887.
-- Bd. 6, p. 197-207.
Edited by Philipp Spitta. Figured bass not realized. Original
Latin text. Notes in German.

2   Quemadmodum desiderat. -- In NSA. -- 1963. -- Bd. 12, p. 69-92. Pub.
no.: BA3666.
Edited by Wilhelm Ehmann. Latin text. Notes in German and English.
Transposed up M2.

3   Quemadmodum desiderat. -- In Kleine geistliche Konzerte. -- Kassel :
Bärenreiter, c1960. -- Heft 19, p. 9-32. Pub. no.: Bärenreiter 3439.
Edited by Wilhelm Ehmann. Continuo realized by Horst Soenke. Latin
text. Notes in German and English. Transposed up M2.

Other editions: Hänssler HE20.336.

SWV 337

[Kleine geistliche Concerte, 2. Theil. Aufer immensam, Deus, aufer iram]

Sacred Latin text. Sources: Aufer immensam, Deus, aufer iram.
Quintet (SATTB) with basso continuo. Ranges of voice parts: d1-e2,
g-a1, d-g1, d-e1, G-c1. Duration: medium.

1   Aufer immensam, Deus, aufer iram. -- In SGA. -- 1887. -- Bd. 6, p.
207-216.
Edited by Philipp Spitta. Figured bass not realized. Original
Latin text. Notes in German.

2   Aufer immensam. -- In NSA. -- 1963. -- Bd. 12, p. 93-114. Pub. no.:
BA3666.
Edited by Wilhelm Ehmann. Latin text. Notes in German and English.
Transposed up M2.

3 Aufer immensam. -- In Kleine geistliche Konzerte. -- Kassel :
Bärenreiter, c1963. -- Heft 19, p. 33-54. Pub. no.: Bärenreiter
3439.
Edited by Wilhelm Ehmann. Continuo realized by Horst Soenke. Latin
text. Notes in German and English by Wilhelm Ehmann. Transposed up
M2.

Other editions: Hänssler HE20.337.

SWV 338

[Teutoniam dudum belli atra pericla molestant]

Secular Latin text. Sources: Schütz, Heinrich. Teutoniam dudum belli
atra pericla molestant.
For chorus (SSATB) with 2 violins and basso continuo. Ranges of
voice parts: d1-f2, e1-g2, d-a1, c#-e1, F#-c1. Duration: medium.

1 Teutoniam dudum belli atra pericla molestant. -- In SGA. -- 1893. --
Bd. 15, p. 27-37.
Edited by Philipp Spitta. Figured bass not realized. Original
Latin text. Notes in German.

2 Teutoniam dudum belli atra pericla molestant. -- In NSA. -- 1971. --
Bd. 38, p. 48-74. Pub. no.: BA4490.
Edited by Werner Bittinger. Latin and German text. Notes in German
and English.

SWV 339

[Ich beschwöre euch, ihr Töchter zu Jerusalem]

Sacred German text. Sources: Song of Solomon 2:17. Song of Solomon 5
:8-10. Song of Solomon 6:1-2. Song of Solomon 3:1.
For chorus (SSSSATB) and basso continuo. Ranges of voice parts:
e1-g2, c1-f2, d1-g2, a-e2, f-a1, c-f1, E-d1. Duration: medium.

1 Ich beschwöre euch, ihr Töchter zu Jerusalem. -- In SGA. -- 1893. --
Bd. 14, p. 65-78.
Edited by Philipp Spitta. Figured bass not realized. Original
German text. Notes in German.

SWV 340

[O du allersüssester und liebster Herr Jesu]

Sacred German text. Sources: Meditationes Augustini.
For chorus (SSATB), 2 violins, and basso continuo. Ranges of voice
parts: d1-f2, c1-d2, f-a1, c-f1, F-bflat. Duration: medium.

1 O du allersüssester und liebster Herr Jesu. -- In SGA. -- 1893. --
Bd. 14, p. 79-92.
Edited by Philipp Spitta. Figured bass not realized. Original
German text. Notes in German.

SWV 341

[Symphoniae sacrae, 2 pars. Mein Herz ist bereit, Gott, dass ich singe]

    Sacred German text. Sources: Psalm 57:7-10.
    Solo for soprano or tenor, 2 violins and continuo. Range of voice part: d1-g2. Duration: medium.

1   Mein Herz ist bereit. -- In SGA. -- 1888. -- Bd. 7, p. 7-10.
    Edited by Philipp Spitta. Figured bass not realized. Original German text. Notes in German.

2   Mein Herz ist bereit. -- In NSA. -- 1964. -- Bd. 15, p. [1]-8. Pub. no.: BA3669.
    Edited by Werner Bittinger. German text. Notes in German and English.

3   Mein Herz ist bereit. -- In Symphoniae sacrae II. -- Kassel : Bärenreiter, c1964. -- Nr. 1. Pub. no.: Bärenreiter 3448.
    Edited by Werner Bittinger. German text. Notes in German.

SWV 342

[Symphoniae sacrae, 2 pars. Singet dem Herren ein neues Lied]

    Sacred German text. Sources: Psalm 96:1-4.
    Solo for soprano or tenor with 2 violins and continuo. Range of voice part: c1-f2. Duration: medium.

1   Singet dem Herren ein neues Lied. -- In SGA. -- 1888. -- Bd. 7, p. 11-15.
    Edited by Philipp Spitta. Figured bass not realized. Original German text. Notes in German.

2   Singet dem Herren ein neues Lied. -- In NSA. -- 1964. -- Bd. 15, p. 9-19. Pub. no.: BA3669.
    Edited by Werner Bittinger. German text. Notes in German and English.

3   Singet dem Herrn ein neues Lied. -- In Symphoniae sacrae II. -- Kassel : Bärenreiter, c1964. -- Nr. 2. Pub. no.: Bärenreiter 3447.
    Edited by Werner Bittinger. German text. Notes in German and English.

SWV 343

[Symphoniae sacrae, 2 pars. Herr unser Herrscher, wie herrlich ist dein Nam]

    Sacred German text. Sources: Psalm 8.
    Solo for soprano or tenor with 2 violins and continuo. Range of voice part: c1-a2. Duration: medium.

1   Herr unser Herrscher, wie herrlich ist dein Nam. -- In SGA. -- 1888.
     -- Bd. 7, p. 16-22.
     Edited by Philipp Spitta. Figured bass not realized. Original
     German text. Notes in German.

2   Herr unser Herrscher. -- In NSA. -- 1964. -- Bd. 15, p. 20-31. Pub.
     no.: BA3669.
     Edited by Werner Bittinger. German text. Notes in German and
     English.

3   Herr unser Herrscher. -- In Symphoniae sacrae II. -- Kassel :
     Bärenreiter, c1964. -- Nr. 3. Pub. no.: Bärenreiter 629.
     Edited by Werner Bittinger. German text. Notes in German.

SWV 344

[Symphoniae sacrae, 2 pars. Meine Seele erhebt den Herren]

     Sacred German text. Sources: Magnificat.
     Solo for soprano with 2 violins, 2 violas or trombones, 2 cornetti
     or trumpets, 2 flutes, and continuo. Range of voice part: c1-f#2.
     Duration: medium.

1   Meine Seele erhebt den Herren. -- In SGA. -- 1888. -- Bd. 7, p.
     23-29.
     Edited by Philipp Spitta. Figured bass not realized. Original
     German text. Notes in German.

2   Meine Seele erhebt den Herren. -- In NSA. -- 1964. -- Bd. 15, p.
     33-46. Pub. no.: BA3669.
     Edited by Werner Bittinger. German text. Notes in German and
     English.

     Other editions: Bärenreiter BA4335.

SWV 345

[Symphoniae sacrae, 2 pars. Herr ist meine Stärke]

     Sacred German text. Sources: Exodus 15:11. Exodus 15:2. Psalm 104
     :33.
     Solo for soprano or tenor with 2 violins and continuo. Range of
     voice part: c1-g2. Duration: short.

1   Der Herr ist meine Stärke. -- In SGA. -- 1888. -- Bd. 7, p. 30-33.
     Edited by Philipp Spitta. Figured bass not realized. Original
     German text. Notes in German.

2   Der Herr ist meine Stärke. -- In NSA. -- 1964. -- Bd. 15, p. 47-54.
     Pub. no.: BA3669.
     Edited by Werner Bittinger. German text. Notes in German and
     English.

3   Der Herr ist meine Stärke. -- Kassel : Bärenreiter, c1956. Pub. no.:
     Bärenreiter-Ausgabe 499.
     Edited by Rudolf Gerber. German text. Words in Gothic type. Notes
     in German.

5   Der Herr ist meine Stärke. -- Stuttgart : Hänssler, [19--]. Pub.
     no.: F. 2570 H.
     Edited by Friedrich Hogner. German text. Transposed up M2.

SWV 346

[Symphoniae sacrae, 2 pars. Ich werde nicht sterben]

     Sacred German text. Sources: Psalm 34:4. Psalm 116:3-4. Psalm 118
     :17.
     Solo for soprano or tenor with 2 violins and continuo. Range of
     voice part: c1-g2. Duration: medium.

1   Ich werde nicht sterben, sondern leben. -- In SGA. -- 1888. -- Bd.
     7, p. 34-38.
     Edited by Philipp Spitta. Figured bass not realized. Original
     German text. Notes in German.

2   Ich werde nicht sterben. -- In NSA. -- 1964. -- Bd. 15, p. 55-64.
     Pub. no.: BA3669.
     Edited by Werner Bittinger. German text. Notes in German and
     English. Transposed up M2.

3   Ich werde nicht sterben. -- In Symphoniae sacrae II. -- Kassel :
     Bärenreiter, c1965. -- Nr. 6-7, p. [5]-14. Pub. no.: Bärenreiter
     446.
     Edited by Werner Bittinger. German text. Notes in German.
     Transposed up M2.

     Other editions: Hänssler 5.109.

SWV 347

[Symphoniae sacrae, 2 pars. Ich danke dir, Herr, von ganzem Herzen]

     Sacred German text. Sources: Psalm 56:13. Psalm 103:2-5. Psalm 111
     :1. Psalm 116:8-9. Psalm 118:17.
     Solo for soprano or tenor with 2 violins and continuo. Range of
     voice part: c1-f2. Duration: medium.

1   Ich danke dir Herr von ganzem Herzen. -- In SGA. -- 1888. -- Bd. 7,
     p. 39-44.
     Edited by Philipp Spitta. Figured bass not realized. Original
     German text. Notes in German.

2   Ich danke dir Herr von ganzem Herzen. -- In NSA. -- 1964. -- Bd. 15,
     p. 65-72. Pub. no.: BA3669.
     Edited by Werner Bittinger. German text. Notes in German and
     English. Transposed up M2.

3 Ich danke dir, Herr, von ganzem Herzen. -- In Symphoniae sacrae II.
   -- Kassel : Bärenreiter, c1965. -- Nr. 6-7, p. [15]-22. Pub. no.:
   Bärenreiter 446.
   Edited by Werner Bittinger. German text. Notes in German.
   Transposed up M2.

   Other editions: Hänssler 5.108.

SWV 348

[Symphoniae sacrae, 2 pars. Herzlich lieb hab ich dich, o Herr, meine
     Stärke]

   Sacred German text. Sources: Psalm 18:1-6.
   Solo for alto with 2 violins and continuo. Range of voice part:
   f#-al. Duration: short.

1 Herzlich lieb hab ich dich, o Herr. -- In SGA. -- 1888. -- Bd. 7, p.
   45-48.
   Edited by Philipp Spitta. Figured bass not realized. Original
   German text. Notes in German.

2 Herzlich lieb hab ich dich, o Herr. -- In NSA. -- 1964. -- Bd. 15,
   p. 73-81. Pub. no.: BA3669.
   Edited by Werner Bittinger. German text. Notes in German and
   English. Transposed up M2.

3 Herzlich lieb hab ich dich, o Herr. -- In Symphoniae sacrae II. --
   Kassel : Bärenreiter, c1963. -- Nr. 8. Pub. no.: Bärenreiter 1724.
   Edited by Werner Bittinger. German text. Notes in German.
   Transposed up M2.

SWV 349

[Symphoniae sacrae, 2 pars. Frohlocket mit Händen und jauchzet dem
     Herren]

   Sacred German text. Sources: Psalm 47:1-6.
   Solo for tenor with 2 violins and continuo. Range of voice part:
   c-el. Duration: short.

1 Frohlocket mit Händen und jauchzet dem Herren. -- In SGA. -- 1888.
   -- Bd. 7, p. 49-53.
   Edited by Philipp Spitta. Figured bass not realized. Original
   German text. Notes in German.

2 Frohlocket mit Händen. -- In NSA. -- 1964. -- Bd. 15, p. 82-89. Pub.
   no.: BA3669.
   Edited by Werner Bittinger. German text. Notes in German and
   English.

   Other editions: Bärenreiter BA5901.

SWV 350

[Symphoniae sacrae, 2 pars. Lobet den Herrn in seinem Heiligtum]

    Sacred German text. Sources: Psalm 150.
    Solo for tenor with 2 violins and continuo. Range of voice part:
    c-g1. Duration: medium.

1   Lobet den Herrn in seinem Heiligtum. -- In SGA. -- 1888. -- Bd. 7,
    p. 54-59.
    Edited by Philipp Spitta. Figured bass not realized. Original
    German text. Notes in German.

2   Lobet den Herrn in seinem Heiligtum. -- In NSA. -- 1964. -- Bd. 15,
    p. 90-101. Pub. no.: BA3669.
    Edited by Werner Bittinger. German text. Notes in German and
    English.

3   Lobet den Herrn in seinem Heiligtum. -- In Symphoniae sacrae II. --
    Kassel : Bärenreiter, c1964. -- Nr. 10. Pub. no.: Bärenreiter 4336.
    Edited by Werner Bittinger. German text. Notes in German.

SWV 351

[Symphoniae sacrae, 2 pars. Hütet euch, dass eure Herzen nicht
    beschweret werden]

    Sacred German text. Sources: Luke 21:34-36.
    Solo for bass with 2 violins and continuo. Range of voice part:
    D-d1. Duration: medium.

1   Hütet euch, dass eure Herzen nicht beschweret werden. -- In SGA. --
    1888. -- Bd. 7, p. 60-64.
    Edited by Philipp Spitta. Figured bass not realized. Original
    German text. Notes in German.

2   Hütet euch. -- In NSA. -- 1964. -- Bd. 15, p. 102-110. Pub. no.:
    BA3669.
    Edited by Werner Bittinger. German text. Notes in German and
    English. Transposed up M2.

SWV 352

[Symphoniae sacrae, 2 pars. Herr, nun lässest du deinen Diener im Friede
    fahren]

    Sacred German text. Sources: Nunc dimittis.
    Solo for bass with 2 violins and continuo. Range of voice part:
    D-d1. Duration: short.

1   Herr, nun lässest du deinen Diener im Friede fahren. -- In SGA. --
    1888. -- Bd. 7, p. 65-68.
    Edited by Philipp Spitta. Figured bass not realized. Original
    German text. Notes in German.

2   Herr, nun lässest du deinen Diener im Friede fahren. -- In NSA. --
    1964. -- Bd. 15, p. 111-117. Pub. no.: BA3669.
       Edited by Werner Bittinger. German text. Notes in German and
    English.

5   Herr, nun lässest du deinen Diener im Frieden fahren = Lord, now
    lettest thy servant. -- Neuhausen-Stuttgart : Hänssler, c1968. Pub.
    no.: HE 20.352.
       Edited by Günter Graulich. Continuo realized by Paul Horn. German
    text with English translation. Notes in German and English.

SWV 353

[Symphoniae sacrae, 2 pars. Was betrübst du dich, meine Seele]

    Sacred German text. Sources: Psalm 42:11.
    Duet (SS or TT) with 2 violins and continuo. Ranges of voice
    parts: c1-e2, bflat-f2. Duration: medium.

1   Was betrübst du dich, meine Seele. -- In SGA. -- 1888. -- Bd. 7, p.
    69-76.
       Edited by Philipp Spitta. Figured bass not realized. Original
    German text. Notes in German.

2   Was betrübst du dich, meine Seele. -- In NSA. -- 1965. -- Bd. 16, p.
    1-11. Pub. no.: BA3670.
       Edited by Werner Bittinger. German text. Notes in German and
    English.

6   Why afflict thyself, o my spirit = Was betrübst du dich, meine
    Seele. -- New York : Mercury Music Corp., c1942. Pub. no.: DCS-20.
       Edited by Paul Boepple. German text with English translation.
    Notes in English. Transposed up M2.

SWV 354

[Symphoniae sacrae, 2 pars. Verleih uns Frieden genädiglich]

    Sacred German text. Sources: Luther, Martin. Verleih uns Frieden
    genädiglich.
    Duet (SS or TT) with 2 violins and continuo. Ranges of voice
    parts: c1g2, bflat-f2. Duration: short.

1   Verleih uns Frieden genädiglich. -- In SGA. -- 1888. -- Bd. 7, p.
    77-82.
       Edited by Philipp Spitta. Figured bass not realized. Original
    German text. Notes in German.

2   Verleih uns Frieden. -- In NSA. -- 1965. -- Bd. 16, p. 12-19. Pub.
    no.: BA3670.
       Edited by Werner Bittinger. German text. Notes in German and
    English.

3   Verleih uns Frieden. -- In Symphoniae sacrae II. -- Kassel :
     Bärenreiter, c1965. -- Nr. 14-15, p. [6]-13. Pub. no.: Bärenreiter
     4338.
         Edited by Werner Bittinger. German text. Notes in German and
     English.

SWV 355

[Symphoniae sacrae, 2 pars. Gib unsern Fürsten und aller Obrigkeit]

     Sacred German text. Sources: Luther, Martin. Verleih uns Frieden
     genädiglich.
         Duet (SS or TT) with 2 violins and continuo. Ranges of voice
     parts: bflat-f2, cl-eflat2. Duration: short.

1   Gieb unsern Fürsten und aller Obrigkeit. -- In SGA. -- 1888. -- Bd.
     7, p. 83-86.
         Edited by Philipp Spitta. Figured bass not realized. Original
     German text. Notes in German.

2   Gieb unsern Fürsten. -- In NSA. -- 1965. -- Bd. 16, p. 20-26. Pub.
     no.: BA3670.
         Edited by Werner Bittinger. German text. Notes in German and
     English.

3   Gib unsern Fürsten. -- In Symphoniae sacrae II. -- Kassel :
     Bärenreiter, c1965. -- Nr. 14-15, p. 14-20. Pub. no.: Bärenreiter
     4338.
         Edited by Werner Bittinger. German text. Notes in German and
     English.

SWV 356

[Symphoniae sacrae, 2 pars. Es steh Gott auf]

     Sacred German text. Sources: Psalm 68:1-3.
         Duet (SS or TT) with 2 violins and continuo. Ranges of voice
     parts: dl-a2, cl-g2. Duration: medium.

1   Es steh Gott auf dass seine Feind zerstreuet werden. -- In SGA. --
     1888. -- Bd. 7, p. 87-97.
         Edited by Philipp Spitta. Figured bass not realized. Original
     German text. Notes in German.

2   Es steh Gott auf. -- In NSA. -- 1965. -- Bd. 16, p. 27-41. Pub. no.:
     BA3670.
         Edited by Werner Bittinger. German text. Notes in German and
     English.

3   Es steh Gott auf. -- In Symphoniae sacrae II. -- Kassel :
     Bärenreiter, c1965. -- Nr. 16. Pub. no.: Bärenreiter 5903.
         Edited by Werner Bittinger. German text. Notes in German and
     English.

SWV 357

[Symphoniae sacrae, 2 pars. Wie ein Rubin in feinem Golde leuchtet]

Sacred German text. Sources: Apocrypha. Ecclesiasticus 32:7-9.
Duet (SA) with 2 violins and continuo. Ranges of voice parts:
d1-f2, g-a1. Duration: short.

1 Wie ein Rubin in feinem Golde leuchtet. -- In SGA. -- 1888. -- Bd.
7, p. 98-102.
Edited by Philipp Spitta. Figured bass not realized. Original
German text. Notes in German.

2 Wie ein Rubin in feinem Golde leuchtet. -- In NSA. -- 1965. -- Bd.
16, p. 42-48. Pub. no.: BA3670.
Edited by Werner Bittinger. German text. Notes in German and
English. Transposed up M2.

3 Wie ein Rubin in feinem Golde leuchtet. -- Kassel : Bärenreiter,
[1936?]. Pub. no.: Bärenreiter-Ausgabe 1086.
Edited by Rudolf Gerber. German text. Words in Gothic type. Notes
in German. Transposed up M2.

SWV 358

[Symphoniae sacrae, 2 pars. Iss dein Brot mit Freuden]

Sacred German text. Sources: Ecclesiastes 3:12-13. Ecclesiastes 8
:15. Ecclesiastes 9:7.
Duet (SB) with 2 violins and continuo. Ranges of voice parts:
d1-f2, G-d1. Duration: medium.

1 Iss dein Brot mit Freuden. -- In SGA. -- 1888. -- Bd. 7, p. 103-109.
Edited by Philipp Spitta. Figured bass not realized. Original
German text. Notes in German.

2 Iss dein Brot mit Freuden. -- In NSA. -- 1965. -- Bd. 16, p. 49-57.
Pub. no.: BA3670.
Edited by Werner Bittinger. German text. Notes in German and
English. Transposed up M2.

3 Iss dein Brot mit Freuden. -- Kassel : Bärenreiter, [1936?]. Pub.
no.: Bärenreiter-Ausgabe 1087.
Edited by Rudolf Gerber. German text. Words in Gothic type. Notes
in German. Transposed up M2.

SWV 359

[Symphoniae sacrae, 2 pars. Herr ist mein Licht und mein Heil]

Sacred German text. Sources: Psalm 27:1-3. Psalm 27:5-6.
Duet (TT) with 2 violins and continuo. Ranges of voice parts:
c-g1, c-g1. Duration: medium.

1   Der Herr ist mein Licht und mein Heil. -- In SGA. -- 1888. -- Bd. 7,
     p. 110-118.
        Edited by Philipp Spitta. Figured bass not realized. Original
     German text. Notes in German.

2   Der Herr ist mein Licht und mein Heil. -- In NSA. -- 1965. -- Bd.
     16, p. 58-70. Pub. no.: BA3670.
        Edited by Werner Bittinger. German text. Notes in German and
     English.

3   Der Herr ist mein Licht und mein Heil. -- In Symphoniae sacrae II.
     -- Kassel : Bärenreiter, c1965. -- Nr. 19. Pub. no.: Bärenreiter
     5904.
        Edited by Werner Bittinger. German text. Notes in German and
     English.

SWV 360

[Symphoniae sacrae, 2 pars. Zweierlei bitte ich, Herr, von dir]

     Sacred German text. Sources: Proverbs 30:7-9.
        Duet (TT) with 2 violins and continuo. Ranges of voice parts:
     c-f1, B-f1. Duration: medium.

1   Zweierlei bitte ich, Herr, von dir. -- In SGA. -- 1888. -- Bd. 7, p.
     119-126.
        Edited by Philipp Spitta. Figured bass not realized. Original
     German text. Notes in German.

2   Zweierlei bitte ich, Herr, von dir. -- In NSA. -- 1965. -- Bd. 16,
     p. 71-82. Pub. no.: BA3670.
        Edited by Werner Bittinger. German text. Notes in German and
     English.

3   Zweierlei bitte ich, Herr, von dir. -- In Symphoniae sacrae II. --
     Kassel : Bärenreiter, c1965. -- Nr. 20. Pub. no.: Bärenreiter 5905.
        Edited by Werner Bittinger. German text. Notes in German and
     English.

SWV 361

[Symphoniae sacrae, 2 pars. Herr, neige deine Himmel und fahr herab]

     Sacred German text. Sources: Psalm 144:5-7. Psalm 144:9.
        Duet (BB) with 2 violins and continuo. Ranges of voice parts:
     D-d1, C-d1. Duration: medium.

1   Herr, neige deine Himmel und fahr herab. -- In SGA. -- 1888. -- Bd.
     7, p. 127-133.
        Edited by Philipp Spitta. Figured bass not realized. Original
     German text. Notes in German.

2   Herr, neige deine Himmel. -- In NSA. -- 1965. -- Bd. 16, p. 83-92.
     Pub. no.: BA3670.
        Edited by Werner Bittinger. German text. Notes in German and
     English. Transposed up M2.

3   Herr, neige deine Himmel. -- In Symphoniae sacrae II. -- Kassel :
     Bärenreiter, c1965. -- Nr. 21. Pub. no.: Bärenreiter 5906.
        Edited by Werner Bittinger. German text. Notes in German and
     English. Transposed up M2.

SWV 362

[Symphoniae sacrae, 2 pars. Von Aufgang der Sonnen bis zu ihrem
        Niedergang]

     Sacred German text. Sources: Psalm 113:2-9.
        Duet (BB) with 2 violins and continuo. Ranges of voice parts:
     D-d1, C-c1. Duration: medium.

1   Von Aufgang der Sonnen bis zu ihrem Niedergang. -- In SGA. -- 1888.
     -- Bd. 7, p. 134-141.
        Edited by Philipp Spitta. Figured bass not realized. Original
     German text. Notes in German.

2   Von Aufgang der Sonnen. -- In NSA. -- 1965. -- Bd. 16, p. 93-104.
     Pub. no.: BA3670.
        Edited by Werner Bittinger. German text. Notes in German and
     English. Transposed up M2.

3   Von Aufgang der Sonnen. -- In Symphoniae sacrae II. -- Kassel :
     Bärenreiter, c1965. -- Nr. 22. Pub. no.: Bärenreiter 5907.
        Edited by Werner Bittinger. German text. Notes in German and
     English. Transposed up M2.

SWV 363

[Symphoniae sacrae, 2 pars. Lobet den Herrn, alle Heiden]

     Sacred German text. Sources: Psalm 117.
        Trio (ATB) with 2 violins and continuo. Ranges of voice parts:
     f-a1, c-f1, D-d1. Duration: medium.

1   Lobet den Herrn, alle Heiden. -- In SGA. -- 1888. -- Bd. 7, p.
     142-147.
        Edited by Philipp Spitta. Figured bass not realized. Original
     German text. Notes in German.

2   Lobet den Herrn, alle Heiden. -- In NSA. -- 1968. -- Bd. 17, p.
     1-12. Pub. no.: BA4470.
        Edited by Werner Bittinger. German text. Notes in German and
     English. Transposed up M2.

3   Lobet den Herrn, alle Heiden. -- In Symphoniae sacrae II. -- Kassel
     : Bärenreiter, c1968. -- Nr. 23. Pub. no.: Bärenreiter 5908.
     Edited by Werner Bittinger. German text. Notes in German and
     English. Transposed up M2.

SWV 364

[Symphoniae sacrae, 2 pars. Die so ihr den Herren fürchtet]

     Sacred German text. Sources: Apocrypha. Ecclesiasticus 2:8-13.
     Trio (ATB) with 2 violins and continuo. Ranges of voice parts:
     g-a1, c-e1, C-c1. Duration: medium.

1   Die so ihr den Herren fürchtet. -- In SGA. -- 1888. -- Bd. 7, p.
     148-154.
     Edited by Philipp Spitta. Figured bass not realized. Original
     German text. Notes in German.

2   Die so ihr den Herren fürchtet. -- In NSA. -- 1968. -- Bd. 17, p.
     13-28. Pub. no.: BA4470.
     Edited by Werner Bittinger. German text. Notes in German and
     English.

3   Die so ihr den Herren fürchtet. -- In Symphoniae sacrae II. --
     Kassel : Bärenreiter, c1968. -- Nr. 24. Pub. no.: Bärenreiter 5909.
     Edited by Werner Bittinger. German text. Notes in German and
     English.

SWV 365

[Symphoniae sacrae, 2 pars. Drei schöne Dinge seind]

     Sacred German text. Sources: Ephesians 5:22. Ephesians 5:28.
     Ephesians 5:32. Galatians 5:14-15. Hebrews 13:4. Apocrypha.
     Ecclesiasticus 25:1-2. Proverbs 27:10. Psalm 133:1-3.
     Trio (TTB) with 2 violins and continuo. Ranges of voice parts:
     c-f1, c-f1, C-d1. Duration: long.

1   Drei schöne Dinge seind. -- In SGA. -- 1888. -- Bd. 7, p. 155-165.
     Edited by Philipp Spitta. Figured bass not realized. Original
     German text. Notes in German.

2   Drei schöne Dinge seind. -- In NSA. -- 1968. -- Bd. 17, p. 29-53.
     Pub. no.: BA4470.
     Edited by Werner Bittinger. German text. Notes in German and
     English.

3   Drei schöne Dinge seind. -- In Symphoniae sacrae II. -- Kassel :
     Bärenreiter, c1968. -- Nr. 25. Pub. no.: Bärenreiter 5910.
     Edited by Werner Bittinger. German text. Notes in German and
     English.

SWV 366

[Symphoniae sacrae, 2 pars. Von Gott will ich nicht lassen]

    Sacred German text. Sources: Helmbold, Ludwig. Von Gott will ich nicht lassen.
    Trio (SSB) with 2 violins and continuo. Ranges of voice parts: c#1-g2, bflat-g2, D-d1. Duration: medium.

1   Von Gott will ich nicht lassen. -- In SGA. -- 1888. -- Bd. 7, p. 166-178.
    Edited by Philipp Spitta. Figured bass not realized. Original German text. Notes in German.

2   Von Gott will ich nicht lassen. -- In NSA. -- 1968. -- Bd. 17, p. 54-81. Pub. no.: BA4470.
    Edited by Werner Bittinger. German text. Notes in German and English.

3   Von Gott will ich nicht lassen. -- In Symphoniae sacrae II. -- Kassel : Bärenreiter, c1964. -- Nr. 26. Pub. no.: Bärenreiter 4337.
    Edited by Werner Bittinger. German text. Notes in German and English.

SWV 367

[Symphoniae sacrae, 2 pars. Freuet euch des Herren, ihr Gerechten]

    Sacred German text. Sources: Psalm 33:1-3.
    Trio (ATB) with 2 violins and continuo. Ranges of voice parts: f-a1, c-g1, C-c1. Duration: medium.

1   Freuet euch des Herren, ihr Gerechten. -- In SGA. -- 1888. -- Bd. 7, p. 179-188.
    Edited by Philipp Spitta. Figured bass not realized. Original German text. Notes in German.

2   Freuet euch des Herren, ihr Gerechten. -- In NSA. -- 1968. -- Bd. 17, p. 82-102. Pub. no.: BA4470.
    Edited by Werner Bittinger. German text. Notes in German and English.

3   Freuet euch des Herren, ihr Gerechten. -- Kassel : Bärenreiter, [1932?]. Pub. no.: Bärenreiter-Ausgabe 631.
    Edited by Herbert Birtner. German text. Words in Gothic type. Notes in German.

SWV 368

[Danklied]

    Secular German text. Sources: Dufft, Christian Timotheus. Danklied.
    Solo for alto with 2 discant instruments and basso continuo. Range of voice part: g-g1. Duration: short.

1   Danklied : Aria : fürstliche Gnade zu Wasser und Lande. -- In SGA.
     -- 1893. -- Bd. 15, p. 86.
        Edited by Philipp Spitta. Figured bass not realized. Original
     Latin text. Notes in German.

2   Danklied. -- In NSA. -- 1970. -- Bd. 37, p. 11-12. Pub. no.: BA4489.
        Edited by Werner Bittinger. German text. Notes in German and
     English.

SWV 369

[Geistliche Chormusik. Es wird das Scepter von Juda nicht entwendet
     werden]

        Sacred German text. Sources: Genesis 49:10-11.
        For chorus (SATTB) and optional basso continuo. Ranges of voice
     parts: el-e2, g-al, c-fl, c-el, G-a. Duration: short.

1   Es wird das Scepter von Juda nicht entwendet werden. -- In SGA. --
     1889. -- Bd. 8, p. 7-10.
        Edited by Philipp Spitta. Figured bass not realized. Original
     German text. Notes in German.

2   Es wird das Scepter von Juda nicht entwendet werden. -- In NSA. --
     1962. -- Bd. 5, no. 1. Pub. no.: Bärenreiter-Ausgabe 500.
        Edited by Wilhelm Kamlah. Continuo line not included. German text.
     Words in Gothic type. Notes in German. Transposed up M2.

3   Es wird das Scepter von Juda nicht entwendet werden. -- Kassel :
     Bärenreiter, [19--]. Pub. no.: Bärenreiter-Ausgabe 501.
        Edited by Wilhelm Kamlah. Continuo line not included. German text.
     Words in Gothic type. Transposed up M2.

5   Es wird das Zepter von Juda nicht entwendet werden. --
     Neuhausen-Stuttgart : Hänssler, c1972. Pub. no.: HE 20.369.
        Edited by Günter Graulich. Continuo realized by Paul Horn. German
     text with English translation.

6   Lo, the scepter from Judah shall not be removed = Es wird das
     Szepter von Juda nicht entwendet werden. -- St. Louis, Mo. :
     Concordia, c1961. Pub. no.: 98-1559.
        Edited by C. Buell Agey. German text with English translation.

SWV 370

[Geistliche Chormusik. Er wird sein Kleid in Wein waschen]

        Sacred German text. Sources: Genesis 49:11-12.
        For chorus (SATTB) and optional basso continuo. Ranges of voice
     parts: cl-e2, g-al, d-fl, c-fl, G-cl. Duration: short.

1   Er wird sein Kleid in Wein waschen. -- In SGA. -- 1889. -- Bd. 8, p.
     11-14.
        Edited by Philipp Spitta. Figured bass not realized. Original
     German text. Notes in German.

2   Er wird sein Kleid in Wein waschen. -- In NSA. -- 1962. -- Bd. 5,
    no. 2. Pub. no.: Bärenreiter-Ausgabe 500.
        Edited by Wilhelm Kamlah. Continuo line not included. German text.
    Words in Gothic type. Notes in German. Transposed up M2.

3   Er wird sein Kleid in Wein waschen. -- Kassel : Bärenreiter, [19--].
    Pub. no.: Bärenreiter-Ausgabe 502.
        Edited by Wilhelm Kamlah. Continuo line not included. German text.
    Words in Gothic type. Transposed up M2.

5   Er wird sein Kleid in Wein waschen = He shall tread out his cloak in
    wine. -- Neuhausen-Stuttgart : Hänssler, c1972. Pub. no.: HE 20.370.
        Edited by Günter Graulich. Continuo realized by Paul Horn. German
    text with English translation.

6   Er wird sein Kleid in Wein waschen. -- Leipzig : VEB Breitkopf &
    Härtel, [1930?]. Pub. no.: Partitur-Bibliothek Nr. 3352.
        Edited by Kurt Thomas. German text. Words in Gothic type. Notes in
    German.

SWV 371

[Geistliche Chormusik. Es ist erschienen die heilsame Gnade Gottes]

    Sacred German text. Sources: Titus 2:11-14.
        For chorus (SSATB) and optional basso continuo. Ranges of voice
    parts: bflat-f2, bflat-f2, d-a1, c-f1, F-bflat. Duration: short.

1   Es ist erschienen die heilsame Gnade Gottes. -- In SGA. -- 1889. --
    Bd. 8, p. 15-20.
        Edited by Philipp Spitta. Figured bass not realized. Original
    German text. Notes in German.

2   Es ist erschienen die heilsame Gnade Gottes. -- In NSA. -- 1962. --
    Bd. 5, no. 3. Pub. no.: Bärenreiter-Ausgabe 500.
        Edited by Wilhelm Kamlah. Continuo line not included. German text.
    Words in Gothic type. Notes in German. Transposed up M2.

3   Es ist erschienen. -- Kassel : Bärenreiter, c1954. Pub. no.:
    Bärenreiter-Ausgabe 503.
        Edited by Wilhelm Kamlah. Continuo line not included. German text.
    Words in Gothic type. Transposed up M2.

5   Es ist erschienen die heilsame Gnade Gottes = Now there appeareth
    the grace of the Lord Almighty. -- Neuhausen-Stuttgart : Hänssler,
    c1969. Pub. no.: HE 20.371.
        Edited by Günter Graulich. Continuo realized by Paul Horn. German
    text with English translation. Notes in German and English.

6   Es ist erschienen die heilsame Gnade Gottes. -- Leipzig : VEB
    Breitkopf & Härtel, [1930?]. Pub. no.: Partitur-Bibliothek Nr. 3353.
        Edited by Kurt Thomas. German text. Words in Gothic type. Notes in
    German.

SWV 372

[Geistliche Chormusik. Verleih uns Frieden genädiglich]

Sacred German text. Sources: Luther, Martin. Verleih uns Frieden
genädiglich.
For chorus (SSATB) and optional basso continuo. Ranges of voice
parts: c#1-f2, d1-eflat2, g-a1, c-d1, F-bflat. Duration: short.

1   Verleih uns Frieden genädiglich. -- In SGA. -- 1889. -- Bd. 8, p.
    20-23.
    Edited by Philipp Spitta. Figured bass not realized. Original
    German text. Notes in German.

2   Verleih uns Frieden genädiglich. -- In NSA. -- 1962. -- Bd. 5, no.
    4. Pub. no.: Bärenreiter-Ausgabe 500.
    Edited by Wilhelm Kamlah. Continuo line not included. German text.
    Words in Gothic type. Notes in German. Transposed up M2.

3   Verleih uns Frieden genädiglich. -- Kassel : Bärenreiter, [19--].
    Pub. no.: Bärenreiter-Ausgabe 504.
    Edited by Wilhelm Kamlah. Continuo line not included. German text.
    Words in Gothic type. Transposed up M2.

5   Verleih uns Frieden genädiglich = O Lord, now grant us thy peace in
    grace. -- Neuhausen-Stuttgart : Hänssler, c1972. Pub. no.: HE
    20.372/02.
    Edited by Günter Graulich. Continuo realized by Paul Horn. German
    text with English translation.

6   Verleih uns Frieden genädiglich = Lord, grant us peace. -- [S.l.] :
    G. Schirmer, c1974. Pub. no.: G. Schirmer's choral church music no.
    12003.
    Edited by Maynard Klein. German text with English translation.
    Transposed up M2.

SWV 373

[Geistliche Chormusik. Gib unsern Fürsten und aller Obrigkeit]

Sacred German text. Sources: Luther, Martin. Verleih uns Frieden
genädiglich.
For chorus (SSATB) and optional basso continuo. Ranges of voice
parts: d1-f2, d1-f2, g-a1, c-f1, F#-bflat. Duration: short.

1   Gieb unsern Fürsten und aller Obrigkeit. -- In SGA. -- 1889. -- Bd.
    8, p. 24-26.
    Edited by Philipp Spitta. Figured bass not realized. Original
    German text. Notes in German.

2   Gib unsern Fürsten und aller Obrigkeit. -- In NSA. -- 1962. -- Bd.
    5, no. 5. Pub. no.: Bärenreiter-Ausgabe 500.
    Edited by Wilhelm Kamlah. Continuo line not included. German text.
    Words in Gothic type. Notes in German. Transposed up M2.

3   Gib unsern Fürsten. -- Kassel : Bärenreiter, c1973. Pub. no.:
    Bärenreiter-Ausgabe 505.
    Edited by Wilhelm Kamlah. Continuo line not included. German text.
    Transposed up M2.

5   Gib unsern Fürsten und aller Obrigkeit Fried und gut Regiment =
    Grant to our people and all who govern us. -- Neuhausen-Stuttgart :
    Hänssler, c1972. Pub. no.: HE 20.373.
    Edited by Günter Graulich. Continuo realized by Paul Horn. German
    text with English translation.

6   Give to our leaders and all ruling powers = Gib unsern Fürsten und
    aller Obrigkeit. -- St. Louis, Mo. : Concordia, c1962. Pub. no.:
    Concordia choral series no. 98-1586.
    Edited by C. Buell Agey. German text with English translation.

SWV 374

[Geistliche Chormusik. Unser keiner lebet ihm selber]

    Sacred German text. Sources: Romans 14:7-8.
    For chorus (SSATB) and optional basso continuo. Ranges of voice
    parts: c1-f2, c1-f2, f-a1, c-eflat1, F-bflat. Duration: short.

1   Unser keiner lebet ihm selber. -- In SGA. -- 1889. -- Bd. 8, p.
    27-31.
    Edited by Philipp Spitta. Figured bass not realized. Original
    German text. Notes in German.

2   Unser keiner lebet ihm selber. -- In NSA. -- 1962. -- Bd. 5, no. 6.
    Pub. no.: Bärenreiter-Ausgabe 500.
    Edited by Wilhelm Kamlah. Continuo line not included. German text.
    Words in Gothic type. Notes in German. Transposed up M2.

3   Unser keiner lebet ihm selber. -- Kassel : Bärenreiter, c1954. Pub.
    no.: Bärenreiter-Ausgabe 506.
    Edited by Wilhelm Kamlah. Continuo line not included. German text.
    Words in Gothic type. Transposed up M2.

5   Unser keiner lebet ihm selber. -- Neuhausen-Stuttgart : Hänssler,
    c1972. Pub. no.: HE 20.374/02.
    Edited by Günter Graulich. Continuo realized by Paul Horn. German
    text with English translation.

6   Unser keiner lebet ihm selber. -- Leipzig : VEB Breitkopf & Härtel,
    [1930?]. Pub. no.: Partitur-Bibliothek Nr. 3356.
    Edited by Kurt Thomas. German text. Words in Gothic type. Notes in
    German.

SWV 375

[Geistliche Chormusik. Viel werden kommen von Morgen und von Abend]

    Sacred German text. Sources: Matthew 8:11-12.
    For chorus (SATTB) and optional basso continuo. Ranges of voice
parts: c1-d2, f-g1, c-eflat1, c-d1, F-a. Duration: short.

1   Viel werden kommen von Morgen und von Abend. -- In SGA. -- 1889. --
    Bd. 8, p. 32-35.
      Edited by Philipp Spitta. Figured bass not realized. Notes in
German.

2   Viel werden kommen von Morgen und von Abend. -- In NSA. -- 1962. --
    Bd. 5, no. 7. Pub. no.: Bärenreiter-Ausgabe 500.
      Edited by Wilhelm Kamlah. Continuo line not included. Notes in
German. Transposed up M2.

3   Viel werden kommen von Morgen und von Abend. -- Kassel :
    Bärenreiter, [19--]. Pub. no.: Bärenreiter-Ausgabe 507.
      Edited by Wilhelm Kamlah. Continuo line not included. German text.
Words in Gothic type. Transposed up M2.

5   Viel werden kommen von Morgen und von Abend = Many shall go there
    from eastward and from westward. -- Neuhausen-Stuttgart : Hänssler,
c1972. Pub. no.: HE 20.375.
      Edited by Günter Graulich. Continuo realized by Paul Horn. German
text with English translation.

SWV 376

[Geistliche Chormusik. Sammlet zuvor das Unkraut]

    Sacred German text. Sources: Matthew 13:30.
    For chorus (SATTB) and optional basso continuo. Ranges of voice
parts: c1-eflat2, g-a1, d-g1, c-e1, F-c1. Duration: short.

1   Sammlet zuvor das Unkraut. -- In SGA. -- 1889. -- Bd. 8, p. 36-38.
      Edited by Philipp Spitta. Figured bass not realized. Original
German text. Notes in German.

2   Sammlet zuvor das Unkraut. -- In NSA. -- 1962. -- Bd. 5, no. 8. Pub.
    no.: Bärenreiter-Ausgabe 500.
      Edited by Wilhelm Kamlah. Continuo line not included. German text.
Words in Gothic type. Notes in German.

3   Sammlet zuvor das Unkraut. -- Kassel : Bärenreiter, [19--]. Pub.
    no.: Bärenreiter-Ausgabe 508.
      Edited by Wilhelm Kamlah. Continuo line not included. German text.
Words in Gothic type.

5   Sammlet zuvor das Unkraut = Go, pull up weeds first. --
    Neuhausen-Stuttgart : Hänssler, c1972. Pub. no.: HE 20.376.
      Edited by Günter Graulich. Continuo realized by Paul Horn. German
text with English translation.

SWV 377

[Geistliche Chormusik. Herr, auf dich traue ich]

Sacred German text. Sources: Psalm 31:1-2.
For chorus (SSATB) and optional basso continuo. Ranges of voice
parts: c1-f2, b-eflat2, g-al, d-el, F-cl. Duration: short.

1 Herr, auf dich traue ich. -- In SGA. -- 1889. -- Bd. 8, p. 39-43.
Edited by Philipp Spitta. Figured bass not realized. Original
German text. Notes in German.

2 Herr, auf dich traue ich. -- In NSA. -- 1962. -- Bd. 5, no. 9. Pub.
no.: Bärenreiter-Ausgabe 500.
Edited by Wilhelm Kamlah. Continuo line not included. German text.
Words in Gothic type. Notes in German. Transposed up M2.

3 Herr, auf dich traue ich. -- Kassel : Bärenreiter, c1954. Pub. no.:
Bärenreiter-Ausgabe 509.
Edited by Wilhelm Kamlah. Continuo line not included. German text.
Transposed up M2.

5 Herr, auf dich traue ich. -- Neuhausen-Stuttgart : Hänssler, c1972.
Pub. no.: HE 20.377/02.
Edited by Günter Graulich. Continuo realized by Paul Horn. German
text with English translation.

6 Lord, in thee do I trust = Herr, auf dich traue ich. -- St. Louis,
Mo. : Concordia, c1968. Pub. no.: 98-1921.
Edited by David Nott. German text with English translation.

SWV 378

[Geistliche Chormusik. Die mit Tränen säen, werden mit Freuden ernten]

Sacred German text. Sources: Psalm 126:5-6.
For chorus (SSATB) and optional basso continuo. Ranges of voice
parts: b-f2, b-e2, f-al, c-el, F-a. Duration: short.

1 Die mit Tränen säen. -- In SGA. -- 1889. -- Bd. 8, p. 44-48.
Edited by Philipp Spitta. Figured bass not realized. Original
German text. Notes in German.

2 Die mit Tränen säen. -- In NSA. -- 1962. -- Bd. 5, no. 10. Pub. no.:
Barenreiter-Ausgabe 500.
Edited by Wilhelm Kamlah. Continuo line not included. German text.
Words in Gothic type. Notes in German. Transposed up M2.

3 Die mit Tränen säen. -- Kassel : Bärenreiter, c1954. Pub. no.:
Bärenreiter-Ausgabe 510.
Edited by Wilhelm Kamlah. Continuo line not included. German text.
Transposed up M2.

5   Die mit Tränen säen = Who in sorrow plant seed. --
    Neuhausen-Stuttgart : Hänssler, c1972. Pub. no.: HE 20.378/02.
    Edited by Günter Graulich. Continuo realized by Paul Horn. German
    text with English translation.

6   He who with weeping soweth = Die mit Tränen säen. -- New York : G.
    Schirmer, c1952. Pub. no.: G. Schirmer octavo no. 10115.
    Edited by Robert Shaw and Klaus Speer. German text with English
    translation.

SWV 379

[Geistliche Chormusik. So fahr ich hin zu Jesu Christ]

    Sacred German text. Sources: Herman, Nicolaus. Wenn mein Stundlein
    vorhanden ist.
    For chorus (SSATB) and optional basso continuo. Ranges of voice
    parts: cl-e2, cl-e2, g-al, c-el, G-cl. Duration: short.

1   So fahr ich hin zu Jesu Christ. -- In SGA. -- 1889. -- Bd. 8, p.
    49-52.
    Edited by Philipp Spitta. Figured bass not realized. Original
    German text. Notes in German.

2   So fahr ich hin zu Jesu Christ. -- In NSA. -- 1962. -- Bd. 5, no.
    11. Pub. no.: Bärenreiter-Ausgabe 500.
    Edited by Wilhelm Kamlah. Continuo line not included. German text.
    Words in Gothic type. Notes in German. Transposed up M2.

3   So fahr ich hin zu Jesu Christ. -- Kassel : Bärenreiter, c1954. Pub.
    no.: Bärenreiter-Ausgabe 511.
    Edited by Wilhelm Kamlah. Continuo line not included. German text.
    Transposed up M2.

5   So fahr ich hin zu Jesu Christ. -- Neuhausen-Stuttgart : Hänssler,
    c1972. Pub. no.: HE 20.379/02.
    Edited by Günter Graulich. Continuo realized by Paul Horn. German
    text with English translation.

6   So I depart = So fahr ich hin. -- New York : S. Fox, c1967. Pub.
    no.: FXCM 27.
    Edited by Roger Granville. German text with English translation.
    Transposed up M2.

7   Now shall I go to Jesus Christ = So fahr ich hin zu Jesu Christ. --
    St. Louis, Mo. : Concordia, c1965. Pub. no.: 98-1761.
    Edited by David Nott. German text with English translation.

SWV 380

[Geistliche Chormusik. Also hat Gott die Welt geliebt]

    Sacred German text. Sources: John 3:16.
    For chorus (SATTB) and optional basso continuo. Ranges of voice
    parts: el-e2, a-al, d-el, d-el, E-a. Duration: short.

1   Also hat Gott die Welt geliebt. -- In SGA. -- 1889. -- Bd. 8, p.
    53-54.
    Edited by Philipp Spitta. Figured bass not realized. Original
    German text. Notes in German.

2   Also hat Gott die Welt geliebt. -- In NSA. -- 1962. -- Bd. 5, no.
    12. Pub. no.: Bärenreiter-Ausgabe 500.
    Edited by Wilhelm Kamlah. Continuo line not included. German text.
    Words in Gothic type. Notes in German.

3   Also hat Gott die Welt geliebt. -- Kassel : Bärenreiter, c1954. Pub.
    no.: Bärenreiter-Ausgabe 512.
    Edited by Wilhelm Kamlah. Continuo line not included. German text.

5   Also hat Gott die Welt geliebt = For God so loved this sinful world.
    -- Neuhausen-Stuttgart : Hänssler, c1968. Pub. no.: HE 20.380/01.
    Edited by Günter Graulich. Continuo realized by Paul Horn. German
    text with English translation. Notes in German and English.

6   Also hat Gott die Welt geliebt. -- Leipzig : VEB Breitkopf & Härtel
    Musikverlag, 1978. Pub. no.: PB3362.
    Edited by Kurt Thomas. German text. Words in Gothic type. Notes in
    German.

7   For God so loved the world = Also hat Gott die Welt geliebt. --
    Springfield, Ohio : Chantry Music Press, c1967. Pub. no.: CLA 6713.
    Edited by Richard T. Gore. English text. Transposed up M2.

8   For God so loved the world = Also hat Gott die Welt geliebt. -- St.
    Louis, Mo. : Concordia, c1959. Pub. no.: 98-1472.
    Edited by C. Buell Agey. German text with English translation.

SWV 381

[Geistliche Chormusik. O lieber Herre Gott, wecke uns auf]

    Sacred German text. Sources: O lieber Herre Gott, wecke uns auf.
    For chorus (SSATTB) and optional basso continuo. Ranges of voice
    parts: d1-f2, c1-f2, g-a1, d-f1, c-f1, F#-bflat. Duration: short.

1   O lieber Herre Gott, wecke uns auf. -- In SGA. -- 1889. -- Bd. 8, p.
    55-63.
    Edited by Philipp Spitta. Figured bass not realized. Original
    German text. Notes in German.

2   O lieber Herre Gott, wecke uns auf. -- In NSA. -- 1962. -- Bd. 5,
    no. 13. Pub. no.: Bärenreiter-Ausgabe 500.
    Edited by Wilhelm Kamlah. Continuo line not included. German text.
    Words in Gothic type. Notes in German.

3   O lieber Herre Gott. -- Kassel : Bärenreiter, c1954. Pub. no.:
    Bärenreiter-Ausgabe 513.
    Edited by Wilhelm Kamlah. Continuo line not included. German text.
    Words in Gothic type.

5   O lieber Herre Gott, wecke uns auf = O thou most gracious Lord. --
Neuhausen-Stuttgart : Hänssler, c1972. Pub. no.: HE 20.381.
   Edited by Günter Graulich. Continuo realized by Paul Horn. German
text with English translation. Notes in German and English.

6   O lieber Herre Gott. -- Leipzig : VEB Breitkopf & Härtel, [1930?].
Pub. no.: Partitur-Bibliothek Nr. 3363.
   Edited by Kurt Thomas. German text. Words in Gothic type. Notes in
German.

7   O dearest Lord God = O lieber Herre Gott. -- St. Louis, Mo. :
Concordia, c1967. Pub. no.: 98-1884.
   Edited by David Nott. German text with English translation.

SWV 382

[Geistliche Chormusik. Tröstet, tröstet mein Volk]

   Sacred German text. Sources: Isaiah 40:1-5.
   For chorus (SSATTB) and optional basso continuo. Ranges of voice
parts: c#1-f2, c1-eflat2, d-a1, d-f1, c-d1, F-g. Duration: medium.

1   Tröstet, tröstet mein Volk. -- In SGA. -- 1889. -- Bd. 8, p. 63-71.
   Edited by Philipp Spitta. Figured bass not realized. Original
German text. Notes in German.

2   Tröstet, tröstet mein Volk. -- In NSA. -- 1962. -- Bd. 5, no. 14.
Pub. no.: Bärenreiter-Ausgabe 500.
   Edited by Wilhelm Kamlah. Continuo line not included. German text.
Words in Gothic type. Notes in German. Transposed up M2.

3   Tröstet, tröstet mein Volk. -- Kassel : Bärenreiter, c1954. Pub.
no.: Bärenreiter-Ausgabe 514.
   Edited by Wilhelm Kamlah. Continuo line not included. German text.
Words in Gothic type. Transposed up M2.

5   Tröstet, tröstet mein Volk = O my people, take heart. --
Neuhausen-Stuttgart : Hänssler, c1972. Pub. no.: HE 20.382.
   Edited by Günter Graulich. Continuo realized by Paul Horn. German
text with English translation.

6   Tröstet mein Volk. -- Leipzig : VEB Breitkopf & Härtel, [1930?].
Pub. no.: Partitur-Bibliothek Nr. 3364.
   Edited by Kurt Thomas. German text. Words in Gothic type. Notes in
German.

7   Tröstet, tröstet mein Volk = Comfort ye, my people. -- New York : G.
Schirmer, c1966. Pub. no.: G. Schirmer octavo no. 11423.
   Edited by C. Buell Agey. German text with English translation.
Notes in English. Transposed up M2.

SWV 383

[Geistliche Chormusik. Ich bin eine rufende Stimme]

Sacred German text. Sources: John 1:23. John 1:26-27.
For chorus (SSATTB) and optional basso continuo. Ranges of voice
parts: c1-f2, c1-d2, f-a1, c#-f1, A-e1, D-a. Duration: medium.

1   Ich bin eine rufende Stimme. -- In SGA. -- 1889. -- Bd. 8, p. 71-80.
    Edited by Philipp Spitta. Figured bass not realized. Original
    German text. Notes in German.

2   Ich bin eine rufende Stimme. -- In NSA. -- 1962. -- Bd. 5, no. 15.
    Pub. no.: Bärenreiter-Ausgabe 500.
    Edited by Wilhelm Kamlah. Continuo line not included. German text.
    Words in Gothic type. Notes in German. Transposed up M2.

3   Ich bin eine rufende Stimme. -- Kassel : Bärenreiter, [19--]. Pub.
    no.: Bärenreiter-Ausgabe 515.
    Edited by Wilhelm Kamlah. Continuo line not included. German text.
    Words in Gothic type. Transposed up M2.

5   Ich bin eine rufende Stimme = See, I am a voice of one crying. --
    Neuhausen-Stuttgart : Hänssler, c1972. Pub. no.: HE 20.383.
    Edited by Günter Graulich. Continuo realized by Paul Horn. German
    text with English translation.

6   Lo, I am the voice of one crying in the wilderness = Ich bin eine
    rufende Stimme. -- New York : Mercury Music, c1963. Pub. no.: MC
    437.
    Edited by C. Buell Agey. German text with English translation.

SWV 384

[Geistliche Chormusik. Kind ist uns geboren]

Sacred German text. Sources: Isaiah 9:6-7.
For chorus (SSATTB) and optional basso continuo. Ranges of voice
parts: d1-eflat2, d1-eflat2, f-g1, c-f1, c-f, F-g. Duration:
short.

1   Ein Kind ist uns geboren. -- In SGA. -- 1889. -- Bd. 8, p. 81-88.
    Edited by Philipp Spitta. Figured bass not realized. Original
    German text. Notes in German.

2   Ein Kind ist uns geboren. -- In NSA. -- 1962. -- Bd. 5, no. 16. Pub.
    no.: Bärenreiter-Ausgabe 500.
    Edited by Wilhelm Kamlah. Continuo line not included. German text.
    Words in Gothic type. Notes in German. Transposed up M2.

3   Ein Kind ist uns geboren. -- Kassel : Bärenreiter, c1954. Pub. no.:
    Bärenreiter-Ausgabe 516.
    Edited by Wilhelm Kamlah. Continuo line not included. German text.
    Words in Gothic type. Transposed up M2.

5   Ein Kind ist uns geboren = A child is born among us. --
     Neuhausen-Stuttgart : Hänssler, c1972. Pub. no.: HE 20.384/02.
     Edited by Günter Graulich. Continuo realized by Paul Horn. German
     text with English translation.

6   To us a child is born = Ein Kind ist uns geboren. -- Bryn Mawr, Pa.
     : T. Presser, c. 1982. Pub. no.: 312-41365.
     Edited by Walter Ehret. German text with English translation.
     Transposed up M2.

7   To us is born a savior. -- Springfield, Ohio : Chantry, c1982. Pub.
     no.: CLA 8217.
     Edited by Richard T. Gore. English text. Transposed up M2.

SWV 385

[Geistliche Chormusik. Wort ward Fleisch und wohnet unter uns]

     Sacred German text. Sources: John 1:14.
     For chorus (SSATTB) and optional basso continuo. Ranges of voice
     parts: c1-e2, c1-e2, g-a1, c-f1, c-f1, F-bflat. Duration: medium.

1   Das Wort ward Fleisch und wohnet unter uns. -- In SGA. -- 1889. --
     Bd. 8, p. 89-95.
     Edited by Philipp Spitta. Figured bass not realized. Original
     German text. Notes in German.

2   Das Wort ward Fleisch und wohnet unter uns. -- In NSA. -- 1962. --
     Bd. 5, no. 17. Pub. no.: Bärenreiter-Ausgabe 500.
     Edited by Wilhelm Kamlah. Continuo line not included. German text.
     Words in Gothic type. Notes in German. Transposed up M2.

3   Das Wort ward Fleisch und wohnet unter uns. -- Kassel : Bärenreiter,
     [19--]. Pub. no.: Bärenreiter-Ausgabe 517.
     Edited by Wilhelm Kamlah. Continuo line not included. German text.
     Words in Gothic type. Transposed up M2.

5   Das Wort ward Fleisch = The word was man. -- Neuhausen-Stuttgart :
     Hänssler, c1972. Pub. no.: HE 20.385/02.
     Edited by Günter Graulich. Continuo realized by Paul Horn. German
     text with English translation.

SWV 386

[Geistliche Chormusik. Himmel erzählen die Ehre Gottes]

     Sacred German text. Sources: Psalm 19:1-6. Gloria Patri.
     For chorus (SSATTB) and optional basso continuo. Ranges of voice
     parts: c1-f2, c1-f2, d-a1, c-f1, c-f1, F-bflat. Duration: medium.

1   Die Himmel erzählen die Ehre Gottes. -- In SGA. -- 1889. -- Bd. 8,
     p. 96-105.
     Edited by Philipp Spitta. Figured bass not realized. Original
     German text. Notes in German.

2   Die Himmel erzählen die Ehre Gottes. -- In NSA. -- 1962. -- Bd. 5,
    no. 18. Pub. no.: Bärenreiter-Ausgabe 500.
        Edited by Wilhelm Kamlah. Continuo line not included. German text.
    Words in Gothic type. Notes in German. Transposed up M2.

3   Die Himmel erzählen die Ehre Gottes. -- Kassel : Bärenreiter, c1973.
    Pub. no.: Bärenreiter-Ausgabe 518.
        Edited by Wilhelm Kamlah. Continuo line not included. German text.
    Transposed up M2.

5   Die Himmel erzählen die Ehre Gottes = The heavens are telling the
    Fathers glory. -- Neuhausen-Stuttgart : Hänssler, c1967. Pub. no.:
    HE 20.386.
        Edited by Günter Graulich. Continuo realized by Paul Horn. German
    text with English translation. Notes in German and English.

6   The heavens are telling = Die Himmel rühmen die Ehre Gottes. --
    Springfield, Ohio : Chantry Music Press, c1972.
        Edited by Richard T. Gore. English text. Notes in English.
    Transposed up M2.

    Other editions: Hänssler 2.047.

SWV 387

[Geistliche Chormusik. Herzlich lieb hab ich dich, o Herr]

    Sacred German text. Sources: Schalling, Martin. Herzlich lieb hab
    ich dich, O Herr.
        For chorus (SSATTB) and optional basso continuo. Ranges of voice
    parts: d1-f2, c1-f2, bflat-a1, c-f1, c-f1, F-bflat. Duration:
    medium.

1   Herzlich lieb hab ich dich, o Herr. -- In SGA. -- 1889. -- Bd. 8, p.
    106-118.
        Edited by Philipp Spitta. Figured bass not realized. Original
    German text. Notes in German.

2   Herzlich lieb hab ich dich, o Herr. -- In NSA. -- 1962. -- Bd. 5,
    no. 19. Pub. no.: Bärenreiter-Ausgabe 500.
        Edited by Wilhelm Kamlah. Continuo line not included. German text.
    Words in Gothic type. Notes in German. Transposed up M2.

3   Herzlich lieb hab ich dich, o Herr. -- [S.l. : s.n., 19--]. Pub.
    no.: Bärenreiter-Ausgabe 519.
        Edited by Wilhelm Kamlah. Continuo line not included. German text.
    Words in Gothic type. Transposed up M2.

5   Herzlich lieb hab ich dich, o Herr. -- Neuhausen-Stuttgart :
    Hänssler, c1972. Pub. no.: HE 20.387.
        Edited by Günter Graulich. Continuo realized by Paul Horn. German
    text with English translation.

SWV 388

[Geistliche Chormusik. Das ist je gewisslich wahr und ein teuer wertes
     Wort]

     Sacred German text. Sources: Timothy, 1st, 1:15-17.
     For chorus (SSATTB) and optional basso continuo. Ranges of voice
     parts: d1-f2, c#1-e2, g-a1, c-g1, c-e1, F-c1. Duration: medium.

1   Das ist je gewisslich wahr und ein theuer werthes Wort. -- In SGA.
     -- 1889. -- Bd. 8, p. 119-130.
     Edited by Philipp Spitta. Figured bass not realized. Original
     German text. Notes in German.

2   Das ist je gewisslich wahr. -- In NSA. -- 1962. -- Bd. 5, no. 20.
     Pub. no.: Bärenreiter-Ausgabe 500.
     Edited by Wilhelm Kamlah. Continuo line not included. German text.
     Words in Gothic type. Notes in German.

3   Das ist je gewisslich wahr. -- Kassel : Bärenreiter, c1954. Pub.
     no.: Bärenreiter-Ausgabe 520.
     Edited by Wilhelm Kamlah. Continuo line not included. German text.
     Words in Gothic type.

5   Das ist je gewisslich wahr und ein teuer wertes Wort = Hear the
     faithful word of God. -- Neuhausen-Stuttgart : Hänssler, c1970. Pub.
     no.: HE 20.388.
     Edited by Günter Graulich. Continuo realized by Paul Horn. German
     text with English translation. Notes in German and English.

SWV 389

[Geistliche Chormusik. Ich bin ein rechter Weinstock]

     Sacred German text. Sources: John 15:1-2. John 15:4-5.
     For chorus (SSATTB) and optional basso continuo. Ranges of voice
     parts: c1-eflat2, c1-eflat2, f-a1, c-f1, c-d1, F-g. Duration: short.

1   Ich bin ein rechter Weinstock. -- In SGA. -- 1889. -- Bd. 8, p.
     130-137.
     Edited by Philipp Spitta. Figured bass not realized. Original
     German text. Notes in German.

2   Ich bin ein rechter Weinstock. -- In NSA. -- 1962. -- Bd. 5, no. 21.
     Pub. no.: Bärenreiter-Ausgabe 500.
     Edited by Wilhelm Kamlah. Continuo line not included. German text.
     Words in Gothic type. Notes in German. Transposed up M2.

3   Ich bin ein rechter Weinstock. -- Kassel : Bärenreiter, c1954. Pub.
     no.: Bärenreiter-Ausgabe 521.
     Edited by Wilhelm Kamlah. Continuo line not included. German text.
     Words in Gothic type. Transposed up M2.

5   Ich bin ein rechter Weinstock = I am the only true vine. --
Neuhausen-Stuttgart : Hänssler, c1973. Pub. no.: HE 20.389.
    Edited by Günter Graulich. Continuo realized by Paul Horn. German
text with English translation. Notes in German and English.

6   The vine most surely I am = Ich bin ein rechter Weinstock.
Springfield, Ohio : Chantry Music Press, c1967.
    Edited by Richard T. Gore. English text. Notes in English.
Transposed up M2.

SWV 390

[Geistliche Chormusik. Unser Wandel ist im Himmel]

    Sacred German text. Sources: Philippians 3:20-21.
    For chorus (SSATTB) and optional basso continuo. Ranges of voice
parts: c1-f2, c1-f2, f-a1, c-f1, c-f1, F-bflat. Duration: short.

1   Unser Wandel ist im Himmel. -- In SGA. -- 1889. -- Bd. 8, p.
137-145.
    Edited by Philipp Spitta. Figured bass not realized. Original
German text. Notes in German.

2   Unser Wandel ist im Himmel. -- In NSA. -- 1962. -- Bd. 5, no. 22.
Pub. no.: Bärenreiter-Ausgabe 500.
    Edited by Wilhelm Kamlah. Continuo line not included. German text.
Words in Gothic type. Notes in German. Transposed up M2.

5   Unser Wandel ist im Himmel = We are citizens of heaven. --
Neuhausen-Stuttgart : Hänssler, c1972. Pub. no.: HE 20.390.
    Edited by Günter Graulich. Continuo realized by Paul Horn. German
text with English translation.

    Other editions: Bärenreiter BA522.

SWV 391

[Geistliche Chormusik. Selig sind die Toten, die in dem Herren sterben]

    Sacred German text. Sources: Revelation 14:13.
    For chorus (SSATTB) and optional basso continuo. Ranges of voice
parts: b-f2, b-f2, g-a1, c-f1, c-d1, E-g. Duration: short.

1   Selig sind die Toten, die im dem Herren sterben. -- In SGA. -- 1889.
-- Bd. 8, p. 145-151.
    Edited by Philipp Spitta. Figured bass not realized. Original
German text. Notes in German.

2   Selig sind die Toten. -- In NSA. -- 1962. -- Bd. 5, no. 23. Pub.
no.: Bärenreiter-Ausgabe 500.
    Edited by Wilhelm Kamlah. Continuo line not included. German text.
Words in Gothic type. Notes in German. Transposed up M2.

3   Selig sind die Toten. -- Kassel : Bärenreiter, c1954. Pub. no.:
     Bärenreiter-Ausgabe 523.
         Edited by Wilhelm Kamlah. Continuo line not included. German text.
     Words in Gothic type. Transposed up M2.

5   Selig sind die Toten, die in dem Herren sterben = Blest are the
     departed. -- Neuhausen-Stuttgart : Hänssler, c1969. Pub. no.: HE
     20.391.
         Edited by Günter Graulich. Continuo realized by Paul Horn. German
     text with English translation. Notes in German and English.

6   Blessed are the faithful = Selig sind die Toten. -- New York : G.
     Schirmer, c1952. Pub. no.: G. Schirmer octavo no. 10114.
         Edited by Robert Shaw and Klaus Speer. German text with English
     translation. Transposed up M2.

     Other editions: Hänssler 1.012.

SWV 392

[Geistliche Chormusik. Was mein Gott will, das g'scheh allzeit]

     Sacred German text. Sources: Was mein Gott will, das g'scheh
     allzeit.
         For chorus (AT), 4 unspecified instruments and optional basso
     continuo. Ranges of voice parts: a-g1, c-e1. Duration: medium.

1   Was mein Gott will, das g'scheh allzeit. -- In SGA. -- 1889. -- Bd.
     8, p. 152-155.
         Edited by Philipp Spitta. Figured bass not realized. Original
     German text. Notes in German.

2   Was mein Gott will, das g'scheh allzeit. -- In NSA. -- 1962. -- Bd.
     5, no. 24. Pub. no.: Bärenreiter-Ausgabe 500.
         Edited by Wilhelm Kamlah. Continuo line not included. German text.
     Words in Gothic type. Notes in German. Transposed up m3.

3   Was mein Gott will, das g'scheh allezeit. -- Kassel : Bärenreiter,
     [19--]. Pub. no.: Bärenreiter-Ausgabe 524.
         Edited by Wilhelm Kamlah. Continuo line not included. German text.
     Words in Gothic type. Transposed up m3.

5   Was mein Gott will, das gscheh allzeit = What my God wills, let that
     be done. -- Neuhausen-Stuttgart : Hänssler, c1972. Pub. no.: HE
     20.392.
         Edited by Günter Graulich. Continuo realized by Paul Horn. German
     text with English translation.

SWV 393

[Geistliche Chormusik. Ich weiss, dass mein Erlöser lebt]

     Sacred German text. Sources: Job 19:25-27.
         For chorus (SSMATRB) and optional basso continuo. Ranges of voice
     parts: d1-g2, c1-e2, g-c2, c-g#1, c-e1, A-e1, E-a. Duration: short.

1   Ich weiss, dass mein Erlöser lebt. -- In SGA. -- 1889. -- Bd. 8, p.
    156-162.
    Edited by Philipp Spitta. Figured bass not realized. Original
    German text. Notes in German.

2   Ich weiss, dass mein Erlöser lebt. -- In NSA. -- 1962. -- Bd. 5, no.
    25. Pub. no.: Bärenreiter-Ausgabe 500.
    Edited by Wilhelm Kamlah. Continuo line not included. German text.
    Words in Gothic type. Notes in German.

3   Ich weiss, dass mein Erlöser lebt. -- Kassel : Bärenreiter, c1954.
    Pub. no.: Bärenreiter-Ausgabe 525.
    Edited by Wilhelm Kamlah. Continuo line not included. German text.

5   Ich weiss, dass mein Erlöser lebt. -- Neuhausen-Stuttgart :
    Hänssler, c1969. Pub. no.: HE 20.393/02.
    Edited by Günter Graulich. Continuo realized by Paul Horn. German
    text with English translation.

6   I know that my Redeemer lives = Ich weiss, dass mein Erlöser lebt.
    -- New York : G. Schirmer, c1967. Pub. no.: G. Schirmer octavo no.
    11386.
    Edited by C. Buell Agey. German text with English translation.
    Notes in English.

SWV 394

[Geistliche Chormusik. Sehet an den Feigenbaum und alle Bäume]

    Sacred German text. Sources: Luke 21:29-31. Luke 21:33.
    For chorus (ST), 5 unspecified instruments, and optional basso
    continuo. Ranges of voice parts: c1-e2, d-e1. Duration: medium.

1   Sehet an den Feigenbaum und alle Bäume. -- In SGA. -- 1889. -- Bd.
    8, p. 163-170.
    Edited by Philipp Spitta. Figured bass not realized. Original
    German text. Notes in German.

2   Sehet an den Feigenbaum. -- In NSA. -- 1962. -- Bd. 5, no. 26. Pub.
    no.: Bärenreiter-Ausgabe 500.
    Edited by Wilhelm Kamlah. Continuo line not included. German text.
    Words in Gothic type. Notes in German. Transposed up M2.

3   Sehet an den Feigenbaum. -- Kassel : Bärenreiter, [19--]. Pub. no.:
    Bärenreiter-Ausgabe 526.
    Edited by Wilhelm Kamlah. Continuo line not included. German text.
    Words in Gothic type. Transposed up M2.

5   Sehet an den Feigenbaum und alle Bäume. -- Neuhausen-Stuttgart :
    Hänssler, c1969. Pub. no.: HE 20.394.
    Edited by Günter Graulich. Continuo realized by Paul Horn. German
    text with English translation.

SWV 395

[Geistliche Chormusik. Engel sprach zu den Hirten]

Sacred German text. Sources: Luke 2:10-11. Isaiah 9:6.
For chorus of two (ST), three (STB) or seven (SATTTBB) with
unspecified instruments on remaining lines and optional basso
continuo. Ranges of voice parts: d1-d2, a-g1, c-d1, c-d1, d-d1, F-a,
F-g. Duration: short.

1   Der Engel sprach zu den Hirten. -- In SGA. -- 1889. -- Bd. 8, p.
     171-176.
     Edited by Philipp Spitta. Figured bass not realized. Original
     German text. Notes in German.

2   Der Engel sprach zu den Hirten. -- In NSA. -- 1962. -- Bd. 5, no.
     27. Pub. no.: Bärenreiter-Ausgabe 500.
     Edited by Wilhelm Kamlah. Continuo line not included. Notes in
     German. Transposed up M2.

3   Der Engel sprach zu den Hirten. -- Kassel : Bärenreiter, c1954. Pub.
     no.: Bärenreiter-Ausgabe 527.
     Edited by Wilhelm Kamlah. Continuo line not included. German text.
     Words in Gothic type. Transposed up M2.

5   Der Engel sprach zu den Hirten = The angel said to the shepherds. --
     Neuhausen-Stuttgart : Hänssler, c1972. Pub. no.: HE 20.395.
     Edited by Günter Graulich. Continuo realized by Paul Horn. German
     text with English translation.

6   Lo, the angel said to the shepherds = Der Engel sprach zu den
     Hirten. -- New York : G. Schirmer, c1961. Pub. no.: G. Schirmer
     octavo no. 10865.
     Edited by C. Buell Agey. German text with English translation.
     Notes in English.

SWV 396

[Geistliche Chormusik. Auf dem Gebirge hat man ein Geschrei gehöret]

Sacred German text. Sources: Matthew 2:18.
For chorus (AA), 5 unspecified instruments, and optional basso
continuo. Ranges of voice parts: g-c1, e-b21. Duration: medium.

1   Auf dem Gebirge hat man ein Geschrei gehöret. -- In SGA. -- 1889. --
     Bd. 8, p. 177-183.
     Edited by Philipp Spitta. Figured bass not realized. Original
     German text. Notes in German.

2   Auf dem Gebirge hat man ein Geschrei gehöret. -- In NSA. -- 1962. --
     Bd. 5, no. 28. Pub. no.: Bärenreiter-Ausgabe 500.
     Edited by Wilhelm Kamlah. Continuo line not included. German text.
     Words in Gothic type. Notes in German. Transposed up M2.

3   Auf dem Gebirge hat man ein Geschrei gehöret. -- Kassel :
     Bärenreiter, [19--]. Pub. no.: Bärenreiter-Ausgabe 528.
     Edited by Wilhelm Kamlah. Continuo line not included. German text.
     Words in Gothic type. Transposed up M2.

5   Auf dem Gebirge hat man ein Geschrei gehöret. -- Neuhausen-Stuttgart
     : Hänssler, c1969. Pub. no.: HE 20.396t.
     Edited by Günter Graulich. Continuo realized by Paul Horn. German
     text with English translation. Transposed up P4.

SWV 397

[Geistliche Chormusik. Du Schalksknecht, alle diese Schuld hab ich dir
     erlassen]

     Sacred German text. Sources: Matthew 18:32-33.
     Solo for tenor, 6 unspecified instruments, and optional basso
     continuo. Range of voice part: d-g1. Duration: short.

1   Du Schalksknecht, alle diese Schuld hab ich dir erlassen. -- In SGA.
     -- 1889. -- Bd. 8, p. 184-188.
     Edited by Philipp Spitta. Figured bass not realized. Original
     German text. Notes in German.

2   Du Schalksknecht, alle diese Schuld hab ich dir erlassen. -- In NSA.
     -- 1962. -- Bd. 5, no. 29. Pub. no.: Bärenreiter-Ausgabe 500.
     Edited by Wilhelm Kamlah. Continuo line not included. German text.
     Words in Gothic type. Notes in German. Transposed up M2.

3   Du Schalksknecht. -- Kassel : Bärenreiter, [19--]. Pub. no.:
     Bärenreiter-Ausgabe 529.
     Edited by Wilhelm Kamlah. Continuo line not included. German text.
     Words in Gothic type. Transposed up M2.

5   Du Schalksknecht, alle diese Schuld hab ich dir erlassen = False
     servant. -- Neuhausen-Stuttgart : Hänssler, c1972. Pub. no.: HE
     20.397.
     Edited by Günter Graulich. Continuo realized by Paul Horn. German
     text with English translation.

SWV 398

[Symphoniae sacrae, 3 pars. Herr ist mein Hirt, mir wird nichts mangeln]

     Sacred German text. Sources: Psalm 23.
     Trio (SAT) with 2 violins and basso continuo with optional chorus
     (SATB) and 4 unspecified instruments. Ranges of voice parts: c1-f2,
     g-bflat1, c-g1/ d1-c2, bflat-a1, e-f1, F-c1. Duration: medium.

1   Der Herr ist mein Hirt. -- In SGA. -- 1891. -- Bd. 10, p. 7-16.
     Edited by Philipp Spitta. Figured bass not realized. Original
     German text. Notes in German.

5   Der Herr ist mein Hirt = The Lord is my shepherd. --
     Neuhausen-Stuttgart : Hänssler, c1970. Pub. no.: HE 20.398.
        Edited by Günter Graulich. Continuo realized by Paul Horn. German
     text with English translation. Notes in German and English.

6   Psalm 23. -- Springfield, Ohio : Chantry Music Press, c1983. Pub.
     no.: CLC 835.
        Edited by Harald Wolff. English text.

SWV 399

[Symphoniae sacrae, 3 pars. Ich hebe meine Augen auf zu den Bergen]

     Sacred German text. Sources: Psalm 121.
        Trio (ATB) with 2 violins and basso continuo with optional chorus
     (SATB) and 4 unspecified instruments. Ranges of voice parts:
     f-bflat1, c-g1, F-d1/ d1-e2, f-a1, c-d1, Eflat-a. Duration: medium.

1   Ich hebe meine Augen auf. -- In SGA. -- 1891. -- Bd. 10, p. 17-26.
        Edited by Philipp Spitta. Figured bass not realized. Original
     German text. Notes in German.

5   Ich hebe meine Augen auf zu den Bergen = I lift up mine eyes to the
     hills. -- Neuhausen-Stuttgart : Hänssler, c1973. Pub. no.: HE
     20.399.
        Edited by Günter Graulich. Continuo realized by Paul Horn. German
     text with English translation. Notes in German and English.

        Other editions: Hänssler 5.005.

SWV 400

[Symphoniae sacrae, 3 pars. Wo der Herr nicht das Haus bauet]

     Sacred German text. Sources: Psalm 127.
        Trio (SSB) with 2 violins or violin and cornettino and basso
     continuo with optional chorus (SATB) and 4 unspecified instruments.
     Ranges of voice parts: c1-g2, c1-g2, D-d1/ e1-e2, a-a1, e-g1, F-d1.
     Duration: long.

1   Wo der Herr nicht das Haus bauet. -- In SGA. -- 1891. -- Bd. 10, p.
     27-41.
        Edited by Philipp Spitta. Figured bass not realized. Original
     German text. Notes in German.

5   Wo der Herr nicht das Haus bauet = If the Lord build not the
     dwelling. -- Neuhausen-Stuttgart : Hänssler, c1972. Pub. no.: HE
     20.400.
        Edited by Günter Graulich. Continuo realized by Paul Horn. German
     text with English translation. Notes in German and English.

SWV 401

[Symphoniae sacrae, 3 pars. Mein Sohn, warum hast du uns das getan?]

Sacred German text. Sources: Luke 2:48-49. Psalm 84:1-2. Psalm 84:4. Trio (SMB) with 2 violins and basso continuo with optional chorus (SATB) and 4 unspecified instruments. Ranges of voice parts: c1-g2, c1-d2, E-c1/ e1-e2, g-a1, d-f1, E-c1. Duration: medium.

1   Mein Sohn, warum hast du uns das getan. -- In SGA. -- 1891. -- Bd. 10, p. 42-53.
    Edited by Philipp Spitta. Figured bass not realized. Original German text. Notes in German.

5   Mein Sohn, warum hast du uns das getan = Jesus in the temple. -- Neuhausen-Stuttgart : Hänssler, c1972. Pub. no.: HE 20.401.
    Edited by Günter Graulich. Continuo realized by Paul Horn. German text with English translation. Notes in German and English.

6   Der zwölfjährige Jesus im Tempel. -- In Drei biblische Szenen. -- Wiesbaden : Breitkopf & Härtel, [19--]. -- p. 18-39. Pub. no.: Edition Breitkopf Nr. 1634.
    Edited by A. Hänlein. German text.

7   Mein Sohn, warum hast du uns das getan = My son, why hast thou so dealt with us?. -- London : Oxford University Press, Music Dept., c1962.
    Edited by Paul Steinitz. German text with English translation. Notes in English.

SWV 402

[Symphoniae sacrae, 3 pars. O Herr hilf, o Herr lass wohl gelingen]

Sacred German text. Sources: Matthew 21:9. Psalm 118:25-26. Trio (SST) with 2 violins and basso continuo. Ranges of voice parts: c1-f2, c#1-f2, c-f1. Duration: short.

1   O Herr hilf, o Herr lass wohl gelingen. -- In SGA. -- 1891. -- Bd. 10, p. 54-57.
    Edited by Philipp Spitta. Figured bass not realized. Original German text. Notes in German.

5   Oh Herr hilf, o Herr lass wohl gelingen = O save us Lord. -- Neuhausen-Stuttgart : Hänssler, c1967. Pub. no.: HE 20.402.
    Edited by Günter Graulich. Continuo realized by Paul Horn. German text with English translation. Notes in German and English.

SWV 403

[Symphoniae sacrae, 3 pars. Siehe, es erschien der Engel des Herren
      Joseph im Traum]

   Sacred German text. Sources: Matthew 2:13-15.
   Quartet (STTB) with 2 violins and basso continuo with optional
chorus (SATB) and 4 unspecified instruments. Ranges of voice parts:
c1-f2, c-g1, c-g1, D-c1/ d1-e2, a-a1, c#-f1, D-c1. Duration: medium.

1   Siehe, es erschien der Engel des Herren Joseph im Traum. -- In SGA.
    -- 1891. -- Bd. 10, p. 58-66.
      Edited by Philipp Spitta. Figured bass not realized. Original
   German text. Notes in German.

5   Siehe, es erschien der Engel des Herren Joseph im Traum = The flight
    into Egypt. -- Neuhausen-Stuttgart : Hänssler, c1967. Pub. no.: XX
    403.
      Edited by Günter Graulich. Continuo realized by Paul Horn. German
   text with English translation. Notes in German and English.

SWV 404

[Symphoniae sacrae, 3 pars. Feget den alten Sauerteig aus]

   Sacred German text. Sources: Corinthians, 1st, 5:7-8.
   Quartet (SATB) with 2 violins and basso continuo. Ranges of voice
parts: bflat-f2, g-a1, c-g1, F-d1. Duration: medium.

1   Feget den alten Sauerteig aus. -- In SGA. -- 1891. -- Bd. 10, p.
    67-76.
      Edited by Philipp Spitta. Figured bass not realized. Original
   German text. Notes in German.

5   Feget den alten Sauerteig aus. -- Stuttgart : Hänssler, [19--]. Pub.
    no.: H. 2572 H.
      Edited by Emil Kübler. German text. Words in Gothic type.
   Transposed up M2.

   Other editions: Hänssler 5.008.

SWV 405

[Symphoniae sacrae, 3 pars. O süsser Jesu Christ, wer an dich recht
      gedenket]

   Sacred German text. Sources: Heermann, Johann. O süsser Jesu Christ,
wer an dich recht gedenket.
   Quartet (SSAT) with 2 violins and basso continuo and optional
chorus (SATB) and 4 unspecified instruments. Ranges of voice parts:
c1-g2, d1-f2, a-bflat1, c-g1/ e1-d2, bflat-g1, e-f1, F#-bflat.
Duration: long.

1   O süsser Jesu Christ, wer an dich recht gedenket. -- In SGA. --
    1891. -- Bd. 10, p. 77-88.
    Edited by Philipp Spitta. Figured bass not realized. Original
    German text. Notes in German.

3   O süsser Jesu Christ. -- Kassel : Bärenreiter, c1956. Pub. no.:
    Bärenreiter-Ausgabe 3369.
    Edited by Werner Bittinger. German text. Words in Gothic type.
    Notes in German.

    Other editions: Hänssler HE20.405.

SWV 406

[Symphoniae sacrae, 3 pars. O Jesu süss, wer dein gedenkt]

    Sacred German text. Sources: O Jesu süss, wer dein gedenkt.
    Quartet (SSTT) with 2 violins and basso continuo. Ranges of voice
    parts: f1-f2, d1-f2, f-f1, c-f1. Duration: medium.

1   O Jesu süss, wer dein gedenkt. -- In SGA. -- 1891. -- Bd. 10, p.
    89-95.
    Edited by Philipp Spitta. Figured bass not realized. Original
    German text. Notes in German.

    Other editions: Hänssler HE20.406.

SWV 407

[Symphoniae sacrae, 3 pars. Lasset uns doch den Herren, unsern Gott,
    loben]

    Sacred German text. Sources: Apocrypha. Ecclesiasticus 50:24.
    Apocrypha. Judith 16:15. Jeremiah 5:24. Jeremiah 33:11. Psalm 34:4.
    Psalm 46:9. Psalm 46:7. Psalm 65:12. Psalm 81:2. Psalm 95:1-2. Psalm
    100:1. Psalm 147:9. Psalm 147:12-14. Psalm 147:7. Psalm 149:1. Psalm
    150:4.
    Quartet (SSTB) with 2 violins and basso continuo with optional
    chorus (SATB) and 4 unspecified instruments. Ranges of voice parts:
    d1-g2, c1-e2, d-g1, D-d1/ e1-e2, a-a1, d-e1, G-c1. Duration: medium.

1   Lasset uns doch den Herren, unsern Gott, loben. -- In SGA. -- 1891.
    -- Bd. 10, p. 96-107.
    Edited by Philipp Spitta. Figured bass not realized. Original
    German text. Notes in German.

5   Lasset uns doch den Herren, unsern Gott, loben = Let us declare the
    glory of the Lord. -- Neuhausen-Stuttgart : Hänssler, c1968. Pub.
    no.: HE 20.407.
    Edited by Günter Graulich. Continuo realized by Paul Horn. German
    text with English translation. Notes in German and English.

SWV 408

[Symphoniae sacrae, 3 pars. Es ging ein Sämann aus zu säen]

Sacred German text. Sources: Luke 8:5-8.
Quartet (SATB) with 2 violins, bassoon and basso continuo with optional chorus (SATB) and 4 unspecified instruments. Ranges of voice parts: dl-f2, g-bflatl, c-fl, E-dl, gl-f2, cl-gl, e-el, E-cl. Duration: long.

1   Es ging ein Sämann aus zu säen. -- In SGA. -- 1891. -- Bd. 11, p. 3-24.
    Edited by Philipp Spitta. Figured bass not realized. Original German text. Notes in German.

3   Es ging ein Sämann aus, zu säen seinen Samen. -- Kassel : Bärenreiter, [1934?]. Pub. no.: Bärenreiter 827.
    Edited by Hans Hoffman. German text. Words in Gothic type. Notes in German. Transposed up m3.

5   Es ging ein Sämann aus zu säen seinen Samen = A sower in his field was sowing. -- Neuhausen-Stuttgart : Hänssler, c1968. Pub. no.: HE 20.408.
    Edited by Günter Graulich. Continuo realized by Paul Horn. German text with English translation. Notes in German and English.

SWV 409

[Symphoniae sacrae, 3 pars. Seid barmherzig, wie auch euer Vater barmherzig ist]

Sacred German text. Sources: Luke 6:36-42.
Quartet (SATB) with 2 violins, bassoon and basso continuo with optional chorus (SATB) and 4 unspecified instruments. Ranges of voice parts: cl-e2, d-al, c-fl, D-dl/ el-e2, b-al, c#-el, E-a. Duration: medium.

1   Seid barmherzig, wie auch euer Vater barmherzig ist. -- In SGA. -- 1891. -- Bd. 11, p. 25-38.
    Edited by Philipp Spitta. Figured bass not realized. Original German text. Notes in German.

3   Seid barmherzig, wie auch euer Vater barmherzig ist. -- Kassel : Bärenreiter, c1956. Pub. no.: Bärenreiter-Ausgabe 3370.
    Edited by Werner Bittinger. German text. Words in Gothic type. Notes in German. Transposed up M2.

5   Seid barmherzig, wie auch euer Vater barmherzig ist = Be ye loving, even as your father hath loved you. -- Neuhausen-Stuttgart : Hänssler, c1969. Pub. no.: HE 20.409/01.
    Edited by Günter Graulich. Continuo realized by Paul Horn. German text with English translation. Notes in German and English.

SWV 410

[Symphoniae sacrae, 3 pars. Siehe, dieser wird gesetzt zu einem Fall]

Sacred German text. Sources: Luke 2:34-35.
Quintet (SSATB) with 2 violins and basso continuo. Ranges of voice parts: a-e2, d1-e2, g-a1, d-e1, E-b. Duration: medium.

1 Siehe, dieser wird gesetzt zu einem Fall. -- In SGA. -- 1891. -- Bd. 11, p. 39-50.
   Edited by Philipp Spitta. Figured bass not realized. Original German text. Notes in German.

5 Siehe, dieser wird gesetzt zu einem Fall = See now, this child has been sent for the downfall. -- Neuhausen-Stuttgart : Hänssler, c1972. Pub. no.: HE 20.410.
   Edited by Günter Graulich. Continuo realized by Paul Horn. German text with English translation. Notes in German and English.

SWV 411

[Symphoniae sacrae, 3 pars. Vater unser, der du bist im Himmel]

Sacred German text. Sources: Lord's prayer.
Quintet (SMTTB) with 2 violins and basso continuo with optional chorus (SATB) and 4 unspecified instruments. Ranges of voice parts: d1-f2, bflat-c2, c-g1, c-f1, D-d1/ f#1-e2, c1-bflat1, f-e1, F-a. Duration: medium.

1 Vater unser, der du bist im Himmel. -- In SGA. -- 1891. -- Bd. 11, p. 51-62.
   Edited by Philipp Spitta. Figured bass not realized. Original German text. Notes in German.

3 Vater unser. -- Kassel : Bärenreiter, c1964. Pub. no.: Bärenreiter 3426.
   Edited by Werner Bittinger. German text. Notes in German.

5 Vater Unser = The Lord's prayer. -- Neuhausen-Stuttgart : Hänssler, c1972. Pub. no.: HE 20.411.
   Edited by Günter Graulich. Continuo realized by Paul Horn. German text with English translation. Notes in German and English.

6 Our Father = Das Vaterunser. -- New York : Broude Brothers, c1954. Pub. no.: B.B. 131.
   Edited by Kurt Stone. German text with English translation. Notes in English. Transposed up M2.

SWV 412

[Symphoniae sacrae, 3 pars. Siehe, wie fein und lieblich ist]

Sacred German text. Sources: Psalm 133.
Quintet (SSATB) with 2 violins, bassoon, basso continuo, and 2 unspecified optional instruments. Ranges of voice parts: c1-g2, b-f2, f-a1, A-f1, Eflat-d1. Duration: medium.

1   Siehe, wie fein und lieblich ist. -- In SGA. -- 1891. -- Bd. 11, p. 62-74.
Edited by Philipp Spitta. Figured bass not realized. Original German text. Notes in German.

6   Siehe, wie fein und lieblich. -- Stuttgart : Hohenheim, [19--]. Pub. no.: H. 3844 H.
Edited by Paul Horn. German text. Notes in German.

Other editions: Hänssler 1.286; 2.049; 2.052; 8.038; 9.005; 44.169.

SWV 413

[Symphoniae sacrae, 3 pars. Hütet euch, dass eure Herzen nicht beschweret werden]

Sacred German text. Sources: Luke 21:34-36.
Sextet (SSATTB) with 2 violins and basso continuo. Ranges of voice parts: a-e2, d1-e2, e-a1, A-e1, c-e1, D-b. Duration: medium.

1   Hütet euch, dass eure Herzen nicht beschweret werden. -- In SGA. -- 1891. -- Bd. 11, p. 75-85.
Edited by Philipp Spitta. Figured bass not realized. Original German text. Notes in German.

5   Hütet euch, dass eure Herzen nicht beschweret werden = Watch and pray. -- Neuhausen-Stuttgart : Hänssler, c1974. Pub. no.: HE 20.413.
Edited by Günter Graulich. Continuo realized by Paul Horn. German text with English translation. Notes in German and English.

SWV 414

[Symphoniae sacrae, 3 pars. Meister, wir wissen, dass du wahrhaftig bist]

Sacred German text. Sources: Matthew 22:16-21.
Quintet (SSATB) with 2 violins, bassoon and basso continuo with optional chorus (SATB) and 4 unspecified instruments. Ranges of voice parts: d1-f2, c1-e2, f-a1, d-f1, F-c1/ f1-f2, bflat-a1, f#-f1,F-c1. Duration: medium.

1   Meister, wir wissen, dass du wahrhaftig bist. -- In SGA. -- 1891. --
    Bd. 11, p. 86-98.
    Edited by Philipp Spitta. Figured bass not realized. Original
    German text. Notes in German.

3   Meister, wir wissen, dass du wahrhaftig bist. -- Kassel :
    Bärenreiter, [1940?]. Pub. no.: Bärenreiter-Ausgabe 1486.
    Edited by Rudolf Holle. German text. Notes in German. Transposed
    up M2.

    Other editions: Hänssler HE20.414.

SWV 415

[Symphoniae sacrae, 3 pars. Saul, Saul, was verfolgst du mich?]

    Sacred German text. Sources: Acts 9:4-5.
    Sextet (SSATBB) with 2 violins, basso continuo and optional
    choruses (SATB/SATB). Ranges of voice parts: c1-f2, a-e2, f-a1,
    d-f#1, G-b, D-a/ d1-d2, g-g1, f#-e1, G-a/ d1-e2, a-a1, d-e1, F-a.
    Duration: short.

1   Saul, Saul, was verfolgst du mich?. -- In SGA. -- 1891. -- Bd. 11,
    p. 99-108.
    Edited by Philipp Spitta. Figured bass not realized. Original
    German text. Notes in German.

3   Saul, Saul, was verfolgst du mich = Saul, Saul, why persecutest thou
    me?. -- Kassel : Bärenreiter, c1966. Pub. no.: Bärenreiter 3466.
    Edited by Werner Bittinger. German text. Notes in German and
    English. Transposed up M2.

5   Saul, Saul, was verfolgst du mich = Saul, Saul, wilt thou injure
    me?. -- Neuhausen-Stuttgart : Hänssler, c1969. Pub. no.: HE 20.415.
    Edited by Günter Graulich. Continuo realized by Paul Horn. German
    text with English translation. Notes in German and English.

6   Saul. -- Minneapolis, Minn. : Augsburg Publishing House, c1963.
    Edited by Frank Pooler. German text with English translation.

SWV 416

[Symphoniae sacrae, 3 pars. Herr, wie lang willt du mein so gar
      vergessen?]

    Sacred German text. Sources: Psalm 13.
    Sextet (SSATTB) with 2 violins, basso continuo and 4 optional
    viols. Ranges of voice parts: c1-e2, c1-e2, g-a1, A-f1, A-e1, E-c1.
    Duration: medium.

1   Herr, wie lang willt du mein so gar vergessen?. -- In SGA. -- 1891.
    -- Bd. 11, p. 109-124.
    Edited by Philipp Spitta. Figured bass not realized. Original
    German text. Notes in German.

Other editions: Hänssler HE20.416.

SWV 417

[Symphoniae sacrae, 3 pars. Komm, heilger Geist, Herre Gott]

    Sacred German text. Sources: Komm, heiliger Geist. Luther, Martin.
Komm, heiliger Geist.
    Sextet (SMTTRB) with 2 violins, basso continuo, and optional
choruses (SATB/SATB). Ranges of voice parts: f1-e2, a-c2, e-g1,
c-e1, c-d1, D-d1, g#1-e2, c1-a1, e-e1, A-a, e1-e2, c1-a1, e-e1, E-a.
Duration: medium.

1   Komm, heilger Geist, Herre Gott. -- In SGA. -- 1891. -- Bd. 11, p.
125-142.
    Edited by Philipp Spitta. Figured bass not realized. Original
German text. Notes in German.

5   Komm, heiliger Geist, Herre Gott = Come, Holy Ghost, Our Lord. --
Neuhausen-Stuttgart : Hänssler, c1974. Pub. no.: HE 20.417.
    Edited by Günter Graulich. Continuo realized by Paul Horn. German
text with English translation. Notes in German and English.

    Other editions: Hänssler 1.675.

SWV 418

[Symphoniae sacrae, 3 pars. Nun danket alle Gott]

    Sacred German text. Sources: Apocrypha. Ecclesiasticus 50:24-26.
    Sextet (SSATTB) with 2 violins and basso continuo with optional
chorus (SATB) and 4 unspecified instruments. Ranges of voice parts:
d1-eflat2, c1-eflat2, g-a1, c-f1, c-e1, F-d1, c1-bflat1, f-e1, d-c1,
F-g. Duration: medium.

1   Nun danket alle Gott. -- In SGA. -- 1891. -- Bd. 11, p. 143-156.
    Edited by Philipp Spitta. Figured bass not realized. Original
German text. Notes in German.

5   Nun danket alle Gott = Let all give thanks to God. --
Neuhausen-Stuttgart : Hänssler, c1975. Pub. no.: HE 20.418.
    Edited by Günter Graulich. Continuo realized by Paul Horn. German
text with English translation. Notes in German and English.

    Other editions: Hänssler 5.010.

SWV 419

[Trauerlied]

    Sacred German text. Sources: Brehm, Christian. Trauerlied.
    For chorus (SATB) a cappella. Ranges of voice parts: e1-e2, b-g#1,
e-e1, A-a. Duration: short.

1   O meine Seel, warum bist du betrübet. -- In SGA. -- 1927. -- Bd. 18,
     p. 115.
     Edited by Heinrich Spitta. Original German text. Notes in German.

2   Ein Trauerlied. -- In NSA. -- 1970. -- Bd. 37, p. 7-8. Pub. no.:
     BA4489.
     Edited by Werner Bittinger. German text. Notes in German and
     English.

SWV 420

[Geistliche Gesänge. Kyrie, Gott Vater in Ewigkeit]

    Sacred German text. Sources: Missa brevis deutsch. Kyrie.
    For chorus (SATB) and optional continuo. Ranges of voice parts:
    d1-e2, g-a1, c-f1, G-c1. Duration: medium.

1   Kyrie Gott Vater in Ewigkeit. -- In SGA. -- 1892. -- Bd. 12, p.
     117-121.
     Edited by Philipp Spitta. Continuo not realized. Original German
     text. Notes in German.

4   Kyrie, Gott Vater in Ewigkeit. -- In SSA. -- 1971. -- Bd. 15, p.
     3-9. Pub. no.: HE 20.915.
     Edited by Günter Graulich. Continuo realized by Paul Horn. German
     text with English translation.

5   Kyrie, Gott Vater in Ewigkeit = Kyrie, God Father throughout all
     time. -- Neuhausen-Stuttgart : Hänssler, c1967. Pub. no.: HE 20.420.
     Edited by Günter Graulich. Continuo realized by Paul Horn. German
     text with English translation. Notes in German and English.

6   Kyrie Gott Vater in Ewigkeit. -- Mainz : B. Schott's Söhne, c1925.
     Pub. no.: C 31 296.
     German text.

SWV 421

[Geistliche Gesänge. Teutsche Gloria in excelsis]

    Sacred German text. Sources: Missa brevis deutsch. Gloria.
    For chorus (SATB) with optional continuo. Ranges of voice parts:
    e1-g2, g-b1, c-g1, G-c1. Duration: medium.

1   Das teutsche Gloria in excelsis : super All Ehr und Lob soll Gottes
     sein. -- In SGA. -- 1892. -- Bd. 12, p. 122-128.
     Edited by Philipp Spitta. Continuo not realized. Original German
     text. Notes in German.

4   All Ehr und Lob soll Gottes sein. -- In SSA. -- 1971. -- Bd. 15, p.
     10-19. Pub. no.: HE 20.915.
     Edited by Günter Graulich. Continuo realized by Paul Horn. German
     text with English translation.

5   All Ehr und Lob soll Gottes sein = Glory to God upon his throne. --
     Neuhausen-Stuttgart : Hänssler, c1968. Pub. no.: HE 20.421/01.
        Edited by Günter Graulich. Continuo realized by Paul Horn. German
     text with English translation. Notes in German and English.

SWV 422

[Geistliche Gesänge. Nicaenische Glaube]

     Sacred German text. Sources: Nicene Creed. German.
        For chorus (SATB) with optional continuo. Ranges of voice parts:
     cl-e2, g-al, c-gl, E-cl. Duration: medium.

1   Der Nicaenische Glaube : Ich gläube an einen einigen Gott. -- In
     SGA. -- 1892. -- Bd. 12, p. 129-134.
        Edited by Philipp Spitta. Continuo not realized. Original German
     text. Notes in German.

4   Ich glaube an einen einigen Gott. -- In SSA. -- 1971. -- Bd. 15, p.
     20-29. Pub. no.: HE 20.915.
        Edited by Günter Graulich. Continuo realized by Paul Horn. German
     text with English translation.

5   Ich glaube an einen einigen Gott = I believe in one God. --
     Neuhausen-Stuttgart : Hänssler, c1969. Pub. no.: HE 20.422.
        Edited by Günter Graulich. Continuo realized by Paul Horn. German
     text with English translation. Notes in German and English.

SWV 423

[Geistliche Gesänge. Wort der Einsetzung des heiligen Abendmahls]

     Sacred German text. Sources: Corinthians, 1st, 11:23-25. Matthew 26
     :26-28.
        For chorus (SMAR) with optional continuo. Ranges of voice parts:
     dl-f2, bflat-c2, g-al, Bflat-dl. Duration: medium.

1   Die Wort der Einsetzung des heiligen Abendmahls. -- In SGA. -- 1892.
     -- Bd. 12, p. 135-139.
        Edited by Philipp Spitta. Continuo not realized. Original German
     text. Notes in German.

4   Unser Herr Jesus Christus in der Nacht, da er verraten ward. -- In
     SSA. -- 1971. -- Bd. 15, p. 30-36. Pub. no.: HE 20.915.
        Edited by Günter Graulich. Continuo realized by Paul Horn. German
     text with English translation.

5   Unser Herr Jesus Christus in der Nacht, da er verraten ward = When
     Our Lord was betrayed. -- Neuhausen-Stuttgart : Hänssler, c1969.
     Pub. no.: HE 20.423.
        Edited by Günter Graulich. Continuo realized by Paul Horn. German
     text with English translation. Notes in German and English.

     Other editions: Hänssler 9.002.

SWV 424

[Geistliche Gesänge. Psalm 111]

Sacred German text. Sources: Psalm 111. Gloria Patri.
For chorus (SMAR) with optional continuo. Ranges of voice parts:
d1-f2, g-c2, f-a1, c-d1. Duration: medium.

1   Der 111. Psalm : Ich danke dem Herrn von ganzem Herzen. -- In SGA.
    -- 1892. -- Bd. 12, p. 140-146.
    Edited by Philipp Spitta. Continuo not realized. Original German
    text. Notes in German.

4   Psalm 111. -- In SSA. -- 1971. -- Bd. 15, p. 37-45. Pub. no.: HE
    20.915.
    Edited by Günter Graulich. Continuo realized by Paul Horn. German
    text with English translation.

5   Ich danke dem Herrn von ganzem Herzen = All thanks to the Lord. --
    Neuhausen-Stuttgart : Hänssler, c1969. Pub. no.: HE 20.424/01.
    Edited by Günter Graulich. Continuo realized by Paul Horn. German
    text with English translation. Notes in German and English.

    Other editions: Hänssler 9.005.

SWV 425

[Geistliche Gesänge. Danksagen wir alle Gott, unserm Herren Christo]

Sacred German text. Sources: Dank sagen wir alle Gott.
For chorus (SMAT) with optional continuo. Ranges of voice parts:
f1-e2, d1-b1, a-g1, c-e1. Duration: short.

1   Danksagen wir alle Gott. -- In SGA. -- 1892. -- Bd. 12, p. 147-148.
    Edited by Philipp Spitta. Continuo not realized. Original German
    text. Notes in German.

3   Danksagen wir alle. -- Kassel : Bärenreiter, c1974. Pub. no.: BA
    996.
    German text. Continuo line not included.

4   Danksagen wir alle Gott, unserm Herren Christo. -- In SSA. -- 1971.
    -- Bd. 15, p. 46-48. Pub. no.: HE 20.915.
    Edited by Günter Graulich. Continuo realized by Paul Horn. German
    text with English translation.

5   Danksagen wir alle Gott, unserm Herren Christo = All thanks be to
    God. -- Neuhausen-Stuttgart : Hänssler, c1968. Pub. no.: HE 20.425.
    Edited by Günter Graulich. Continuo realized by Paul Horn. German
    text with English translation. Notes in German and English.

    Other editions: Hänssler HE20.425.

SWV 426

[Geistliche Gesänge. Magnificat]

Sacred German text. Sources: Magnificat.
For chorus (SATB) with optional continuo. Ranges of voice parts:
d1-e2, g-a1, d-e1, G-c1. Duration: medium.

1   Magnificat : meine Seele erhebt den Herren. -- In SGA. -- 1892. --
    Bd. 12, p. 149-157.
       Edited by Philipp Spitta. Continuo not realized. Original German
    text. Notes in German.

4   Meine Seele erhebt den Herren. -- In SSA. -- 1971. -- Bd. 15, p.
    49-60. Pub. no.: HE 20.915.
       Edited by Günter Graulich. Continuo realized by Paul Horn. German
    text with English translation.

5   Meine Seele erhebt den Herren = The German Magnificat 1657. --
    Neuhausen-Stuttgart : Hänssler, c1968. Pub. no.: HE 20.426.
       Edited by Günter Graulich. Continuo realized by Paul Horn. German
    text with English translation. Notes in German and English.

6   Magnificat for four voices from Twelve sacred songs, 1657. --
    Springfield, Ohio : Chantry Music Press, c1966.
       Edited by Richard T. Gore. German text with English translation.
    Notes in English. Transposed up m2.

SWV 426

[Geistliche Gesänge. Magnificat. Ehre sei dem Vater]

7   Gloria Patri = Ehre sei dem Vater = Glory to the Father. --
    Neuhausen-Stuttgart : Hänssler, c1969. Pub. no.: HE 20.426/1.
       Chorus (SATB) with optional continuo. Concluding chorus from SWV
    426. Edited by Günter Graulich. Continuo realized by Paul Horn.
    German text with English translation.

8   Ehre sei dem Vater = Glory to the Father. -- New York, N.Y. : Tetra
    Music Corp., c1977.
       Edited by Kurt Stone. German text with English translation.
    Transposed up m3.

9   Ehre sei dem Vater. -- Augsburg : A. Böhm, c1971. Pub. no.: 11487.
       For chorus (SATB) a capella. Continuo line not included.
    Concluding chorus from SWV 426. Edited by Gerhard Kronberg. German
    text. Transposed up M2.

       Other editions: Bärenreiter BA581 (Ehre sei); Hänssler 44.721
    (Ehre sei).

SWV 427

[Geistliche Gesänge. Des H. Bernhardi Freuden-Gesang]

Sacred German text. Sources: Heermann, Johann. O süsser Jesu Christ, wer an dich recht gedenket.
For chorus (SMAR) and optional continuo or alternating choruses (SMAR/SMAR) and optional continuo. Ranges of voice parts: e1-f2, a-d2, g-a1, A-d1. Duration: medium.

1 Des H. Bernhardt Freuden-Gesang. -- In SGA. -- 1892. -- Bd. 12, p. 158-162.
Edited by Philipp Spitta. Continuo not realized. Original German text. Notes in German.

4 O süsser Jesu Christ, wer an dich recht gedenket : des heiligen Bernhard Freudengesang. -- In SSA. -- 1971. -- Bd. 15, p. 61-66. Pub. no.: HE 20.915.
Edited by Günter Graulich. Continuo realized by Paul Horn. German text with English translation.

5 O süsser Jesu Christ, wer an dich recht gedenket = Oh, Jesus Christ, my Lord, I beg thee, do not leave me. -- Neuhausen-Stuttgart : Hänssler, c1968. Pub. no.: HE 20.427.
Edited by Günter Graulich. Continuo realized by Paul Horn. German text with English translation. Notes in German and English.

SWV 427

[Geistliche Gesänge. Des H. Bernhardi Freuden-Gesang. Nun sei dem Vater Dank]

6 Nun sei dem Vater Dank. -- Neuhausen-Stuttgart : Hänssler, c1969. Pub. no.: HE 20.427/10.
For chorus (SATB) and optional continuo. Closing movement of SWV 427. Edited by Günter Graulich. Continuo realized by Paul Horn. German text with English translation.

Other editions: Hänssler 2.049 (Nun sei).

SWV 428

[Geistliche Gesänge. Teutsche gemeine Litaney]

Sacred German text. Sources: Luther, Martin. Deutsche Litanei.
For chorus (SATB) with optional continuo. Ranges of voice parts: d1-a1, f-f1, d-f1, F-bflat. Duration: medium.

1 Die teutsche gemeine Litaney. -- In SGA. -- 1892. -- Bd. 12, p. 163-170.
Edited by Philipp Spitta. Continuo not realized. Original German text. Notes in German.

4   Die deutsche Litanei. -- In SSA. -- 1971. -- Bd. 15, p. 67-81. Pub.
     no.: HE 20.915.
         Edited by Günter Graulich. Continuo realized by Paul Horn. German
     text with English translation.

5   Die deutsche Litanei = The Litany. -- Neuhausen-Stuttgart :
     Hänssler, c1969. Pub. no.: HE 20.428.
         Edited by Günter Graulich. Continuo realized by Paul Horn. German
     text with English translation. Notes in German and English.

SWV 429

[Geistliche Gesänge. Benedicite vor dem Essen]

     Sacred German text. Sources: Psalm 145:15-16. Lord's prayer. Luther,
     Martin. Herre Gott, himmlischer Vater.
         For chorus (SATB) with optional continuo. Ranges of voice parts:
     c1-e2, g-a1, c-f1, E-bflat. Duration: medium.

1   Das Benedicite vor dem Essen. -- In SGA. -- 1892. -- Bd. 12, p.
     171-175.
         Edited by Philipp Spitta. Continuo not realized. Original German
     text. Notes in German.

4   Das Benedicite vor dem Essen. -- In SSA. -- 1971. -- Bd. 15, p.
     82-87. Pub. no.: HE 20.915.
         Edited by Günter Graulich. Continuo realized by Paul Horn. German
     text with English translation.

5   Das Benedicite vor dem Essen. -- Neuhausen-Stuttgart : Hänssler,
     c1969. Pub. no.: HE 20.429.
         Edited by Günter Graulich. Continuo realized by Paul Horn. German
     text with English translation. Notes in German and English.

6   Das Benedicite und Vaterunser = Benediction and the Lord's prayer.
     -- New York : Tetra Music Corp., c1977. Pub. no.: A.B. 402.
         Edited by Kurt Stone. German text with English translation.

SWV 429

[Geistliche Gesänge. Benedicite vor dem Essen. Aller Augen warten auf
     dich]

7   Aller Augen warten auf dich, Herre. -- Neuhausen-Stuttgart :
     Hänssler, c1969. Pub. no.: HE 20.429/1.
         For chorus (SATB) with optional continuo. Opening movement of SWV
     429. Edited by Günter Graulich. Continuo realized by Paul Horn.
     German text with English translation.

8   Aller Augen warten auf dich. -- Neuhausen-Stuttgart : Hänssler,
     c1968. Pub. no.: HE 6.082.
         Continuo line not included. German text. Transposed up M2.

9   Aller Augen warten auf dich. -- Kassel : Bärenreiter, 1964.
         Continuo line not included. German text. Words in Gothic type.

10 Ev'ry eye waiteth upon thee = Aller Augen warten auf dich. -- In
    Three chorales. -- Fort Lauderdale, Fla. : Music 70, c1975. -- p.
    3-4. Pub. no.: M70-153.
        Edited by John Kingsbury. German text with English translation.
    Transposed up M3.

SWV 429

[Geistliche Gesänge. Benedicite vor dem Essen. Herre Gott, himmlischer
    Vater]

11 Herre Gott, himmlischer Vater. -- Neuhausen-Stuttgart : Hänssler,
    c1969. Pub. no.: HE 20.429/3.
        For chorus (SATB) and optional continuo. Closing movement of SWV
    429. Edited by Günter Graulich. Continuo realized by Paul Horn.
    German text with English translation.

SWV 429

[Geistliche Gesänge. Benedicite vor dem Essen. Vater unser]

12 Vater unser = Lord's prayer. -- Neuhausen-Stuttgart : Hänssler,
    c1969. Pub. no.: HE 20.429/20.
        For chorus (SATB) and optional continuo. Second movement of SWV
    429. Edited by Günter Graulich. Continuo realized by Paul Horn.
    German text with English translation.

13 The Lord's prayer. -- Fremont, Ohio : Chantry Music Press, c1950.
    English text.

14 Our Father, which art in heaven = Vater unser, der du bist im
    Himmel. -- New York : S. Fox, c1965. Pub. no.: CM 1.
        Edited by Roger Granville. German text with English translation.
    Transposed up M2.

        Other editions: Bärenreiter BCh33 (Aller Augen); Hänssler
    20.429/30 (Herre Gott).

SWV 430

[Geistliche Gesänge. Deo gratias nach dem Essen]

    Sacred German text. Sources: Psalm 136:1. Psalm 136:26. Psalm 147
    :9-11. Lord's prayer. Luther, Martin. Wir danken dir, Herr Gott.
        For chorus (SATB) with optional continuo. Ranges of voice parts:
    c1-e2, g-a1, c-f1, E-c1. Duration: medium.

1   Das Deo gratias nach dem Essen. -- In SGA. -- 1892. -- Bd. 12, p.
    175-178.
        Edited by Philipp Spitta. Continuo not realized. Original German
    text. Notes in German. Part 2 of SWV 430 is identical to part 2 of
    SWV 429.

4   Das Deo gratias nach dem Essen. -- In SSA. -- 1971. -- Bd. 15, p. 88-94. Pub. no.: HE 20.915.
     Edited by Günter Graulich. Continuo realized by Paul Horn. German text with English translation.

5   Das Deo gratias nach dem Essen = The Lord be praised. -- Neuhausen-Stuttgart : Hänssler, c1969. Pub. no.: HE 20.430.
     Edited by Günter Graulich. Continuo realized by Paul Horn. German text with English translation. Notes in German and English.

SWV 430

[Geistliche Gesänge. Deo gratias nach dem Essen. Danket dem Herren]

6   Danket dem Herren, denn er ist sehr freundlich. -- Neuhausen-Stuttgart : Hänssler, c1969. Pub. no.: HE20.430/1.
     For chorus (SATB) and optional continuo. Opening movement of SWV 430. Edited by Günter Graulich. Continuo realized by Paul Horn. German text with English translation.

SWV 430

[Geistliche Gesänge. Deo gratias nach dem Essen. Wir danken dir, Herr Gott, himmlischer Vater]

7   Wir danken dir, Herr Gott, himmlischer Vater. -- Neuhausen-Stuttgart : Hänssler, c1969. Pub. no.: HE20.430/3.
     For chorus (SATB) and optional continuo. Closing movement of SWV 430. Edited by Günter Graulich. German text with English translation.

SWV 431

[Geistliche Gesänge. Christe fac ut sapiam]

     Sacred German text. Sources: Hymnus ante lectionem pro vera sapientia ad Jesum Christum Deum Optimum Maximum in auditoriis et scholis.
     For chorus (SATB) and optional continuo or alternating choruses (SATB/SATB) and optional continuo. Ranges of voice parts: d1-c2, a-a1, g-e1, E-c1. Duration: medium.

1   Christe fac ut sapiam. -- In SGA. -- 1892. -- Bd. 12, p. 179-182.
     Edited by Philipp Spitta. Continuo not realized. Original German text. Notes in German.

4   Christe fac ut sapiam. -- In SSA. -- 1971. -- Bd. 15, p. 95-100. Pub. no.: HE 20.915.
     Edited by Günter Graulich. Continuo realized by Paul Horn. Latin text with German translation.

5   Christe fac ut sapiam = Christe, lass mich weise sein. --
     Neuhausen-Stuttgart : Hänssler, c1969. Pub. no.: HE 20.431.
       Edited by Günter Graulich. Continuo realized by Paul Horn. Latin
     text with German translation. Notes in German and English.

SWV 432

[Canticum B. Simeonis, SWV 432]

       Sacred German text. Sources: Nunc dimittis.
         For chorus (SSATTB) and optional basso continuo. Ranges of voice
       parts: d1-eflat2, c1-d2, bflat-a1, c-d1, c-d1, F-bflat. Duration:
       short.

1   Canticum B. Simeonis, I. -- In SGA. -- 1892. -- Bd. 12, p. 201-204.
       Edited by Philipp Spitta. Figured bass not realized. Original
     German text. Notes in German.

2   Herr, nun lassest du deinen Diener in Friede fahren. -- In NSA. --
     1970. -- Bd. 31, p. 73-81. Pub. no.: BA4483.
       Edited by Werner Breig. German text. Notes in German and English.

3   Herr, nun lassest du deinen Diener in Friede fahren. -- Kassel :
     Bärenreiter, c1970. Pub. no.: BA 5919.
       Edited by Werner Breig. German text. Notes in German.

5   Herr, nun lassest du deinen Diener im Frieden fahren = The German
     Nunc dimittis I 1656. -- Neuhausen-Stuttgart : Hänssler, c1967. Pub.
     no.: XX 432.
       Edited by Günter Graulich. Continuo realized by Paul Horn. German
     text with English translation. Notes in German and English.

SWV 433

[Canticum B. Simeonis, SWV 433]

       Sacred German text. Sources: Nunc dimittis.
         For chorus (SSATTB) and optional basso continuo. Ranges of voice
       parts: e1-f2, c1-e2, g-a1, d-e1, c-e1, E-c1. Duration: short.

1   Canticum B. Simeonis, II. -- In SGA. -- 1892. -- Bd. 12, p. 204-207.
       Original German text. Notes in German.

2   Herr, nun lassest du deinen Diener in Friede fahren. -- In NSA. --
     1970. -- Bd. 31, p. 82-91. Pub. no.: BA4483.
       Edited by Werner Breig. German text. Notes in German and English.

5   Herr, nun lassest du deinen Diener im Frieden fahren = The German
     Nunc dimittis II 1656. -- Neuhausen-Stuttgart : Hänssler, c1967.
     Pub. no.: XX 433.
       Edited by Günter Graulich. Continuo realized by Paul Horn. German
     text with English translation. Notes in German and English.

SWV 434

[Wie wenn der Adler sich aus seiner Klippe schwingt]

    Secular German text. Sources: Schirmer, David. Wie wenn der Adler sich aus seiner Klippe schwingt.
    Solo for soprano with basso continuo. Range of voice part: f1-e2. Duration: short.

1   Aria : Wie wenn der Adler sich aus seiner Klippe schwingt. -- In SGA. -- 1893. -- Bd. 15, p. 87.
    Edited by Philipp Spitta. Figured bass not realized. Original German text. Notes in German.

2   Wie wenn der Adler sich aus seiner Klippe schwingt. -- In NSA. -- 1970. -- Bd. 37, p. 3. Pub. no.: BA4489.
    Edited by Werner Bittinger. German text. Notes in German and English.

SWV 435

[Historia von der Geburt Jesu Christi]

    Sacred German text. Sources: Luke 2:1-21. Luke 2:40. Matthew 2. Dank sagen wir alle Gott.
    For chorus (SSATTB in mvnt. 5; AAA in mvnt. 7; BBBB in mvnt. 11; SATB in mvnt. 19), evangelist (tenor), angel (soprano), wise men (TTT), Herod (bass), violetta I and II, violin I and II, viola I and II, bassoon, clarino I and II or cornetto I and II, trombone I and II, and continuo. Ranges of voice parts: e1-g2, c1-g2, g-bflat1, c-g1, c-f1, F-d1/ b-a1, g-a1, f-f1/ c-d1, G-bflat, D-bflat, D-bflat/ f1-eflat2, bflat-f1, d-f1, F-d1/ d-f1/ c1-g2/ d-f1, eflat-eflat1, c-c1/F-d1. Duration: long.

1   Historia von der Geburt Jesu Christi. -- In SGA. -- [1909?]. -- Bd. 17.
    Edited by Arnold Schering. Figured bass not realized. Original German text. Notes in German. Partial edition, consisting of evangelist's part only, also appears in Bd. 1 of the SGA.

2   Historia der Geburt Jesu Christi. -- In NSA. -- 1955. -- Bd. 1. Pub. no.: Bärenreiter-Ausgabe 1709.
    Edited by Friedrich Schöneich. German text. Notes in German.

3   Historia der Geburt Jesu Christi = History of the birth of Jesus Christ. -- Kassel : Bärenreiter, c1955. Pub. no.: TP 132.
    Edited by Friedrich Schöneich. Miniature score. German text. Notes in German and English.

6   The Christmas story = Historia von der Geburt Jesu Christi. -- New York : G. Schirmer, c1949. Pub. no.: Ed. 1930.
    Edited by Arthur Mendel. German text with English translation. Notes in English. Transposed up M2.

7 Historia von der Geburt Jesu Christi. -- [S.l.] : Kalmus, c1966.
Pub. no.: Kalmus vocal scores 6435.
German text with English translation.

8 Historia von der Geburt Jesu Christi. -- Leipzig : VEB Breitkopf &
Härtel, [19--]. Pub. no.: Edition Breitkopf Nr. 3131.
Continuo realized by Otto Taubmann. German text.

9 Weihnachts-Historie = Histoire de Noël = Christmas story. -- London
; New York : Eulenburg, [19--]. Pub. no.: Edition Eulenburg no. 981.
Miniature score. Edited by Fritz Stein. German text. Notes in
German and English.

SWV 435

[Historia von der Geburt Jesu Christi. Intermedium 2]

11 Chorus of the angels. -- Ft. Lauderdale, Fla. : Music 70, c1970.
Pub. no.: M70-241.
Edited by Jerry Wesely Harris. English text.

12 Ehre sei Gott in der Höhe. -- Neuhausen-Stuttgart : Hänssler, c1969.
Pub. no.: HE 20.435/1.
Edited by Günter Graulich. German text with English translation.

SWV 435

[Historia von der Geburt Jesu Christi. Intermedium 3]

13 Joyfully we go now to Bethlehem. -- Melville, N.Y. : Pro Art
Publications, c1982. Pub. no.: PROCH 3022.
Edited by Jerry Wesley Harris. German text with English
translation. Transposed up P5.

SWV 435

[Historia von der Geburt Jesu Christi. Intermedium 4]

14 Where is the newborn king of Israel. -- Melville, N.Y. : Pro Art
Publications, c1982. Pub. no.: PROCH 3023.
Edited by Jerry Wesley Harris. German text with English
translation. Transposed up M2.

SWV 435

[Historia von der Geburt Jesu Christi. Beschluss]

15 Now let all men thank thee = Dank sagen wir alle Gott. -- New York :
S. Fox, c1967. Pub. no.: XCM 18.
Edited by Roger Granville. German text with English translation.

16 Now let us all give thanks = Dank sagen wir alle Gott. -- Glen Rock,
    N.J. : J. Fischer, c1966. Pub. no.: J.F. & B. 9614.
       Edited by Lewis Niven. German text with English translation. Notes
    in English.

17 Dank sagen wir alle Gott. -- Neuhausen-Stuttgart : Hänssler, c1969.
    Pub. no.: HE 20.435/20.
       Edited by Günter Graulich. Continuo realized by Paul Horn. German
    text with English translation.

    Other editions: Bärenreiter BA1709; BA996 (Dank sagen).

SWV 436

[Ego autem sum Dominus]
    For solo voice and basso continuo.

1   Ego autem sum Dominus : [continuo line]. -- In SGA. -- 1927. -- Bd.
    18, p. xvii-xviii.
       Edited by Heinrich Spitta. Figured bass not realized. Notes in
    German.

SWV 437

[Veni, Domine]
    For solo voice and basso continuo.

1   Veni, Domine : [continuo line]. -- In SGA. -- 1927. -- Bd. 18, p.
    xviii.
       Edited by Heinrich Spitta. Figured bass not realized. Notes in
    German.

SWV 438

[Erde trinkt fur sich]

    Secular German text. Sources: Opitz, Martin. Erde trinkt fur sich.
       Duet (AT) with basso continuo. Ranges of voice parts: f-a1, c-d1.
    Duration: short.

1   Madrigal : die Erde trinkt fur sich. -- In SGA. -- 1893. -- Bd. 15,
    p. 84-85.
       Edited by Philipp Spitta. Figured bass not realized. Original
    German text. Notes in German.

2   Die Erde trinkt fur sich. -- In NSA. -- 1970. -- Bd. 37, p. 37-40.
    Pub. no.: BA4489.
       Edited by Werner Bittinger. German text. Notes in German and
    English. Transposed up M2.

SWV 439

[Heute ist Christus geboren]

Sacred German text. Sources: Heute ist Christus der Herr geboren.
For coro favorito (SSS) and basso continuo with possible optional
choir (original parts not extant). Ranges of voice parts: f1-g2,
d1-a2, a-f2. Duration: medium.

1   Heute ist Christus geboren. -- In SGA. -- 1893. -- Bd. 14, p.
101-105.
Edited by Philipp Spitta. Figured bass not realized. Original
German text. Notes in German.

3   Heute ist Christus der Herr geboren. -- Kassel : Bärenreiter, c1963.
Pub. no.: Bärenreiter 3445.
Edited by Werner Bittinger. German text. Notes in German and
English. Transposed down m3.

5   Heute ist Christus der Herr geboren = This happy morning was Christ
the Lord born. -- Neuhausen-Stuttgart : Hänssler, c1967. Pub. no.:
HE 20.439.
Edited by Günter Graulich. Continuo realized by Paul Horn. German
text with English translation. Notes in German and English.

SWV 440

[Güldne Haare, gleich Aurore]

Secular German text. Sources: Schutz, Heinrich. Guldne Haare, gleich
Aurore.
Duet (SS) with 2 violins and basso continuo. Ranges of voice
parts: g1-g2, c1-f2. Duration: medium.

1   Canzonetta : güldne Haare. -- In SGA. -- 1893. -- Bd. 15, p. 91-94.
Edited by Philipp Spitta. Figured bass not realized. Original
German text. Notes in German.

2   Güldne Haare, gleich Aurore. -- In NSA. -- 1970. -- Bd. 37, p.
13-19. Pub. no.: BA4489.
Edited by Werner Bittinger. German text. Notes in German and
English. Transposed down m3.

SWV 441

[Liebster, sagt in sussem Schmerzen]

Sacred German text. Sources: Opitz, Martin. Himmlische Hirtenlieder.
Duet (SS) with 2 violins and basso continuo. Ranges of voice
parts: d1-g2, c#1-f2. Duration: medium.

1   Madrigal : Liebster, sagt in sussem Schmerzen. -- In SGA. -- 1893.
    -- Bd. 15, p. 38-44.
        Edited by Philipp Spitta. Figured bass not realized. Original
    German text. Notes in German.

2   Liebster, sagt in sussem Schmerzen. -- In NSA. -- 1970. -- Bd. 37,
    p. 53-62. Pub. no.: BA4489.
        Edited by Werner Bittinger. German text. Notes in German and
    English.

3   Liebster, sagt in sussem Schmerzen. -- Kassel : Bärenreiter, c1970.
    Pub. no.: BA 6457.
        Edited by Werner Bittinger. German text. Notes in German and
    English.

SWV 442

[Tugend ist der beste Freund]

    Secular German text. Sources: Opitz, Martin. Tugend ist der beste
    Freund.
        Duet (SS) with 2 violins and basso continuo. Ranges of voice
    parts: b-e2, b-e2. Duration: medium.

1   Madrigal : Tugend ist der beste Freund. -- In SGA. -- 1893. -- Bd.
    15, p. 74-82.
        Edited by Philipp Spitta. Figured bass not realized. Original
    German text. Notes in German.

2   Tugend ist der beste Freund. -- In NSA. -- 1970. -- Bd. 37, p.
    63-73. Pub. no.: BA4489.
        Edited by Werner Bittinger. German text. Notes in German and
    English.

3   Tugend ist der beste Freund. -- Kassel : Bärenreiter, c1970. Pub.
    no.: BA 6457.
        Edited by Werner Bittinger. German text. Notes in German and
    English.

SWV 443

[Dialogo per la pascua]

    Sacred German text. Sources: John 20:13. John 20:16-17.
        For chorus (SSAT) and basso continuo. Ranges of voice parts:
    c1-g2, b-f2, g-g2, c-e1. Duration: medium.

1   Dialogo per la pascua : Weib, was weinest du?. -- In SGA. -- 1893.
    -- Bd. 14, p. 60-64.
        Edited by Philipp Spitta. Figured bass not realized. Original
    German text. Notes in German.

3   Dialogo per la pascua : Weib, was weinest du?. -- Kassel :
    Bärenreiter, c1968. Pub. no.: Bärenreiter 3444.
    Edited by Werner Bittinger. German text. Notes in German and
    English.

5   Osterdialog. -- Stuttgart : Hänssler, [1963?]. Pub. no.: 1.500.
    Edited by Günter Graulich. Continuo realized by Paul Horn. German
    text. Notes in German.

6   Easter dialogue. -- New York : Bourne, c1968.
    Edited by Richard Lamb. English text. Transposed down M2.

7   Oster-Dialog. -- In Drei biblische Szenen. -- Wiesbaden : Breitkopf
    & Härtel, [19--]. -- p. 9-17. Pub. no.: Edition Breitkopf Nr. 1634.
    Edited by A. Hänlein. German text.

SWV 444

[Es gingen zweene Menschen hinauf]

    Sacred German text. Sources: Luke 18:10-14.
    For chorus (SSAR) and basso continuo. Ranges of voice parts:
    d1-f2, b-e2, g-a1, A-e1. Duration: medium.

1   Es gingen zweene Menschen hinauf. -- In SGA. -- 1893. -- Bd. 14, p.
    55-59.
    Edited by Philipp Spitta. Figured bass not realized. Original
    German text. Notes in German.

3   Es gingen zweene Menschen hinauf. -- Kassel : Bärenreiter, c1968.
    Pub. no.: Bärenreiter 3444.
    Edited by Werner Bittinger. German text. Notes in German and
    English.

6   Pharisaer und Zollner. -- In Drei biblische Szenen. -- Wiesbaden :
    Breitkopf & Härtel, [19--]. -- p. 1-8. Pub. no.: Edition Breitkopf
    Nr. 1634.
    Edited by A. Hänlein. German text. Transposed down M2.

    Other editions: Hänssler 1.499.

SWV 445

[Ach bleib mit deiner Gnade]
    No longer attributed to Schutz.

SWV 446

[In dich hab ich gehoffet, Herr]
    No longer attributed to Schutz.

SWV 447

[Erbarm dich mein, o Herre Gott]

> Sacred German text. Sources: Hegenwald, Erhard. Erbarm dich mein, o
> Herre Gott.
> Solo for soprano with 2 violins, 2 violas, double bass, and basso
> continuo. Range of voice part: c1-e2. Duration: medium.

1   Erbarm dich mein, o Herre Gott. -- In SGA. -- 1927. -- Bd. 18, p.
    111-114.
    Edited by Heinrich Spitta. Figured bass not realized. Original
    German text. Notes in German.

2   Erbarm dich mein, o Herre Gott. -- In NSA. -- 1971. -- Bd. 32, p.
    20-29. Pub. no.: BA4484.
    Edited by Werner Breig. German text. Notes in German and English.

5   Erbarm dich mein, o Herre Gott = Have mercy Lord, o Saviour dear.
    -- Neuhausen-Stuttgart : Hänssler, c1967. Pub. no.: XX 447.
    Edited by Gunter Graulich. Continuo realized by Paul Horn. German
    text with English translation. Notes in German and English.

SWV 448

[Gesang der drei Männer im feurigen Ofen]

> Sacred German text. Sources: Daniel 3:52-90.
> For coro favorito (SSATB) and basso continuo with optional coro
> capella (SSATB) and or 2 violins, 2 violas, and double bass/and 2
> optional cornetti and 3 optional trombones. Ranges of voice parts:
> c#1-g2, c1-f2, d-a1, c-e1, D-c1/ c1-g2, c1-f2, d-g1, c-e1, C-g.
> Duration: medium.

1   Gesange der drei Männer im feurigen Ofen. -- In SGA. -- 1893. -- Bd.
    13, p. 177-218.
    Edited by Philipp Spitta. Figured bass not realized. Original
    German text. Notes in German.

5   Gesang der drei Männer im feurigen Ofen = The song of the three holy
    children. -- Neuhausen-Stuttgart : Hänssler, c1977. Pub. no.:
    HE20.448/02.
    Edited by Günter Graulich. Continuo realized by Paul Horn. German
    text with English translation.

    Other editions: Hänssler 1.456.

SWV 449

[Psalm 8]

> Sacred German text. Sources: Psalm 8.
> For quintet (SSATB) and basso continuo with optional cornettino,
> violin, 4 trombones, and chorus at times doubling the quintet.

Sacred German text. Sources: Psalm 8.
For quintet (SSATB), and basso continuo with optional cornettino, violin, 4 trombones, and chorus at times doubling the quintet. Ranges of voice parts: d1-f2, a-f2, g-a1, c-f1, D-bflat. Duration: medium.

1   Der 8. Psalm. -- In SGA. -- 1893. -- Bd. 13, p. 29-44.
     Edited by Philipp Spitta. Figured bass not realized. Original German text. Notes in German.

2   Herr, unser Herrscher. -- In NSA. -- 1970. -- Bd. 27, p. 55-74. Pub. no.: Bärenreiter Ausgabe BA4479.
     Edited by Werner Breig. German text. Notes in German and English.

SWV 450

[Ach Herr, du Schöpfer aller Ding]

Sacred German text. Sources: Luther, Martin. Vom Himmel hoch da komm ich her.
For chorus (SATTB) and basso continuo. Ranges of voice parts: d1-e2, g-a1, c-e1, d-f1, E-a. Duration: short.

1   Madrigale spirituale. -- In SGA. -- 1893. -- Bd. 14, p. 105-107.
     Edited by Philipp Spitta. Figured bass not realized. Original German text. Notes in German.

2   Ach Herr, du Schöpfer aller Ding. -- In NSA. -- 1971. -- Bd. 32, p. 13-19. Pub. no.: BA4484.
     Edited by Werner Breig. German text. Notes in German and English.

3   Ach Herr, du Schöpfer aller Ding. -- Kassel : Bärenreiter, c1963. Pub. no.: Bärenreiter 1723.
     Edited by Werner Bittinger. German text. Notes in German.

5   Ach Herr, du Schöpfer aller Ding = O Lord, creator of all things. -- Neuhausen-Stuttgart : Hänssler, c1967. Pub. no.: XX 450.
     Edited by Gunter Graulich. Continuo realized by Paul Horn. German text with English translation. Notes in German and English.

6   O Lord, creator of us all = Ach Herr, du Schöpfer aller Ding. -- Bryn Mawr, Pa. : T. Presser, c1978. Pub. no.: 312-41183.
     Edited by Robert Field. German text with English translation.

SWV 451

[Nachdem ich lag in meinem öden Bette]

Sacred German text. Sources: Opitz, Martin. Himmlische Hirtenlieder.
Duet (SB) with 2 violins, 2 unspecified instruments, and basso continuo. Ranges of voice parts: c#1-e2, F-c1. Duration: medium.

1   Madrigal : nachdem ich lag in meinem öden Bette. -- In SGA. -- 1893.
    -- Bd. 15, p. 45-50.
       Edited by Philipp Spitta. Figured bass not realized. Original
    German text. Notes in German.

2   Nachdem ich lag in meinem öden Bette. -- In NSA. -- 1970. -- Bd. 37,
    p. 74-84. Pub. no.: BA4489.
       Edited by Werner Bittinger. German text. Notes in German and
    English.

SWV 452

[Lasst Salomon sein Bette nicht umgeben]

    Sacred German text. Sources: Opitz, Martin. Himmlische Hirtenlieder.
    Duet (SB) with 2 violins, 2 unspecified instruments, and basso
    continuo. Ranges of voice parts: c#1-e2, G-bflat. Duration: medium.

1   Madrigal : lasst Salomon sein Bette nicht umgeben. -- In SGA. --
    1893. -- Bd. 15, p. 51-57.
       Edited by Philipp Spitta. Figured bass not realized. Original
    German text. Notes in German.

2   Lasst Salomon sein Bette nicht umgeben. -- In NSA. -- 1970. -- Bd.
    37, p. 85-97. Pub. no.: BA4489.
       Edited by Werner Bittinger. German text. Notes in German and
    English.

SWV 453

[Freue dich des Weibes deiner Jugend]

    Sacred German text. Sources: Proverbs 5:18-19.
    For chorus (SATB), 2 cornetti, 3 trombones, and basso continuo.
    Ranges of voice parts: d1-e2, g-a1, c-f1, D-a. Duration: medium.

1   Freue dich des Weibes deiner Jugend. -- In SGA. -- 1893. -- Bd. 14,
    p. 156-163.
       Edited by Philipp Spitta. Figured bass not realized. Original
    German text. Notes in German.

SWV 454

[Nun lasst uns Gott dem Herren]
    No longer attributed to Schutz.

SWV 455

[Psalm 19]

Sacred German text. Sources: Psalm 19:1-6.
Sextet (SSATTB) with basso continuo with optional chorus (SSATTB) and/or instruments at times doubling sextet. Ranges of voice parts: c1-f2, c1-f2, f-a1, c-f1, c-eflat1, F-bflat/ d1-f2, c1-f2, a-a1, d-d1, d-d1, G-bflat. Duration: short.

1   Der 19. Psalm. -- In SGA. -- 1893. -- Bd. 14, p. 180-187.
    Edited by Philipp Spitta. Figured bass not realized. Original
    German text. Notes in German.

2   Die Himmel erzählen die Ehre Gottes. -- In NSA. -- 1970. -- Bd. 27,
    p. 104-114. Pub. no.: BA4479.
    Edited by Werner Breig. Edited by Werner Breig. German text. Notes
    in German and English.

5   Die Himmel erzählen die Ehre Gottes = The heavens are telling the
    Fathers glory. -- Neuhausen-Stuttgart : Hänssler, c1969. Pub. no.:
    HE 20.455.
    Edited by Günter Graulich. Continuo realized by Paul Horn. German
    text with English translation. Notes in German and English.

SWV 456

[Hodie Christus natus est]

Sacred Latin text. Sources: Hodie Christus natus est.
For chorus (SSATTB) and basso continuo. Ranges of voice parts:
d1-f2, c1-g2, f-a1, c-f1, c-f1, F-a. Duration: medium.

1   Hodie Christus natus est. -- In SGA. -- 1893. -- Bd. 14, p. 92-100.
    Edited by Philipp Spitta. Figured bass not realized. Original
    Latin text. Notes in German.

3   Hodie Christus natus est. -- Kassel : Bärenreiter, c1963. Pub. no.:
    Bärenreiter 3446.
    Edited by Werner Bittinger. Latin text. Notes in German and
    English.

5   Hodie Christus natus est = Christ, der Herr, ist heute geborn. --
    Neuhausen-Stuttgart : Hänssler, c1967. Pub. no.: HE 20.456.
    Edited by Günter Graulich. Continuo realized by Paul Horn. Latin
    text with German translation. Notes in German and English.

6   Hodie Christus natus est = On this day Christ the Lord is born. --
    [S.l.] : G. Schirmer, c1973. Pub. no.: G. Schirmer's choral church
    music no. 11972.
    Edited by Maynard Klein. Latin text with English translation.
    Transposed up m3.

SWV 457

[Ich weiss, dass mein Erlöser lebt]

Sacred German text. Sources: Job 19:25-27.
For chorus (SSATTB) and optional basso continuo. Ranges of voice
parts: c1-g2, b-e2, e-a1, A-e1, A-e1, D-c1. Duration: medium.

3   Ich weiss, dass mein Erlöser lebt. -- Kassel : Bärenreiter, [19--].
Pub. no.: Bärenreiter 985.
Edited by Hans Joachim Moser. German text. Words in Gothic type.
Notes in German and English.

5   Ich weiss, dass mein Erlöser lebt. -- Neuhausen-Stuttgart :
Hänssler, c1972. Pub. no.: HE 20.457.
Edited by Günter Graulich. Continuo realized by Paul Horn. German
text with English translation.

SWV 458

[Litania]

Sacred German text. Sources: Luther, Martin. Deutsche Litanei.
For chorus (SSATTB) and basso continuo. Ranges of voice parts:
c1-f2, e1-e2, a-a1 d-f1, d-f1, D-c1. Duration: medium.

1   Litania. -- In SGA. -- 1892. -- Bd. 12, p. 185-197.
Edited by Philipp Spitta. Figured bass not realized. Original
German text. Notes in German.

3   Litania. -- Kassel : Bärenreiter, c1960. Pub. no.:
Bärenreiter-Ausgabe 3531.
Edited by Christiane Engelbrecht. German text. Notes in German.

SWV 459

[Saget den Gästen]

Sacred German text. Sources: Matthew 22:4.
For chorus (SATB), 2 violins, bassoon, and basso continuo. Ranges
of voice parts: c1-f2, e-a1, c-g1, F-c1. Duration: medium.

1   Saget den Gästen. -- In SGA. -- 1893. -- Bd. 14, p. 43-54.
Edited by Philipp Spitta. Figured bass not realized. Original
German text. Notes in German.

5   Saget den Gästen = Tell all the bidden. -- Neuhausen-Stuttgart :
Hänssler, c1967. Pub. no.: XX 459.
Edited by Günter Graulich. Continuo realized by Paul Horn. German
text with English translation. Notes in German and English.

SWV 460

[Itzt blicken durch des Himmels Saal]

    Secular German text. Sources: Opitz, Martin. Nachtklag.
    For chorus (SSATB) with 2 violins and basso continuo. Ranges of
voice parts: d1-g2, c1-e2, f-a1, c-f1, E-bflat. Duration: medium.

1   Madrigal : itzt blicken durch des Himmels Saal. -- In SGA. -- 1893.
    -- Bd. 15, p. 58-73.
      Edited by Philipp Spitta. Figured bass not realized. Original
German text. Notes in German.

2   Itzt blicken durch des Himmels Saal. -- In NSA. -- 1970. -- Bd. 37,
    p. 98-122. Pub. no.: BA4489.
      Edited by Werner Bittinger. German text. Notes in German and
English. Transposed up M2.

    Other editions: Bärenreiter BA565.

SWV 461

[Psalm 85]

    Sacred German text. Sources: Psalm 85. Gloria Patri.
    For quintet (SSTTB), 2 violins, 3 trombones, and basso continuo
with optional chorus (SATB). Ranges of voice parts: d1-g2, d1-f#2,
d-g1, c-g1, F-d1/ d1-f2, g-a1, d-f1, G-c1. Duration: long.

1   Der 85. Psalm. -- In SGA. -- 1893. -- Bd. 13, p. 80-131.
      Edited by Philipp Spitta. Figured bass not realized. Original
German text. Notes in German.

2   Herr, der du bist vormals genädig gewest. -- In NSA. -- 1971. -- Bd.
    28, p. 1-60. Pub. no.: Bärenreiter Ausgabe BA4480.
      Edited by Werner Breig. Latin text. Notes in German and English.

SWV 462

[Psalm 7]

    Sacred German text. Sources: Psalm 7.
    For double chorus (SATB/SATB) and basso continuo with optional
instrumental ensemble of 2 violins, viola, cornetto, and 3
trombones. Ranges of voice parts: c1-g2, g-a1, c-f1, E-c1/ c1-f2,
f-a1, c-e1, D-c1. Duration: long.

1   Der 7. Psalm. -- In SGA. -- 1893. -- Bd. 13, p. 45-79.
      Edited by Philipp Spitta. Figured bass not realized. Original
German text. Notes in German.

2   Auf dich, Herr, traue ich. -- In NSA. -- 1970. -- Bd. 27, p. 17-54.
    Pub. no.: Bärenreiter Ausgabe BA4479.
      Edited by Werner Breig. German text. Notes in German and English.

SWV 463

[Cantate Domino canticum novum]

Sacred Latin text. Sources: Psalm 96:1-2.
For chorus (SATB/SATB) and basso continuo. Ranges of voice parts:
c1-g2, f#1-bflat1, c-d1, D-bflat/ c1-eflat2, f-a1, c-d1, F-bflat.
Duration: short.

1   Cantate Domino : [reference]. -- In SGA. -- 1927. -- Bd. 18, p. xvi.
    Edited by Heinrich Spitta. Notes in German.

5   Cantate Domino canticum novum = Lobsinget Gott dem Herrn ein neues
    Lied. -- Neuhausen-Stuttgart : Hänssler, c1967. Pub. no.: HE
    20.463/02.
    Edited by Günter Graulich. Continuo realized by Paul Horn.

SWV 464

[Ich bin die Auferstehung und das Leben]

Sacred German text. Sources: John 11:25-26.
For chorus (SATB/SATB) and optional basso continuo. Ranges of
voice parts: c#1-e2, d-b1, A-f1, F-c1/ c#1-e2, d-b1, A-e1, D-c1.
Duration: short.

2   Ich bin die Auferstehung und das Leben. -- In NSA. -- 1970. -- Bd.
    31, p. 1-12. Pub. no.: BA4483.
    Edited by Werner Breig. German text. Notes in German and English.

3   Ich bin die Auferstehung und das Leben. -- Kassel : Bärenreiter,
    c1970. Pub. no.: BA 5919.
    Edited by Werner Breig. German text. Notes in German.

5   Ich bin die Auferstehung und das Leben = I am the resurrection and
    new being. -- Neuhausen-Stuttgart : Hänssler, c1972. Pub. no.: HE
    20.464/02.
    Edited by Günter Graulich. Continuo realized by Paul Horn. German
    text with English translation.

SWV 465

[Da pacem, Domine, in diebus nostris]

Sacred Latin text. Sources: Da pacem, Domine.
For chorus I (5 violas with 1 or 2 optional voices), chorus II
(SATB), optional chorus (SSATB) and basso continuo. Ranges of voice
parts: d1-e2, f-a1, c-f1, D-c1/ d1-f2, c1-e2, f-a1, c-e1, D-bflat.
Duration: medium.

1   Da pacem, Domine. -- In SGA. -- 1893. -- Bd. 15, p. 17-26.
    Edited by Philipp Spitta. Figured bass not realized. Original
    Latin text. Notes in German.

2   Da pacem, Domine, in diebus nostris. -- In NSA. -- 1971. -- Bd. 38, p. 75-103. Pub. no.: BA4490.
     Edited by Werner Bittinger. Latin and German text. Notes in German and English. Transposed up M2.

5   Da pacem Domine = Gib Frieden Herre Gott. -- Neuhausen-Stuttgart : Hänssler, c1969. Pub. no.: HE 20.465.
     Edited by Günter Graulich. Continuo realized by Paul Horn. Latin text with German translation. Notes in German, English and French.

SWV 466

[Psalm 15]

    Sacred German text. Sources: Psalm 15.
    For chorus I (alto and bass line with 2 violins and double bass), chorus II (soprano and tenor line with 3 trombones) and basso continuo. Ranges of voice parts: g-a1, D-a/ b-f2, A-g1. Duration: medium.

1   Der 15. Psalm. -- In SGA. -- 1893. -- Bd. 13, p. 157-168.
     Edited by Philipp Spitta. Original German text. Notes in German.

2   Herr, wer wird wohnen in deiner Hütten. -- In NSA. -- 1970. -- Bd. 27, p. 75-103. Pub. no.: Bärenreiter Ausgabe BA4479.
     Edited by Werner Breig. German text. Notes in German and English.

SWV 467

[Wo Gott der Herr nicht bei uns halt]

    Sacred German text. Sources: Jonas, Justus. Wo Gott, der Herr, nicht bei uns halt.
    For chorus I (soprano with lute), chorus II (soprano with 3 viols), chorus III (soprano with 3 trombones) and basso continuo. Range of voice part: d1-g2/ d1-f2/ d1-f2. Duration: medium.

1   Wo Gott der Herr nicht bei uns halt. -- In SGA. -- 1893. -- Bd. 13, p. 169-176.
     Edited by Philipp Spitta. Figured bass not realized. Original German text. Notes in German.

2   Wo Gott der Herr nicht bei uns halt. -- In NSA. -- 1971. -- Bd. 32, p. 30-57. Pub. no.: BA4484.
     Edited by Werner Breig. German text. Notes in German and English.

    Other editions: Bärenreiter BA5916.

SWV 468

[Magnificat anima mea Dominum]

Sacred Latin text. Sources: Magnificat.
For coro favorito (SATB), 2 violins, double bass, 3 trombones and basso continuo with optional choruses (SATB/SATB). Ranges of voice parts: c1-g2, e-a1, A-f1, D-d1/ e1-d2, e-a1, d-e1, F-a/ d1-e2, a-a1, d-e1, F-a. Duration: long.

1   Magnificat. -- In SGA. -- 1927. -- Bd. 18, p. 51-91.
    Edited by Heinrich Spitta. Figured bass not realized. Original Latin text. Notes in German.

3   Magnificat. -- Kassel : Bärenreiter, c1962. Pub. no.: Bärenreiter 4334.
    Edited by Wilhelm Ehmann. Continuo realized by Jorg Neithardt Keller. Latin text. Notes in German and English.

5   Magnificat anima mea Dominum = Hoch rühmt und ehrt meine Seele Gott den Herren. -- Neuhausen-Stuttgart : Hänssler, c1968. Pub. no.: HE 20.468.
    Edited by Günter Graulich. Continuo realized by Paul Horn. Latin text with German translation. Notes in German and English.

6   Magnificat. -- Leipzig : VEB Breitkopf & Härtel, c1927. Pub. no.: Edition Breitkopf Nr. 5422.
    Continuo realized by Heinrich Spitta. Latin text.

SWV 469

[Surrexit pastor bonus]

Sacred Latin text. Sources: Surrexit pastor bonus.
For chorus (SSATTB), 2 violins, 3 trombones, and basso continuo with optional choruses (SATB/SATB). Ranges of voice parts: d1-eflat2, c1-eflat2, g-a1, c-f1, c-d1, F-bflat/ g1-eflat2, c1-a1, d-e1, F-a/ e1-c2, b-f#1, d-d1, F-a. Duration: short.

1   Surrexit pastor bonus. -- In SGA. -- 1893. -- Bd. 14, p. 1-15.
    Edited by Philipp Spitta. Figured bass not realized. Original Latin text. Notes in German.

SWV 470

[Christ ist erstanden von der Marter alle]

Sacred German text. Sources: Christ ist erstanden von der Marter alle.
Trio (SAT), 3 viols, 4 trombones and basso continuo with optional chorus (SATB/SATB). Ranges of voice parts: d-e2, a-a1, d-f1/ f#1-d2, a-a1, f-e1, G-a/ e1-e2, a-a1, d-d1, D-f. Duration: medium.

1   Christ ist erstanden. -- In SGA. -- 1893. -- Bd. 14, p. 167-179.
     Edited by Philipp Spitta. Figured bass not realized. Original
     German text. Notes in German.

2   Christ ist erstanden von der Marter alle. -- In NSA. -- 1971. -- Bd.
     32, p. 137-164. Pub. no.: BA4484.
     Edited by Werner Breig. German text. Notes in German and English.

3   Christ ist erstanden. -- Kassel : Bärenreiter, c1971. Pub. no.:
     Bärenreiter 5917.
     Edited by Werner Breig. German text. Notes in German and English.

SWV 471

[O bone Jesu, fili Mariae]

     Sacred Latin text. Sources: Jesu, dulcis memoria.
     For chorus (SSAATB), 2 violins, 4 violas, optional double bass,
     and basso continuo. Ranges of voice parts: f1-f2, e1-f2, g-a1, f-f1,
     d-f1, D-a. Duration: medium.

1   O bone Jesu, fili Mariae. -- In SGA. -- 1927. -- Bd. 18, p. 93-110.
     Edited by Heinrich Spitta. Figured bass not realized. Original
     Latin text. Notes in German.

5   O bone Jesu, fili Mariae = O mein Herr Jesus. -- Neuhausen-Stuttgart
     : Hänssler, c1967. Pub. no.: HE 20.471.
     Edited by Gunter Graulich. Continuo realized by Paul Horn. Latin
     text with German translation. Notes in German and English.

SWV 472

[Herr Gott, dich loben wir]
 German text.
     No longer attributed to Schutz.

SWV 473

[Psalm 127]

     Sacred German text. Sources: Psalm 127.
     For chorus I (SSATB), chorus II (SATB), 2 violins, 3 trombones,
     and basso continuo. Ranges of voice parts: a-f2, c1-e2, f-a1, c-e1,
     D-c1/ a-d2, e-a1, c-e1, D-bflat. Duration: long.

1   Der 127. Psalm. -- In SGA. -- 1893. -- Bd. 13, p. 132-156.
     Edited by Philipp Spitta. Figured bass not realized. Original
     German text. Notes in German.

2   Wo der Herr nicht das Haus bauet. -- In NSA. -- 1971. -- Bd. 28, p.
     118-150. Pub. no.: BA4480.
     Edited by Werner Breig. German text. Notes in German and English.

SWV 474

[Ach wie soll ich doch in Freuden leben]

    Secular German text. Sources: Schütz, Heinrich. Ach wie soll ich
doch in Freuden leben.
    For chorus I (lute), chorus II (3 viols), chorus III (3
trombones), chorus IV (violin and cornetto), chorus V (ATB), with
basso continuo. Ranges of voice parts: g-g1, f-d1, Eflat-g.
Duration: medium.

1   Ach wie soll ich doch in Freuden leben. -- In SGA. -- 1927. -- Bd.
18, p. 117-126.
    Edited by Heinrich Spitta. Figured bass not realized. Original
German text. Notes in German.

2   Ach wie soll ich doch in Freuden leben. -- In NSA. -- 1971. -- Bd.
38, p. 1-21. Pub. no.: BA4490.
    Edited by Werner Bittinger. German text. Notes in German and
English.

SWV 475

[Veni, sancte Spiritus]

    Sacred Latin text. Sources: Veni sancte Spiritus.
    For chorus I (SS and bassoon), chorus II (B and 2 cornetti or 2
violins), chorus III (TT and 3 trombones), chorus IV (AT with violin
or cornetto, flute or cornetto, and double bass) and basso continuo.
Ranges of voice parts: d1-g2, c1-g2/ D-c1/ d-f1, c-e1/ g-a1, e-f1.
Duration: long.

1   Veni, sancte spiritus. -- In SGA. -- 1893. -- Bd. 14, p. 16-42.
    Edited by Philipp Spitta. Figured bass not realized. Notes in
German.

2   Veni, sancte Spiritus. -- In NSA. -- 1971. -- Bd. 32, p. 101-136.
Pub. no.: BA4484.
    Edited by Werner Breig. German text. Notes in German and English.

5   Veni sancte Spiritus = Komm herab, o heilger Geist. --
Neuhausen-Stuttgart : Hänssler, c1967. Pub. no.: XX 475.
    Edited by Günter Graulich. Continuo realized by Paul Horn. Latin
text with German translation. Notes in German and English.

SWV 476

[Psalm 24]

Sacred Latin text. Sources: Psalm 24.
For coro favorito (SATB/SATB) doubled at times by coro capella
(SATB/SATB) with 2 cornetti, 5 bassoons, 2 violins, 4 trombones, and
basso continuo with optional third coro capella (SSATTB) at times
doubling cornetti. Ranges of voice parts: d1-f2, g-a1, c-e1, D-c1/
d1-f2, g-a1, c-f1, C-bflat/f1-f2, g-a1, c-e1, D-a/ d1-f2, g-a1,
c-d1, D-a/ a1-a2, g1-a2, b-a1, d-e1, c-e1, F-a. Duration: long.

1   Der 24. Psalm. -- In SGA. -- 1893. -- Bd. 13, p. 1-28.
    Edited by Philipp Spitta. Original Latin text. Notes in German.

2   Domini est terra. -- In NSA. -- 1970. -- Bd. 27, p. 115-158. Pub.
    no.: Bärenreiter Ausgabe BA4479.
    Latin text. Edited by Werner Breig.

5   Domini est terra = Gottes ist der Erdkreis. -- Neuhausen-Stuttgart :
    Hänssler, c1969. Pub. no.: HE 20.476.
    Edited by Günter Graulich. Continuo realized by Paul Horn. Latin
    text with German translation. Notes in German, English, and French.

SWV 477

[Vater Abraham, erbarme dich mein]

    Sacred German text. Sources: Luke 16:24-31.
    For soloists (SSATB), 2 violins, 2 flutes, and basso continuo.
    Ranges of voice parts: f1-g2, eflat1-f2, f-bflat1, c-f1, C-d1.
    Duration: long.

1   Vater Abraham, erbarme dich mein. -- In SGA. -- 1927. -- Bd. 18, p.
    37-50.
    Edited by Heinrich Spitta. Figured bass not realized. Original
    German text. Notes in German.

5   Vater Abraham, erbarme dich mein = Father Abraham, have mercy on me.
    -- Neuhausen-Stuttgart : Hänssler, c1967. Pub. no.: XX 477.
    Edited by Günter Graulich. Continuo realized by Paul Horn. German
    text with English translation. Notes in German and English.

SWV 478

[Sieben Worte Kristi am Kreuz]

    Sacred German text. Sources: John 19:25-28. John 19:30. Luke 23:34.
    Luke 23:46. Luke 23:39-43. Mark 15:25. Matthew 27:46. Matthew 27:48.
    Da Jesus an dem Kreuze stund.
    For solo voices (SATTB), 5 unspecified instruments, basso continuo
    and optional chorus (SATTB). Ranges of voice parts: c1-e2, g-a1,
    c-e1, d-e1, E-a. Duration: long.

1   Die Sieben Wortte unsers lieben Erlösers und Seligmachers Jesu
    Christi. -- In SGA. -- 1885. -- Bd. 1, p. 147-158.
    Edited by Philipp Spitta. Figured bass not realized. Original
    German text. Notes in German.

2   Die sieben Worte Jesu Christi am Kreuz. -- In NSA. -- 1957. -- Bd.
2, p. 3-31. Pub. no.: Bärenreiter-Ausgabe 3662.
    Edited by Bruno Grusnick. German text. Words in Gothic type. Notes
in German.

3   Die sieben Worte Jesu Christi am Kreuz. -- Kassel : Bärenreiter,
c1965. Pub. no.: Bärenreiter-Ausgabe 1577.
    Edited by Bruno Grusnick. German text. Words in Gothic type.

5   Die sieben Worte Jesu Christi am Kreuz = The seven last words of
Jesu on the Cross. -- Stuttgart : Hänssler, c1967. Pub. no.: XX 478.
    Edited by Günter Graulich. Continuo realized by Paul Horn. German
text with English translation. Notes in German and English.

6   Die sieben Worte Jesu Christi am Kreuz. -- Leipzig : VEB Breitkopf &
Härtel, [19--]. Pub. no.: Edition Breitkopf Nr. 1770.
    Edited by Albrecht Hänlein. German text.

7   The seven words of Christ on the Cross. -- Saint Louis, Miss. :
Concordia Publishing House, c1950. Pub. no.: S 621.
    Edited by Richard T. Gore. English text. Transposed up m3.

8   The seven last words. -- New York : G. Schirmer, c1890.
    Edited by Carl Riedel. English translation.

9   Die sieben Worte Jesu Christ am Kreuz = The seven words of Jesus
Christ on the Cross. -- Boston, Mass. : E.C. Schirmer, c1970. Pub.
no.: E.C.S. choral music no. 2756.
    Edited by Daniel Pinkham. German text with English translation.
Notes in English. Transposed up M2.

10   The seven last words.-- New York, N.Y. : Kalmus, [19--]. Pub. no.:
Kalmus vocal scores 6434.
    English text.

11   The seven last words from the Cross. -- London : Oxford University
Press, Music Dept., c1961.
    Edited by Paul Steinitz. German text with English translation.
Notes in English.

12   The seven words of Jesus Christ = Die sieben Worte Jesu Christi. --
London ; New York : Eulenburg, [19--]. Pub. no.: Edition Eulenburg
No. 977.
    Edited by Fritz Stein. Figured bass not realized. German text.
Notes in German and English.

13   The seven words of Christ on the Cross. -- St. Louis, Miss. :
Concordia, [19--]. Pub. no.: 98-1627.
    Edited by Richard T. Gore. Chorus score. English text. Transposed
up m3.

SWV 478

[Sieben Worte Kristi am Kreuz. Conclusio]

14 Praise God's Son who redeems us. -- Fort Lauderdale, Fla. : Music
    70, c1983. Pub. no.: M70-342.
      For chorus (SATTB); keyboard reduction of vocal parts. Concluding
    chorus from "Die sieben Worte Kristi am Kreuz". Edited by Elwood
    Coggin. English text.

SWV 478

[Sieben Worte Kristi am Kreuz. Introitus]

15 Since Christ Our Lord was crucified. -- Boston, Mass. : E.C.
    Schirmer, c1926. Pub. no.: Concord series no. 88.
      For chorus (TTBB) a cappella; keyboard reduction of vocal parts.
    Arrangement of the opening chorus of "Die sieben Worte Kristi am
    Kreuz". Arranged by A.T.D. English text.

16 Since Christ His head in sorrow bowed. -- Boston, Mass. : E.C.
    Schirmer, c1936. Pub. no.: E.C.S. no. 994.
      For chorus (SATTB); keyboard reduction of vocal parts. Opening
    chorus of "Die Sieben Worte Kristi am Kreuz". Edited by A.T.D.
    English text.

SWV 479

[St. Matthew Passion]

    Sacred German text. Sources: Matthew 26. Matthew 27. Ehre sei dir,
    Christe, der du littest Not.
      For solo voices (SAATTTTTBB) and chorus (SATB) a cappella. Ranges
    of voice parts: d1-g2, g-c2, c-g1, F-d1. Duration: long.

1   Historia des Leidens und Sterbens unsers Herrn und Heylandes Jesu
    Christi nach dem Evangelisten St. Matthaeus. -- In SGA. -- 1885. --
    Bd. 1, p. 49-72.
      Edited by Philipp Spitta. Original German text. Solo parts in
    plainsong notation. Notes in German.

2   Die Matthäus-Passion. -- In NSA. -- 1957. -- Bd. 2, p. 109-144. Pub.
    no.: Bärenreiter-Ausgabe 3662.
      Edited by Fritz Schmidt. German text. Words in Gothic type. Solo
    parts in plainsong notation. Notes in German.

3   Die Matthaeus-Passion. -- Kassel : Bärenreiter, [1929?]. Pub. no.:
    Bärenreiter-Ausgabe 300.
      Edited by Fritz Schmidt. German text. Words in Gothic type. Solo
    parts in plainsong notation. Notes in German.

6   The passion according to St. Matthew. -- London : Oxford University
     Press, Music Dept., c1965.
         Edited by Peter Pears and Imogen Holst. Chorus score. English
     text. Solo parts in plainsong notation.

7   The passion according to St. Matthew. -- St. Louis, Mo. : Concordia,
     c1955. Pub. no.: 97-7573.
         Edited by Richard T. Gore. Keyboard reduction of vocal parts.
     English text. Solo parts in plainsong notation. Notes in English.

8   Historia des Leidens und Sterbens ... -- Leipzig : VEB Breitkopf &
     Härtel, [19--]. Pub. no.: Edition Breitkopf No. 720.
         Edited by Arnold Mendelssohn. Keyboard accompaniment added. German
     text.

9   Matthäus-passion = St Matthew passion. -- London ; New York :
     Eulenburg, [19--]. Pub. no.: Edition Eulenburg No. 976.
         Edited by Fritz Stein. Miniature score. German text. Solo parts in
     plainsong notation. Notes in German and English.

10   Historia des Leidens und Sterbens ... -- Neuhausen-Stuttgart :
     Hänssler, c1973. Pub. no.: HE 20.479/05.
         Edited by Günter Graulich. Chorus score. German text with English
     translation.

SWV 479

[St. Matthew Passion. Beschluss]

11   Glory be to Christ, the Lord = Ehre sei dir, Christe. -- New York :
     G. Schirmer, c1976. Pub. no.: G. Schirmer octavo no. 12058.
         Edited by C. Buell Agey. Keyboard reduction of vocal parts. German
     text with English translation.

12   Ehre sei dir, Christe = Christ, be thine the glory. -- New York : G.
     Schirmer, c1951. Pub. no.: G. Schirmer octavo no. 10123.
         Edited by Robert Shaw. Keyboard reduction of vocal parts. German
     text with English translation.

13   Christ, to thee be glory. -- New York : Mercury Music Corp., c1960.
     Pub. no.: MC375.
         Edited by Arthur Hilton. Keyboard reduction of vocal parts.
     English text.

14   Praise to thee, Lord Jesus. -- [S.l.] : Novello, c1935. Pub. no.:
     Novello's octavo anthems 1202.
         Edited by W.H. Harris. Keyboard reduction of vocal parts. English
     text.

15   Christ, to thee be glory. -- St. Louis, Mo. : Concordia, c1956. Pub.
     no.: 98-1355.
         For chorus (TTBB). Edited by Fred L. Precht. Keyboard reduction of
     vocal parts. German text with English translation.

16   Ehre sei dir, Christe. -- Neuhausen-Stuttgart : Hänssler, c1968.
     Pub. no.: HE 20.479/10.
     Edited by Günter Graulich. Keyboard reduction of vocal parts by
     Paul Horn. German text with English translation.

     Other editions: Hänssler HE20.479.

SWV 480

[St. Luke Passion]

     Sacred German text. Sources: Luke 22. Luke 23. Da Jesus an dem
     Kreuze stund.
     For solo voices (SATTTBBB) and chorus (SATB) a cappella. Ranges of
     voice parts: c1-e2, e-bflat1, c-g1, F-c1. Duration: long.

1   Historia des Leidens und Sterbens unsers Herrn und Heylandes Jesu
     Christi nach dem Evangelisten St. Lucas. -- In SGA. -- 1885. -- Bd.
     1, p. 99-122.
     Edited by Philipp Spitta. Original German text. Solo parts in
     plainsong notation. Notes in German.

2   Die Lukas-Passion. -- In NSA. -- 1957. -- Bd. 2, p. 37-71. Pub. no.:
     Bärenreiter-Ausgabe 3662.
     Edited by Wilhelm Kamlah. German text. Words in Gothic type. Notes
     in German.

3   Die Lukas-Passion. -- Kassel : Bärenreiter, 1935. Pub. no.:
     Bärenreiter-Ausgabe 696.
     Edited by Wilhelm Kamlah. German text. Words in Gothic type. Solo
     parts in plainsong notation. Notes in German.

6   The St. Luke Passion. -- London : Oxford University Press, Music
     Dept., c1956.
     Edited by Paul Steinitz. Chorus score. Keyboard reduction of vocal
     parts. English text. Solo parts in plainsong notation. Notes in
     English.

7   Historia des Leidens und Sterbens ... : Lukas-Passion. -- Leipzig :
     VEB Breitkopf & Härtel, c1927. Pub. no.: EB 5346.
     Edited by Arnold Mendelssohn. Keyboard accompaniment added. German
     text. Transposed up M2.

8   St. Luke Passion = Lukas-Passion. -- London ; New York : Eulenburg,
     [19--]. Pub. no.: Edition Eulenburg no. 978.
     Edited by Fritz Stein. German text. Notes in German and English.

9   Historia des Leidens und Sterbens ... -- Neuhausen-Stuttgart :
     Hänssler, c1971. Pub. no.: HE 20.480.
     Edited by Günter Graulich. Chorus score. German text with English
     translation.

SWV 480

[St. Luke Passion. Beschluss]

10 Wer gottes Marter in Ehren hat. -- Neuhausen-Stuttgart : Hänssler,
c1969. Pub. no.: HE 20.480/1.
Edited by Günter Graulich. Keyboard accompaniment added by Paul
Horn. German text with English translation.

Other editions: Hänssler HE20.480.

SWV 481

[St. John Passion]

Sacred German text. Sources: John 19:1-30. Weisse, Michael. Christus
der uns selig macht.
For solo voices (STTTBB) and chorus (SATB) a cappella. Ranges of
voice parts: c1-e2, g-a1, c-f1, G-c1. Duration: long.

1 Historia des Leidens und Sterbens unsers Herrn und Heilandes Jesu
Chrisi nach dem Evangelisten St. Johannes. -- In SGA. -- 1885. --
Bd. 1, p. 125-144.
Edited by Philipp Spitta. Original German text. Solo parts in
plainsong notation. Notes in German.

2 Die Johannes-Passion. -- In NSA. -- 1957. -- Bd. 2, p. 75-104. Pub.
no.: Bärenreiter-Ausgabe 3662.
Edited by Wilhelm Kamlah. German text. Words in Gothic type. Notes
in German.

3 Die Johannes-Passion. -- Kassel : Bärenreiter, 1969. Pub. no.:
Bärenreiter-Ausgabe 960.
Edited by Wilhelm Kamlah. German text. Words in Gothic type. Solo
parts in plainsong notation.

5 Johannespassion = Passion according to St. John. --
Neuhausen-Stuttgart : Hänssler, c1967. Pub. no.: HE 20.481/01.
Edited by Günter Graulich. Solo parts in plainsong notation.
German text with English translation. Notes in German and English.

6 The passion according to St. John. -- Chicago, Ill. : G.I.A.
Publications, c1980. Pub. no.: G-2377.
Edited by Stephen Rosolack. Keyboard reduction of vocal parts.
English text. Solo parts in plainsong notation. Notes in English.

7 The passion according to St. John. -- London : Oxford University
Press, Music Dept., c1963.
Edited by Peter Pears and Imogen Holst. Chorus score. English
text. Solo parts in plainsong notation. Notes in English.

8 The passion according to Saint John. -- Springfield, Ohio : Chantry
Music Press, c1962. Pub. no.: PAS 621.
Edited by William H. Reese. English text. Solo parts in plainsong
notation. Notes in English.

9   Historia des Leidens und Sterbens ... : Johannes-Passion. -- Leipzig
     : VEB Breitkopf & Härtel, [19--]. Pub. no.: EB 1250.
     Edited by Arnold Mendelssohn. Keyboard accompaniment added. German
     text.

10   Johannes-Passion = Passion selon St. Jean = St. John passion. --
     London ; New York : Eulenburg, [1934?]. Pub. no.: Edition Eulenburg
     No. 979.
     Edited by Fritz Stein. Miniature score. German text. Solo parts in
     plainsong notation. Notes in German and English.

SWV 481

[St. John Passion. Beschluss]

11   O hilf, Christe, Gottes Sohn = Help us, Jesu, Son of God. --
     Neuhausen-Stuttgart : Hänssler, c1969. Pub. no.: HE 20.481/10.
     Concluding chorus from SWV 481. Edited by Günter Graulich.
     Keyboard accompaniment added by Paul Horn. German text with English
     translation.

12   Help us, Jesus Christ, God's Son = O hilf, Christe, Gottes Sohn. --
     Dayton, Ohio : Sacred Music Press, c1973. Pub. no.: S-135.
     Edited by Walter Ehret. Keyboard reduction of vocal parts. German
     text with English translation.

13   O help, Jesus, Son of God. -- Fremont, Ohio : Chantry Music Press,
     c1956.
     Edited by William H. Reese. Keyboard reduction of vocal parts.
     German text with English translation.

14   Hjälp mig, Jesus. -- Stockholm : Svenska Kyrkans Diakonistyrelses
     Bokförlag, [19--]. Pub. no.: S.K.D.B. 207.
     Swedish text.

SWV 482

[Wohl denen, die ohne Wandel leben]

     Sacred German text. Sources: Psalm 119:1-16. Gloria Patri.
     For eight soloists (SATB/SATB) or chorus (SATB/SATB) and basso
     continuo. Ranges of voice parts: d1-f2, c1-a1, e-f1, F-d1/ e1-e2,
     a-a1, d-f1, E-c1. Duration: medium.

2   Aleph und Beth : Wohl denen, die ohne Wandel leben. -- In NSA. --
     c1984. -- Bd. 39, p. 1-16. Pub. no.: BA 5951.
     Edited by Wolfram Steude. German text. Notes in German and
     English.

5   Wohl denen, die ohne Tadel leben. -- Neuhausen-Stuttgart : Hänssler,
     c1967. Pub. no.: HE 20.482.
     Edited by Heinrich Spitta and Günter Graulich. Continuo realized
     by Paul Horn. German text with English translation.

     Other editions: Bärenreiter BA5921.

SWV 483

[Tue wohl deinem Knechte]

> Sacred German text. Sources: Psalm 119:17-32. Gloria Patri.
> For eight soloists (SATB/SATB) or chorus (SATB/SATB) and basso
> continuo. Ranges of voice parts: c1-f2, g-a1, d-f1, G-d/ c1-f2,
> a-a1, e-g1, G#-d. Duration: medium.

2   Gimel und Daleth : Tue wohl deinem Knechte, dass ich lebe. -- In
> NSA. -- c1984. -- Bd. 39, p. 17-34. Pub. no.: BA 5951.
> Edited by Wolfram Steude. German text. Notes in German and
> English.

SWV 484

[Zeige mir, Herr, den Weg deiner Rechte]

> Sacred German text. Sources: Psalm 119:33-48. Gloria Patri.
> For eight soloists (SATB/SATB) or chorus (SATB/SATB) and basso
> continuo. Ranges of voice parts: c1-f2, a-b1, d-g1, G-c1/ d1-e2,
> g-h1, f-g1, F-c1. Duration: medium.

2   He und Vav : Zeige mir, Herr, den Weg deiner Rechte. -- In NSA. --
> c1984. -- Bd. 39, p. 35-52. Pub. no.: BA 5951.
> Edited by Wolfram Steude. German text. Notes in German and
> English.

> Other editions: Bärenreiter BA5922.

SWV 485

[Gedenke deinem Knecht an dein Wort]

> Sacred German text. Sources: Psalm 119:49-64. Gloria Patri.
> For eight soloists (SATB/SATB) or chorus (SATB/SATB) and basso
> continuo. Ranges of voice parts: c1-e2, a-a1, d-g1, F-c1/ d1-e2,
> f#-b1, e-g1, F-c1. Duration: medium.

2   Dsain und Chet : Gedenke deinem Knechte an dein Wort. -- In NSA. --
> c1984. -- Bd. 39, p. 53-74. Pub. no.: BA 5951.
> Edited by Wolfram Steude. German text. Notes in German and
> English.

SWV 486

[Du tust Guts deinem Knechte]

> Sacred German text. Sources: Psalm 119:65-80. Gloria Patri.
> For eight soloists (SATB/SATB) or chorus (SATB/SATB) and basso
> continuo. Ranges of voice parts: d1-e2, e-a1, e-f1, F-c1/ b-e2,
> e-g1, d#-g1, D-c1. Duration: medium.

2   Thet und Jod : Du tust Guts deinem Knechte. -- In NSA. -- c1984. --
     Bd. 39, p. 75-96. Pub. no.: BA 5951.
        Edited by Wolfram Steude. German text. Notes in German and
     English.

SWV 487

[Meine Seele verlanget nach deinem Heil]

    Sacred German text. Sources: Psalm 119:81-96. Gloria Patri.
      For eight soloists (SATB/SATB) or chorus (SATB/SATB) and basso
    continuo. Ranges of voice parts: c1-f2, f-a1, d-e1, D-c1/ c#-f2,
    f-a1, c-g1, D-bflat. Duration: medium.

2   Caph und Lamed : Meine Seele verlanget nach deinem Heil. -- In NSA.
     -- c1984. -- Bd. 39, p. 97-118. Pub. no.: BA 5951.
        Edited by Wolfram Steude. German text. Notes in German and
     English.

SWV 488

[Wie habe ich dein Gesetze so lieb]

    Sacred German text. Sources: Psalm 119:97-112. Gloria Patri.
      For eight soloists (SATB/SATB) or chorus (SATB/SATB) and basso
    continuo. Ranges of voice parts: d1-g2, g-bflat1, c-f1, D-d1/ d1-f2,
    f-a1, c-f1, D-bflat. Duration: medium.

2   Mem und Nun : Wie habe ich dein Gesetze so lieb. -- In NSA. --
     c1984. -- Bd. 39, p. 119-142. Pub. no.: BA 5951.
        Edited by Wolfram Steude. German text. Notes in German and
     English.

SWV 489

[Ich hasse die Flattergeister]

    Sacred German text. Sources: Psalm 119:113-128.
      For eight soloists (SATB/SATB) or chorus (SATB/SATB) and basso
    continuo. Ranges of voice parts: c#1-e2, f-a1, c-f1, F-c1/ d1-e2,
    e-a1, c-e1, D-c1. Duration: medium.

2   Samech und Ain : Ich hasse die Flattergeister. -- In NSA. -- c1984.
     -- Bd. 39, p. 143-162. Pub. no.: BA 5951.
        Edited by Wolfram Steude. German text. Notes in German and
     English.

SWV 490

[Deine Zeugnisse sind wunderbarlich]

Sacred German text. Sources: Psalm 119:129-144. Gloria Patri.
For eight soloists (SATB/SATB) or chorus (SATB/SATB) and basso
continuo. Ranges of voice parts: e1-e2, a-a1, c-f1, F-c1/ d1-e2,
e-a1, c-e1, D-c1. Duration: medium.

2   Pe und Zade : Deine Zeugnisse sind wunderbarlich. NSA. -- c1984. --
    Bd. 39, p. 163-182. Pub. no.: BA 5951.
    Edited by Wolfram Steude. German text. Notes in German and
    English.

SWV 491

[Ich rufe von ganzem Herzen]

Sacred German text. Sources: Psalm 119:145-160. Gloria Patri.
For eight soloists (SATB/SATB) or chorus (SATB/SATB) and basso
continuo. Ranges of voice parts: c1-e2, g-a1, A-f1, D-c1/ d1-e2,
g-a1, c-f1, D-c1. Duration: medium.

2   Koph und Resch : Ich rufe von ganzem Herzen. -- In NSA. -- c1984. --
    Bd. 39, p. 183-204. Pub. no.: BA 5951.
    Edited by Wolfram Steude. German text. Notes in German and
    English.

    Other editions: Bärenreiter BA5923.

SWV 492

[Fürsten verfolgen mich ohne Ursach]

Sacred German text. Sources: Psalm 119:161-176. Gloria Patri.
For eight soloists (SATB/SATB) or chorus (SATB/SATB) and basso
continuo. Ranges of voice parts: d1-f2, g-a1, c-f1, D-bflat/ c1-f2,
g-a1, c-f#1, D-c1. Duration: medium.

2   Schin und Tav : Die Fürsten verfolgen mich ohne Ursach. -- In NSA.
    -- c1984. -- Bd. 39, p. 205-228. Pub. no.: BA 5951.
    Edited by Wolfram Steude. German text. Notes in German and
    English.

SWV 492

[Fürsten verfolgen mich ohne Ursach. Ehre sei dem Vater und dem Sohn]

6   Ehre sei dem Vater und dem Sohn = Glory to the Father and the Son.
    -- Neuhausen-Stuttgart : Hänssler, c1969. Pub. no.: HE 20.492/1.
    Concluding chorus from SWV 492. Edited by Heinrich Spitta and
    Günter Graulich. Continuo realized by Paul Horn. German text with
    English translation.

SWV 493

[Psalm 100]

    Sacred German text. Sources: Psalm 100. Gloria Patri.
     For eight soloists (SATB/SATB) or chorus (SATB/SATB) and basso
    continuo. Ranges of voice parts: c1-f2, g-a1, c-f1, D-d1/ d1-f#2,
    a-a1, c-f1, D-bflat. Duration: medium.

2   Jauchzet dem Herren, alle Welt. -- In NSA. -- c1984. -- Bd. 39, p.
    229-252. Pub. no.: BA 5951.
     Edited by Wolfram Steude. German text. Notes in German and
    English.

     Other editions: Bärenreiter BA5924.

SWV 494

[Deutsches Magnificat]

    Sacred German text. Sources: Magnificat.
     For double choruses (SATB/SATB) and basso continuo. Ranges of
    voice parts: d1-e2, e-a1, c-g1, D-c1/ d1-e2, a-a1, d-f1, D-c1.
    Duration: medium.

2   Meine Seele erhebt den Herren. -- In NSA. -- c1984. -- Bd. 39, p.
    253-273. Pub. no.: BA 5951.
     Edited by Wolfram Steude. German text. Notes in German and
    English.

3   Deutsches Magnificat. -- Kassel : Bärenreiter, c1950. Pub. no.:
    Bärenreiter-Ausgabe 2155.
     Edited by Konrad Ameln. Continuo line not included. German text.
    Notes in German.

5   Deutsches Magnificat = The German Magnificat. -- Neuhausen-Stuttgart
    : Hänssler, c1967. Pub. no.: HE 20.494.
     Edited by Günter Graulich. Continuo realized by Paul Horn. German
    text with English translation. Notes in German and English.

6   Deutsches Magnificat. -- Leipzig : VEB Breitkopf & Härtel
    Musikverlag, [19--]. Pub. no.: PB 2685.
     German text. Transposed up M2.

7   German Magnificat = Deutsches Magnificat. -- London : Oxford
    University Press, Music Dept., c1966.
     Edited by Paul Steinitz. Notes in English. Transposed up M2.

8   My soul doth magnify the Lord. -- New York : G. Schirmer, c1967.
    Pub. no.: Ed. 2665.
     Edited by Maynard Klein. Keyboard reduction of vocal parts. German
    text with English translation. Notes in English. Transposed up M2.

9   Meine Seele erhebt den Herren. -- In NSA. -- Kassel : Bärenreiter,
    1971. -- Bd. 28, p. 183-206. Pub. no.: Bärenreiter Ausgabe BA4480.
    Edited by Werner Breig. German text. Notes in German and English.

SWV 495

[Unser Herr Jesus Christus]

    Sacred German text. Sources: Corinthians, 1st, 11:23-25. Matthew 26
    :26-28.
    For chorus (SATB/SATB) a cappella. Ranges of voice parts: c#1-f2,
    g-a1, c-f1, F-d1/ c1-e2, g-a1, d-f1, D-c1. Duration: medium.

3   Unser Herr Jesus Christus in der Nacht da er verraten ward. -- 2.
    Aufl. -- Kassel ; New York : Bärenreiter, 1964, c1961. Pub. no.:
    Bärenreiter-Ausgabe 1722.
    Edited by Werner Braun. German text. Notes in German.

SWV 496

[Esaja dem Propheten das geschah]

    Sacred German text. Sources: Luther, Martin. Jesaja dem Propheten
    das geschah.

2   Esaja dem Propheten das geschah : [fragment]. -- In NSA. -- 1971. --
    Bd. 32, p. 168-170. Pub. no.: BA4484.
    Edited by Werner Breig. German text. Notes in German and English.

SWV Anh. 1

[Vier Hirtinnen, gleich jung, gleich schön]

    Secular German text. Sources: Vier Hirtinnen, gleich jung, gleich
    schön.
    For chorus (SSAT) and basso continuo. Ranges of voice parts:
    e1-g2, c1-f2, g-a1, c-f1. Duration: medium.

1   Vier Hirtinnen, gleich jung, gleich schön. -- In SGA. -- 1927. --
    Bd. 18, p. 127-132.
    Edited by Heinrich Spitta. Figured bass not realized. Original
    German text. Notes in German.

2   Vier Hirtinnen, gleich jung, gleich schön. -- In NSA. -- 1970. --
    Bd. 37, p. 41-50. Pub. no.: BA 4489.
    Edited by Werner Bittinger. German text. Notes in German and
    English.

    Other editions: Bärenreiter BA1271.

SWV Anh. 2

[Ach Herr, du Sohn Davids]
    No longer attributed to Schütz.

SWV Anh. 3

[Gott Abraham]
    No longer attributed to Schütz.

SWV Anh. 4

[Stehe auf, meine Freundin]
    No longer attributed to Schütz.

SWV Anh. 5

[Benedicam Dominum in omni tempore]
    No longer attributed to Schütz.

SWV Anh. 6

[Freuet euch mit mir]
    No longer attributed to Schütz.

SWV Anh. 7

[Herr, höre mein Wort]

    Sacred German text. Sources: Psalm 5.
    For eight soloists (SATB/SATB) with optional doubling chorus
    (SATB/SATB) and basso continuo. Ranges of voice parts: c#1-f2, g-a1,
    e-f1, E-c1/ b-e2, e-a1, d#-f1, E-c1. Duration: medium.

2   Herr, höre mein Wort. -- In NSA. -- 1970. -- Bd. 27, p. 1-16. Pub.
    no.: BA 4479.
        Edited by Werner Breig. German text. Notes in German and English.

SWV Anh. 8

[Machet die Tore weit]
    No longer attributed to Schütz.

SWV Anh. 9

[Sumite psalmum]
    No longer attributed to Schütz.

SWV Anh. 10

[Dominus illuminatio mea]
    No longer attributed to Schütz.

SWV Anh. 11

[Es erhub sich ein Streit im Himmel]
    No longer attributed to Schütz.

TITLE INDEX

Account of the Resurrection of Jesus Christ SWV 50

Ach Gott, der du vor dieser Zeit SWV 157

Ach Gott vom Himmel, sieh darein SWV 108

Ach Gott, warum verstösst du nun SWV 187

Ach Herr, du Schöpfer aller Ding SWV 450

Ach Herr, es ist der Heiden Heer SWV 176

Ach Herr, mein Gott, straf mich doch nicht SWV 102

Ach Herr, straf mich nicht in deinem Zorn SWV 24

Ach Herr, verwirf mich nicht SWV 54

Ach Herr, wie lang willt du denn noch SWV 109

Ach, mein Sohn Absalon SWV 269

Ach, meine Seele schmilzt in Wonne hin SWV 263

Ach treuer Gott, sie doch darein SWV 156

Ach wie gross ist der Feinde Rott SWV 99

Ach wie soll ich doch in Freuden leben SWV 474

Ad Dominum, cum tribularer clamavi SWV 71

Adjuro vos, filiae Hierusalem SWV 264

Adveniunt pascha pleno concelebranda triumpho SWV 338

Aleph und Beth SWV 482

All Ehr und Lob soll Gottes sein SWV 421

All our eyes do wait, o Lord, upon thee SWV 429

All thanks be to God SWV 425

All thanks to the Lord SWV 424

Allein Gott in der Höh sei Ehr SWV 327

Alleluia! lobet den Herrn in seinem Heiligtum SWV 38

Alleluia, worship Jehovah SWV 38

Aller Augen warten auf dich, Herr SWV 88

Aller Augen warten auf dich SWV 429

Alma afflitta, che fai? SWV 4

Als das Volk Israel auszog SWV 212

Als ich Gott den Herrn gesucht SWV 268

Also hat Gott die Welt geliebt SWV 380

An den Wassern zu Babel sassen wir SWV 37

An Wasserflüssen Babylon SWV 242

Angel said to the shepherds SWV 395

Anima mea liquefacta est SWV 263

Annunciation according to St. Luke SWV 333

Aspice pater piissimum filium SWV 73

Attendite, popule meus, legem meam SWV 270

Auf dein Wort will ich trauen SWV 243

Auf dem Gebirge hat man ein Geschrei gehoret SWV 396

Auf dich, Herr, trau ich allezeit SWV 168

Auf dich, Herr, traue ich SWV 462

Auf dich, trau ich, mein Herr und Gott SWV 103

Auf Hügeln, Bergen weit und breit
    SWV 169
Auf und blaset am Fest des
    Neumonds die Tuba SWV 275
Aufer immensam, Deus, aufer iram
    SWV 337
Auferstehungs-Historie SWV 50
Aus der Tiefe, ruf ich Herr, zu
    dir SWV 25
Aus meines Herzen Grunde SWV 243
Aus tiefer Not schrei ich zu dir
    SWV 235
Aus unsers Herzens Grunde SWV 172
Ave Maria, gratia plena SWV 334
Be swift to do His will SWV 201
Be ye loving, even as your father
    hath loved you SWV 409
Beckerscher Psalter SWV 97-256
Benedicam Dominum in omni tempore
    SWV 267
Benedicite und Vaterunser SWV 429
Benedicite vor dem Essen SWV 429
Benediction and the Lord's prayer
    SWV 429
Bewahr mich, Gott, ich trau auf
    dich SWV 112
Blessed are all those who fear God
    SWV 30
Blessed are the faithful SWV 391
Blessed is he who walks not in the
    paths of godlessness SWV 290
Blessed they who keep not the law
    of the ungodly SWV 28
Blest are the departed SWV 391
Blest he who goes not after words
    of the godless SWV 290
Blut Jesu Christi, des Sohnes
    Gottes SWV 298
Bone Jesu, verbum Patris SWV 313
Bringt Ehr und Preis dem Herren
    SWV 126
Bringt her dem Herren, ihr
    Gewaltigen SWV 283
Buccinate in neomenia tuba SWV 275
Calicem salutaris accipiam SWV 60
Canconetta SWV 278
Cantabo Domino in vita mea SWV 260
Cantate Domino canticum novum SWV
    81
Cantate Domino SWV 463
Canticum B. Simeonis SWV 281 432
    433
Cantiones sacrae SWV 53-93
Canzonetta SWV 440
Caph und Lamed SWV 487
Child is born among us SWV 384

Child is born unto us SWV 302
Child to us is born SWV 302
Chorus of the angels SWV 435
Christ, der Herr, ist heute
    geboren SWV 456
Christ ist erstanden von der
    Marter alle SWV 470
Christ, to thee be glory SWV 479
Christe Deus adjuva SWV 295 295
Christe, fac ut sapiam SWV 431
Christe, lass mich weise sein SWV
    431
Christmas history SWV 435
Christmas story SWV 435
Come, Holy Ghost, Our Lord SWV 417
Comfort ye, my people SWV 382
Concert in Form einer teutschen
    Begräbnis-Missa SWV 279
Concert mit 11. Stimmen SWV 21
Concerto in the form of a German
    Requiem SWV 279
Confitemini, Domino, quoniam ipse
    bonus SWV 91
Cosi morir debb'io SWV 5
D'orrida selce alpina SWV 6
Da pacem, Domine SWV 465
Dank sagen wir alle Gott SWV 435
Danket dem Herren SWV 91
Danket dem Herren, denn er ist
    freundlich SWV 32 45
Danket dem Herren, denn er ist
    sehr freundlich SWV 430
Danket dem Herren, erzeigt ihm Ehr
    SWV 204
Danket dem Herren, gebt ihm Ehr
    SWV 241
Danket dem Herren, lobt ihn frei
    SWV 203
Danket dem Herren, unserm Gott SWV
    205
Danklied SWV 368
Danksagen wir alle Gott, unserm
    Herren Christo SWV 425
Das ist je gewisslich wahr SWV 277
    388
Das ist mir lieb, dass der Herr
    mein Stimm und Flehen höret SWV
    51
De vitae fugacitate SWV 94
Dein Wort, Herr, nicht vergehet
    SWV 221
Deine Zeugnisse sind wunderbarlich
    SWV 490
Demütig will ich mich dir ergeben
    SWV 79
Den enda glädje, som jag vet SWV
    163

Den Herren lobt mit Freuden SWV 239

Dennoch hat Israel zum Trost SWV 170

Deo gratias nach dem Essen SWV 430

Der ist furwahr ein selig Mann SWV 210

Des H. Bernhardi Freuden-Gesang SWV 427

Des Nachts auf meinem Lager SWV 272

Deus misereatur nobis, et benedicat nobis SWV 55

Deutsche Litanei SWV 428

Deutsches Magnificat SWV 494

Di marmo siete voi SWV 17

Dialogo per la pascua SWV 443

Die lieben dein Gesetze SWV 224

Die mit Tränen säen SWV 42 378

Die nur vertrauend stellen SWV 230

Die so ihr den Herren fürchtet SWV 364

Dir gbuhrt allein die Ehre SWV 223

Dir, o Herr, gilt all mein Hoffen SWV 259

Discedite a me omnes operamini SWV 87

Domine Deus, pater coelestis, benedic nobis SWV 90

Domine, labia mea aperies SWV 271

Domine, ne in furore tuo arguas me SWV 85

Domine, non est exaltatum cor meum SWV 78

Domini est terra SWV 476

Drei schöne Dinge seind SWV 365

Dsain und Chet SWV 485

Du Hirt Israel, höre uns SWV 177

Du liebster, Herr, du Allergütigster, Christe SWV 67

Du Schalksknecht, alle diese Schuld hab ich dir erlassen SWV 397

Du tust Guts deinem Knechte SWV 486

Du tust viel guts beweisen SWV 220

Dulcissime et benignissime Christe SWV 67

Dunque addio, care selve SWV 15

Easter dialogue SWV 443

Ecce advocatus meus apud te, Deus patrem SWV 84

Ego autem sum Dominus SWV 436

Ego dormio, et cor meum vigilat SWV 63

Ego enim inique egi SWV 58

Ego sum tui plaga doloris SWV 57

Ehre sei dem Vater SWV 426

Ehre sei dem Vater und dem Sohn SWV 492

Ehre sei dir, Christe SWV 479

Ehre sei Gott in der Hohe SWV 435

Eil Herr, mein Gott, zu retten mich SWV 167

Eile mich, Gott zu erreten SWV 282

Eins bitte ich vom Herren SWV 294

Engel sprach zu den Hirten SWV 395

Er wird sein Kleid in Wein waschen SWV 370

Erbarm dich mein, o Herre Gott SWV 148 447

Erd und was sich auf ihr regt SWV 121

Erde trinkt für sich SWV 438

Erhör mein Gbet, du treuer Gott SWV 152

Erhör mein Stimm, Herr, wenn ich klag SWV 161

Erhör mich, wenn ich ruf zu dir SWV 100

Erhöre mich, wenn ich dich rufe, Gott meiner Gerechtigkeit SWV 289

Erzürn dich nicht so sehre SWV 134

Es ging ein Sämann aus zu säen SWV 408

Es gingen zweene Menschen hinauf SWV 444

Es ist ein Freud dem Herzen mein SWV 227

Es ist erschienen die heilsame Gnade Gottes SWV 371

Es ist furwahr ein kostlich Ding SWV 190

Es spricht der Unweisen Mund wohl SWV 110 150

Es steh Gott auf dass seine Feind zerstreuet werden SWV 165 356

Es wird das Scepter von Juda nicht entwendet werden SWV 369

Es woll uns Gott genädig sein SWV 164

Esaja dem Propheten das geschah SWV 496

Et ne despicias humiliter te petentem SWV 54

Every eye waiteth upon thee SWV 429

Exquisivi Dominum et exaudivit me SWV 268

Exultavit cor meum in Domino SWV 258

Eyes of all wait upon thee SWV 88
False servant SWV 397
Father Abraham, have mercy on me
    SWV 477
Fear of the Lord God is the source
    of wisdom SWV 318
Feget den alten Sauerteig aus SWV
    404
Feind haben mich oft gedrängt SWV
    234
Feritevi, ferite, viperette
    mordacci SWV 9
Fest ist gegründet Gottes Stadt
    SWV 184
Feste Burg ist unser Gott SWV 143
Fiamma ch'allacia e laccio SWV 10
Fili mi, Absalon SWV 269
Flight into Egypt SWV 403
For God so loved the world SWV 380
For God so loved this sinful world
    SWV 380
Freude und Gluck bewegt mich SWV
    258
Freue dich des Weibes deiner
    Jugend SWV 453
Freuet euch des Herren, ihr
    Gerechten SWV 367
Freut euch des Herrn, ihr Christen
    all SWV 130
Frohlocket mit Händen und jauchzet
    dem Herren SWV 349
Frohlockt mit Freud, ihr Volker
    all SWV 144
From the depths have I cried to
    thee, Lord SWV 25
Fuggi o mio core SWV 8
Für solch grosses Mysterium SWV 77
Fürcht des Herren ist der Weisheit
    Anfang SWV 318
Furcht störet, doch nicht
    zerstöret den Trost SWV 70
Furchte dich nicht, ich bin mit
    dir SWV 296
Fürsten verfolgen mich ohne Ursach
    SWV 492
Fürstliche Gnade zu Wasser und
    Lande SWV 368
Gedenke deinem Knecht an dein Wort
    SWV 485
Geistliche Chormusik SWV 369-397
Geistliche Gesänge SWV 420-431
Gelobet sei der Herr, mein Hort
    SWV 249
German Magnificat SWV 494
German Magnificat 1657 SWV 426

German Nunc dimittis I 1656 SWV
    432
German Nunc dimittis II 1656 SWV
    433
Gesang der drei Manner im feurigen
    Ofen SWV 448
Gib Frieden Herre Gott SWV 465
Gib unsern Fürsten und aller
    Obrigkeit SWV 355 373
Gimel und Daleth SWV 483
Giunto e pur, Lidia, giunto SWV 18
Give ear, O Lord SWV 289
Give ear to me when I call thee
    SWV 289
Give God the glory SWV 283
Give to Jehovah SWV 283
Give to our leaders and all ruling
    powers SWV 373
Gleichwie ein Hirsch eilt mit
    Begier SWV 139
Gloria Patri SWV 426
Glory be to Christ, the Lord SWV
    479
Glory to God upon his throne SWV
    421
Glory to the Father SWV 426
Glory to the Father and the Son
    SWV 492
Glück zu dem Helikon SWV 96
Go, pull up weeds first SWV 376
God, be merciful unto us SWV 55
God's might recall, ye people all
    SWV 215
Gott, führ mein Sach und richte
    mich SWV 140
Gott, gieb dem König auserkorn
    Recht SWV 169
Gott hilf mir, denn das Wasser
    dringt SWV 166
Gott, man lobt dich in der Still
    SWV 162
Gott, mein Geschrei erhöre SWV 158
Gott, schweig du nicht so ganz und
    gar SWV 180
Gott sei Dank, der uns den Sieg
    gegeben hat SWV 50
Gott unser Herr, mächtig durchs
    Wort SWV 147
Gottes ist der Erdkreis SWV 476
Gottseligkeit ist zu allen Dingen
    nutz SWV 299
Grant to our people and all who
    govern us SWV 373
Gratias agimus tibi, Domine Deus
    Pater SWV 93
Great is our Lord SWV 286

Great is the Lord SWV 286
Grimmige Gruft, so hast du dann
    SWV 52
Gross ist der Herr und hoch
    gepreist SWV 145
Güldne Haare, gleich Aurore SWV
    440
Gutes und Barmherzigkeit SWV 95
Habe deine Lust an dem Herren SWV
    311
Hast verwundet mein Herze SWV 64
Hasten, O Lord, to redeem me SWV
    282
Haus und Güter erbet man von
    Eltern SWV 21
Have mercy Lord, o Saviour dear
    SWV 447
He shall tread out his cloak in
    wine SWV 370
He und Vav SWV 484
He who weeping soweth SWV 42
Hear the faithful word of God SWV
    388
Hearken unto my cry SWV 61
Heavens are telling the Father's
    glory SWV 386 455
Heilige Gemeine SWV 254
Help us, Jesu, Son of God SWV 481
Herr, auf dich traue ich SWV 377
Herr, der du bist vormals genädig
    gewest SWV 461
Herr der du vormals gnädig warst
    SWV 182
Herr, der du vormals hast dein
    Land SWV 182
Herr, dich lob die Seele mein SWV
    202
Herr, du erforschst meine Sinne
    SWV 244
Herr erhör dich in der Not SWV 116
Herr Gott, dem alle Rach heimfällt
    SWV 192
Herr Gott, des ich mich ruhmte
    viel SWV 207
Herr Gott, erhör die Grechtigkeit
    SWV 113
Herr Gott, erzeig mir Hilf und
    Gnad SWV 153
Herr Gott, hilf und erbarm dich
    unser SWV 55
Herr Gott himmlischer Vater SWV 90
Herr Gott, mein Heiland, Nacht und
    Tag SWV 185
Herr Gott Vater im hochsten Thron
    SWV 188
Herr, hader mit den Hadrern mein
    SWV 132

Herr hör, was ich will bitten dich
    SWV 101
Herr, höre mein Wort SWV Anh. 7
Herr, ich hoffe darauf, dass du so
    gnädig bist SWV 312
Herr ist gross und sehr löblich
    SWV 286
Herr ist König herrlich schon SWV
    191
Herr ist König überall SWV 195
Herr ist mein getreuer Hirt SWV
    120
Herr ist mein Hirt SWV 33
Herr ist mein Hirt, mir wird
    nichts mangeln SWV 398
Herr ist mein Licht und mein Heil
    SWV 359
Herr ist meine Stärke SWV 345
Herr König und regiert SWV 197
Herr, mein Gebet erhor in Gnad SWV
    248
Herr, mein Gemüt und Sinn du
    weisst SWV 236
Herr, mein Gott, ach nicht in
    deinem Zorn SWV 85
Herr, mein Gott, nicht vermessen
    dränget mein Herze SWV 78
Herr, mein Gott, wenn ich ruf zu
    dir SWV 246
Herr, neig zu mir dein gnädigs Ohr
    SWV 183
Herr, neige deine Himmel und fahr
    herab SWV 361
Herr, nun lassest du deinen Diener
    SWV 281 352 432 433
Herr, schaff mir Recht, nimm dich
    mein an SWV 123
Herr schauet vom Himmel auf der
    Menschen Kinder SWV 292
Herr sprach zu meim Herzen SWV 208
Herr sprach zu meinem Herren SWV
    22
Herr, straf mich nicht in deinem
    Zorn SWV 135
Herr unser Herrscher, wie herrlich
    ist dein Nam SWV 27 343 449
Herr, wann ich nur dich habe SWV
    321
Herr, wenn ich nur dich habe SWV
    280
Herr, wer wird wohnen in deiner
    Hütten SWV 466
Herr, wie lang willt du mein so
    gar vergessen? SWV 416
Herre Gott, himmlischer Vater SWV
    429
Herzlich lieb hab ich dich, o
    Herr, meine Stärke SWV 348

Herzlich lieb hab ich dich, O Herr
  SWV 387
Heu mihi, Domine, quia peccavi
  nimis SWV 65
Heute ist Christus geboren SWV 439
Hilf mir, Gott, durch den Namen
  dein SWV 151
Himmel erzählen die Ehre Gottes
  SWV 386 455
Himmel, Herr preisen sehr SWV 115
Himmel und Erde vergehen SWV 300
Histoire de la Resurrection SWV 50
Histoire de Noël SWV 435
Historia der Auferstehung Jesu
  Christi SWV 50
Historia von der Geburt Jesu
  Christi SWV 435
History of the birth of Jesus
  Christ SWV 435
Hjälp mig, Jesus SWV 481
Hoch freuet sich der König SWV 117
Hoch rühmt und ehrt meine Seele
  Gott den Herren SWV 468
Hodie Christus natus est SWV 315
  456
Hoffe, Israel SWV 80
Hör mein Gebet und lass zu dir SWV
  200
Hör, mein Volk, mein Gesetz und
  Weis SWV 175
Höre mich, Herr SWV 86
Hört zu, ihr Völker insgemein SWV
  146
How lovely is thine own dwelling
  place SWV 29
How pleasant are thy dwellings SWV
  181
Hütet euch, dass eure Herzen nicht
  beschweret werden SWV 351 413
I am the only true vine SWV 389
I am the resurrection and new
  being SWV 464
I believe in one God SWV 422
I bow and bend the knee unto the
  Father of Lord Jesus Christ SWV
  319
I call to thee, Lord Jesu Christ
  SWV 326
I know that my Redeemer lives SWV
  393
I lift up mine eyes to the hills
  SWV 31 399
I love the Lord SWV 51
Ich beschwöre euch, ihr Tochter zu
  Jerusalem SWV 339
Ich beuge meine Knie gegen dem
  Vater SWV 319

Ich bin die Auferstehung und das
  Leben SWV 324 464
Ich bin ein rechter Weinstock SWV
  389
Ich bin eine rufende Stimme SWV
  383
Ich bin jung gewesen und bin alt
  worden SWV 320
Ich bin verstummet ganz und still
  SWV 136
Ich danke dem Herrn von ganzem
  Herzen SWV 34 284
Ich danke dir, Herr, von ganzem
  Herzen SWV 347
Ich flehe euch an, Töchter von
  Jerusalem SWV 264
Ich freu mich des das mir geredt
  ist SWV 26
Ich glaube an einen einigen Gott
  SWV 422
Ich hab mein Sach Gott
  heimgestellt SWV 94 305
Ich harrete des Herren SWV 137
Ich hasse die Flattergeister SWV
  222 489
Ich heb mein Augen auf zu dir SWV
  228
Ich heb mein Augen sehnlich auf
  SWV 226
Ich hebe meine Augen auf zu den
  Bergen SWV 31 399
Ich lieb dich, Herr, von Herzen
  sehr SWV 114
Ich liege und schlafe und erwache
  SWV 310
Ich, nur ich bin der Missetater
  SWV 58
Ich, o ich bin die Qual deiner
  Schmerzen SWV 57
Ich preis dich, Herr, zu aller
  Stund SWV 127
Ich rief zum Herrn SWV 71
Ich ruf zu dir, Herr Gott, mein
  Hort SWV 125
Ich ruf zu dir, Herr Jesu Christ
  SWV 326
Ich ruf zu dir, mein Herr und Gott
  SWV 225
Ich ruf zu Gott mit meiner Stimm
  SWV 174
Ich rufe von ganzem Herzen SWV 491
Ich sags von Grund meins Herzen
  frei SWV 133
Ich schrei zu meinem lieben Gott
  SWV 247
Ich singe dem Herren SWV 260
Ich trau auf Gott, was solls denn
  sein SWV 107

Ich singe dem Herren SWV 260

Ich trau auf Gott, was solls denn sein SWV 107

Ich weiss, dass mein Erlöser lebt SWV 393 457

Ich weiss, woran ich glaube SWV 243

Ich werde nicht sterben, sondern leben SWV 346

Ich will bei meinem Leben SWV 131

Ich will den Herren loben allezeit SWV 306

Ich will den Kelch des Heiles nehmen mit Dank SWV 60

Ich will sehr hoch erhöhen dich SWV 250

Ich will, so lang ich lebe SWV 131

Ich will verkündgen in der Gmein SWV 119

Ich will von Gnade singen SWV 186

Ich will von Herzen danken Gott dem Herren SWV 209

If the Lord build not the dwelling SWV 400

Ihr Heiligen, lobsinget dem Herren SWV 288

In den Armen des Heilandes und Herren SWV 82

In dich, Gott, hab ich gehoffet SWV 66

In dich hab ich gehoffet, Herr SWV 128

In Gnaden, Herr, wollst eindenk sein SWV 237

In Juda ist der Herr bekannt SWV 173

In lectulo per noctes SWV 272

In meinem Herzen hab ich mir SWV 136

In te, Domine, speravi SWV 66 259

In thee, O Lord, do I put my trust SWV 66

Inter brachia Salvatoris mei SWV 82

Invenerunt me custodes civitatis SWV 273

Io moro, ecco ch'io moro SWV 13

Is God for us SWV 329

Is not Ephraim my precious son? SWV 40

Iss dein Brot mit Freuden SWV 358

Ist Gott für uns, wer mag wider uns sein? SWV 329

Ist nicht Ephraim mein teurer Sohn? SWV 40

Itzt blicken durch des Himmels Saal SWV 460

Jauchzet dem Herren SWV 47

Jauchzet dem Herren alle Welt SWV 36 198

Jauchzet dem Herren, alle Welt SWV 493

Jauchzet Gott alle Lande sehr SWV 163

Jesus in the temple SWV 401

Johannes Passion SWV 481

Joseph, du Sohn David SWV 323

Joseph, you David's son, be not afraid SWV 323

Joyfully we go now to Bethlehem SWV 435

Jubilate Deo in chordis et organo SWV 276

Jubilate Deo omnis terra SWV 262 332

Kind ist uns geboren SWV 302 384

Klaglicher Abschied SWV 52

Kleine geistliche Concerte, 1. Theil SWV 282-305

Kleine geistliche Concerte, 2. Theil SWV 306-337

Komm doch, Geliebter mein SWV 274

Komm herab, o heilger Geist SWV 475

Komm, heilger Geist, Herre Gott SWV 417

Komm, ich bitt dich, in mein Herze SWV 83

Kommt alle zu mir SWV 261

Kommt herzu, lasst uns frohlich sein SWV 193

Koph und Resch SWV 491

Kyrie, God Father throughout all time SWV 420

Kyrie Gott Vater in Ewigkeit SWV 420

Lamb of God SWV 78

Lass mir Gnad widerfahren SWV 219

Lasset uns doch den Herren, unsern Gott loben SWV 407

Lasst Salomon sein Bette nicht umgeben SWV 452

Lasst uns Gott, unserm Herren SWV 216

Let all give thanks to God SWV 418

Let the people give thanks SWV 205

Let us declare the glory of the Lord SWV 407

Liebster, sagt in süssem Schmerzen SWV 441

Litania SWV 458

Litany SWV 428

Lo, I am the voice of one crying in the wilderness SWV 383

Lo, the angel said to the shepherds SWV 395

Lo, the scepter from Judah shall not be removed SWV 369

Lob und Ehre zollt dem Herren SWV 262

Lobe den Herrn meine Seele SWV 39

Lobet den Herren, der zu Zion wohnet SWV 293

Lobet den Herrn, alle Heiden SWV 363

Lobet den Herrn in seinem Heiligtum SWV 350

Lobet, ihr Himmel, Gott den Herrn SWV 253

Lobet, ihr Knecht, den Herren SWV 211

Lobsinget Gott dem Herrn ein neues Lied SWV 463

Lobt den Herren SWV 276

Lobt Gott in seinem Heiligtum SWV 255

Lobt Gott mit Schall, ihr Heiden all SWV 215

Lobt Gott von Herzengrunde SWV 240

Lord, and whom but thee have I SWV 280

Lord be praised SWV 430

Lord, create in me a cleaner heart SWV 291

Lord God our Father SWV 90

Lord, grant us peace SWV 372

Lord, if I have thee only SWV 321

Lord, in thee do I trust SWV 377

Lord is my shepherd SWV 398

Lord, my hope is in thee SWV 312

Lord, now lettest thou thy servant SWV 281 352

Lord's prayer SWV 411 429

Love of God is most useful in all things SWV 299

Lukas Passion SWV 480

Madrigals SWV 1-19

Magnificat SWV 426 468

Many shall go there from eastward and from westward SWV 375

Master, thou laboring all the night SWV 317

Matthäus Passion SWV 479

May God attend thee in thy distress SWV 116

Meas dicavi res Deo SWV 305

Meim Herzen ists ein grosse Freud SWV 214

Mein Gott, mein Gott, ach Herr mein Gott SWV 118

Mein Herz dichtet ein Lied mit Fleiss SWV 142

Mein Herz ist bereit, Gott, dass ich singe SWV 341

Mein Herz ist gerüstet SWV 257

Mein Licht und Heil ist Gott der Herr SWV 124

Mein Seel ist still in meinem Gott SWV 159

Mein Seel soll loben Gott den Herrn SWV 251

Mein Sohn, warum hast du uns das getan SWV 401

Meine Seele erhebt den Herren SWV 344 426 494

Meine Seele verlanget nach deinem Heil SWV 487

Meine Worte höre in Gnaden an SWV 61

Meister, wir haben die ganze Nacht gearbeitet SWV 317

Meister, wir wissen, dass du wahrhaftig bist SWV 414

Mem und Nun SWV 488

Mensch vor Gott wohl selig ist SWV 129

Merkt auf, die ihr an Gottes Statt SWV 179

Mi saluta costei SWV 12

Mine eyes I lift SWV 226

Mit Dank wir sollen loben SWV 104

Mit fröhlichem Gemute SWV 105

Mit rechtem Ernst und frohem Mut SWV 206

Musicalische Exequien SWV 279-281

My son, why hast thou so dealt with us SWV 401

My soul doth magnify the Lord SWV 494

Nach dir verlangt mich, Herr mein Gott SWV 122

Nachdem ich lag in meinem öden Bette SWV 451

Nacket bin ich von Mutterleibe kommen SWV 279

Nicaenische Glaube SWV 422

Nicht uns Herr, sondern deinem Namen gib Ehre SWV 43

Nicht uns, nicht uns, Herr lieber Gott SWV 213

Nonne hic est, mi Domine, innocens ille SWV 74

Now let all men thank thee SWV 435

Now let us all give thanks SWV 435
Now shall I go to Jesus Christ SWV
   379
Now there appeareth the grace of
   the Lord Almighty SWV 371
Nun danket alle Gott SWV 418
Nun komm, der Heiden Heiland SWV
   301
Nun lob, mein Seel, den Herren SWV
   41 201
O blessed Lord our God SWV 287
O bone Jesu, fili Mariae SWV 471
O bone, o dulcis, o benigne Jesu
   SWV 53
O dearest Lord God SWV 381
O der grossen Wundertaten SWV 278
O dolcezze amarissime d'amore SWV
   2
O du allersüssester und liebster
   Herr Jesu SWV 340
O God, be merciful unto us SWV 55
O Gott, du mein getreuer Gott SWV
   160
O gracious Lord God, may we be
   vigilant and ready SWV 287
O guter, o lieber, freundlicher
   Herr Jesu SWV 53
O help, Christ, thou Son of God
   SWV 295
O help, Jesus, Son of God SWV 481
O Herr hilf, o Herr lass wohl
   gelingen SWV 297 402
O hilf, Christe, Gottes Sohn SWV
   295 481
O how fair are all thy courts SWV
   29
O Jesu, nomen dulce SWV 308
O Jesu suss, wer dein gedenkt SWV
   406
O Jesus Christ, my Lord, I beg
   thee, do not leave me SWV 427
O Jesus, thou Son of God SWV 295
O lieber Herre Gott, wecke uns auf
   SWV 287 381
O Lord, creator of all things SWV
   450
O Lord, creator of us all SWV 450
O Lord, in thy wrath rebuke me not
   SWV 24
O Lord, now grant us thy peace in
   grace SWV 372
O may the eyes of all SWV 88
O mein Herr Jesus SWV 471
O meine Hoffnung, Jesus SWV 69
O meine Seel, warum bist du
   betrübet SWV 419
O mighty God, Our Lord SWV 287

O misericordissime Jesu SWV 309
O my people, take heart SWV 382
O nimm an mein Gebet SWV 62
O praise the Lord, ye people all
   SWV 215
O primavera, gioventù de l'anno
   SWV 1
O quam tu pulchra es, amica mea
   SWV 265
O save us Lord SWV 297 402
O sing ye unto the Lord SWV 81
O Sohn des Höchsten, wie tief hast
   du wollen erniedrigt sein SWV
   59
O süsser Jesu Christ, wer an dich
   recht gedenket SWV 405 427
O süsser, o freundlicher, o
   gütiger Herr Jesu Christe SWV
   285
O thou most gracious Lord SWV 381
O weh mir, Herr, mein Gott SWV 65
   66
O wie beruckend, wie schon du bist
   SWV 265
Oculi omnium in te sperant, Domine
   SWV 88
Öffne du mir meine Lippen,
   Allmächtiger SWV 271
Oh Lord, have mercy upon us SWV 55
Ohn alle Schuld SWV 74
On this day Christ the Lord is
   born SWV 456
One thing I ask of the Lord SWV
   294
Oster-Dialog SWV 443
Our Father SWV 89 411 429
Paratum cor meum, Deus SWV 257
Passion according to St. John SWV
   481
Passion according to St. Matthew
   SWV 479
Passion selon St. Jean SWV 481
Pater noster SWV 89 92
Pe und Zade SWV 490
Pharisaer und Zollner SWV 444
Praise God's Son who redeems us
   SWV 478
Praise to the Lord God SWV 293
Praise to thee, Lord Jesus SWV 479
Praise ye Jehovah SWV 293
Praise ye the Lord SWV 288
Praise ye the Lord, my soul SWV 39
Preisen will ich allezeit den
   Herren in der Höh SWV 267
Pro hoc magno mysterio pietatis
   SWV 77

Psalm 7 SWV 462
Psalm 8 SWV 449
Psalm 15 SWV 466
Psalm 24 SWV 476
Psalm 100 SWV 493
Psalm 111 SWV 424
Psalm 127 SWV 473
Psalmen Davids SWV 22-47
Quando se claudunt lumina SWV 316
Quella damma son io SWV 11
Quemadmodum desiderat cervus ad
    fontes aquarum SWV 336
Quid commisisti, o dulcissime
    puer? SWV 56
Quid detur tibi aut quid apponatur
    tibi SWV 72
Quo, nate Dei, quo tua descendit
    humilitas SWV 59
Quoniam ad te clamabo, Domine SWV
    62
Quoniam non est in morte qui memor
    sit tui SWV 86
Reduc, Domine Deus meus, oculos
    majestatis tuae SWV 75
Response to the psalms SWV 256
Responsorium SWV 256
Resurrection history SWV 50
Ride la primavera SWV 7
Rorate coeli desuper SWV 322
Saget den Gästen SWV 459
Samech und Ain SWV 489
Sammlet zuvor das Unkraut SWV 376
Saul, Saul, was verfolgst du mich?
    SWV 415
Saul, Saul, why persecutest thou
    me SWV 415
Schaffe in mir, Gott, ein reines
    Herz SWV 291
Schaue doch, Vater, den Sohn SWV
    73
Schin und Tav SWV 492
See, I am a voice of one crying
    SWV 383
See, I have an advocate in Heaven
    SWV 304
See now, this child has been sent
    for the downfall SWV 410
Seele Christi heilige mich SWV 325
Sehet an den Feigenbaum und alle
    Bäume SWV 394
Sei gegrüsset Maria, du holdselige
    SWV 333
Sei mir gnadig, o Gott, mein Herr
    SWV 154
Seid barmherzig, wie auch euer
    Vater barmherzig ist SWV 409

Selig sind die Toten, die im dem
    Herren sterben SWV 391
Selve beate, se sospirando in
    flebili susurri SWV 3
Seven last words of Jesu on the
    Cross SWV 478
Show yourselves joyful to the Lord
    SWV 47
Si non humiliter sentiebam SWV 79
Sicut Moses serpentem in deserto
    exaltavit SWV 68
Sieben Worte Kristi am Kreuz SWV
    478
Siehe, dieser wird gesetzt zu
    einem Fall SWV 410
Siehe, es erschien der Engel des
    Herren Joseph im Traum SWV 403
Siehe, mein Fürsprecher ist im
    Himmel SWV 84 304
Siehe, wie fein und lieblich ist
    SWV 412
Since Christ his head in sorrow
    bowed SWV 478
Since Christ Our Lord was
    crucified SWV 478
Sing a new song SWV 194
Sing and be joyful SWV 36
Sing, o my soul, the Father's
    praises SWV 39
Singet dem Herrn ein neues Lied
    SWV 35 194 196 342
Singet ein neues Lied, jauchzet
    dem Herrn SWV 81
Singet mit Freuden unserm Gott SWV
    178
So fahr ich hin zu Jesu Christ SWV
    379
So höre doch, meine Gemeinde SWV
    270
So I depart SWV 379
So weit, Herr Gott, der Himmel
    reicht SWV 133
So wie Moses die Schlange in der
    Wüste hat erhöhet SWV 68
Song of the three holy children
    SWV 448
Sospir che del bel petto SWV 14
Soul of Christ now sanctify me SWV
    325
Sower in his field was sowing SWV
    408
Speret Israel in Domino SWV 80
Spes mea, Christe Deus, hominum tu
    dulcis amator SWV 69
St. John Passion SWV 481

St. Luke Passion SWV 480
St. Matthew Passion SWV 479
Steige herab von den Bergen SWV 266
Stimm des Herren gehet auf den Wassern SWV 331
Supereminet omnem scientiam, o bone Jesu SWV 76
Surrexit pastor bonus SWV 469
Symphoniae sacrae, 1 pars SWV 257-276
Symphoniae sacrae, 2 pars SWV 341-367
Symphoniae sacrae, 3 pars SWV 398-418
Syncharma musicum SWV 49
Te Christe supplex invoco SWV 326
Tell all the bidden SWV 459
Teutoniam dudum belli atra pericla molestant SWV 338
Teutsche gemeine Litaney SWV 428
Thet und Jod SWV 486
This happy morning was Christ the Lord born SWV 439
Thou art my hope, Christ Jesus SWV 69
To God alone on high be praise SWV 327
Tornate o cari baci SWV 16
Trauerlied SWV 419
Tröst uns, Gott, unser Zuversicht SWV 177
Tröstet, tröstet mein Volk SWV 382
Tu wohl, Herr, deinem Knechte SWV 218
Tue wohl deinem Knechte SWV 483
Tugend ist der beste Freund SWV 442
Turbabor, sed non perturbabor SWV 70
Über alle Erkenntnis erhebet sich SWV 76
Und es trafen mich dort in der Stadt die Wächter SWV 273
Unser Herr Jesu Christus SWV 495
Unser Herr Jesus Christus in der Nacht, da er verraten ward SWV 423
Unser keiner lebet ihm selber SWV 374
Unser Wandel ist im Himmel SWV 390
Vasto mar, nel cui seno SWV 19
Vater Abraham, erbarme dich mein SWV 477
Vater unser SWV 89 92 411 429
Veni de Libano, amica mea SWV 266

Veni, dilecte mi, in hortum meum SWV 274
Veni, Domine SWV 437
Veni redemptor gentium SWV 301
Veni, rogo in cor meum SWV 83
Veni, sancte Spiritus SWV 328 475
Venite ad me, omnes qui laboratis SWV 261
Verba D. Pauli SWV 277
Verba mea auribus percipe, Domine SWV 61
Verbum caro factum est SWV 314
Verleih uns Frieden genädiglich SWV 354 372
Viel werden kommen von Morgen und von Abend SWV 375
Vier Hirtinnen, gleich jung, gleich schon SWV Anh. 1
Vine most surely I am SWV 389
Voice of the Lord sounds upon the waters SWV 331
Von Aufgang der Sonnen bis zu ihrem Niedergang SWV 362
Von Gnad und Recht soll singen SWV 199
Von Gott will ich nicht lassen SWV 366
Vor bösen Menschen rette mich SWV 245
Vulnerasti cor meum, filia charissima SWV 64
Wann unsre Augen schlafen ein SWV 316
War Gott nicht mit uns diese Zeit SWV 229
Warum toben die Heiden SWV 23
Warum verstösst du uns so gar SWV 171
Was betrübst du dich, meine Seele SWV 335 353
Was er dir geben möge SWV 72
Was haben doch die Leut im Sinn SWV 98
Was hast du verwirket, liebster, freundlicher Herre SWV 56
Was hast du verwirket, o du allerholdseligster Knab SWV 307
Was mein Gott will, das g'scheh allzeit SWV 392
Was trotzst denn du, Tyrann, so hoch SWV 149
Watch and pray SWV 413
We are citizens of heaven SWV 390
Weib, was weinest du? SWV 443
Weichet hinweg von mir SWV 87
Weihnachts-Historie SWV 435

Wende, du unser Richter, deinen
  Blick SWV 75
Wenn Gott einmal erlosen wird SWV
  231
Wenn ich schlafend ruh, wachet
  doch mein liebend Herz SWV 63
Wenn sich der Herr Gott Zebaoth
  SWV 173
Wer gottes Marter in Ehren hat SWV
  480
Wer nicht sitzt im Gottlosen Rat
  SWV 97
Wer sich des Höchsten Schirm
  vertraut SWV 189
Wer will uns scheiden von der
  Liebe Gottes SWV 330
Wer wird, Herr, in der Hütten dein
  SWV 111
What has bowed you down, o my
  spirit SWV 335
What my God wills, let that be
  done SWV 392
When Our Lord was betrayed SWV 423
Where is the newborn king of
  Israel? SWV 435
Who in sorrow plant seed SWV 378
Who shall separate us SWV 330
Who then can part us from the love
  God gives us? SWV 330
Why afflict thyself, o my spirit
  SWV 353
Wie ein Rubin in feinem Golde
  leuchtet SWV 357
Wie habe ich dein Gesetze so lieb
  SWV 488
Wie ists so fein, lieblich und
  schon SWV 238
Wie lieblich sind deine Wohnungen
  SWV 29
Wie meinst du's doch, ach Herr
  mein Gott SWV 106
Wie nun, ihr Herren, seid ihr
  stumm SWV 155
Wie sehr lieblich und schöne SWV
  181
Wie wenn der Adler sich aus seiner
  Klippe schwingt SWV 434
Wir danken dir, Herr Gott,
  himmlischer Vater SWV 93 430

Wir glauben all an einen Gott SWV
  303
Wir haben, Herr, mit Fleiss gehört
  SWV 141
With God for us, who can be
  against us? SWV 329
Wo der Herr nicht das Haus bauet
  SWV 400 473
Wo Gott der Herr nicht bei uns
  Hält SWV 467
Wo Gott nicht selbst bei uns wäre
  SWV 49
Wo Gott zum Haus nicht gibt sein
  Gunst SWV 232
Wohl dem, den Gott hat erwählt SWV
  162
Wohl dem, der den Herren fürchtet
  SWV 30 44
Wohl dem, der ein tugendsam Weib
  hat SWV 20
Wohl dem, der in Gottesfurcht
  steht SWV 233
Wohl dem, der nicht wandelt im Rat
  SWV 28 290
Wohl denen, die da leben SWV 217
Wohl denen, die ohne Tadel leben
  SWV 482
Wohl denen, die ohne Wandel leben
  SWV 482
Wohl mag der sein ein selig Mann
  SWV 138
Word was man SWV 385
Wort Jesus Syrach SWV 20
Wort der Einsetzung des heiligen
  Abendmahls SWV 423
Wort ward Fleisch und wohnet unter
  uns SWV 385
Zion spricht, der Herr hat mich
  verlassen SWV 46
Zu Lob und Ehr mit Freuden singt
  SWV 252
Zweierlei bitte ich, Herr, von dir
  SWV 360
Zwölfjährige Jesus im Tempel SWV
  401
19. Psalm SWV 455
85. Psalm SWV 461
133. Psalm SWV 48
166. Psalm SWV 51

SOURCE INDEX

Acts 9:4-5 SWV 415

Agricola, Johann. Ich ruf zu dir, Herr Jesu Christ SWV 326

Alber, Erasmus. Christe, der du bist der helle Tag SWV 316

Aligieri, Alessandro. D'orrida selce alpina SWV 6

Ambrose, Saint. Veni redemptor gentium SWV 301

Apocrypha. Ecclesiasticus 2:8-13 SWV 364

Apocrypha. Ecclesiasticus 25:1-2 SWV 365

Apocrypha. Ecclesiasticus 26:1-4 SWV 20

Apocrypha. Ecclesiasticus 26:21 SWV 20

Apocrypha. Ecclesiasticus 32:7-9 SWV 357

Apocrypha. Ecclesiasticus 50:24 SWV 407

Apocrypha. Ecclesiasticus 50:24-26 SWV 418

Apocrypha. Judith 16:15 SWV 407

Apocrypha. Wisdom of Solomon 3:1-3 SWV 279

Apocrypha. Wisdom of Solomon 3:1 SWV 281

Aufer immensam, Deus, aufer iram SWV 337

Brehm, Christian. Trauerlied SWV 419

Christ ist erstanden von der Marter alle SWV 470

Corinthians, 1st, 5:7-8 SWV 404

Corinthians, 1st, 11:23-25 SWV 423 495

Corinthians, 1st, 15:57 SWV 50

Da pacem Domine SWV 465

Da Jesus an dem Kreuze stund SWV 478 480

Daniel 3:52-90 SWV 448

Dank sagen wir alle Gott SWV 425 435

Decius, Nicolaus. Allein Gott in der Höh sei Ehr SWV 327

Domine Deus, pater coelestis, benedic nobis SWV 90 93

Dufft, Christian Timotheus. Danklied SWV 368

Ecclesiastes 3:12-13 SWV 358

Ecclesiastes 8:15 SWV 358

Ecclesiastes 9:7 SWV 358

Ehre sei dir, Christe, der du littest Not SWV 479

Ephesians 3:14-17 SWV 319

Ephesians 5:22 SWV 365

Ephesians 5:28 SWV 365

Ephesians 5:32 SWV 365

Exodus 15:11 SWV 345

Exodus 15:2 SWV 345

Galatians 5:14-15 SWV 365

Gatti, Alessandro. Fiamma ch'allacia e laccio SWV 10

Genesis 32:26 SWV 279

Genesis 49:10-11 SWV 369

Genesis 49:11-12 SWV 370

Gigas, Johannes. Ach wie elend ist unsre Zeit SWV 279

Gloria Patri SWV 22 23 24 25 26 27 28 30 34 35 36 37 386 424 461 482 483 484 485 486 487 488 490 491 492 493

Graumann, Johann. Nun lob, mein Seel, den Herren SWV 41

Guarini, Battista. Pastor fido SWV 1 2 3 5 11 15

Hebrews 13:4 SWV 365

Heermann, Johann. O süsser Jesu
 Christ, wer an dich recht
 gedenket SWV 405 427
Hegenwald, Erhard. Erbarm dich
 mein, o Herre Gott SWV 447
Helmbold, Ludwig. Nun lasst uns
 Gott dem Herren SWV 279
Helmbold, Ludwig. Von Gott will
 ich nicht lassen SWV 366
Herman, Nicolaus. Wenn mein
 Stündlein vorhanden ist SWV 279
 379
Heu mihi Domino, qui peccavi nimis
 SWV 65
Heute ist Christus der Herr
 geboren SWV 439
Hodie Christus natus est SWV 315
 456
Hymnus ante lectionem pro vera
 sapientia ad Jesum Christum
 Deum Optimum Maximum in
 auditoriis et scholis SWV 431
Isaiah 1:18 SWV 279
Isaiah 9:6-7 SWV 302 384
Isaiah 9:6 SWV 395
Isaiah 26:20 SWV 279
Isaiah 40:1-5 SWV 382
Isaiah 41:10 SWV 296
Isaiah 45:8 SWV 322
Isaiah 49:14-16 SWV 46
Jeremiah 5:24 SWV 407
Jeremiah 31:20 SWV 40
Jeremiah 33:11 SWV 407
Jesu, dulcis memoria SWV 308 471
Job 1:21 SWV 279
Job 19:25-26 SWV 279
Job 19:25-27 SWV 393 457
John 1:14 SWV 314 385
John 1:23 SWV 383
John 1:26-27 SWV 383
John 1:29 SWV 279
John 3:14-15 SWV 68
John 3:16 SWV 279 380
John 11:25-26 SWV 324 464
John 15:1-2 SWV 389
John 15:4-5 SWV 389
John 19:1-30 SWV 481
John 19:25-28 SWV 478
John 19:30 SWV 478
John 20:2-17 SWV 50
John 20:13 SWV 443
John 20:16-17 SWV 443
John 20:19-23 SWV 50
John, 1st, 1:7 SWV 279 298
Jonas, Justus. Wo Gott, der Herr,
 nicht bei uns halt SWV 467

Komm, heiliger Geist SWV 417
Leon, Johann. Ich hab mein Sach
 Gott heimgestellt SWV 94 279 305
Lord's prayer SWV 89 92 411 429
 430
Luke 1:28-38 SWV 333 334
Luke 2:1-21 SWV 435
Luke 2:10-11 SWV 395
Luke 2:34-35 SWV 410
Luke 2:40 SWV 435
Luke 2:48-49 SWV 401
Luke 5:5 SWV 317
Luke 6:36-42 SWV 409
Luke 8:5-8 SWV 408
Luke 16:24-31 SWV 477
Luke 18:10-14 SWV 444
Luke 21:29-31 SWV 394
Luke 21:33 SWV 300 394
Luke 21:34-36 SWV 351 413
Luke 22 SWV 480
Luke 23 SWV 480
Luke 23:34 SWV 478
Luke 23:39-43 SWV 478
Luke 23:46 SWV 478
Luke 23:55-56 SWV 50
Luke 24:3-35 SWV 50
Luke 24:1 SWV 50
Luke 24:37-38 SWV 50
Luther, Martin. Deutsche Litanei
 SWV 279 428 458
Luther, Martin. Herre Gott,
 himmlischer Vater SWV 429
Luther, Martin. Jesaja dem
 Propheten das geschah SWV 496
Luther, Martin. Komm, heiliger
 Geist SWV 417
Luther, Martin. Mit Fried und
 Freud ich fahr dahin SWV 279
Luther, Martin. Nun freut euch,
 lieben Christen gmein SWV 279
Luther, Martin. Nun komm, der
 Heiden Heiland SWV 301
Luther, Martin. Verleih uns
 Frieden genädiglich SWV 354 355
 372 373
Luther, Martin. Vom Himmel hoch
 da komm ich her SWV 450
Luther, Martin. Wir danken dir,
 Herr Gott SWV 430
Magnificat SWV 344 426 468 494
Manuale Augustini SWV 82 83 285
Marino, Giambattista. Saluto
 nocevole SWV 12
Marino, Giambattista. Baci cari
 SWV 16
Marino, Giambattista. Bacio

chiesto con arguzia SWV 13
Marino, Giambattista. Bella mano
   veduta SWV 8
Marino, Giambattista. Guerra di
   baci SWV 9
Marino, Giambattista. Partita
   dell'amante SWV 18
Marino, Giambattista. Partita
   dell'amata SWV 4
Marino, Giambattista. Somiglianza
   tra l'amante e l'amata SWV 17
Marino, Giambattista. Sospiro
   della sua donna SWV 14
Marino, Giambattista. Stagioni
   contrarie alla sua ninfa SWV 7
Mark 15:25 SWV 478
Mark 16:1-6 SWV 50
Mark 16:8-11 SWV 50
Mark 16:13-14 SWV 50
Matthew 1:20-21 SWV 323
Matthew 2 SWV 435
Matthew 2:13-15 SWV 403
Matthew 2:18 SWV 396
Matthew 8:11-12 SWV 375
Matthew 11:28-30 SWV 261
Matthew 13:30 SWV 376
Matthew 18:32-33 SWV 397
Matthew 21:9 SWV 402
Matthew 22:16-21 SWV 414
Matthew 22:4 SWV 459
Matthew 26 SWV 479
Matthew 26:26-28 SWV 423 495
Matthew 27 SWV 479
Matthew 27:46 SWV 478
Matthew 27:48 SWV 478
Matthew 28:2-4 SWV 50
Matthew 28:6-15 SWV 50
Meditationes Augustini SWV 53 54
   56 57 58 59 67 69 70 73 74 75 76
   77 84 304 307 309 313 340
Missa brevis deutsch. Gloria SWV
   421
Missa brevis deutsch. Kyrie SWV
   420
Nicene Creed. German SWV 303 422
Nunc dimittis SWV 281 352 432 433
O lieber Herre Gott, wecke uns auf
   SWV 287 381
O Jesu süss, wer dein gedenkt SWV
   406
Opitz, Martin. Erde trinkt für
   sich SWV 438
Opitz, Martin. Glück zu dem
   Helikon SWV 96
Opitz, Martin. Himmlische
   Hirtenlieder SWV 441 451 452

Opitz, Martin. Nachtklag SWV 460
Opitz, Martin. Tugend ist der
   beste Freund SWV 442
Philippians 1:21 SWV 279
Philippians 3:20-21 SWV 279 390
Proverbs 5:18-19 SWV 453
Proverbs 18:22 SWV 21
Proverbs 19:14 SWV 21
Proverbs 27:10 SWV 365
Proverbs 30:7-9 SWV 360
Psalm 1 SWV 28 97
Psalm 1:1-3 SWV 290
Psalm 2 SWV 23 98
Psalm 3 SWV 99
Psalm 3:5-8 SWV 310
Psalm 4 SWV 100
Psalm 4:1 SWV 289
Psalm 5 SWV 101 Anh. 7
Psalm 5:1-2 SWV 61
Psalm 5:2-3 SWV 62
Psalm 5:2 SWV 289
Psalm 6 SWV 24 102
Psalm 6:1-4 SWV 85
Psalm 6:5-7 SWV 86
Psalm 6:8-10 SWV 87
Psalm 7 SWV 103 462
Psalm 8 SWV 27 104 343 449
Psalm 9 SWV 105
Psalm 9:11-12 SWV 293
Psalm 10 SWV 106
Psalm 11 SWV 107
Psalm 12 SWV 108
Psalm 13 SWV 109 416
Psalm 13:5-6 SWV 312
Psalm 14 SWV 110
Psalm 14:2-3 SWV 292
Psalm 15 SWV 111 466
Psalm 16 SWV 112
Psalm 17 SWV 113
Psalm 18 SWV 114
Psalm 18:1-6 SWV 348
Psalm 19 SWV 115
Psalm 19:1-6 SWV 386 455
Psalm 20 SWV 116
Psalm 21 SWV 117
Psalm 22 SWV 118 119
Psalm 23 SWV 33 120 398
Psalm 23:6 SWV 95
Psalm 24 SWV 121 476
Psalm 25 SWV 122
Psalm 26 SWV 123
Psalm 27 SWV 124
Psalm 27:1-3 SWV 359
Psalm 27:5-6 SWV 359
Psalm 27:4 SWV 294
Psalm 28 SWV 125

Psalm 29 SWV 126
Psalm 29:1-2 SWV 283
Psalm 29:3-9 SWV 331
Psalm 30 SWV 127
Psalm 30:4-5 SWV 288
Psalm 31 SWV 128
Psalm 31:1-2 SWV 66 377
Psalm 31:2-3 SWV 259
Psalm 32 SWV 129
Psalm 33 SWV 130
Psalm 33:1-3 SWV 367
Psalm 34 SWV 131
Psalm 34:1-3 SWV 267
Psalm 34:1-4 SWV 306
Psalm 34:4-5 SWV 268
Psalm 34:4 SWV 346 407
Psalm 34:6 SWV 306
Psalm 35 SWV 132
Psalm 36 SWV 133
Psalm 37 SWV 134
Psalm 37:1-5 SWV 311
Psalm 37:25 SWV 320
Psalm 38 SWV 135
Psalm 39 SWV 136
Psalm 40 SWV 137
Psalm 41 SWV 138
Psalm 42 SWV 139
Psalm 42:11 SWV 335 353
Psalm 43 SWV 140
Psalm 44 SWV 141
Psalm 45 SWV 142
Psalm 46 SWV 143
Psalm 46:7 SWV 407
Psalm 46:9 SWV 407
Psalm 47 SWV 144
Psalm 47:1-6 SWV 349
Psalm 48 SWV 145
Psalm 49 SWV 146
Psalm 50 SWV 147
Psalm 51 SWV 148
Psalm 51:10-12 SWV 291
Psalm 51:15 SWV 271
Psalm 52 SWV 149
Psalm 53 SWV 150
Psalm 54 SWV 151
Psalm 55 SWV 152
Psalm 56 SWV 153
Psalm 56:13 SWV 347
Psalm 57 SWV 154
Psalm 57:7-10 SWV 341
Psalm 58 SWV 155
Psalm 59 SWV 156
Psalm 60 SWV 157
Psalm 61 SWV 158
Psalm 62 SWV 159
Psalm 63 SWV 160

Psalm 64 SWV 161
Psalm 65 SWV 162
Psalm 65:12 SWV 407
Psalm 66 SWV 163
Psalm 66:4 SWV 283
Psalm 67 SWV 164
Psalm 67:1 SWV 55
Psalm 68 SWV 165
Psalm 68:1-3 SWV 356
Psalm 69 SWV 166
Psalm 70 SWV 167 282
Psalm 71 SWV 168
Psalm 72 SWV 169
Psalm 73 SWV 170
Psalm 73:25-26 SWV 279 280 321
Psalm 74 SWV 171
Psalm 75 SWV 172
Psalm 76 SWV 173
Psalm 77 SWV 174
Psalm 78 SWV 175
Psalm 78:1-3 SWV 270
Psalm 79 SWV 176
Psalm 80 SWV 177
Psalm 81 SWV 178
Psalm 81:1 SWV 275
Psalm 81:2 SWV 407
Psalm 81:3 SWV 275
Psalm 82 SWV 179
Psalm 83 SWV 180
Psalm 84 SWV 29 181
Psalm 84:1-2 SWV 401
Psalm 84:4 SWV 401
Psalm 85 SWV 182 461
Psalm 86 SWV 183
Psalm 87 SWV 184
Psalm 88 SWV 185
Psalm 89 SWV 186 187
Psalm 90 SWV 188
Psalm 90:10 SWV 279
Psalm 91 SWV 189
Psalm 92 SWV 190
Psalm 93 SWV 191
Psalm 94 SWV 192
Psalm 95 SWV 193
Psalm 95:1-2 SWV 407
Psalm 96 SWV 194
Psalm 96:1-2 SWV 463
Psalm 96:1-4 SWV 342
Psalm 96:11 SWV 47
Psalm 97 SWV 195
Psalm 98 SWV 35 196
Psalm 98:4-6 SWV 47
Psalm 98:4 SWV 276
Psalm 98:6 SWV 275
Psalm 99 SWV 197
Psalm 100 SWV 36 198 262 332 493.

Psalm 100:1 SWV 407
Psalm 101 SWV 199
Psalm 102 SWV 200
Psalm 103 SWV 201
Psalm 103:1-4 SWV 39
Psalm 103:2-5 SWV 347
Psalm 104 SWV 202
Psalm 104:33 SWV 260 345
Psalm 105 SWV 203
Psalm 106 SWV 204
Psalm 107 SWV 205
Psalm 108 SWV 206
Psalm 108:1-3 SWV 257
Psalm 109 SWV 207
Psalm 110 SWV 22 208
Psalm 111 SWV 34 209 284 424
Psalm 111:1 SWV 347
Psalm 111:10 SWV 318
Psalm 112 SWV 210
Psalm 113 SWV 211
Psalm 113:2-9 SWV 362
Psalm 114 SWV 212
Psalm 115 SWV 43 213
Psalm 116 SWV 51 214
Psalm 116:3-4 SWV 346
Psalm 116:8-9 SWV 347
Psalm 116:13-14 SWV 60
Psalm 117 SWV 47 215 363
Psalm 118 SWV 216
Psalm 118:17 SWV 346 347
Psalm 118:25-26 SWV 297 402
Psalm 119 SWV 217 218 219 220 221
    222 223 224
Psalm 119:1-16 SWV 482
Psalm 119:17-32 SWV 483
Psalm 119:33-48 SWV 484
Psalm 119:49-64 SWV 485
Psalm 119:65-80 SWV 486
Psalm 119:81-96 SWV 487
Psalm 119:97-112 SWV 488
Psalm 119:113-128 SWV 489
Psalm 119:129-144 SWV 490
Psalm 119:145-160 SWV 491
Psalm 119:161-176 SWV 492
Psalm 120 SWV 225
Psalm 120:1-2 SWV 71
Psalm 120:3-4 SWV 72
Psalm 121 SWV 31 226 399
Psalm 122 SWV 26 227
Psalm 123 SWV 228
Psalm 124 SWV 229
Psalm 125 SWV 230
Psalm 126 SWV 231
Psalm 126:5-6 SWV 42 378
Psalm 127 SWV 232 400 473
Psalm 128 SWV 30 44 233

Psalm 129 SWV 234
Psalm 130 SWV 25 235
Psalm 131 SWV 236
Psalm 131:1 SWV 78
Psalm 131:2 SWV 79
Psalm 131:3 SWV 80
Psalm 132 SWV 237
Psalm 133 SWV 238 412
Psalm 133:1-3 SWV 48 365
Psalm 134 SWV 239
Psalm 135 SWV 240
Psalm 136 SWV 32 45 241
Psalm 136:1 SWV 91 430
Psalm 136:25 SWV 91
Psalm 136:26 SWV 430
Psalm 137 SWV 37 242
Psalm 138 SWV 243
Psalm 139 SWV 244
Psalm 140 SWV 245
Psalm 141 SWV 246
Psalm 142 SWV 247
Psalm 143 SWV 248
Psalm 144 SWV 249
Psalm 144:5-7 SWV 361
Psalm 144:9 SWV 361
Psalm 145 SWV 250
Psalm 145:3-4 SWV 286
Psalm 145:15-16 SWV 88 429
Psalm 146 SWV 251
Psalm 147 SWV 252
Psalm 147:9-11 SWV 91 430
Psalm 147:12-14 SWV 407
Psalm 147:7 SWV 407
Psalm 147:9 SWV 407
Psalm 148 SWV 253
Psalm 148:1 SWV 47
Psalm 149 SWV 254
Psalm 149:1-3 SWV 81
Psalm 149:1 SWV 407
Psalm 150 SWV 38 255 350
Psalm 150:4 SWV 47 276 407
Revelation 14:13 SWV 281 391
Romans 8:31-34 SWV 329
Romans 8:35 SWV 330
Romans 8:38-39 SWV 330
Romans 14:7-8 SWV 374
Romans 14:8 SWV 279
Samuel, 1st, 2:1-2 SWV 258
Samuel, 2nd, 18:33 SWV 269
Schalling, Martin. Herzlich lieb,
    hab ich dich, O Herr SWV 387
Schirmer, David. Wie wenn der
    Adler sich aus seiner Klippe
    schwingt SWV 434
Schütz, Heinrich. Ach wie soll
    ich doch in Freuden leben SWV
    474

Schütz, Heinrich. Güldne Haare,
  gleich Aurore SWV 440
Schütz, Heinrich. Klaglicher
  Abschied SWV 52
Schütz, Heinrich. Syncharma
  musicum SWV 49
Schütz, Heinrich. Teutoniam dudum
  belli atra pericla molestant SWV
  338
Seele Christi heilige mich SWV 325
Soliloquia Augustini SWV 336
Song of Solomon 2:10 SWV 266
Song of Solomon 2:14 SWV 263
Song of Solomon 2:17 SWV 339
Song of Solomon 3:1-2 SWV 272
Song of Solomon 3:3-4 SWV 273
Song of Solomon 4:1-5 SWV 265
Song of Solomon 4:16 SWV 274
Song of Solomon 4:8 SWV 266
Song of Solomon 4:9 SWV 64
Song of Solomon 5:8-10 SWV 339
Song of Solomon 5:1 SWV 274
Song of Solomon 5:13 SWV 263
Song of Solomon 5:2 SWV 63 265 266
Song of Solomon 5:6 SWV 263
Song of Solomon 5:8 SWV 264
Song of Solomon 6:1-2 SWV 339
Song of Solomon 3:1 SWV 339
Stiehler, Caspar. Te Christe
  supplex invoco SWV 326
Surrexit pastor bonus SWV 469
Timothy, 1st, 4:8 SWV 299
Timothy, 1st, 1:15-17 SWV 277 388
Titus 2:11-14 SWV 371
Veni sancte Spiritus SWV 328 475
Vier Hirtinnen, gleich jung,
  gleich schön SWV Anh. 1
Was mein Gott will, das g'scheh
  allzeit SWV 392
Weisse, Michael. Christus der uns
  selig macht SWV 295 481

PERFORMING FORCES INDEX

Solos or solo ensembles

1 Voice

A Continuo	SWV 284 307
A Violin, bassoon or trombone, and continuo	SWV 259
A 2 discant instruments, continuo	SWV 368
A 2 violins and continuo	SWV 348
B Continuo	SWV 310
B 2 violins and continuo	SWV 351–352
B 2 violins or 2 flutes and continuo	SWV 262
B 4 trombones or 2 violins and 2 trombones and continuo	SWV 269–270
M Continuo	SWV 283
S Continuo	SWV 52 282 285 306 434
S 2 violins and continuo	SWV 257–258 341–343 345–347
S 2 violins, 2 violas or trombones, 2 cornetti or trumpets, 2 flutes, and continuo	SWV 344
S 2 violins, 2 violas, double bass, continuo	SWV 447
S 4 violas, continuo	SWV 447
T Continuo	SWV 282 285 308–310 368

T 2 violins and continuo   SWV 260-261 341-343
                                                                345-347 349-350

                        2 Voices

AA Continuo   SWV 293

AT Continuo   SWV 96 438

BB Continuo   SWV 296 319-320

BB 2 violins and continuo   SWV 361-362

MA 3 cornetti, 3 trombones, continuo   SWV 40

SA Continuo   SWV 290

SA 2 violins and continuo   SWV 357 440

SA 3 bassoons or 3 viola da gamba and continuo   SWV 272-273

SA 3 cornetti, 3 trombones, continuo   SWV 40

SB Continuo   SWV 292 316

SB Violin, 3 viols da gamba, continuo   SWV 451-452

SB 2 violins and continuo   SWV 358

SB 2 violins, 2 unspecified instruments,
   continuo   SWV 451-452

SS Continuo   SWV 286-289 311-314

SS 2 violins and continuo   SWV 353-356 440-442

SS 5 unspecified instruments, continuo   SWV 396

ST Continuo   SWV 291 315

ST Cornetto or violin, trombone, bassoon and
   continuo   SWV 271

TA 3 cornetti, 3 trombones, continuo   SWV 40

TR 2 violins and continuo   SWV 265-266

TT Continuo   SWV 294-295 317-318

TT 2 cornettino or 2 fiffaro and continuo   SWV 263-264

TT 2 violins and continuo   SWV 353-356 359-360

3 Voices

ATB Continuo   SWV 325

ATB Lute, 3 viols, 3 trombones, violin,
  cornetto, continuo   SWV 474

ATB 2 violins and continuo with 4 optional
  unspecified instruments   SWV 399

ATB 2 violins and continuo   SWV 363-364 367

BBB Continuo   SWV 300

SAT 2 violins and continuo with 4 optional
  unspecified instruments   SWV 398

SAT 3 viols, 4 trombones, continuo   SWV 470

SMB 2 violins and continuo with 4 optional
  unspecified instruments   SWV 401

SSA Continuo   SWV 439

SSB Continuo   SWV 298 322

SSB 2 violins and continuo   SWV 366

SSB 2 violins or violin and cornettino and
  continuo with 4 optional unspecified
  instruments   SWV 400

SSR Continuo   SWV 299 323

SSS Continuo   SWV 439

SSS Lute, 3 viols, 3 trombones, continuo   SWV 467

SST Continuo   SWV 297 321

SST 2 violins and continuo   SWV 402

SST 3 trombones and continuo   SWV 274

STB Cornetto or violin and continuo   SWV 267-268

TTB Continuo   SWV 324

TTB Cornetto, trombetta or cornetto, bassoon,
  and continuo   SWV 275-276

TTB 2 violins and continuo   SWV 365

4 Voices

ABST 2 violins, double bass, 3 trombones,

continuo	SWV 466
SATB Continuo	SWV 302 304 329-332 443
SATB 2 violins and basso continuo	SWV 404
SATB 2 violins, bassoon, continuo, and 4 optional unspecified instruments	SWV 408-409
SATB 2 violins, double bass, 3 trombones, continuo	SWV 468
SATB 5 viols, continuo	SWV 465
SMTA Cornetto or trombone, 3 trombones, continuo	SWV 40
SSAT Continuo	SWV Anh. 1
SSAT 2 violins and continuo with 4 optional unspecified instruments	SWV 405
SSBB Continuo	SWV 301
SSSR Continuo	SWV 326
SSSS 2 violins, continuo	SWV 278
SSTB Continuo	SWV 303
SSTB 2 violins and continuo with 4 optional unspecified instruments	SWV 407
SSTT Continuo	SWV 327-328
SSTT 2 violins, continuo	SWV 406
STST 2 trombones and continuo	SWV 274
STST 3 cornetti and bassoon, 4 trombones, continuo	SWV 46
STST 6 trombones and continuo	SWV 42
STTB 2 violins and continuo with 4 optional unspecified instruments	SWV 403

5 Voices

ATSTS 2 flutes or 2 cornetti, bassoon, violin, 2 viols, continuo	SWV 47
SATB and 1 optional voice 5 viols, continuo	SWV 465
SATTB Continuo	SWV 336-337

SATTB SATTB instruments, continuo   SWV 478

SMTTB 2 violins, continuo, and 4 optional
  unspecified instruments   SWV 411

SSATB Continuo and 5 unspecified instruments   SWV 333-334

SSATB Continuo   SWV 305 335 448-449

SSATB 2 violins and basso continuo   SWV 410

SSATB 2 violins, bassoon, continuo, and 2
  optional unspecified instruments   SWV 412

SSATB 2 violins, bassoon, continuo, and 4
  optional unspecified instruments   SWV 414

SSATB 2 violins, 2 flutes, continuo   SWV 477

SSTTB 2 violins, 3 trombones, continuo   SWV 461

TTSSB 3 trombones or bassoons, 3 cornetti or
  violins, continuo   SWV 21

6 Voices

SATB and 2 optional voices 5 viols, continuo   SWV 465

SMTTRB 2 violins and continuo   SWV 417

SSAATB 2 violins, 4 violas, optional double
  bass, continuo   SWV 471

SSATBB 2 violins and continuo   SWV 415

SSATTB Continuo   SWV 279 455

SSATTB 2 violins and continuo   SWV 413

SSATTB 2 violins, continuo, and 4 optional
  unspecified instruments   SWV 418

SSATTB 2 violins, continuo, and 4 optional
  viols   SWV 416

SSATTB 2 violins, 3 trombones, continuo   SWV 469

TTSSSB 3 cornetti or 2 cornetti and trombone,
  3 bassoons, continuo   SWV 49

7 Voices

SSATTTB Bassoon, 2 cornetti or 2 violins, 3
  trombones, violin or cornetto, flute or

cornetto, double bass, continuo (4 different groups)	SWV 475

8 Voices

SATBSATB Continuo	SWV 22-26 34-38 41 482-494 Anh. 7
SATBSATB SATB/SATB instruments, continuo	SWV 23
SATBSATB SATB/SATB instruments	SWV 23
SATBSATB SMAB/SMAB instruments, continuo	SWV 34
SATBSATB SSAB/SSAB instruments, continuo	SWV 23
SATBSATB SSATB instruments, continuo	SWV 22
SATBSATB SSMB/SSMB instruments, continuo	SWV 26
SATBSATB 2 cornetti, 5 bassoons, 2 violins, 4 trombones, continuo	SWV 476
SATBSATB 2 violins, 2 violas, double bass, 4 cornetti, trombone, continuo	SWV 41
SATBSATB 3 cornetti and trombone or 3 violins and bassoon and cornetto or flute and 2 trombones and trombone or bassoon	SWV 38
SMARATTB Continuo	SWV 28
SMARATTB SMAR/ATTB instruments, continuo	SWV 28
SSARTTRB Continuo	SWV 29
SSARTTRB SSAR/TTRB instruments, continuo	SWV 29
SSATATRB Continuo	SWV 27 30
SSATATRB SSAT/ATRB instruments, continuo	SWV 27 30
SSATATRB SSAT/ATRB/SSATB instruments, continuo	SWV 27
SSATATRB SSATB instruments, continuo	SWV 27
SSMTATTB Continuo	SWV 32
SSMTATTB SATB/SSMT instruments, continuo	SWV 32

9 Voices

SSSAATTRB 4 viols, 8 optional unspecified instruments, continuo	SWV 50

Choruses

1-part chorus

T Chorus 6 unspecified instruments and continuo	SWV 397
T Chorus 6 unspecified instruments	SWV 397
Unison voices Continuo	SWV 283

2-part chorus

AA Chorus 5 unspecified instruments and continuo	SWV 396
AA Chorus 5 unspecified instruments	SWV 396
AT Chorus 4 unspecified instruments and continuo	SWV 392
AT Chorus 4 unspecified instruments	SWV 392
SA Chorus Continuo	SWV 293
ST Chorus 5 unspecified instruments and continuo	SWV 394-395
ST Chorus 5 unspecified instruments	SWV 394-395
TB Chorus Continuo	SWV 293

3-part chorus

ATB Chorus Continuo	SWV 86
ATB Chorus Lute, 3 viols, 3 trombones, violin, cornetto, continuo	SWV 474
SSA Chorus 2 violins, cello	SWV 435
STB Chorus 4 unspecified instruments and continuo	SWV 395
STB Chorus 4 unspecified instruments	SWV 395

4-part chorus

SAAR Chorus A cappella	SWV 83
SAAR Chorus Continuo	SWV 83

SATB Chorus A cappella   SWV 54-66 68-82 88-93
                                                         97-100 102-104
                                                         106-256 419-422
                                                         428-431

SATB Chorus A Solo B Solo S Solo SATB Solo T
  Solo Continuo   SWV 31

SATB Chorus AT Solo B Solo SS Solo SSATB Solo
  2 violins, 3 trombones, continuo   SWV 473

SATB Chorus ATB Solo 2 violins and continuo
  with 4 optional unspecified instruments   SWV 399

SATB Chorus Continuo   SWV 53-66 68-82 84-85
                                                         87-93 97-100 102
                                                         -104 106-256 420
                                                         -422 428-431 443

SATB Chorus Flute and string bass   SWV 194

SATB Chorus RA Solo 3 cornetti, 3 trombones,
  continuo   SWV 43

SATB Chorus SAATTTTTBB Solo A cappella   SWV 479

SATB Chorus SAT Solo 2 violins and continuo
  with 4 optional unspecified instruments   SWV 398

SATB Chorus SATB Solo Continuo   SWV 39 304

SATB Chorus SATB Solo 2 violins, bassoon,
  continuo, and 4 optional unspecified
  instruments   SWV 408-409

SATB Chorus SATTTBBB Solo A cappella   SWV 480

SATB Chorus SMB Solo 2 violins and continuo
  with 4 optional unspecified instruments   SWV 401

SATB Chorus SMTTB Solo 2 violins, continuo,
  and 4 optional unspecified instruments   SWV 411

SATB Chorus SSAT Solo Continuo   SWV 33

SATB Chorus SSAT Solo 2 violins and continuo
  with 4 optional unspecified instruments   SWV 405

SATB Chorus SSATB Solo 2 violins, bassoon,
  continuo, and 4 optional unspecified
  instruments   SWV 414

SATB Chorus SSATTB Solo 2 violins, continuo,
  and 4 optional unspecified instruments   SWV 418

SATB Chorus SSB Solo 2 violins or violin and
  cornettino and continuo with 4 optional

unspecified instruments   SWV 400

SATB Chorus SSTB Solo 2 violins and continuo
  with 4 optional unspecified instruments   SWV 407

SATB Chorus SSTTB Solo 2 violins, 3 trombones,
  continuo   SWV 461

SATB Chorus STTB Solo 2 violins and continuo
  with 4 optional unspecified instruments   SWV 403

SATB Chorus STTTBB Solo A cappella   SWV 481

SATB Chorus T Solo 3 cornetti, continuo   SWV 20

SATB Chorus TA Solo 3 cornetti, 3 trombones,
  continuo   SWV 43

SATB Chorus TA Solo 4 cornetti, violin, 3
  trombones, continuo   SWV 44

SATB Chorus 2 cornetti, 3 trombones, continuo   SWV 453

SATB Chorus 2 violins, bassoon, continuo   SWV 459

SMAR Chorus A cappella   SWV 53-55 67 76-77 81
                                                                     97 101 105 423
                                                                     -424 427

SMAR Chorus Continuo   SWV 53-55 67 76-77 81
                                                                     97 101 105 423
                                                                     -424 427

SMAT Chorus A cappella   SWV 425

SMAT Chorus Continuo   SWV 425

SSAR Chorus Continuo   SWV 444

SSAT Chorus A cappella   SWV 426

SSAT Chorus Continuo   SWV 426 443 Anh. 1

SSMT Chorus A cappella   SWV 66-67 83 88-93

SSMT Chorus Continuo   SWV 66-67 83 88-93

SSSB Chorus TT Solo 3 cornetti or 2 cornetti
  and trombone, 3 bassoons, continuo   SWV 49

SSTB Chorus Continuo   SWV 444

SSTT Chorus Continuo   SWV 443

TTBB Chorus A cappella   SWV 478-479

5-part chorus

MATTB Chorus SSR Solo Continuo	SWV 281
SATB/T Chorus 3 cornetti, continuo	SWV 20
SATBB Chorus Continuo	SWV 450
SATTB Chorus A cappella	SWV 1-17 369-370 375 -376 380
SATTB Chorus A Solo B Solo S Solo SATTB Solo T Solo T Solo SATTB instruments, continuo	SWV 478
SATTB Chorus Continuo	SWV 450
SATTB Chorus Continuo	SWV 369-370 375-376 380
SATTB Chorus 2 violins, continuo	SWV 338
SMATB Chorus A cappella	SWV 6
SSATB Chorus A cappella	SWV 1-3 7-18 51
SSATB Chorus ATSTS Solo 2 flutes or 2 cornetti, bassoon, violin, 2 viols, continuo	SWV 47
SSATB Chorus Continuo	SWV 94
SSATB Chorus Cornetto or violin, violin or flute, double bass or bassoon, continuo	SWV 48
SSATB Chorus Optional continuo	SWV 371-374 377-379
SSATB Chorus SA Solo Continuo and 5 unspecified instruments	SWV 333-334
SSATB Chorus SATBSATB Solo Continuo	SWV 22
SSATB Chorus SATBSATB Solo SSATB instruments, continuo	SWV 22
SSATB Chorus SSAT/A Solo 3 trombones, trombetta and timpani, continuo	SWV 45
SSATB Chorus SSATATRB Solo Continuo	SWV 27
SSATB Chorus SSATATRB Solo SSAT/ATRB instruments, continuo	SWV 27
SSATB Chorus SSATATRB Solo SSAT/ATRB/SSATB instruments, continuo	SWV 27
SSATB Chorus SSATATRB Solo SSATB instruments, continuo	SWV 27

SSATB Chorus SSATB Solo Continuo   SWV 305

SSATB Chorus SSATB Solo Cornettino, violin, 4
  trombones, continuo   SWV 449

SSATB Chorus SSATB Solo 2 violins, 2 violas,
  double bass, 2 cornetti, 3 trombones,
  continuo   SWV 448

SSATB Chorus 2 violins, continuo   SWV 340 460

SSMAR Chorus A cappella   SWV 7-8 12-15 17-18

STTTB Chorus A cappella   SWV 4-5

TTSSB Chorus 3 trombones or bassoons, 3
  cornetti or violins, continuo   SWV 21

                         6-part chorus

SSAATB Chorus A Solo S Solo SSA Solo T Solo 2
  violins, 4 violas, optional double bass,
  continuo   SWV 471

SSATTB Chorus A cappella   SWV 381-391 432-433
                                                                       457

SSATTB Chorus AAA Solo B Solo BBB Solo S Solo
  T Solo TTT Solo 2 violettas, 2 violins, 2
  violas, bassoon, 2 clarini, 2 trombones,
  continuo   SWV 435

SSATTB Chorus Continuo   SWV 95 277 381-391
                                                                       432-433 456-458

SSATTB Chorus SSATTB Solo Continuo   SWV 279

SSATTB Chorus SSATTB Solo Optional unspecified
  instruments, continuo   SWV 455

SSMAAR Chorus Continuo   SWV 95

                         7-part chorus

SATTTBB Chorus A cappella   SWV 395

SATTTBB Chorus Continuo   SWV 395

SSAATBB Chorus A cappella   SWV 393

SSAATBB Chorus Continuo   SWV 393

SSMATRB Chorus A cappella   SWV 393

SSMATRB Chorus Continuo   SWV 393

SSSSATB Chorus Continuo   SWV 339

                    8-part chorus

MATTB/SSR Chorus Continuo   SWV 281

SATB/SATB Chorus A cappella   SWV 19 280 464 495

SATB/SATB Chorus A Solo B Solo S Solo SATB
  Solo T Solo Continuo   SWV 31

SATB/SATB Chorus Continuo   SWV 23 280 431 462
                                                 -464 482-494

SATB/SATB Chorus MA Solo 3 cornetti, 3
  trombones, continuo   SWV 40

SATB/SATB Chorus SA Solo 3 cornetti, 3
  trombones, continuo   SWV 40

SATB/SATB Chorus SAT Solo 3 viols, 4
  trombones, continuo   SWV 470

SATB/SATB Chorus SATB Solo Continuo   SWV 39 41

SATB/SATB Chorus SATB Solo 2 violins, double
  bass, 3 trombones, continuo   SWV 468

SATB/SATB Chorus SATB Solo 2 violins, 2
  violas, double bass, 4 cornetti, trombone,
  continuo   SWV 41

SATB/SATB Chorus SATB/SATB instruments,
  continuo   SWV 23

SATB/SATB Chorus SATB/SATB Solo Continuo   SWV 23 Anh. 7

SATB/SATB Chorus SATB/SATB Solo SATB/SATB
  instruments, continuo   SWV 23

SATB/SATB Chorus SATB/SATB Solo 2 cornetti, 5
  bassoons, 2 violins, 4 trombones, continuo   SWV 476

SATB/SATB Chorus SMTA Solo Cornetto or
  trombone, 3 trombones, continuo   SWV 40

SATB/SATB Chorus SMTTRB Solo 2 violins,
  continuo   SWV 417

SATB/SATB Chorus SSATBB Solo 2 violins,
  continuo   SWV 415

SATB/SATB Chorus SSATTB Solo 2 violins, 3
  trombones, continuo   SWV 469

SATB/SATB Chorus SSSAATTRB Solo 4 viols, 8
    optional unspecified instruments, continuo   SWV 50

SATB/SATB Chorus ST/ST Solo 3 cornetti and
    bassoon, 4 trombones, continuo   SWV 46

SATB/SATB Chorus TA Solo 3 cornetti, 3
    trombones, continuo   SWV 40

SATB/SATB Chorus TA Solo 4 cornetti, violin, 3
    trombones, continuo   SWV 44

SATB/SATB Chorus 2 violins, viola, cornetto, 3
    trombones, continuo   SWV 462

SATB/SATB Chorus 3 trumpets and trombone, 2
    trumpets, 2 trombones   SWV 38

SATB/SSMT Chorus SSMT/ATTB Solo Continuo   SWV 32

SATB/SSMT Chorus SSMTATTB Solo SATB/SSMT
    instruments, continuo   SWV 32

SMAB/SMAB Chorus SATB/SATB Solo Continuo   SWV 34

SMAB/SMAB Chorus SATB/SATB Solo SMAB/SMAB
    instruments, continuo   SWV 34

SMAR/SMAR Chorus Continuo   SWV 427

SSAB/SSAB Chorus SATB/SATB Solo Continuo   SWV 23

SSAB/SSAB Chorus SATB/SATB Solo SSAB/SSAB
    instruments, continuo   SWV 23

SSAT/SATB Chorus SSAT Solo Continuo   SWV 33

SSAT/TTBB Chorus   SWV 29

SSMB/SATB Chorus SATB/SATB Solo Continuo   SWV 38

SSMB/SATB Chorus 3 cornetti and trombone or 3
    violins and bassoon and cornetto or flute
    and 2 trombones and trombone or bassoon   SWV 38

SSMB/SSMB Chorus SATB/SATB Solo Continuo   SWV 26

SSMB/SSMB Chorus SATB/SATB Solo SSMB/SSMB
    instruments, continuo   SWV 26

STTB/STTB Chorus A cappella   SWV 19

9-part chorus

SSATB/SATB Chorus Continuo   SWV 465

SSATB/SATB Chorus 2 violins, 3 trombones,
  continuo   SWV 473

10-part chorus

SATRB/SATRB Chorus Continuo   SWV 42

SSAAATTBBB Chorus B Solo S Solo T Solo TTT
  Solo 2 violettas, 2 violins, 2 violas,
  bassoon, 2 clarini, 2 trombones, continuo   SWV 435

12-part chorus

SATB/SATB/SATB Chorus Continuo   SWV 36

SATB/SATB/SATB Chorus 2 violins, double bass,
  3 trombones, continuo   SWV 468

14-part chorus

MATTB/SSR/SSR/SSR Chorus Continuo   SWV 281

SATB/SATB/SSATTB Chorus SATB/SATB Solo 2
  cornetti, 5 bassoons, 2 violins, 4
  trombones, continuo   SWV 476

SSATTB/SATB/SATB Chorus 2 violins, 3
  trombones, continuo   SWV 469

About the Compilers

D. DOUGLAS MILLER is Associate Professor of Music at Pennsylvania State University and Music Director/Conductor of the State College Choral Society and Choral Society Madrigal Singers. He has contributed to *American Music Teacher*.

ANNE L. HIGHSMITH is Head of the Copy Cataloging Department of the Sterling C. Evans Library of Texas A&M University. She has contributed to *Journal of Academic Librarianship, Peasant Studies,* and *Proceedings of the Fifth National Online Meeting.*